BOOKS BY FITZROY MACLEAN

Take Nine Spies (1978)

To Caucasus (1977)

To the Back of Beyond (1975)

A Concise History of Scotland (1970)

Jugoslavia (1969)

Back to Bokhara (1959)

A Person from England (1958)

Disputed Barricade (1957)

Eastern Approaches (1950)

TAKE NINE SPIES

Fitzroy Maclean

TAKE NINE SPIES

Really, Commissaire, you seem to have been reading too many romantic thrillers. This is no romance, my dear sir, this is reality.

FREDERICK FORSYTH *The Day of the Jackal*

ATHENEUM   *NEW YORK*

1978

Library of Congress Cataloging in Publication Data

Maclean, Fitzroy, Sir; bart., date
    Take nine spies.

    Bibliography: p.
    1. Spies—Biography. 2. Espionage—History. I. Title.
UB270.M28 1978   327'.12'0922[B]   77-15315
ISBN 0-689-10854-0

FOR SUKIE AND DEREK

CONTENTS

ILLUSTRATIONS

TAKE NINE SPIES

'Life', observed Samuel Butler, rather characteristically, 'is the art of drawing sufficient conclusions from insufficient premises.' His dictum applies a fortiori to the subject of this book. Spies are by nature creatures of the dark, lurking in the shadows, shunning unnecessary illumination. To serve their purpose, they must either escape notice altogether or else appear to be what they are not. Even when it is all over, when the decorations have been distributed or the firing squads have done their work, it is usually too much to hope for a balanced, objective account of what happened. The secret services of the world do not, as a rule, throw their archives open to researchers. Real or imaginary considerations of security, humanity, policy, diplomacy or quite simply prestige blur the issue and confuse the truth. And the fog of history descends at its densest.

To draw valid conclusions from conflicting evidence or no evidence at all, to follow trails that as often as not lead nowhere is a tantalizing task. Here the writer of fiction is at an advantage. Instead of shadowy, indeterminate figures with confused motives and indistinct personalities, he creates convincing characters of flesh and blood. Their motives are clear, their behaviour logical and decisive, their courage or villainy unquestioned. We are told what they wear, whether it be slouch hats and dirty mackintoshes or the confections of Christian Dior and Savile Row. We know what they order for dinner: whether oysters and pink champagne or baked beans and tea.

By contrast, anyone who attempts to reconstruct a real spy from a handful of mouldering bones in a prison yard or the ramblings of some elderly pensioner in scarcely less mouldy exile or retirement has a far harder task. Confused by the duplicity of double agents, forever following carefully planted clues deliberately designed to lead nowhere or false trails which only lead back to the fertile imagination of previous investigators, blinded by smokescreens and baffled by strategems, he faces a far tougher and more frustrating assignment.

Nor is it even easy to discover whether these 'queer people', as that famous, if somewhat muddle-headed spy-catcher Sir Basil Thompson rather condescendingly calls them, were ever really spies at all, or, if they were, for whom they were spying and what set them on their lonely and devious course in the first place, whether they drifted into espionage from avarice or greed, under irresistible pressure of one kind or another, from loyalty (or lack of loyalty) to some cause or simply from a love of excitement and an urge to escape from whatever they were doing before. As Sir Robert Baden Powell once remarked, with more than a hint of ambiguity, 'for anyone who is tired of life, the thrilling life of a spy should be the finest recuperation.'

For my own part, though I have in my time encountered a number of spies and spymasters of varying nationalities and allegiances, I cannot really claim any very special knowledge of or insight into my subject. Espionage is something I have always been careful to keep clear of. All I have done in the present instance is take nine spies, sift through such evidence as I could find about them, discard what seemed to me obvious nonsense, and, from what remained, piece together the sequence of events and attempt some sort of estimate of the personalities involved and of their motives or lack of motives. Even within these limitations, I have found the task a fascinating one and can only hope that I may have succeeded in imparting some of its fascination to my readers.

One last word. The reader may perhaps notice that in one way or another the Russians seem to play a preponderant part in this little book. This is only natural. To quote one of our most respected Kremlin-watchers, Mr Edward Crankshaw: 'The Russians, not to put too fine a point on it, have always been nuts about espionage and counter-espionage.'

One

EYE OF THE MORNING

O what a tangled web we weave,
When first we practice to deceive

SIR WALTER SCOTT

On the evening of 13 March 1905 an unusually select audience assembled at the Musée Guimet on the Place d'Iena in the fashionable sixteenth *arrondissement* of Paris. Not, as one might imagine, to admire the collection of oriental works of art which its founder, Monsieur Emile-Etienne Guimet, had assembled there over the years, but, instead, to watch a display of eastern dances to be given by a young dancer called, it seemed, Lady MacLeod, whom Monsieur Guimet had met some weeks earlier, and by whom the old gentleman had been utterly captivated. Only on this occasion Lady MacLeod was appearing for the first time under a new and more exotic name, being announced to the assembled guests as Mata Hari, 'the Eye of the Morning'.

Monsieur Guimet, who opened the proceedings with a few well-chosen words, had spared no efforts to make the occasion a success. The museum's pillared library, skilfully lit and wreathed in flowers, had become a kind of eastern shrine, while some of the more exotic exhibits, dramatically illuminated, had been left in their places to heighten the generally oriental effect.

Lady MacLeod, a tall, supple, well-built, amber-skinned young woman with strong features and a generous mouth, wore an oriental costume especially picked by Monsieur Guimet from his own extensive collection: a richly jewelled brassiere, a couple of bracelets and a few diaphanous draperies loosely knotted well below her hips. A glittering diadem set off her glossy swept-back black hair. Four black-robed nautch-girls acted as her attendants. 'I saw,' wrote an onlooker, 'the form of a beautiful woman materialize behind shimmering gauze of gold and silver. Softly, almost imperceptibly, with infinite grace she began to dance.' As she danced, an orchestra somewhere in the background accompanied her with what purported to be eastern music.

She was an immediate, a sensational success. 'You can scarcely,' wrote

3

one member of her audience, 'credit the mystic frenzy produced by her lascivious attitudes . . . From her great sombre eyes, half-closed in sensuous ecstasy, there gleamed an uncanny light, like phosphorescent flowers. She seemed to embrace an invisible being in her long, shapely arms.' 'Nude dancing', commented another, even more explicitly, 'is designed to arouse passion and desire. But Mata Hari made you feel that you were actually satisfying your desire with her.'

From this point onwards she went from strength to strength. That spring she danced, usually against a background of palm trees, oriental carpets, banks of flowers and clouds of incense, in the houses of the rich, fashionable and famous. From the drawing-rooms of the *beau monde* she soon graduated to the professional stage and by August was playing to packed audiences at the Théâtre Olympia in the Boulevard des Capucines.

Who, in fact, was Lady MacLeod? Apart from a general assumption that her background was in some way oriental, no one seems to have probed very closely into it. She, on the other hand, was always ready to oblige with new and glamorous details of her early life, details which varied every time she told the story. 'I was born', went one version, 'in the south of India, on the coast of Malabar, in the holy city of Jaffnapatam, the child of a family within the sacred caste of Brahma. My father was called Assirvadam, which means "the blessing of God", because of his piety and pureness of heart. My mother was a glorious *bayadère* in the Temple of Kanda-Swany. She died when she was fourteen, on the day that I was born. The priests of the temple, having cremated my mother, adopted me under the baptismal name of Mata Hari, "the Eye of the Morning". In the great pagoda of Siva I was trained to follow my mother's footsteps in the holy rites of the dance – long monotonous hours of practice, for every gesture of the dance has its spiritual meaning. Then, at the age of thirteen, on the threshold of womanhood, I was initiated into the mystery of faith and love on the night of Sakty-Pudja, at the coming of spring. There, before the purple granite altar of Kanda-Swany, I danced for the first time, completely nude.' One day, her narrative continued, she was carried off by a handsome young British officer. She bore him a son; the baby was poisoned by a fanatical native servant. With her own hands she strangled the assassin. Her husband died of fever. Unable to return to the Temple of Kanda-Swany, she made her way to Europe, bringing with her the secrets of the sacred rites of Siva.

To other people she told other, widely differing versions of her story. Passed with improvements from one salon to another, picked up and embroidered by every newspaper in the world, the legend of Mata Hari soon reached fantastic proportions. The plain, unvarnished truth was somewhat different.

．　　．　　．　　．　　．

The future Mata Hari had been born twenty-nine years before, on 7 August 1876, in the little town of Leeuwarden in Holland, where her father, Adam Zelle (a heavily-bearded man of rather flamboyant tastes which his daughter, it soon became clear, had inherited), kept a hat shop. Adam and his wife, formerly Antje van der Meulen, gave their daughter the name of Margaretha. In 1890 Margaretha's father and mother separated. Shortly after this her mother died. Her father, whose once flourishing business had failed, moved to Amsterdam and to all intents and purposes out of her life. In due course Margaretha, slender, with black hair and bold eyes and a taste for showy clothes and bright colours, was sent to the Hague to stay with an uncle.

At seventeen Margaretha looked older than her age, was extremely pretty, and knew it. In March 1895, glancing idly through the personal column of the Amsterdam *Daily News* she came upon a classified advertisement which told her that an officer on leave from the Dutch East Indies would like to meet a suitable young lady with a view to matrimony. Having nothing better to do, she answered it, enclosing a photograph.

The advertisement had been put in, partly as a joke, by a friend of one Rudolph or, as he was more usually called, John MacLeod, a thirty-eight-year-old officer of Scottish extraction then serving in the Dutch colonial forces and at present on leave from the East Indies. John MacLeod was intrigued by Margaretha's answer and even more so by the photograph she enclosed. He suggested a *rendez-vous* at the Rijksmuseum in Amsterdam. This was an immediate success. Captain MacLeod was at once attracted to the tall, strikingly handsome, dark-haired girl with her good figure and generous mouth, while Margaretha's love of military uniforms and the excitement of the whole thing helped her to overlook her suitor's almost total baldness (which was, however, balanced by a fine moustache) and the substantial difference in their ages. By the end of the month they were engaged to be married and on 11 July 1895, just three and a half months after their first meeting in the nearby Rijksmuseum, the couple were declared man and wife in Amsterdam City Hall: John, with bald pate and bristling moustache, buttoned into his best uniform, carrying his sword, wearing a couple of medals and showing every single one of his thirty-nine years; on his arm the eighteen-year-old Greta in her bridal veil.

Eighteen months later, at the end of January 1897, a son was born to Margaretha MacLeod and three months after that she and her husband sailed for the Dutch East Indies. A photograph, taken on board the S.S. *Prinses Amalia*, shows a rather elegant, interesting-looking Margaretha sitting with a group of other, much less interesting-looking passengers, while John, in uniform, wearing his képi and two medals, stands stiffly behind her. Less than a year after their arrival another child was born to the

MacLeods: a daughter, called Jeanne Louise. For Margaretha this first journey to the East opened up a whole new world, which until now she had only dreamed of – a world, incidentally, in which good-looking young white women were at a premium and where she received from all sides the admiration she felt was her due.

But already the MacLeods' marriage was beginning to show signs of strain. Even before they left Holland, their friends, without blaming either of them, had noticed the tension between them. In June 1899 the death of their little son, Norman, poisoned apparently by a disgruntled servant, brought them briefly together, but only for a time. To John it was a shattering, disillusioning blow. Other misfortunes followed. Margaretha fell ill. The climate and all the other limitations of colonial life were fast becoming too much for both of them. In sweltering heat, amid clouds of insects, nerves are on edge and minor causes of irritation are easily magnified out of all proportion. John by this time knew that he would never be promoted to colonel. By the end of 1900 he had decided to resign his commission.

There followed eighteen months during which they remained in the Indies, quarrelling savagely and deeply unhappy together. For both of them the East had lost any charm it had ever had. By now Margaretha was talking openly of her determination to return to Europe. John, too, was tired of the Indies. It was almost the only thing they were agreed on. In March 1902 they sailed for Holland.

They did not remain together for long after their return. In August Margaretha applied for a legal separation which was quickly granted. It was to be followed four years later by a divorce. For a time she stayed in Amsterdam, and then went back to her uncle in the Hague. Their daughter, now five years old, went to live with her father. Money was short. Margaretha could not find work. The alimony John was supposed to pay her never materialized. She had long wanted to see Paris. Now at last she was a free agent. One day she simply took a ticket and went there.

But Margaretha's first trip to Paris was a disaster. She had no work and no money and, to the penniless unemployed, Paris, like most cities, is not very welcoming. She tried to find work as an artist's model, but this proved uncongenial and unrewarding. Soon she was back in Holland, only to find that for a young woman with no money Holland did not have much to offer either. But Margaretha was not easily put off. She now possessed a little more experience of life. In 1904 she went back to Paris, determined this time to succeed.

Her new approach was a bold one: though practically penniless, she put up at the Grand Hotel. In Sumatra she had learned to ride and soon she was appearing at the Cirque Molier in the Rue Benouville. She was a natural horsewoman and her turns were a success, but the proprietor,

Ernest Molier, appreciating her charms at their proper value, had a better idea for her: she should dance. Her experience in this field was limited, but this, she quickly realized, need not matter. All she needed was a pretext, a myth, a story-line. And here, apart from a sense of rhythm and a remarkable body, she had three immense assets: her five years in the Far East, sufficient effrontery, and an enormously fertile imagination.

She was fortunate, too, in the moment of her arrival and in the mood prevailing in Paris at the time. The threat of war still seemed remote; money was plentiful; society was at its most brilliant; all kinds of excesses were accepted as a matter of course; art in all its manifestations was flourishing – the more luxuriant and exotic, the more successful. What better place or moment in history could there be for the début of what one English writer called 'a woman from the Far East who had come to Europe, laden with perfume and jewels, to introduce some of the richness of oriental colour and life into the satiated society of European cities'? And he went on to speak of 'veils encircling and discarded' and – the phrase is typical of the period – 'just a suggestion of naughtiness'.

In that first winter of 1904 to 1905 the stage could not have been better set for Margaretha Zelle's début in the role of Lady MacLeod: exotic, aristocratic and romantic with, on top of everything else, that additional 'suggestion of naughtiness' which utterly made the evening. Little wonder that the sixty-nine-year-old Monsieur Guimet lost no time in approaching her on behalf of his museum. As the great Colette was to write later with a woman's eye for essentials, 'The moment when Mata Hari, freed of her last girdle fell modestly forward upon her belly, carried the male – and a good proportion of the female – spectators to the extreme limit of decent attention.'

In a matter of weeks the hatter's daughter from Leeuwarden, the discarded wife of Major John MacLeod, had achieved instant, phenomenal success. Her wildest dreams had come true. She was in demand everywhere, not simply as a dancer but as a guest, a social celebrity and, needless to say, as a mistress.

Meanwhile offers of every description were beginning to pour in from London, St Petersburg, Vienna and Berlin. Save in the stuffiest strongholds of the Faubourg Saint-Germain, no party was complete without her. Colette, sharp-eyed and acidulous as usual (she had already made the malicious observation that on stage, while revealing everything else, Mata Hari managed to keep her breasts 'prudently hidden'), met her at a garden party: 'A loud, strongly-stressed voice calling me by my *nom de plume* made me turn round. I found a lady in a black and white check suit, her bust held high by a boned cuirass of stays, a veil with velvet chenille dots upon her nose, holding out a tightly-gloved hand in white glacé kid stitched with black.

7

I also remember a frilled shirt with a stiff collar and a pair of shoes of a bright egg colour. I remember my amazement. The lady laughed heartily, displaying a set of strong, white teeth, gave me her name, wrung my hand, expressed the hope that we might meet again and did not move a muscle as the voice of Lady W. rang out beside us, loud and clear: "She an Oriental! Don't be silly! Hamburg or Rotterdam, or possibly Berlin".'

But most people – men in particular – raved about her and there is certainly nothing in her contemporary photographs to justify Colette's suggestion of brash vulgarity. As for her breasts, she usually seems to have kept them covered in public, possibly because of their less than perfect shape, though most experts deny the story that they had been bitten off by Major MacLeod in a fit of jealousy.

If Mata Hari was to make the most of her opportunities – artistic, social and, not least, financial – she clearly needed professional advice. This, in the event, was provided by a prominent member of the Paris bar, Maître Edouard Clunet, who was henceforth to become her legal adviser and friend. Another friend was Gabriel Astruc, a leading French impresario, who launched her on a truly spectacular career. In January 1906, she was dancing in Madrid. In February she was at Monte Carlo. Later that year she was in Berlin. In Berlin, Mata does not seem to have danced, at any rate professionally. While there, however, she became the mistress of Lieutenant Alfred Kiepert of the Eleventh Regiment of Hussars from Krefeld in Westphalia, who set her up for a time in an apartment in the smartest quarter of the capital. In December she went on to Vienna, where she danced both in tights and in the nude, causing, it appears, a sensation in both. She also gave, for the benefit of anyone who cared to listen, one or two imaginative new accounts of her origins and background. Like the French and the Spaniards, the Viennese were captivated by her. Leaving Vienna at the beginning of 1907 she spent the next couple of months travelling. Then, at the end of 1907, having broken with Lieutenant Kiepert, she returned to Paris, where, as the New York *Herald* of 12 December duly reported she put up at the altogether admirable Hotel Meurice in the Rue de Rivoli.

Thanks to her own earnings and to the generosity of her many admirers, Mata Hari now had plenty to spend and had become one of the best-dressed (and most-photographed) women in Paris. At the Grand Prix d'Automne at Longchamps in October 1908, she wore a sensational velvet dress with an elaborately embroidered corsage, a high neck and ruched sleeves, an immense fur-lined velvet muff and a fur-trimmed velvet hat, set off by a twelve-inch plume of osprey feathers. The photographer has skilfully captured the ripe, assured beauty and elegance of the *femme de trente ans*, as she stands, with all eyes on her, amid the crowd of dressed-up race-goers.

In January 1910 she again danced in Monte Carlo, this time as Cleopatra to the music of Rimski-Korsakov. After which, for much of 1910 and 1911, she to all intents and purposes disappeared from circulation. In fact, for the next year or so, she seems to have spent most of her time living quietly in the country at a château near Tours, where she had been set up in style by a prosperous stockbroker. Horses and riding still meant a lot to her and, now that she had time, she would go for long rides in the country. In August 1911 she went to Vittel to take the cure, attending the Concours Hippique in an elegant white Brussels lace summer dress and a large picture hat lavishly garnished with ostrich feathers, shaded to match her parasol and the trimmings of her dress – an outfit which clearly delighted the photographers (as did everything else she did or did not wear).

Returning to Paris towards the end of 1911, Mata Hari moved into the Villa Rémy, a mock-Tudor or possibly Norman villa, in the Rue Windsor at Neuilly. During the winter season of 1911–12 she danced in two ballets at the Scala in Milan, thus, after barely six years, setting the seal on her career as a professional dancer.

By this time her rich stockbroker had run out of money and disappeared from her life. She therefore wrote to Gabriel Astrue, asking if he knew anyone with some money who would care to give protection to artists. She herself, she went on, urgently needed 30,000 francs to give security to her art. Meanwhile, to the casual observer, Mata Hari gave few signs of financial embarrassment. Life at Neuilly went on as usual and in the leafy avenues of the Bois de Boulogne, where she went riding every day, no one was better dressed or better mounted. Among those who admired her as she cantered by was the Minister of War, General Messimy, who also went riding in the Bois and who had met her with his old friend Monsieur Guimet. 'She was', he said long afterwards, 'a splendid looking, mysterious creature. She used to smile at me in the most engaging manner . . . But I didn't set much store by this, knowing perfectly well that it was my job rather than me personally that she was interested in. My friends tried to warn me against her, saying that she was not only a terrible man-eater but a terrible money-eater as well.'

Mata certainly spent a lot of money. In the event no likely benefactor with 30,000 francs to spare materialized. Nor did any lucrative engagements come her way. With nothing to take her abroad, she stayed in Paris, dancing here and there and, as usual, talking volubly about herself and her dances. These now seem to have taken on an Indian, rather than an East Indian flavour, being accompanied by a turbaned orchestra. In September 1913 the London *Tatler* devoted a double-page picture feature to them beneath the caption 'Lady MacLeod dances in the light of the moon to her friends'. Lady MacLeod, it went on to explain, 'had been brought up in India, which inspires so many of her dances. Recently her ladyship gave a wonderful *soirée d'art* at her magnificent *hôtel* at Neuilly near Paris to which only a few special friends were invited. The dances which she performed were most suggestive of religious rites and love and passion and were brilliantly executed'. Three months later American *Vogue*, then at the very start of its career, published a similar set of photographs and also an article about her under the headline 'As danced before Buddha. Concerning Lady MacLeod, the Mata Hari, who brought the sacred dances to the Uninitiated West'. This vividly described her childhood not in India but on the Isle of Marouda, where her grandfather was Regent and where 'like a child of the people she passed from one temple to another until the different gods . . . were as familiar to her as to a native' and she 'gained an understanding of the hidden meaning and deep-seated influence of the Buddhist religions'. After which she 'married Lord MacLeod when barely seventeen and left her native land to go with him to Scotland'. And so on and so forth. 'Of course,' the article concluded, 'like all dramatic artists, she hopes eventually to come to America.'

Meanwhile for Mata Hari money was still short and the summer of 1913 found her, at the age of thirty-seven, accepting engagements, not at the Scala or the Berlin Opera, but at the Folies Bergères and, worse still, in Palermo. But there were better times ahead, or so it must have seemed. Early in 1914 she went to Berlin, where she was due to open in a play at the beginning of September. Soon the German papers were full of her, reporting in particular that she and her old love, Herr Kiepert, were together again.

Herr Kiepert, as it happened, was not the only German with whom Mata Hari was seen in Berlin. The 1st of August 1914 found her driving through the streets of the capital in a motor car belonging to another of her lovers, a senior police officer called Griebel. Suddenly they heard a distant roar and, making for the Imperial Palace, came on an immense crowd cheering the Kaiser. The crisis which for a month or more had threatened Europe had come to a head. A few hours later Germany was at war.

On learning that war had been declared, Mata Hari's first instinct seems to have been to get out of Germany. But travel in wartime Europe was far from easy. Fortunately for her a friendly Dutchman she met in the hotel took pity on one so pretty and in such obvious distress and managed to get her a sleeper on the night train to Amsterdam. Knowing her reputation and being a married man, he was careful, however, not to travel with her himself.

A few days later she arrived in Amsterdam with no money and very few belongings. Being Mata Hari, she did not, however, stay stranded for long. To another instant admirer, whom she happened to meet in the street, she explained with the ready inventiveness which always stood her in such good stead and in charming Slav-accented French that she was a Russian. For the good Dutchman the prospect of an affair with a glamorous Russian had instant appeal. Soon she was well provided for. And by the time her benefactor discovered that she was as Dutch as he was, her immediate difficuties had been solved.

To be living in Holland again amongst her own people after all that had happened in the last ten years was a strange experience for the former Margaretha Zelle. But by the end of the year, she was dancing to packed houses at the Theatre Royal in the Hague, and other engagements followed. Soon she had found a new and influential lover, *'un Colonel-Baron'*, as one authority describes him, and by the summer of 1915 was comfortably installed in a neat little house in the Hague. That December, travelling by ship to England and back across the Channel to France (for Belgium was occupied by the Germans), she paid a short visit to Paris in order to move her belongings out of the Villa Rémy. Some possessions she sold and others she took back with her to Holland, whither she returned early in 1916 by way of Spain and Portugal.

Mata Hari's new lover, the Colonel-Baron van der Capellen, seems to have been a relatively rich man and very much part of the Dutch establishment. But, in spite of the security her new liaison afforded her and of the Baron's frequent visits to her comfortable little house, Mata Hari, for one reason or another, still hankered after Paris. After the life she had become accustomed to there was so little to do in the Hague, so little going on, so few amusing people. She was even quite glad, when she met him at parties, of an occasional chat with the German Consul, Herr Krämer, a quiet sort of man, who before the war had been some kind of merchant.

So in the spring of 1916, having obtained a new Dutch passport, she applied to the French Consul for a French visa and to the British Consul for a British visa – both necessary for a wartime journey to Paris. But though the French visa was granted without difficulty, the British visa was for some reason refused. And so Mata Hari decided to travel instead by way of Spain, sailing towards the end of May and arriving in Paris from Madrid around the middle of June.

During her stay in Paris Mata Hari, now approaching forty, made no pretence of remaining faithful to the Colonel-Baron or indeed to anyone else. One of her lovers at this time was the Marquis de Beaufort, whom she had met at the Grand Hotel on her previous visit. Another was Jean Hallaure, a French cavalry officer, whom she had met before the war at the Cirque Molier and who, after being wounded, now had been given a job on the

Staff. A third was a twenty-five-year-old Russian, Captain Vadim Maslov. Vadim, by all accounts, she loved best of all, but there were also, it was noticed by those whose business it was to keep track of such things, an Italian, two Irishmen, four Englishmen and a Montenegrin, not to mention a couple more Frenchmen, one of whom was a general.

In the summer of 1916 Captain Maslov had been wounded and was convalescing at Vittel, where Mata had spent some enjoyable weeks taking the waters five years earlier. Being anxious to join him there she asked her friend on the Staff, Hallaure, how to get permission to visit Vittel, which was in a military Zone. Either on this or on some other pretext, he appears to have suggested that she should go and see someone at 282 Boulevard St Germain. What happened next is not entirely clear, but the office in which she found herself on arriving at No. 282 turned out to be a section of the French Intelligence Service or Deuxième Bureau, presided over by a certain Captain Georges Ladoux, a short, rather squat man of forty with hair *en brosse*, steel-rimmed spectacles and a short, rather straggly moustache.

According to Ladoux's own account the suggestion that she should pay him a visit had been put to her at his instance by her friend Jean Hallaure. He also seems, on the strength of repeated warnings received from the British, to have half suspected her of being a German spy and to have formed the project either of setting a trap for her or of using her as a double agent. Whatever the truth of the matter, the conversation which now took place between Mata Hari and Captain Ladoux quickly took an intriguing turn.

Ladoux has himself described Mata's arrival in his office, wearing a dark tailor-made suit and an enormous straw hat adorned with a single grey ostrich feather. Like so many others, he was immediately struck by the way she moved with all the grace and assurance of an experienced actress and, in addition, with a provocative swaying of the hips, which at once revealed the exotic dancer.

'*Que voulez-vous de moi?*' she inquired as she calmly sat down opposite him. After which she quickly followed up her advantage by suggesting with a charming smile that, as it was such a hot day, he might tell the police-spies who were following her to go and drink her health at the *bistro* across the way. In any case, she went on, why *was* she being followed and why had her hotel room been ransacked? Did they think she was a *spy*? Had they any reason to suspect her? 'No', replied Ladoux, wondering by his own admission whether the British really had any grounds for their assertion that this calm, self-assured, charming lady was a spy. 'We don't share the suspicions of our English friends and that is why we are going to allow you to go to Vittel.' And he went on to say that he had done his best, through Lieutenant Hallaure, to bring about her present visit to him. He knew, he hinted, of her affairs with Hallaure and that Maslov was another of her lovers. He even half-implied that he might want her to work for him. Their conversation had throughout been agreeable and light-hearted in tone. Before she left, Mata promised to come and see him again when she got back to Paris.

Arriving at Vittel in early September, Mata Hari spent the next few weeks there, taking the waters and seeing a great deal of Maslov, who, according to one account, actually asked her to marry him. On her return from Vittel she again went to see Captain Ladoux. She was, she said, after a few preliminary exchanges, ready to work for him. But being now anxious to marry Captain Maslov (*'peut-etre le seul amour de ma vie'*) and live happily ever after, she would need a lot of money, one million francs, mainly in order to impress Captain Maslov's father, an admiral who came of a most distinguished family. But her services, she explained, would be well worth it. She had any number of useful contacts in Holland and in German-occupied Belgium, too. She even knew the German Crown-Prince. *'Et si je devenais la maîtresse du Kronprinz,'* she asked, *'vous me le donneriez . . . mon million?'* And more in the same vein.

By the time she left Ladoux's office, they were agreed in principle. Next morning they made more detailed plans. Ladoux wanted her, he said, to go to Holland for him, travelling via Spain. He would book her a passage. Just what other instructions he gave her, then or later, does not appear, though he evidently let her know that he still half-believed her to be working for the Germans.

Early in November 1916, Mata Hari entered Spain at Irun. Thence she travelled by train to Madrid. In Madrid she again found that she was being followed by a French agent, whom she at once recognized for what he was. She accordingly went up to him in the hall of the hotel, told him with her most charming smile that she was proposing to stay in Madrid another day and asked him to 'be a gentleman' and not to follow her that afternoon, as she was supposed to meet someone very dear to her between two and four. To this the agent politely agreed, but quickly sent a colleague of his to follow her instead. His colleague, aged thirty-six, was disguised as a sexagenarian bicyclist. According to his report, Mata Hari then took a horse-cab to a café, whence she made two telephone calls. Following her on his bicycle, the second agent later claimed to have traced these calls to the Deutsche Bank in Madrid and to the German Consul in Vigo.

From Madrid, Mata Hari next caught the train to Vigo where she embarked on the S.S. *Hollandia*, bound for Rotterdam via the British port of Falmouth. At Falmouth, however, the *Hollandia* was boarded by British security officers. After looking at her passport, which was made out in her own name, they accused her of being in fact Clara Benedict, a well-known German spy from Hamburg. An inspector from Scotland Yard then appeared, arrested her and, after taking her by train to London, committed her to jail. Thence she immediately addressed a despairing appeal for help to the Dutch Minister in London, to whom it was in due course forwarded by Basil Thomson, the Assistant Commissioner of Police.

While she was in London, Mata Hari was twice interviewed by Mr Thomson. She clearly made a considerable impression on him. 'I expected,' he writes in his book *Queer People*, 'to see a lady who would bring the whole battery of her charms to bear upon the officers who were to question her. There walked into the room a severely practical person who was prepared to answer any question with a kind of reserved courtesy, who felt so sure of herself and of her innocence that all that remained in her was a desire to help her interrogators. The only thing graceful about her was her walk and the carriage of her head. She made no gestures and, to say truth, time had a little dimmed the charms of which we had heard so much . . . I have said she was openness itself. She was ready with an answer to every question and of all the people that I examined during the course of the War she was the quickest on the uptake.'

At their second meeting the interview took a rather unexpected turn.

'I see how it is,' said Mata Hari. 'You suspect me . . . Very well then. I am going to make a confession to you. I am a spy, but not, as you think for the Germans, but one of your allies – the French.'

But, even though he had by this time presumably satisfied himself that Mata Hari was not a German and that the passport on which she was travelling was her own and genuine, Mr Thomson still felt sure that she was a spy. 'We were convinced,' he writes, 'that she was acting for the Germans and that she was on her way to Germany with information which she had committed to memory.

'On the other hand,' he continues, 'she had no intention of landing on British soil or of committing any act of espionage in British jurisdiction and, with nothing to support our view, we could not very well detain her in England; so at the end of the second interview I said to her, "Madame [she spoke no English], we are going to send you back to Spain and, if you will take the advice of someone nearly twice your age, give up what you have been doing." She said, "Sir, I thank you from my heart. I shall not forget your advice. What I have been doing I will do no more. You may trust me implicitly."'

After which, Mata Hari was released by Scotland Yard (who, I find, are still reluctant to answer questions about her) and, discriminating as ever, moved a few hundred yards along the Embankment to the Savoy Hotel.

Just what passed between Basil Thomson and Georges Ladoux at this or any other stage is still far from clear. According to Ladoux the British sent him a signal notifying him of Mata Hari's arrest and her claim to be working for the French. To this he replied with true Gallic nonchalance: *'Comprends rien. Refoulez Mata Hari en Espagne'*. Which is what in fact was done.

On the face of it, it seems likely that something had happened earlier in the War to make the British security authorities (who, it will be recalled, had already refused her a visa in the spring of 1916) suspect that Mata was a German agent and that they so informed their French colleagues and that they were therefore pained and surprised when they found that the Deuxième Bureau were using her as an agent. It also seems possible that a certain element of rivalry entered into their mutual relations and influenced the decisions of both. As for Mata Hari, she followed one part of Mr Thomson's advice and left for Spain, and by 10 December was safely installed at the Palace Hotel in Madrid. There she remained until the beginning of January for what she claimed were 'sentimental reasons'.

Mata certainly did not waste her time in Madrid. Spain was neutral and both the Germans and the Allies made plentiful use of Madrid as an espionage centre. Spying, she was beginning to realize, had a definite appeal for her and she wanted to get to work. It was not long before she had made contact with Major Kalle, the German Military Attaché, and soon after that she became his mistress. Exactly what passed between them must remain a matter of speculation. There can be little doubt that Kalle thought that he had recruited her as an agent. He also certainly gave her money. At this stage of the war the Germans were trying to make trouble for the French in Morocco and for this purpose were secretly landing soldiers and agents from submarines along the coast. These operations came within Major Kalle's sphere of activities and according to Mata were one of the subjects they discussed when not otherwise engaged.

At about the same time Mata made another conquest. The French Military Attaché, Colonel Denvignes, a senior officer, soon to be promoted General, proved as susceptible to her charms as his German opposite number and took the first opportunity of congratulating her on the majestic entry he had seen her make by the main staircase of the Ritz. It was not long, we are told, before he was *'amoureux comme un sous-lieutenant'*. Once again, business mingled with pleasure. While seeking (and possibly obtaining) her favours, Colonel Denvignes evidently imagined in his turn that he was recruiting her as an agent. At any rate she seems to have passed on to him and indeed to Ladoux what Kalle had told her about the secret landings in Morocco. What she certainly gave Denvignes was a ribbon from her corset or, according to another account, from the bunch of violets she wore in her cleavage. This, we learn from more than one source, excited him immensely and became one of his most prized and frequently displayed possessions.

Meanwhile, hearing nothing from Georges Ladoux and gaining the general impression that the French were suspicious of her, Mata lost patience and, early in January, took the train back to Paris. At the Gare d'Austerlitz she briefly encountered Colonel Denvignes returning to Madrid after a quick visit to Paris. His obvious embarrassment on meeting her and the sudden change in his attitude towards her came as a shock to her. Clearly someone had said something to him. Captain Ladoux, too, when she eventually managed to obtain an interview, was a great deal less forthcoming than he had been.

But Mata, as always, had other fish to fry. Paris in 1917 was full of old friends and glamorous uniforms. After first putting up briefly at the Plaza Athénée, she took a room at the Elysée-Palace Hotel on the Champs Elysées and was soon back in the swim. Amongst the old friends who sought her out was her beloved Vadim Maslov, her *amant de coeur*, whom she had not seen since the previous autumn. Only one thing cast a slight shadow on her happiness – an uneasy feeling that she was under suspicion. Even Vadim had been warned against her.

The rest of January went by and the first twelve days of February. On the night of 12 February Mata went to bed as usual in her room at the Elysée-Palace. Next morning there was a loud knock at her door. She opened it to find several policemen in the passage. They told her to get dressed: she was under arrest. Their chief, Commissaire Albert Priolet, then read out the charge against her: she was accused of spying and having dealings with the enemy. Downstairs a car was waiting to take her to the prison of Saint Lazare.

Ever since their original encounter in August 1916 and by his own account long before that, Captain Ladoux had been working hard on Mata Hari's dossier. There had been the reports of the various agents who had followed her in France and Spain. There had in all probability been exchanges with Basil Thomson. And, most important of all, there had of late been a number of signals passing between Madrid and Berlin, which, intercepted by the French monitoring station on the Eiffel Tower and deciphered, seemed to him without any doubt to concern Mata Hari, who was referred to in them as agent H21, employed by the German Intelligence Centre in Cologne. In them her movements were accurately described and reference made to substantial sums of money which had been paid to her.

According to Ladoux, the first of these signals, sent by Major Kalle to Berlin, ran roughly as follows: 'Agent H21 just arrived in Madrid; managed to get recruited by the French, but was turned back by the British and is now requesting instructions and money.' To this Berlin had apparently replied promptly, promising a substantial payment to the agent in question. From Agent H21 the representative of the German Intelligence Service in Madrid had, it seemed, obtained a certain amount of not very definite information. There was a reference to Princess George of Greece (born Bonaparte), who lived in Paris. There was talk of an Allied offensive in the spring. And so on. It was none of it very precise or even very up-to-date news. It was also news that could easily have been gleaned without difficulty from chance conversations or from the public press. But, with a few adjustments, it could be made to fit into the case which Captain Ladoux was busily building up.

On the day of her arrest Mata Hari was immediately taken from prison to the Chancellerie, adjoining the Palais de Justice on the Quai de l'Horloge, for interrogation. The investigating officer or *rapporteur militaire* was Captain Pierre Bouchardon, a typical French functionary in his forties with a legal background, a narrow face, a narrow moustache and a dome-like forehead. This was the first of more than a dozen sessions which were to extend over the next four months.

According to Bouchardon's own account, after complaining of her arrest and asking that her old friend Maître Clunet should act for her, she began by declaring her complete loyalty to France. She a German spy! What an idea! On the contrary, it was in the interests of France that she had made contact with Major Kalle. By methods for which she was rightly famous, she had utterly enslaved the officer in question. And, once she had him in her power, it had been child's play to wheedle information out of him. And this information, particularly that concerning the German landings by submarine on the coast of Morocco, she had immediately passed on to Colonel Denvignes, who, she did not attempt to disguise, had also been rather taken with her.

During further sessions, which were spread over several weeks, Mata gave her interrogator a racy and thoroughly characteristic account of her activities during the past two or three years. For his part, he could not help admiring her. Her French, he was to recall many years later, though perhaps not always strictly grammatical, was vivid and *plein de saveur*. She had the right word for everything. And then what style! What irony! What a gift for repartee! *'Elle fit'*, he writes, *'une belle défense.'*

Meanwhile a couple of months had gone by and Bouchardon was obliged to admit that he was not making much progress, when on 21 April the Ministry of War belatedly backed up its original charge against Mata Hari by making available to him the complete series of intercepted signals which had passed between Major Kalle and Berlin between 13 December 1916 and 8 March 1917, and which Bouchardon had apparently not seen before. As far as Bouchardon was concerned, these clinched the matter. He now felt that he had an open-and-shut case.

After studying this new material for ten days, he fixed his next encounter with Mata Hari for 1 May, when he shut himself up with his *greffier* and the prisoner in what he calls 'a kind of cellar', stacked with the incriminating evidence now at his disposal. He then charged her directly with being Agent H21 and with having deliberately deceived Captain Ladoux, while all the time she was being paid by the Germans and furnishing them with valuable information. On 4 November, he said, referring to his file, she had received 5,000 francs through the Dutch Consul. This came from Germany. In Madrid in December Major Kalle, on instructions from Berlin, had paid her 3,500 pesetas. Finally, in a signal to Berlin, Kalle had announced that on her return to Paris H21 wanted to be paid a further 5,000 francs via the German Consul in Amsterdam, her maid, Anna Lintjens, and the Dutch Consul in Paris. And this she had actually drawn.

From this point onwards, according to Bouchardon, Mata Hari did herself less than justice. Confronted with this evidence, she for once floundered wildly, seeking to suggest that Major Kalle could have bribed the porter at her hotel in Madrid in order to find out about her contacts and her private arrangements, and trying desperately to make out that any money she had been paid had come from her various lovers. But Bouchardon was remorseless, coming back again and again to her number, H21, and to the three payments made to her. Even supposing, he said, that two German women spies had had the same number, only one of them could have had a maid called Anna Lintjens. And again and again he kept bringing her back to the same inescapable facts.

In the end Mata's usually strong nerves showed signs of giving way. 'How pitiless you are,' she said through her tears, 'to torture a poor woman like this and ask her all these horrid questions!' But Bouchardon, as was his habit when interrogating a prisoner, kept walking relentlessly up and down, firing questions at her, first from one position and then from another. It became more than she could bear. *'Ah! Si vous saviez, mon capitaine,'* she screamed, *'ce que vous m'agacez à marcher toujours comme ça!'* And, having asked for some water to drink, she threw what was left of it all over his trousers.

As far as Bouchardon was concerned, his investigation was virtually closed, but, allowing a suitable interval to elapse, he sent for her again. This time she took a different line. He has left a detailed account of what she said.

'Today,' she began, 'I have decided to tell you the truth. My reason for not speaking sooner was that I was rather ashamed of myself. In May 1916

I was in my house at the Hague. It was late and my old maid, Anna Lintjens, had already gone to bed. There was a ring at the door. I opened it myself and recognized Herr Krämer, the German Consul at Amsterdam, who had in fact written to me to say he was coming to see me but without giving any reason. As it happened, Herr Krämer knew I had applied for a visa to go to France. He now put a question to me. "Will you do something for us?" he asked. "What we would like you to do is to collect any information while you are there that might interest us. If you agree, I have 20,000 francs for you."

'"That isn't much," I replied. "I agree," he said. "If you want more you will have to show what you are capable of. It's entirely up to you how much you earn." I asked for a few days to think it over.'

And Mata Hari went on to explain that, having thought it over, she decided to accept.

'I remembered" she said with exquisite feminine logic, 'that at the theatre I had danced at in Berlin, they had kept some very valuable furs of mine and I came to the conclusion that it would be *de bonne guerre* to reimburse myself in this way. I accordingly wrote to Krämer to say that I accepted and he came round immediately with the 20,000 francs in French banknotes. "You will have to correspond with us in invisible ink which no one except us can read", he said, "and sign yourself H21."'

He handed her three little bottles, of which two contained a white liquid, while the third was absinthe-green. He then moistened a sheet of paper with the first liquid; wrote on it with the second; and effaced it with the third. When she wanted to send him a secret message, he said she was to write it out in invisible ink and then, on top of it, write an ordinary letter about anything she liked addressed to him at the Hotel de l'Europe, Amsterdam.

'Having pocketed the 20,000 francs,' she concluded, 'I paid my respects to the Consul who, I can assure you, had a long wait for any letters from me. As for his three bottles, I threw them into the canal between Amsterdam and the open sea.'

These revelations did not, as it turned out, make quite the impression Mata Hari had hoped for or do anything to change Captain Bouchardon's mind. As he saw it, it was very unlikely that Krämer would have paid her as much as he had if she had not already been working for the Germans. Besides, he remembered that she had also visited Paris in December 1915 and had spoken to Major Kalle of two missions to France. Equally, if, having pocketed Krämer's 20,000 francs in May, she had really given the Germans no further sign of life, was it likely that they would have paid her another 5,000 francs on 4 November, not to mention the 3,500 pesetas she had had from Kalle and the second 5,000 francs she had been paid on reaching Paris? No, he concluded, in all three instances she was quite certainly being paid by the enemy after the event for services well and truly rendered.

Having, as it seemed to him, completed his case to his own satisfaction, Captain Bouchardon now amused himself by questioning Mata Hari about her life with the Colonel-Baron who had been her lover in Holland, the Belgian Marquis who had followed him and literally dozens of others, all of whom had paid lavishly for her favours. But even more interesting from his point of view were the various young officers she had picked up at the Grand Hotel in Paris who could not afford to pay her anything but no doubt had more to tell her about the situation at the front.

'I just love officers,' she said. 'I've loved them all my life. There's nothing I like better than sleeping with them, without worrying about the money. And then I simply adore comparing the physique and temperament of one race or nation with that of another.'

But Bouchardon, for his part, was taking all this in quite a different spirit, thinking not so much of the sexual prowess or otherwise of Mata's lovers as of all the different scraps of vital information a woman like her could extract from such a varied succession of military lovers, comparing and collating it all, and fitting it all together.

In one instance only was Captain Bouchardon convinced that Mata Hari was genuinely in love and that was with her young Russian lover, Vadim Maslov. Hearing, after her arrest, that Vadim had again been wounded, she begged Bouchardon for news of him. 'Thank you for sending me news of Captain Maslov,' she wrote; 'I am still worried and cry so much. Be kind, I beg you, and look for him at the hospital at Epernay. I can't bear the thought that he may have died and that I wasn't with him or that he thought I had forgotten him. You don't know how miserable I am. Get me out of here. I can't bear it.'

But, whatever her feelings for Maslov, Maslov's feelings for her do not seem to have been very deep. Far from being wounded, he was perfectly well and, when invited to make a statement about their relationship, sent a message to say that it had never amounted to much and he had been on the point of breaking it off when he heard of her arrest.

Returning to her cell once the hearings were over, Mata Hari felt that she had put up a good fight and was full of hope that she would be acquitted. But by now Bouchardon had begun to write his report to the Third War Council and his mind was already made up. His prisoner exactly fitted his idea of a spy. 'Speaking five languages,' he wrote afterwards, 'with lovers in every capital of Europe, moving in any number of different worlds and finding discreet accomplices in all of them, Mata Hari could justly claim to be *une femme internationale* – indeed it was one of the last things she said in my office.' For him, at least, there could be no doubt of her guilt. '*Elle était*,' he writes, '*l'espionne-née*' – a born spy.

The trial of Mata Hari opened at the Palais de Justice on 24 July 1917 at one o'clock in the afternoon. Things were not going well for the French that summer. All through 1916 they had suffered terrible casualties and everywhere morale was low. Russia was by now virtually out of the war and the Germans were able to concentrate their forces on the Western Front. That spring the British break-through had been halted and General Nivelle's offensive thrown back. Defeatist and pacifist propaganda was rampant. There had been mutinies in a large number of units and more seemed imminent. In a desperate attempt to save the situation, General Nivelle had been replaced as Commander-in-Chief by General Pétain, who was now ruthlessly restoring order.

Spy-fever in France, as elsewhere, was at its height (Captain Ladoux himself was to be denounced and arrested only four months later). A scapegoat was badly needed, if only to distract attention from the front and help explain such a succession of disasters. In the circumstances, what could have been more welcome than a sensational spy trial? A trial which would give the French an excuse to cry with even more conviction than usual, '*Nous sommes trahis!*' To a great many of those concerned it must have seemed that the forthcoming trial of Mata Hari exactly filled the bill.

Mata Hari was tried by a Military Tribunal, consisting of seven members of the Third Permanent War Council, appointed by the Military Governor of Paris and presided over by the most senior officer among them, Lieutenant-Colonel Albert-Ernest Somprou of the Garde Républicaine.

The prosecuting Counsel was Lieutenant Mornet, a thin, ascetic-looking man with a big beard, who some thirty years later was to prosecute General Pétain himself and some other members of his government on a charge of high treason and collaboration with the enemy.

Mata Hari's defence was undertaken by her old friend Maître Clunet, now seventy-four years of age, looking, Captain Bouchardon thought, like a Venetian Doge and wearing the medal he had won in the Franco–Prussian War of 1870. At the disposal of the Court was Captain Bouchardon's voluminous report to the Council of War. The Military Governor of Paris was represented by Major Emile Massard.

Mata Hari was brought into the courtroom wearing a blue dress with a considerable *décolletage* and a smart three-cornered hat, which gave her, according to one observer, an almost military air. As soon as she had given her particulars and the other immediate formalities had been completed, the President of the Court gave instructions for the Court to be cleared of the press and public. The interrogation of the prisoner then began.

She was charged with having been in touch with the Germans since 1915, with having come to France to spy for them and with having delivered Allied secrets to German agents in Spain and Holland. Basing himself on Captain Bouchardon's report, Lieutenant Mornet began by asking the prisoner about the money she had received from the Germans and the secret number they had given her. To his question she replied as she had replied to Captain Bouchardon, admitting that she had had communication with the Germans and even that she had received money from them, but refusing to admit that she had ever done anything to help them or to damage France's national interests.

The moment now came to call the witnesses. Several were unable to be present but one old friend, Jules Cambon, now Permanent Head of the Ministry of Foreign Affairs, appeared in person and testified that the prisoner had never asked him any questions of political or military significance. Another witness called by the defence, General Messimy, the former Minister of War, had got his wife to write on his behalf saying that her husband, being *'en pleine crise de rhumatisme'*, could not leave his room and in any case had never known the person in question. At this Mata burst out laughing. *'Ah! Il ne m'a jamais connue, celui-là!'* she said, *'Eh bien! Il a un riche toupet!'* And for a moment the court laughed with her.

That evening, after sitting for six hours, the Court was adjourned until eight-thirty the following morning, while the prisoner was taken under guard to a cell in the adjoining building.

Next day, 25 July, Lieutenant Mornet opened at some length for the prosecution, asking that the defendant should be found guilty on all charges. He began by saying that he was frankly embarrassed by the strength of his own case. Two plus two made four. What he was trying to prove was as simple as that and there was no answer to it. And more in the same vein.

Asked if she had anything to say, Mata Hari once more maintained that she was innocent. After which Maître Clunet launched into a rambling speech for the defence, which lasted for most of the long sultry afternoon. The prisoner was then led out, while the members of the Tribunal briefly withdrew to deliberate. On their return, they unanimously condemned her to death.

Neither Maître Clunet nor his client seem to have expected more than a spell of imprisonment, if that. On hearing the sentence, Maître Clunet broke down and wept, while Mata Hari, taken aback, said in a low voice, *'C'est impossible!'* and then again, *'C'est impossible!'*

From the Palais de Justice Mata Hari was taken back to her cell at Saint Lazare. The trial had lasted barely a day and a half. On 27 September the case came before the Court of Appeal and was summarily dismissed. A special appeal to the President of the French Republic for a pardon was rejected.

At six o'clock on the evening of Sunday 14 October, Major Massard at Military Government Headquarters received his copy of the official order for the execution of Mata Hari, signed by her former interrogator, Captain Bouchardon. The execution was to be carried out next morning at first light. At 4 a.m. an official car would pick up Captain Bouchardon at his home to take him to Saint Lazare. At 5 a.m. another car would call at the prison for Mata Hari.

Shortly after four next morning Captain Bouchardon arrived at the prison in his official car. He was followed soon after by Dr Bizard and Dr Bralez, the two doctors who had been attending Mata Hari. Major Massard, representing the Military Governor of Paris, did not appear until 4.45 a.m. (it was, he recalls, still dark as he drove up to the great gate of the prison). They were joined in due course by Colonel Somprou, by Maître Clunet, pale and shakier than ever, and by a number of other officers and officials. It was a cold, foggy morning, but there was already quite a crowd outside the prison, including a number of newspaper men.

An old nun, Sister Léonide, who had been at Saint Lazare for more than fifty years, took Dr Bizard and one or two of the others along the long rat-infested gaslit passage to cell twelve, where Mata Hari had been confined since the trial and where she was now sleeping with two other women. Mata Hari, to whom Doctor Bizard had given a strong sleeping draught the night before, did not wake when they entered the cell. But the other two women, realizing at once what was happening, started to cry. Mata Hari was then shaken awake and propped herself up in bed on her elbows. After this, she was told that her appeal for a pardon had been rejected. *'Ce n'est pas possible!'*, she exclaimed. Then, noticing Sister Léonide's distress, 'Don't worry, Sister,' she said, 'I shall know how to die. *Vous allez voir une belle mort.*' And when a nun hinted that she was showing too much leg while putting her stockings on in front of Dr Bizard: 'It's not the time to bother about that sort of thing' – a remark which stuck in the old doctor's mind in later years.

Of the men only Dr Bizard stayed in the cell while she dressed. 'Thank you, Doctor,' she said when he offered her his smelling-salts. 'As you can see, I don't need them.' She then asked for the Protestant chaplain, the Pasteur Darboux, who spent a few minutes with her and, according to one account, baptized her. After which the others came back. She was now dressed and ready.

23

She was wearing a blue tailor-made dress, trimmed with white, with a long jacket, a straw boater with a veil, gloves and a smart pair of shoes (*des fines bottines*, Major Massard remembered). '*J'ai toujours aimé à être bien chaussée*', she said. Once again she soothed Sister Léonide, who seemed on the verge of tears. To the formal and in this case clearly superfluous inquiry as to whether she was pregnant required under the French Criminal Code, she replied impatiently that she was not – how could she be? (It had, it appeared, been a desperate stratagem of Maître Clunet to try and save her.) After that she was taken to the *greffe* on the first floor, where for seven or eight minutes she wrote some letters. 'Whatever you do, don't get the addresses mixed up,' she said with a laugh, 'that could lead to no end of trouble!' She was then handed over to the Military Police, who took her to the car that was waiting for her below. Outside, it was now colder than ever. Seeing the crowd in the street, Mata smiled. '*Oh! Que de monde!*' she said. '*Quel succès!*'

It was a long drive from the prison to the Château of Vincennes and beyond it to the Polygon, a stretch of rough ground used for cavalry manoeuvres, where a number of troops were on parade. A bugle sounded and Mata helped Sister Léonide out of the car. The old nun then walked with her to where a stake had been driven into the ground, kissed her and left her there.

Now alone, she found herself facing a firing squad of twelve Zouaves wearing greatcoats and steel helmets. It was a few minutes after six and the sun was just rising. Majestically she refused to be blindfolded or tied to the stake, and the rope was simply looped round her waist. Then the *greffier* read out the sentence of death: '*Par arrêt du Troisème Conseil de Guerre la femme Zelle a été condamnée à mort pour l'espionnage.*' As the officer in charge gave the order to take aim, Mata Hari waved to the little group of onlookers. Then came the order to fire and twelve shots rang out, followed, a minute or two later, by a thirteenth, as an orderly with a pistol administered the *coup de grâce*.

'*Personne ne réclame le corps?*' asked the *greffier*. But none of Mata Hari's former friends claimed her body, which over the years had given such pleasure to so many of them, nor had anyone made any arrangements for a funeral. And so what remained of her was lifted into a rough deal box and taken off to one of the Paris hospitals for the medical students to cut up.

Looking back sixty years later, what conclusions or indeed what moral can one draw from this sad little tale?

Though with the years she has become the archetype of the Beautiful Spy (a destiny which could scarcely fail to please her), one cannot help asking oneself whether Mata Hari ever did any serious spying at all.

One can so easily see her on that evening in May 1916 when Consul Krämer came to call: still fretting about the loss of her precious furs, left behind in Germany two years before; as usual, short of cash; bored, now that she was back there, with the Hague and with her distinguished, but far from exciting lover, the Colonel-Baron. What, in the circumstances, could have been more welcome than the excitement of that half-expected knock on the door, of the offer of 20,000 francs simply for going to Paris (where she wanted to go anyway) and for doing, as she was the first to grasp, practically nothing?

And then, three months later, Captain Ladoux, whom she discovered half by chance in his office at 282 Boulevard St Germain. So keen, for his part, that she should try to do what in fact she had already done and infiltrate the German Secret Service. And, like Krämer, ready (or so it seemed) to pay her in good hard cash. All this would mean that, having reached the age of forty, she could now marry her true love and live happily for the rest of her days.

Little wonder that, by the time she reached Madrid, it meant nothing to her to shuttle back and forth between the French and German Military Attachés, bearing tales of royal intrigue and secret landings from submarines. One feels, even, that she may have quite enjoyed her unexpected encounter with Mr (shortly after to become Sir) Basil Thomson, that in some ways rather disappointing product of Eton and New College.

Who, after all, she must have reflected, could possibly be better than herself at keeping all these odd characters happy? Was that not precisely what she had been doing with all her many lovers for the past dozen years? It was just a question of using her charm, of drawing on that fantastically fertile imagination of hers or, when all else failed, of falling back on some half-remembered bit of gossip or faded file of old newspapers. Of dreaming up, in short, bedtime stories that could not possibly do anyone any harm or, for that matter, very much good.

The only trouble was that at the height of a European war, when millions of lives were at stake, not to mention political and military careers, such stories had a way of being taken more seriously than they deserved, of bringing in an unexpected bonus or, alternatively, of turning suddenly sour.

In the Palace Hotel in Madrid in December 1916, the next room to Mata Hari was occupied by a young Frenchwoman called Marthe Richer. Just as Mata Hari became the mistress of the German Military Attaché, Major Kalle, so Marthe, who was also working for Captain Ladoux, had become the mistress of the German Naval Attaché, Baron von Krohn (and, incidentally, made, she tells us, an appalling scene on reading a newspaper story which reported that the latter had also been Mata Hari's lover). And, just as Major Kalle paid Mata Hari out of German Secret Service funds, so his naval colleague likewise dipped into the same funds to reward Marthe for whatever services she happened to render. The main difference between the two stories lies in the ending. Mata Hari was shot. Marthe was awarded the Légion d'Honneur. Both, it may be added, later had films made about them. But, whereas Marthe's part was taken by some now-forgotten actress, the part of Mata (and this, one feels, would have been some consolation) was played by Greta Garbo herself.

And what, one is tempted to ask, of the spy-masters and spy-catchers, the intelligence and counter-intelligence officers, who, from their desks, in theory at any rate, controlled or tried to control the activities and destinies of all these 'queer people'? How do they come out of it all? What sort of figure do they cut? Consul Krämer and Captain Ladoux, Major Kalle and Colonel Denvignes, or, for that matter, Mr Basil Thomson, who, by sowing doubts in Ladoux's mind, may ultimately have been responsible for Mata Hari's terrible and possibly undeserved fate?

Here, once more, the writer of fiction scores every time. One can never help being impressed by the grizzled, decisive, utterly dependable father-figure with his direct manner and his direct line to the Prime Minister, sitting in his comfortable office looking out over St James's Park or Regent's Park, as the case may be. Again the reality is different.

Basil Thomson, later to be caught by his own police doing something he shouldn't in the park with a lady bearing the slightly improbable name of Thelma de Lava, was apparently the first to suspect Mata Hari, though on what grounds neither he nor anyone else ever made clear. And yet, when he caught her travelling quite openly on her own perfectly genuine passport, he mistook her for Clara Benedict, and then, when he had found out who she really was, advised her for no very good reason to stop working for the French and go to Spain.

Captain Ladoux, who in October 1917, the very month when Mata Hari was shot, was himself arrested as a spy, released, re-arrested and finally released again and awarded the Légion d'Honneur (after his chauffeur, who had accused him of treachery, had himself been shot as an enemy agent), may conceivably have been playing some incredibly deep game. He may have known much more about Mata Hari than has ever emerged, enough to justify shooting her six times over. But on the face of it this seems inherently improbable. What appears much more likely is that he was determined not to be outdone by Basil Thomson as a spy-catcher. And so, to save his own face, he did what can always be done with a double-agent: he had her shot simply for being in communication with the enemy. For, despite the intercepted telegrams, despite the various testimonies of this kind or that, the one thing that no one seems to have done was to produce hard evidence that she had ever given the Germans any information that was really of any value to them.

As for Major Kalle, combining business with pleasure, and Colonel Denvignes, with his purloined ribbon, they are frankly figures of fun, both reading each other's telegrams and both forcing their unwelcome attentions on the forty-year-old Mata Hari, who should from the first have been suspect to both. By their behaviour both can be said to have brought the reputedly respectable post of Military Attaché into total disrepute, while simultaneously Baron von Krohn was doing the same for that of Naval Attaché only a few doors away.

Of Consul Krämer, on the other hand, a merchant in civilian life and the man who in a sense started it all, we know nothing discreditable. In trying to recruit Mata Hari for his masters in Berlin without, apparently, trying to win her favours for himself (though this has been questioned), he behaved quite sensibly. In paying her 20,000 francs for her services, possibly rather less so. But then how could he, a simple merchant, be expected to guess that behind that impressive façade and all that talk, she would, with the best will in the world, never make much of a spy?

Two

MORE LIVES THAN ONE

For he who lives more lives than one
More deaths than one must die.

OSCAR WILDE.

On 1 October 1900 Captain Alfred Victor Redl was appointed to the Evidenzbureau or Intelligence Department of the Austro–Hungarian Imperial and Royal General Staff in Vienna, then directed by Colonel Baron Giesl von Gieslingen. Captain Redl, who had returned earlier that year from an eighteen-months' Russian language course and attachment to the Russian Army at the old Tartar town of Kazan on the Volga, had two functions in the Evidenzbureau. He was in charge of the important Russian Section, which was responsible for collecting information about Russia, at that time Austria's main potential adversary. He was also Chief of the even more important Operations Section or Kundschafterstelle. This was responsible for the despatch of secret agents and for the co-ordination and distribution of the intelligence material they collected to other branches of the General Staff. It was also responsible for security and counter-intelligence. In fact, as Captain Redl very soon realized, whoever controlled the Operations Section could very quickly control the Evidenzbureau as a whole.

Captain Redl, who at this time was just thirty-six, was extremely well thought of by his superiors. Indeed he was regarded as one of the ablest younger officers in the Imperial and Royal Army. Fair haired, pleasant looking and slightly built with a smartly brushed-up moustache, his outstanding ability had led to his advancement to the key appointment which he now held. In the Imperial and Royal Army noble birth or a sizeable fortune both helped to advance an officer's career. Alfred Redl had neither. He was one of the fourteen children of Franz Redl, a poor railway official from Lemberg or Lwow, who had died when Alfred was eleven, leaving his large family in extremely reduced circumstances.

Before transferring to the railways shortly after his marriage, Alfred's

28

father had served for eleven years as a lieutenant in the Imperial and Royal Army, for which he retained a certain nostalgia. Lemberg, the Headquarters of the 11th Army Corps, was a garrison town, full of uniforms and brass bands. Alfred's elder brother Oscar was already in the Army. It was thus perhaps only natural that Alfred, having at the age of fourteen successfully passed into the Lemberg Cadet School, should have decided to make the Army his career. But he did so with conscious enthusiasm and with utter determination to succeed.

Having passed out of the Cadet School in 1882, Alfred was posted as a non-commissioned officer to the 9th Galician Infantry Regiment, one of the 102 infantry regiments of the Imperial and Royal Army. Five years later, at the age of twenty-three, he was commissioned as a second lieutenant in the same regiment at a ceremonial parade held on 1 May 1887 in Lemberg in the presence of the Corps Commander and the Governor of Galicia. It was a big moment in his life, marking as it did the attainment of something he had striven for since childhood, his emergence from the poverty and squalor that had marked his early life and the first step in what he was already convinced would be a brilliant career.

Smart, hard-working and invariably agreeable, Alfred made an excellent platoon-commander. Two years later, in the spring of 1889, he was promoted lieutenant and appointed battalion adjutant. As adjutant he added still further to his reputation. 'A strong, staunch character, quiet, good-natured, capable, quick, accurate', said one report. 'Zealous and industrious', said another. 'Friendly, tactful, popular, modest', said a third. 'A very fine and able officer', was the colonel's final verdict.

On the strength of these opinions and of his performance in the previous written examinations, Alfred Redl was in October 1892 admitted to the Kaiserliche und Königliche Kriegsschule, the Imperial and Royal Staff College, founded some forty years before by the famous Marshal Radetsky in order to provide the necessary number of officers for posts on the Imperial and Royal General Staff. Alfred Redl was extremely able and extremely ambitious. For ability and ambition the General Staff, with its bottle-green uniforms, double row of buttons and double gold braid offered infinitely more scope than any other branch of the service. Numbering no more than four hundred officers out of a total of twenty-eight thousand, it was, in every sense of the word, a *corps d'élite*.

Two years later on 30 October 1894, having completed the long and strenuous course, Alfred graduated from the Staff College. 'On the basis of natural talents, zeal and thoroughness,' wrote the commandant, 'he promises to become a very able General Staff officer.' A few days later he was provisionally assigned to the General Staff in Vienna and some months after that began a two-years' tour of duty as General Staff officer of the

61st Brigade in Budapest, a city in its way scarcely less glamorous than Vienna itself.

In the spring of 1897 Alfred was promoted captain and transferred to the 30th Infantry Regiment in Galicia as a company commander. After what he had seen of life as a staff officer in Budapest and Vienna, regimental duty, especially in the remote provinces, had begun to lose some of its charm for him. A year later, having discovered that he was eligible to be sent on a Russian language course at Kazan, he made formal application to the Chief of the Personnel Branch of the Imperial and Royal General Staff for a posting to Kazan in the spring of 1899, adding that he already had a good grasp of Russian and wished to perfect his knowledge of that language. In due course the application was accepted, Alfred was transferred back to the General Staff and General von Klepsch, the Austrian Military Attaché in St Petersburg, was instructed to make the necessary arrangements with the Russian Army for the arrival in Kazan in May of Captain Alfred Redl and of another Austrian staff captain, Adalbert Dani von Gyarmata.

The two young officers travelled to Kazan by train by way of Warsaw and Vilna, St Petersburg, Moscow and Nizhni Novgorod. It was a long, leisurely journey in a cumbrous but comfortable sleeping car, lumbering along at twenty or thirty miles an hour, and punctuated by lengthy stops at the railway station restaurants where, in accordance with Russian custom, copious and elaborate meals were set before the travelling public. By now it was spring. The winter snows had melted. Along the railway line the silver birches were brilliantly green; in every direction the vast Russian plain stretched endlessly away and the gilded onion-domes of the Orthodox churches standing out above the roofs of the peasants' houses lent the landscape a different, more exotic look. On a young man of intelligence and imagination (and Alfred was well endowed with both) this first journey to Russia, remote, mysterious and equivocal, was bound to make a strong impression. This, in a sense, was enemy territory, where, as he had been duly warned before leaving Vienna, everyone, however hospitable and friendly, would inevitably be watching him with the close attention the Russians have always devoted to visitors from abroad. while he himself, as a keen staff officer, would necessarily be keeping his eyes wide open for anything of the slightest military or political interest.

At the turn of the century Kazan was a town of some 180,000 inhabitants, of whom less than one sixth were Tartars. Indeed by this time almost the only remaining indication of its Tartar origins was the tall seven-tiered Tartar tower, rising high above the walls of the Kremlin, from which the Khan's beautiful daughter was said to have cast herself down in despair after the city's capture by Ivan the Terrible. Besides the Kremlin and several old Orthodox churches, Kazan could boast three or four modern hotels and restaurants, strung out along the main street, two public parks, a theatre or two, a university and the headquarters of the 16th Army Corps. Like most garrison towns, it was the scene of much lively, if rather provincial, social life. Russians have always been fascinated by foreigners. Alfred and Adalbert, elegant in their bottle-green and double rows of buttons, soon found themselves, like their predecessors on the course, much in demand with the hostesses of Kazan. They also found that their monthly allowance of two hundred and fifty roubles, while adequate for their ordinary living expenses, was nothing like enough to enable them to play the part expected of them in local society.

In October 1899, six months or so after their arrival, Alfred, who for his part was entirely without private means, sat down to compose two long letters, one to the Chief of the Imperial and Royal General Staff and another to the officer in charge of the Personnel Section, Colonel Viktor Dankl.

The Austro–Hungarian General Staff officers [he wrote to the latter] occupy a particularly excellent and respectable position here in the highest society; they are very welcome in all salons and are very favourably regarded guests. One is overwhelmed with favours of every sort from all sides which naturally must be returned. The most fitting way to do this, albeit expensive, is to participate in or appear at charitable fêtes, of which there are an infinite number here; and we are absolutely obliged to attend fifteen or twenty of them. Here it counts as a matter of honour for each social leader to arrange annually at least one of these fêtes and since we are acquainted with most of these persons, frequently enjoy their hospitality, we are as a rule personally invited by them to appear at the bazaar. It is thus, so to say, impossible for us to stay away. Consider also that on such occasions one is forced to buy something from each lady one knows (around forty of them) and in addition since most ladies compete as much as possible for charitable purposes, one is invited or challenged to expensive purchases.

They also, he pointed out, needed money for extra clothes when not in uniform and for furs with which to face the Russian winter. 'Finally,' he concluded, 'I report that we are at present in good health and are industriously continuing the study of the Russian language under a well-trained and experienced teacher.'

Alfred's closely reasoned case produced the desired result. By return each of them was sent five hundred roubles, with the warning, however, that they would have to make this do. For the moment his financial problem was less acute.

As a good staff officer, Alfred Redl did not stay in Kazan for the whole of the eighteen months he spent in Russia. With the help of an allowance especially provided for this purpose, he used the time at his disposal to travel extensively in European Russia, visiting the Upper Volga, the Karma and Viatka Rivers, Warsaw in Russian Poland, Kiev and Odessa in the

Ukraine, Tiflis and Baku in Transcaucasia, the shores of the Black Sea and the Caspian, parts of Western Siberia and, of course, St Petersburg and Moscow; in short he got to know the country and the people. All of which, together with his improved knowledge of Russian, was duly noted down by those concerned as making him eminently suitable for appointment to the Evidenzbureau.

For many years now the Evidenzbureau, like so many other Viennese institutions, had simply continued on its easy-going way. The staff officers responsible for collecting information about different parts of the world had done so from the reports sent in by the Military Attachés in the various capitals and from the public press, which they studied in some detail. As for the Operations Section, the Kundschafterstelle, it had, under Alfred Redl's predecessor, taken things easier still, relying for the most part on help from its far more active German counterpart enthusiastically directed by Major Walther Nicolai. Such spies as it employed in Russia were almost certainly kept under continuous observation by Major Nikolai Stepanovich Batyushin, the dynamic director of the Russian Intelligence Centre West in Warsaw, while, as for picking up foreign spies, it had in the past twenty years only managed to catch four of the large number who were undoubtedly operating in various interests up and down the length and breadth of the Austro–Hungarian Empire.

Alfred Redl, keen, energetic, clear-thinking and ambitious, was determined to change all this. It was not long before he submitted to his chief, Colonel Baron von Giesl, plans for the reorganization of the Kundschafterstelle on rather more realistic lines with the object of enabling it to hold its own in the highly competitive world of international espionage. The Colonel, who had always had a high opinion of Redl, was much impressed by the proposals he now put forward and authorized him to go ahead with them, at the same time relieving him of his duties as head of the Russian Section, in order that he might henceforth concentrate all his energies on the work of the Operations Section.

This he did, working day and night, applying for increased funds, employing more agents, checking and double-checking on every one of them, improving his administration and security arrangements, visiting his outposts in the provinces, gradually bringing the central control, not only of the Operations Section, but of the entire Evidenzbureau, into his own capable hands. By the spring of 1901 the Directorate of Intelligence as already a very different place from the sleepy backwater to which he had been appointed six months earlier and Alfred's reputation as a promising young officer had been still further enhanced. Sufficiently enhanced, with-

32

out any doubt, to warrant the close attention of his opposite numbers on the other side of the hill, for in Russia they were quite certainly well aware of him and had been watching him since his tour of duty at Kazan two years earlier.

Not only was the Austrian Intelligence Service thus renovated and refurbished, but the Counter-Intelligence and Security Services as well. Spying on behalf of Austria's enemies was no longer the safe occupation it once had been. Suddenly spy-trial followed spy-trial and at most of them the key witness was Captain Alfred Redl, whose testimony generally tipped the balance for or, more usually, against the man in the dock. It was he, for example, who in January 1901 secured a verdict of guilty and a sentence of four and a half years hard labour for Captain Alexander von Carina, a former Austrian cavalry officer charged with passing secret information to the French and probably to the Russians as well. 'The verdict of guilty,' wrote the *Neue Freie Presse*, 'depended largely on the opinion of Staff Captain Alfred Redl.' Then there was Joseph Zaleski, a locksmith, and his stepfather, Peter Schuster, both sentenced to periods of hard labour in May of that year for giving the Russians particulars of roads, fortifications and other installations in the frontier area in Galicia. In January 1903 one Anton Alois Burghardt and three accomplices were found guilty of having tried to obtain the mobilization plans of the 10th Army Corps in Przemysl. In February Theophil Fedyk, a deserter from the Austrian Army, was convicted of having sold information concerning frontier fortifications in Galicia. In March Dr Bronislaus Ossolinsky was arrested in Lemberg. In August, having been interrogated by Alfred Redl, he confessed to stealing the rail mobilization plans for Galicia and was sentenced to a year's imprisonment. Most of these cases, it will be noticed, followed much the same pattern: the espionage was carried out in Galicia and those convicted received relatively light sentences.

The Russians, it may be observed, also had their successes in this field. In June 1902 Lieutenant-Colonel Grimm of the Russian Imperial General Staff was sentenced to twelve years hard labour at a secret court martial in Warsaw, while at about the same time Major Erwin Müller, the Austrian Military Attaché in St Petersburg, was hastily recalled to Vienna. These two events, quite clearly, were not unconnected.

Nor was this Colonel Müller's only such exploit. On an official visit to the Tsar with the Archduke Franz Ferdinand, the Heir Apparent, he had been approached while in St Petersburg by Colonel Cyril Petrovich Laikov of the Russian General Staff with an offer to sell him the Russian Army's plan of attack against Austria. Although he had been especially warned by the Archduke not to dabble in espionage on this occasion, the temptation had been too much for him and he had concluded the deal. On his next visit to

St Petersburg, however, he had found himself cold-shouldered by his friends in the Russian Army. Thinking that this might mean that they knew of his deal with Colonel Laikov, he felt momentarily uneasy and made some discreet inquiries. The reason for their attitude, he discovered, was quite different. Someone – his Russian friends assumed quite wrongly that it was he – had betrayed Laikov and the poor fellow had been obliged to commit suicide.

As for Captain Redl, every trial of a Russian spy was grist to his mill. At each trial, he was the hero, the star witness, the man whose evidence, whose special knowledge, had brought this or that traitor to justice. And with each trial his grasp of the situation and the extent of his special knowledge increased still further. He now knew as much as anyone about the frontier fortifications of Galicia or the mobilization plan for the 10th Army Corps, knowledge which for so keen an officer was bound sooner or later to have its uses.

It was thus only natural that, when in the summer of 1903 the time came for him to return to regimental duty, Colonel Eugen Hordliczka, who, after a spell in the key post of Austrian Military Attaché in Belgrade, had succeeded Baron von Giesl as Head of the Kundschafterstelle should have made a special request to General Beck, the Chief of the General Staff, for him to be left where he was. This, most exceptionally, was agreed to and he now became an established authority on espionage and counter-espionage, writing treatises on the subject, lecturing to the General Staff and to the police, and travelling all over Austria–Hungary on tours of inspection and investigation.

On first being posted to Vienna three years earlier, Alfred had taken a furnished flat on the top floor of a house at No. 50 in the Florianigasse in the Josephstadt or Eighth District, an easy half hour's walk from the Ministry of War. Now he moved a couple of houses along the same street to a larger and more commodious apartment at No. 48, again on the top floor. In his private as well as his official life he was launching out in a discreet and entirely suitable manner. Colonel Hordliczka was as pleased with him as Baron von Giesl had been. '. . . strong, honourable, straightforward,' he wrote, 'with a quiet even temperament . . . extremely hard-working and zealous and an easy man to get on with; respectful to his superiors, friendly and tactful with his contemporaries. Demanding and strict with his subordinates, but at the same time kind and thoughtful.' As a tactician he was equally impressive. 'He judged tactical situations correctly,' wrote Hordliczka of his performance on manoeuvres. 'He is clear and precise, a quick and accurate worker. Entirely suitable for Chief of Staff of an infantry division.' Off duty he was no less of a paragon: 'Helpful and modest with senior officers; very friendly, has excellent manners and only frequents the best society. Very popular and most correct in his behaviour . . . an excellent influence on younger officers.'

Nor was this last observation just imagination on the part of Colonel Hordliczka. Alfred was prepared to take any amount of trouble with young officers, and with young men generally, especially if he liked the look of them. For example, a former servant of his, now a bank-messenger, had asked him whether he could help the son of one of his fellow messengers to get into the Army. Having interviewed the boy, Stefan Hromodka, a slim, brown-eyed youth of fourteen, and formed a favourable opinion of him, Alfred took endless trouble to get him through the medical examination and into the Vienna Cadet School, even going so far as to suggest that he was his nephew, which, though not strictly true, was naturally a considerable help, and also made it simpler for the two to meet should the need arise. And so thanks to Alfred, in the autumn of 1903 young Stefan, whose father was a bank-messenger and whose mother kept a vegetable stall, was duly admitted to the Vienna Cadet School, with every prospect of becoming in due course an officer of the Imperial and Royal Army and with a generous allowance from his new-found benefactor, Captain Alfred Redl.

Towards the end of 1903, the Austrian Foreign Office seem to have received by way of their Embassy in St Petersburg information to the effect that the Russians were in possession of their northern war plans and in particular of their Northern Deployment Orders which, it seemed probable, had been betrayed to the Russians by an Austrian officer. Amid the consternation caused by this discovery, the task of tracking down the traitor was as a matter of course entrusted to Captain Redl as the officer in charge of counter-intelligence.

Once again Alfred's superiors were not disappointed. In due course he produced, with apparent ease, evidence which seemed to show that the plans had been passed to the Russians by a certain Lieutenant-Colonel Sigmund Hekailo, formerly Judge Advocate of the 43rd Landwehr Division based on Lemberg. This consisted of secret documents and photographs of secret documents sent by Hekailo to a cover address in Warsaw – in fact, to the house-keeper of a Russian staff officer there. To gain possession of these, he was careful to explain, had cost him twenty-nine thousand crowns, a sum which was naturally at once reimbursed to him out of secret funds by the Minister of Defence.

There was only one difficulty. Some time before this, Colonel Hekailo had come under suspicion of embezzling official and other funds, and, before any action could be taken against him, had promptly disappeared, presumably abroad.

It was now clear that in addition to stealing public funds he had also been peddling official secrets. The difficulty was to find him. But again Captain Redl had the requisite information up his sleeve. Sigmund Hekailo, it seemed, was living in Brazil under the name of Karl Weber. While under the Austrian extradition treaty with Brazil he could not be extradited for espionage, he could quite well be extradited for fraud and embezzlement. The necessary machinery was accordingly set in motion and in due course Karl Weber was arrested by the Brazilian Police.

When they came for him, Weber at first displayed a Russian passport and claimed that he was a subject of the Tsar, but on searching the house they discovered an Austrian full-dress uniform and knew they had found the right man. Having read somewhere of the Austrian sense of honour, they now generously left a loaded revolver in his cell, but Hekailo, who held a different view of the matter, did not avail himself of the opportunity thus offered. Nor did he take an equally strong hint that he should jump overboard on his way to Rio de Janeiro. Disappointed, the Brazilians shipped him back to Trieste battened down in the hold of a collier from which he emerged somewhat chastened, but still well aware of his legal rights.

Legally, as Hekailo knew, the Austrians could not have him extradited for embezzlement and then try him for espionage. On the other hand they could (and did) interrogate him about anything they chose. They found him ready enough to talk, often far into the night. It was quite true, he said, that, in addition to embezzling public funds he had sold a good many secret documents to the Russians. But not, he insisted, the Northern Deployment Plan, to which, as Judge Advocate, he had naturally not had access.

The commission which investigated Colonel Hekailo's case consisted of Major Wilhelm Haberditz, Captain Redl and Lieutenant Hans Seeliger of the Judge Advocates' Department, who took shorthand notes of the proceedings. Lieutenant Seeliger was much struck by Captain Redl's grasp of the subjects under discussion and also by his obvious determination to get Hekailo to confess that he had sold the Northern Deployment Plan to the Russians. But Hekailo, aware of the legal position and having relatively little to fear, kept calm. 'Where in the world could I have obtained this deployment plan, Captain?' he inquired coolly. 'Surely only someone on the General Staff in Vienna could have sold that to the Russians?' Happening to glance at Captain Redl as Hekailo said this, Seeliger thought he saw him wince slightly and turn pale, possibly at the insult to the Bottle-Green Corps. But only for a moment. Then, muttering something under his breath, he started to search busily through the papers in the folder in front of him.

In the end, after a long tussle, Hekailo revealed the name of one of his accomplices, Major von Wieckowski, an Austrian Pole serving at the time at Stanislav in Galicia and next day the investigating commission left for Galicia to arrest Major von Wieckowski.

Major von Wieckowski was duly arrested at his desk at Army Headquarters. But no amount of interrogation could break down his stoutly maintained claim that he was entirely innocent. Nor did a search of his office bring anything incriminating to light. At Redl's suggestion, the commission next went to his house – rather a fine one. Here, again, after searching for several hours, they found nothing. But Redl was not so easily put off. Quickly making friends with Wieckowski's six-year-old daughter, with whom he chattered fluently in her native Polish, he took her into the library and there by a trick induced her to show him where her father kept his papers. Pressure on a concealed button in the desk now revealed a secret compartment full of papers. These afforded plentiful proof of Major von Wieckowski's guilt. The method employed to obtain this particular piece of evidence had perhaps not been in quite the best traditions of the Imperial and Royal Army, but it had nevertheless produced the desired result.

The papers discovered in Wieckowski's desk made it clear that he had been receiving secret material from someone in the Lemberg garrison. The commission accordingly proceeded to Lemberg. There the most likely suspect turned out to be the garrison commander's personal assistant, Captain Alexander Acht, who was responsible for the safekeeping of all classified material. After further investigation, Acht was in his turn duly arrested and sent to Vienna.

Meanwhile a sudden and serious difference of opinion had arisen between Major Haberditz and Captain Redl. All at once Redl, who had played such an active part in tracking down Major von Wieckowski, had actually begun to argue that officer's innocence and that of Captain Acht. Surprised and irritated at this sudden volte-face, Major Haberditz tried to have Alfred Redl taken off the Commission. This Colonel Hordliczka refused to contemplate, but undertook to have a word with Redl in confidence. After this, things went more smoothly. Alfred Redl remained on the Commission and even volunteered to procure from one of his agents in Russia an additional piece of evidence which would still further incriminate Wieckowski. But now, for once, things seemed to go wrong and a saddened Redl was obliged to report that one of his best agents, a Russian staff-major, had been caught removing the material in question from the files and, after a summary investigation, had been sentenced to death and executed.

In the late summer of 1904 Hekailo, Wieckowski and Acht were tried *in camera*, found guilty and sentenced to twelve, ten and eight years of hard labour respectively. It was, on the face of it, yet another triumph for Alfred Redl. True, his two colleagues on the Investigating Commission might momentarily have had doubts about his seemingly inconsistent behaviour. But as Major Haberditz himself most strongly emphasized to Lieutenant Seeliger at the time, Captain Redl was not a man whose soundness or loyalty could possibly be called in question.

And sure enough, towards the end of July 1904, even before Hekailo and his accomplices had been brought to trial, Captain Redl had once more acquitted himself brilliantly as chief military expert witness at the trial of two more men accused of spying for Russia, Simon Lavrov and Bronislaus Dyrcz, both found guilty, as the *Neue Freie Presse* pointed out, 'chiefly on the testimony of military expert witness Redl'.

Not all the spies caught by Alfred Redl were working for the Russians. In the summer of 1905 came the cases of Auguste Doré, a spy in the pay of France, and Pierre Contin, who was found to be spying for Italy, making rather attractive little sketches of the frontier area in pen and ink and wash. In September, just after he had started investigating the latter case, Alfred Redl, now forty-one, was promoted to Major, awarded the Military Service Cross and appointed Chief of Staff of the 13th Landwehr Division. In this appointment, which kept him in Vienna and which he held for two years, Alfred as usual won high praise from his superiors and indeed from all with whom he came in contact. On manoeuvres he proved himself as successful as divisional Chief of Staff as he had done in the field of intelligence. 'Experienced, exceptionally able and extremely resourceful', wrote his divisional commander. In the course of 1906 he added the Military Service Medal with its black and yellow ribbon and a Spanish decoration to his Military Service Cross. He also moved to a considerably larger apartment on the top floor of Florianigasse 42.

One of his friends at this time was another young General Staff officer named Theodor Körner von Siegringen, who years later was to become a politician and Bundespräsident of a much diminished Austria. 'Like everyone else who knew him,' said Theodor Körner looking back over half a century or more, 'I liked Alfred very much. He was always dignified – very much a gentleman, but in a very friendly way ... He knew a great deal about military and international affairs. But, over and above that, his knowledge of human behaviour was amazing.' Had he not, after all, wheedled the six-year-old Sylvana Wieckowska into revealing to him the secret drawer where her father kept hidden the evidence of his treachery? And how could he have done that without a good grasp of child psychology?

In the spring of 1907 Alfred, feeling no doubt that he had earned a holiday, took a steamer-trip from Pola to Fiume and Trieste. With him went handsome young Stefan Hromodka, who had passed out of the Vienna

Cadet School the year before and was now accepted by all and sundry as his nephew.

In October 1907, after an absence of two years, Alfred was posted back to the Evidenzbureau, this time as deputy to its Director, Colonel Hordliczka. Under him, in charge of counter-espionage, was his friend and protégé, Captain Maximilian Ronge, small, bald and an unusually intelligent young officer. Attached to the Bureau in an advisory capacity was Lieutenant-Colonel August Urbanski von Ostrymiecz, recently returned from Macedonia.

There was also a new Chief of the Imperial and Royal General Staff. General von Beck had been succeeded by General Baron Conrad von Hötzendörf, a small, neat, good-looking, hard-riding officer who firmly believed in power politics and fancied the idea of short, sharp preventive wars against Russia, Serbia and even Austria's own not very dependable ally, Italy. In Baron von Aerenthal Austria had a Foreign Minister who also favoured a forward policy. Russia's Foreign Minister Izvolski had his eye on the Straits and on much else besides. In Turkey the Young Turks had come to power. There was perpetual unrest in the Balkans. In Germany Kaiser Wilhelm was scarcely a stabilizing influence. Facing him, Great Britain, France and Russia were loosely linked in a defensive alliance. Everywhere the stage was set for trouble and each of the next seven years was to be marked by at least one international incident which took Europe a step nearer to the impending conflagration.

In October 1908 a prolonged crisis, directly or indirectly involving almost every country in Europe, was caused by Austria's decision to annex Bosnia and Herzegovina, two Slav-populated frontier provinces, which, though already under her protection, were still nominally part of the Ottoman Empire and, to complicate things still further, were regarded with longing eyes by Russia's ally Serbia as part of a future South Slav State. Serbian subversive activities in both provinces and in neighbouring Croatia and Dalmatia, countered by vigorous repressive measures on the part of Austria, aggravated matters still further. Meanwhile Russian agents poured into Hungary, the Bukovina and Galicia, in preparation for a possible Russian attack on Austria in support of Serbia.

All this naturally kept the Kundschafterstelle busier than ever and afforded Alfred Redl innumerable fresh opportunities of proving his worth. Impressed by the excellence of his work, General Conrad von Hötzendörf in agreement with the Minister of War decreed that in the very likely event of hostilities breaking out, he should, despite his relative lack of seniority, at once be put in charge of the whole Directorate of Intelligence. In fact, the crisis resolved itself peacefully and Redl remained Colonel Hordliczka's Deputy. Even so, in May 1909 he was promoted to Lieutenant-Colonel and, on General Conrad's personal recommendation, awarded the Order of the Iron Crown. 'During the Balkan crisis,' ran Conrad's citation, 'he showed exemplary effort and striking capabilities.'

Colonel Hordliczka had now been Director of the Kundschafterstelle for six years and was clearly due for promotion. It was surely not too much to hope that, when the time came, that star performer Alfred Redl would succeed him.

Meanwhile there was plenty to keep Colonel Redl busy. The continuing crisis meant intensified efforts both in the field of espionage and of counter-espionage. In 1908 the total number of suspected spies arrested in Austria–Hungary had been sixty. In 1909 it exceeded eleven hundred. Fortunately the capable Captain Ronge was able to relieve Alfred of much of the counter-espionage work, while he himself concentrated on the collection of positive intelligence and on the briefings called for by General Conrad and the Imperial Chancellery.

With the increased likelihood of war, Austria's military co-operation with her ally Germany had become closer than ever. Following an exchange of letters between the two Chiefs of Staff, General Conrad von Hötzendörf and General von Moltke, concerning their common plan of attack, Colonel Redl was sent to Berlin for far-ranging discussions with the German Director of Military Intelligence. These proved most successful and in October 1909, not long after his return to Vienna, Redl was informed that the Germans had awarded him the Royal Prussian Order of the Crown, a much coveted decoration normally only given to generals.

Alfred, meanwhile, remained his usual hard-working, affable self. Many years later Captain von Hubka, formerly Military Attaché in Montenegro and now one of his subordinates in charge of the Italian section of the Directorate who also had rooms at No. 42 Florianigasse, was to recall the impression he made at this time. 'Despite his burden of work and the heavy responsibility of his position,' he said, 'he remained the same friendly if dignified officer whom everyone liked and respected. Sometimes we would spend an evening at the Volksgarten Restaurant. Several officers from the Directorate were usually present ... and on at least two occasions young Hromodka, whom we all believed to be Redl's nephew.'

Young Stefan was also to recall that October, when he was granted two weeks leave after graduating from the Military Academy at Wiener Neustadt as a Second-Lieutenant. 'I saw Redl nearly every day,' he said. 'He was very nice to me during my leave – took me everywhere and paid for everything. The night before I left for Brünn he told me that he was going to give me an allowance of fifty crowns a month. We talked about my future.

He warned me of all the pitfalls that faced a young officer and told me especially to have nothing to do with women. He said that he hoped he would soon be in a position to help me to get ahead faster.'

In November came the long-expected announcement that Colonel Hordliczka was leaving the Directorate, but not, as Alfred Redl had hoped, the news that he himself was going to succeed him. Instead, Colonel August Urbanski von Ostrymiecz, who had been attached to the Directorate since leaving Macedonia in 1907, was to become its Director and Alfred was to continue for a time as his deputy. Urbanski was, as it happened, a connection by marriage of General Conrad von Hötzendörf, the Chief of the General Staff. For Alfred, who knew that he had actually been earmarked to take charge of the Directorate in case of war and who for two years now had been its Deputy Director and mainstay, this could only be a sad disappointment.

To make up for this, however, he had about this time a stroke of good luck – or so he told his friends. An uncle of his had died, he said, and left him a not inconsiderable inheritance. Certainly, his way of life became noticeably more lavish. His new apartment in the Florianigasse was luxuriously furnished. His new bright red Austro-Daimler phaeton with its smartly-uniformed chauffeur, gleaming brasswork, initials and what looked like a coronet on the side-panels was the admiration of all his friends and it was not long before he put in an order for another of these expensive vehicles, apparently as a present for his young protégé, Stefan Hromodka.

Alfred Redl's disappointment at not being made Director of Intelligence was only temporary. Colonel Urbanski was often away from Vienna and during the next eighteen months Alfred was for much of the time in charge of the Directorate. In the spring of 1911, during a momentary lull in the international situation, he was posted to the 99th Infantry Regiment as Commander of its 4th Battalion, while remaining, however, an officer of the General Staff.

As his battalion headquarters were in Vienna, life for Alfred continued much as before. At about this time he moved to another, even larger apartment on the top floor of a rather handsome house at No. 10 Wickenburgstrasse, not far from where he had lived before. It was, in the words of one of his guests 'a luxurious establishment with costly furnishings that were definitely on the feminine side'. Here he gave champagne parties for his fellow officers at which he showed himself an excellent host.

A frequent guest at Alfred's parties was Stefan Hromodka, now an officer in the 7th Uhlans, whom he as usual introduced as his nephew. After the parties Alfred's chauffeur would sometimes drive Stefan back to the furnished apartment Alfred had taken for him at Stockerau, but quite often he would stay the night. In addition to the apartment and the Daimler he had given or lent him, Alfred was now paying Stefan an allowance of six hundred crowns a month – more than his own pay as a Lieutenant-Colonel. In the 7th Uhlans Stefan's Daimler and his private apartment caused some surprise, said one of the officers' wives later, 'But when Stefan said they were presents from his rich uncle, no one thought any more about it. Colonel Redl had called on him several times and did seem rich.'

On the occasion of Alfred's transfer to the 99th Infantry Regiment, Colonel Urbanski, like all his previous commanding officers, was loud in his praises, writing in his confidential report of his first-class brain, his knowledge of human nature and his tact and skill in personal relationships. Nor was he forgotten by General Conrad, who, as Chief of the Imperial and Royal General Staff, personally recommended him for yet another high honour, the Emperor's Expression of Supreme Satisfaction and the special medal which went with it. These were duly awarded to him that April.

Some staff officers, while excellent in their own field, do not possess the qualities which make a good regimental officer. Alfred Redl showed himself equally successful in both capacities. 'In two or three weeks,' according to one of his younger brother officers, 'he was easily the most popular officer in the regiment. Always dignified, he was very friendly to junior officers. He went out of his way to help us and we worshipped him.'

The autumn manoeuvres that year gave him further opportunities of distinguishing himself. The officer commanding the 99th happened to be ill and it fell to Alfred to take his place. 'Exceptionally well-suited to command a regiment' was the verdict of the General commanding 2nd Corps. In May 1912 he was promoted to full colonel and in the following October posted to Prague as Chief of Staff to 8th Corps, at this time under the command of General Baron Giesl von Gieslingen, his former chief in the Directorate of Intelligence. It was a key appointment and one which held brilliant promise for the future, for under Plan III 8th Corps was to form the spearhead of the Austrian attack against Serbia in the all too likely event of war.

For Alfred Redl, at forty-eight, now a trifle more portly, but with his carefully tended hair still kept blond by one means or another and his moustache still magnificently brushed and waxed upwards, things had never looked rosier. It really seemed as though there were now no heights to which he might not rise. Indeed people already spoke of him as a future chief of the Imperial and Royal General Staff.

In Prague Alfred Redl moved into a small but convenient apartment that went with the job, next door to the Headquarters building. It comprised two bedrooms, a living-room, a servant's room and a harness-room. It was not long before he had it decorated in the same flamboyant, rather equivocal style which had characterized the various apartments he had occupied in Vienna.

In his living-room the walls and curtains were of a rich red, the furniture baroque and ormolu, the easy chairs and sofas luxuriously upholstered. A heavy fragrance of scent and incense hung on the air. On the occasional tables stood ornaments of bronze and alabaster. Amongst them was the statuette of a lady draped in an ermine cape, which, at the touch of a concealed button, would drop to reveal a shapely nude, typifying the turn of the century and that peculiar blend of Teutonic heavy-handedness and synthetic Latin frivolity which was at the time the hall-mark of Vienna. Clearly an ideal talking-point for one of Alfred's champagne parties, if he ever had time to give any. A bronze bust of Napoleon stood on his desk which was fitted with special English locks. In one of its compartments, strangely enough, was a packet of strychnine, bearing the date 1902. The bookshelves were filled with expensively bound works on military subjects, the bill for which, still unpaid, lay in one of the drawers of the desk.

In Alfred's bedroom stood a great four-poster bed, with sheets of pure silk and a profusion of rose-red quilts and draperies. On the dressing-table was a wide range of cosmetics and toiletries, including a selection of dyes to give his fair hair exactly the right shade and a curling iron for the ends of that more than military moustache. Three roomy closets contained his lavish military and civilian wardrobe: one hundred and ninety-five dress shirts, ten silk-lined uniform greatcoats, ten fur-trimmed civilian greatcoats, ten mackintoshes, twenty-five pairs of uniform trousers, ten pairs of patent-leather shoes, four hundred pairs of suede gloves. In a special compartment, to which Alfred kept the key and which was only opened on special occasions, there was also, strangely enough, a selection of women's clothing: silk stockings, blouses, embroidered kimonos and so on. In the harness-room, in addition to six fine new saddles and bridles for the three horses stabled out behind, was a collection of up-to-date photographic equipment. Alfred, it appeared, when the mood took him, was a keen amateur photographer. In his carefully locked desk upstairs in the livingroom were numerous specimens of his work of one kind or another.

But just now, while he was still getting to grips with his new and arduous job, the time available to Alfred for photography or for any other relaxation – if photography was a relaxation – was limited. Nor did he go out much or receive more than his most intimate friends in the perfumed seclusion of his apartment. As Chief of Staff of an Army Corps under an elderly Corps Commander at a time of international tension, he had a large headquarters to run, war plans to review and bring up to date and an Intelligence Section to bring into being more or less from scratch, not to mention the overall supervision and control of two infantry divisions, a cavalry brigade and a brigade of artillery. Indeed it was only at night, when he returned to his apartment after a long day's work, that he could and did turn his attention to other activities.

Such was Alfred Redl's life during that doom-laden winter of 1912 (the First Balkan War had begun in October, a harbinger of worse to come). Once or twice a month, usually at weekends, he would take his red Daimler and drive the two hundred miles to Vienna. There he would stay not far away from the Ministry of War at the Hotel Klomser in the Herrengasse, a small but good class of hotel of forty rooms or so, where he was well known to the management and staff. On his visits to Vienna he would resume contacts with his wide range of friends and acquaintances. Usually Stefan would get leave from the 7th Uhlans and come into Vienna to see him. Sometimes, too, he would take a drive into the country with Dr Victor Pollak, a well known Vienna lawyer, whom he had first met nearly ten years before when Dr Pollak had been prosecuting attorney at the trial of the two Russian spies Lavrov and Dyrcz and with whom he had since made friends. He would also sometimes meet other people, shadowy, furtive figures with no names or names that did not really belong to them, hovering in alleyways and at street corners, the sort of people with whom a Deputy Director of Intelligence might at a pinch have found it necessary to consort in the line of duty, but whom it was more surprising to find in the company of the Chief of Staff of the 8th Army Corps.

In the spring of 1913 Alfred Redl's friend and former subordinate Max Ronge was, after six years, still in charge of counter-espionage at the Kundschafterstelle. A contemporary account enables us to judge just how up-to-date, thanks to Alfred Redl, the methods and equipment of the Kundschafterselle now were. Cameras had been concealed behind two of the pictures on the wall, so that any visitor could be photographed full-face and in profile without his realizing it. The cigar-box, lighter and ashtrays had all been especially treated to take fingerprints. 'Have a cigar,' the officer on duty would say, lifting the telephone and pointing to the cigar-box; the visitor would help himself and his fingerprints would be on record. For non-smokers there was a similarly treated box of sweets. For those who resisted both these temptations, there was something which no real spy and very few Military Attachés could possibly resist – a dummy file marked SECRET. The duty officer had only to leave the room for a minute or two to be quite certain of getting his set of prints. The room was also wired for sound, so that every word spoken there could be taken down in shorthand or recorded on a gramophone record in the adjoining room. And naturally all the resulting photographs, fingerprints and recordings would be ticketed and docketed and consigned to an all-embracing filing system. At least this branch of the Imperial and Royal General Staff was well ahead of its time.

At the beginning of April 1913 Major Max Ronge received a letter from his opposite number in Berlin, Major Walther Nicolai, of Section IIIb (Intelligence) of the German General Staff. In it Major Nicolai enclosed a typewritten letter bearing a Berlin postmark and addressed as follows:

Herrn Nikon Nizetas
Oesterreich,
WIEN

Hauptpost. Postlagernd

According to Major Nicolai the letter had lain for several weeks unclaimed at the Central Post Office in Vienna, after which it had been returned to its place of origin, Berlin. There it had been opened by the security authorities who found that it contained the sum of six thousand crowns and two addresses, believed by Major Nicolai to be those of espionage centres, one in Paris and another in Geneva. Clearly this would be of interest to the Austrians and Nicolai had accordingly passed it on to Major Ronge under the terms of the agreement for mutual co-operation in counter-intelligence matters, which Alfred Redl had negotiated with the Germans in 1909.

After discussing the matter with his chief, Colonel Urbanski, Major Ronge, as efficient as ever, undertook a careful study of the letter, comparing the type used with others in the collection he had inherited from Alfred Redl and further investigating the two addresses. In Paris he drew a blank. The Geneva address led him, however, to a French agent: a certain Monsieur Larguier, operating against Austria out of Switzerland, whom in the end the Swiss agreed to expel.

The next thing was to establish the identity of Herr Nikon Nizetas, who by the sound of it, could well be a spy of some importance. For some time now the General Staff had had indications that there was a high-level leak somewhere in the Imperial and Royal Army. Nizetas could conceivably be the source of it and Max Ronge accordingly decided to set a trap for him, should he ever call to collect his letter. Through the Chief of Police, Regierungsrat Gayer, he arranged that two detectives, Herr Ebinger and Herr Steidl, should sit each day from eight in the morning to six at night in a back room at the post office which was connected by an electric bell with the counter from which customers collected letters addressed poste restante.

For a month or so Herr Ebinger and Herr Steidl sat for ten hours a day in the room at the post office, but there was still no sign of Herr Nizetas. Then,

45

at the beginning of May, two more letters arrived at the Central Post Office addressed to Herr Nizetas, dated 7 and 9 May respectively and each containing seven thousand crowns in notes.

Hochgeehrter Herr Nizetas, [ran the second of these] You will by now have received my letter of 7 May, apologizing for my delay in despatching the money. Unfortunately it was not possible for me to send it to you sooner.

I now have the honour, *Verehrter Herr Nizetas,* to transmit to you 7000 crowns, which I am taking the risk of sending in this ordinary letter.

As for your proposals, they are all acceptable.

Hochachtungsvoll,
F. Dietroch

P.S. I would ask you to be good enough to write to me again c/o Fr. Elise Kjernlie, Rosenborggate No. 1, Kristiania, Norway.

After steaming the two letters open and reading them, Major Ronge gummed them up again and returned them to the post office, to await collection by the addressee, at the same time persuading Regierungsrat Gayer and his two detectives to maintain their watch for a further period.

Around the middle of May, not long after the arrival in Vienna of the two letters addressed to Herr Nikon Nizetas, Colonel Alfred Redl, at 8th Corps Headquarters in Prague, received a routine request from an officer in his former regiment, the 99th Foot, applying for authority to take the cure at Marienbad, which, as it happened, was under the jurisdiction of 8th Corps. To this he replied that there was unfortunately no vacancy at Marienbad, but that if one became available he would most certainly notify him.

Some days later he received another letter. This was from young Stefan Hromodka, announcing that he wished to leave the Army in order to get married. The news came as a shattering blow to Colonel Redl, who at once sat down to answer Stefan's letter. *'Mein lieber, lieber Stefan,'* he began. It was even harder to decide what should follow, how he could best express his amazement, his horror, his disgust, how, even now, he could best hope to avert disaster and keep Stefan. Stefan, whom he loved more than life itself.

I can't believe [he wrote] that you really want to leave me . . . I can only repeat that marriage will bring you nothing but unhappiness . . . women interfere in everything. The only things they understand are what they are not meant to understand . . . I am in despair . . . What I should like best of all is to go off on a trip with you (Davos?) . . . I could get you leave . . . I think I could also buy you the Austro-Daimler touring car I promised you. . . .

But it was no good. The words would not come – not the right words, at any rate. There was only one thing for it. Hastily pushing into the drawer of his desk what he had written and then crossed out and rewritten two or three times over, he went off to tell the Corps Commander that he would like to spend the weekend in Vienna, leaving early the following morning. He then let Stefan know that he was coming and asked him to meet him at the Hotel Klomser, where he would be staying. Finally, being even at such a time as this a conscientious staff officer, he dispatched a telegram to the officer in the 99th Foot to notify him that there was now a vacancy for him at Marienbad. At an early hour next morning, Saturday, the 24th of May 1913, he was on his way to Vienna.

As it turned out, young Stefan proved more amenable than Alfred could reasonably have hoped. He was more heavily in debt than usual and, having wheedled his lover into agreeing to pay his debts for him and also buy him a new Daimler touring-car, undertook to forget about marriage for the time being and soldier on in the Army. Alfred, as it happened, was himself heavily in debt at this time, owing over forty thousand crowns against total assets that amounted to less than half that sum – some four thousand crowns' worth of securities and fourteen thousand crowns in notes in a sealed envelope in his desk. But Stefan mattered to him more than anything and for the time being Stefan, at the price of several thousand more crowns, was prepared to remain his.

That evening he had arranged to have dinner quietly at the Restaurant Riedhof in the Josefstadt with his friend Dr Pollak. But before that he had another errand to perform, an errand rendered all the more imperative by the events of that afternoon and by his consequent urgent need for more money.

Putting on a civilian suit, he left the Hotel Klomser a little before six and took a taxi to the Central Post Office in the Postgasse. At the poste restante counter, he asked the clerk on duty whether there was anything for Nikon Nizetas. Pressing hard on the button which Regierungsrat Gayer had had installed under the counter and taking as long as he decently could over what he was doing, the clerk duly produced F. Dietroch's two letters of 7 and 9 May, now neatly sealed up again and complete with their valuable contents. Taking possession of them, Alfred signed 'Nikon Nizetas' in the register and walked straight out of the door. All the two detectives could see as, pulling themselves hastily together, they came rushing in several minutes too late, was the back of his taxi disappearing down the street, giving them barely time to take its number before it vanished round the corner.

In his pocket Alfred had a little knife in a grey sheath, given to him as a present by Stefan. Taking this out, he used it to slit open the two envelopes with their complement of banknotes. At the near-by Café Kaiserhof (which was the address he had given the driver) he got out and, walking across the square, hailed another taxi. 'Hotel Klomser,' he said.

Meanwhile the two detectives, appalled by the thought that through their lack of promptness they had let their man escape, had been left gaping disconsolately outside the Central Post Office. Before they had finally decided what to do, they noticed an empty taxi coming down the street. Their powers of perception sharpened by their sense of failure, they also noticed something else: it's number. They could not believe their eyes. It was the very same taxi in which Nikon Nizetas had taken his departure, not many minutes before. 'Police!' they shouted, intercepting it. 'Where did you take your last passenger?' 'To the Café Kaiserhof,' said the driver. 'To the Café Kaiserhof!' they echoed, 'as fast as you can go.' And then, left behind in the cab, they noticed the little grey sheath of a pocket-knife, which one of them, feeling it might come in useful, promptly put in his pocket.

At the Café Kaiserhof there was no one who looked at all like the man the post office clerk had described. Once again the trail had gone cold on them. But once again chance took a hand. On the near-by cab-rank was an old man, employed to wash the cabs, who remembered seeing a gentleman get into a cab. 'Where did he go?' they asked. 'To the Hotel Klomser.'

Having arrived at the Hotel Klomser the two detectives displayed more intelligence and resourcefulness than they had shown hitherto. Giving the little grey knife-sheath to the hall-porter, they asked him to inquire of each guest as he came down from his room whether he had lost it. Then they sat down to wait and watch.

They did not have to wait long. A little before seven Alfred Redl came down from his room, having changed back into the bottle-green uniform of a staff colonel. As he handed in his key, the hall-porter held up the little grey knife-sheath and asked him whether it was his. Yes, he said, it was, and he put it in his pocket.

No sooner were the words out of his mouth than it dawned on him that he had made a terrible mistake. But there was nothing to be done about it now and, trying to look completely unmoved, he walked straight out of the hotel entrance and into the Herrengasse. After him, as he quickly noticed, came the two detectives. But not before one of them had called police headquarters and given the startling news of his identity to Regierungsrat Gayer.

As he walked along, his two followers saw Alfred Redl put his hand in the pocket of his tunic, take out some papers, tear them up and throw them away. While one of them snatched them from the gutter and rushed them to Police Headquarters, the other kept on following Colonel Redl. When the Colonel hailed a taxi and told the driver to take him to the Restaurant

Riedhof, the detective picked up another and went after him. From the Riedhof he called Headquarters to say that Colonel Redl was dining with Dr Pollak and that he had them under observation.

By this time Regierungsrat Gayer had communicated with Major Ronge. There could no longer be any doubt about it. The proof of Redl's guilt was irrefutable. Rushing round to the Central Post Office, Max Ronge had at once recognized the signature with which Nikon Nizetas had signed for the two letters as being in Colonel Redl's handwriting, while among the papers which Redl had torn up and thrown away were a number of receipts for registered mail sent to what were known to be the cover addresses of Russian intelligence agents. Having duly inspected these, Major Ronge immediately reported his conclusions to his chief, Colonel Urbanski, who then went straight to the Grand Hotel to pass on the appalling news to General Conrad von Hötzendörf, the Chief of the Imperial and Royal General Staff, who happened to be dining there with some friends, to the strains, he remembered afterwards, of a *pot-pourri* from Franz Lehar's latest opera, *Der Graf von Luxemburg.*

The effect on these two senior officers of the news, the unbelievable news, that he brought them is not difficult to imagine. General Conrad, who had greeted him affably, went as white as chalk when he was told what had happened. That any member of the Imperial and Royal General Staff should be a traitor was bad enough. That Colonel Alfred Redl, that outstanding officer, who for years now had had at his fingertips all Austria–Hungary's innermost defence secrets should turn out to be an enemy spy, and at such a time as this, simply did not bear thinking about.

But even so, what weighed even heavier with them was the disgrace which Redl's treachery would bring on the Bottle-Green Corps and the scandal which the news would cause. Their first and strongest impulse was to hush things up, to keep the whole horrible business secret. General Conrad's immediate reaction was that his deputy, General von Höfer, Urbanski, Ronge and a legal officer should at once constitute themselves an arrest commission and arrest Alfred Redl. From this it followed automatically that Alfred Redl must not survive his arrest a minute longer than was necessary. Everyone concerned must take an oath of absolute secrecy.

Meanwhile Colonel Redl and Dr Pollak were finishing their dinner at the Riedhof. To the detective watching them it appeared that Colonel Redl was in a state of extreme agitation. He was not mistaken. Almost as soon as they met, he had explained to Dr Pollak that he was in the worst sort of trouble (though without going into details) and had finally asked him to communicate on his behalf with Regierungsrat Gayer. On Gayer's advice they had returned together to the Hotel Klomser, reaching it at eleven-thirty. There Redl had taken leave of Dr Pollak, and gone to his room.

About an hour later there was a knock on Alfred Redl's door and he found himself facing four officers in uniform: General von Höfer, Colonel Urbanski, Major Ronge and Major Wenzel Vorlicek, a Judge Advocate. He was ready for them. 'I know why you have come,' he said. 'My life is over, finished, and I am writing my farewell letters.' On the table in front of him lay a letter to his brother and another, half finished, to General von Giesl. Asked who his accomplices were, he replied that he had none. Asked for details of his treachery, he said that they would find all the proof they needed in his apartment in Prague.

'Have you any kind of firearm, Herr Redl?' inquired one of them.

'No,' came the answer.

'You may ask for one, Herr Redl.'

'May I, then, be given a revolver?'

But none of them was carrying a revolver and in the end one of them was obliged to go home and get one. A quarter of an hour later he returned with a Browning, which he handed to Redl. After that they left him and went and stood outside the hotel on the corner of the Herrengasse and the Bankgasse. It was after all conceivable that he would not do what was expected of him, that he would somehow try to escape. He was not, they now knew, at all a reliable man.

From where they were, they could not see the window of room No. 1 which looked out on to an inner courtyard. At first each of them took it in turn to keep watch, while the others went to the Café Central round the corner to drink black coffee. After a time the Café Central closed. They stood about in the street, an unhappy little group. Hour after hour went by. Still nothing happened: no sound of a shot, no disturbance. Eventually, so as to be less noticeable, they took turns to go home and change into civilian clothes.

In the end, at five in the morning, they could bear it no longer and summoned one of the two detectives who had followed Redl from the Post Office and who was also sworn to secrecy. Him they sent into the hotel. He was to tell the night porter that he had an urgent message for Colonel Redl, to be delivered to him personally. A couple of minutes later he was back, visibly shaken. He had, he said, found the door of Redl's room open and the Colonel on the floor dead. He had managed to slip out of the hotel again without anybody noticing, or so he thought.

It was, they decided, important that the body should be discovered before first light. Using an assumed name, one of them accordingly now rang up the Hotel Klomser and asked to speak urgently to Colonel Redl. Then he rang off. A few minutes later the police were notified of Colonel Redl's suicide by a startled hotel management. The four officers did not need to wait any longer. A solution to their problem had been found. It was almost exactly twelve hours since Alfred Redl had set out for the Central Post Office – a very full twelve hours.

The two police doctors who arrived shortly afterwards at the hotel had no difficulty in confirming that this was a case of suicide. Standing in front of the mirror, Alfred Redl had put the barrel of the Browning into his mouth and pulled the trigger. The bullet had passed through the roof of his mouth, traversed the brain from right to left and lodged in the cranium. There had been some bleeding from the left nostril. The body had slumped beside the sofa.

On the writing table were two letters, to his brother and to Baron von Giesl. There was also a sheet of paper on which the dead man had written a final message. 'Frivolity and passion,' it ran, 'have destroyed me. Pray for me. I am paying for my sins with my life. Alfred.' Underneath he had written: 'It is a quarter to two. I am about to die. Please do not allow a post-mortem examination of my body. Pray for me.'

The next person to appear on the scene was Colonel Redl's soldier servant, Private Josef Sladek. In halting German (for he was a Czech) he questioned very strongly whether the Colonel had in fact killed himself. He had, he said, made quite a number of plans for the following day and was proposing to drive back to Prague on Tuesday. Besides, the Browning did not belong to him. Clearly he had been murdered.

No one wanted a fuss – the hotel least of all. But the case certainly had some strange features: the four high-ranking officers who had called on Colonel Redl at midnight and the unexplained man with a message who had insisted on going up to his room at five-thirty in the morning. And now this. The seeds of doubt had been sown in a good many people's minds. But the authorities stuck to their guns. A scandal was to be avoided at all costs.

On being shown Redl's body, the police performed a post-mortem and at once notified the military authorities. That same morning the military staffs of the Emperor and Heir Apparent were duly informed of the Colonel's suicide. As yet, however, nothing was said of the true reason for it, which was still kept a close secret. Next morning short notices of it would appear in the press suggesting that it had been due to overwork and neurasthenia. It was also announced that Colonel Redl would be buried with full military honours.

For the General Staff it was vital to discover without delay the full extent of the damage which Redl had done. Early on Sunday morning, while Redl's body was on its way to the mortuary, Colonel Urbanski and Major Wendel Vorlicek had, on General Conrad's instructions, caught the train to

Prague. They had lunched with Corps Commander General von Giesl and then set to work.

The first necessity was to gain access to Redl's apartment. For this purpose it was necessary to force the lock. It was a Sunday and no one could be found to do it. In the end a local locksmith called Wagner was found. He was due to play in an important football match that afternoon and was far from keen to take on the job. However he was finally prevailed upon to help, produced his tools and, on Colonel Urbanski's instructions, forced the lock of the front door.

The dead man's apartment, with its rose-red draperies and cloying smell of scent, made an unpleasant impression on Colonel Urbanski. 'Disgusting' is the word he used in one of his reports. Another spoke of 'sybaritic sensuality', while General von Giesl, who accompanied him, was also deeply shocked. Neither, until this moment, had realized that there was anything odd about Redl. After Wagner had forced the special English locks on Redl's desk. it also became all too clear that his treachery had been on a far larger scale than anyone had at first suspected. Taking with him two large suitcases filled with official documents and photographs of such documents, all smelling strongly of scent, Urbanski left for Vienna that night, leaving Major Vorlicek to continue the investigation in Prague.

In addition to official documents, Urbanski found plentiful, and, to him, deeply unpleasant evidence of Colonel Redl's sexual proclivities, love letters, obscene photographs of himself and his various male lovers, women's clothes to satisfy his transvestite inclinations, and so on. Evidence sufficient amongst other things to warrant the immediate arrest of Lieutenant Stefan Hromodka of the 7th Uhlans. There were finally some rather plaintive letters from a lady named Ludmilla, whom most people believed (and were meant to believe) was the Colonel's mistress, asking for money on the grounds that 'the standards of behaviour he imposed on her had cut off her most important source of income'.

Meanwhile in the eyes of the General Staff the need for secrecy remained an overriding consideration. So far, it had been possible to limit the number of those aware of the full circumstances of the case to no more than eight or nine. But already it was becoming more and more difficult to keep up the story that Colonel Redl's reason for killing himself had simply been overwork or nervous stress. There had been Josef Sladek and the hotel staff. Now there was Taumann, the young officer in the 99th Foot, to whom Redl a day or two before had wired the news that there was a vacancy for him at Marienbad. Was that, he kept asking, the action of a man at the end of his tether? General von Giesl, too, had noticed his 'usual easy attitude' the previous week. 'One could not notice in him the slightest sign of abnormality or depression,' he said unhelpfully. Even the Heir Apparent, the Archduke Franz Ferdinand and his Military Assistant, Colonel Bandolff, had been struck of late by the exceptional brilliance and lucidity of Colonel Redl's work.

But worst of all there was the press, always on the lookout for a story and now beginning to sniff round. And here again chance was to intervene in a way which no one could have foreseen. On Monday, 26 May the *Prager Tageblatt* carried the following account of the previous day's football match between OBC Sturm I and SK Union V, which Sturm, after a half-time score of three all, had lost five to seven. 'Sturm,' the sports correspondent had written, 'were from the start the stronger team, as the rate of their scoring showed. But owing to the absence of Marecek and Wagner, their defence was so weak that Atja was unable to prevent Union breaking through it.'

It was accordingly a mortified and rather downcast full-back who later that same Monday called on the captain of his team to explain his absence and make his apologies. The team captain, who happened to be an extremely bright young newspaperman, greeted him with a marked lack of enthusiasm. Nor was he particularly impressed by full-back Wagner's story of having been summoned to force a lock, which, as he at once pointed out, was something you could do in five minutes. Indeed it was only when Wagner started to explain that this lock was a special one and that the apartment he had had to break into had belonged to some general or other who had died in Vienna the day before, that the team captain stopped worrying about Sunday's football match and began to sit up and listen.

And Wagner's story, as he soon realized, was well worth listening to. Wagner had, it seemed, forced not just the lock of the front door, but those of every drawer and every cupboard in the place. After which, two gentlemen from Vienna had searched every inch of the apartment for Russian documents and photographs of plans. And the Colonel from Vienna had shown each photograph to the Corps Commander, who kept shaking his head and saying: 'Terrible, terrible . . . who could have believed it?' And the place had looked more like a woman's apartment, full of cosmetics and bottles of scent. And the letters, which reeked of scent, were all from men. And the two officers from Vienna had taken a note of all their names. And so on.

By this time the keen young reporter had grasped that he was on to the story of a lifetime. Having read the news of Colonel Redl's suicide (together with a flattering obituary notice) in that morning's paper, he had quickly realized that the apartment which had been searched by these high-ranking officers from Vienna must be his. And from this, putting two and two together, he was able to draw a number of fascinating and all too accurate conclusions.

The question was how to make use of his scoop. If he printed it straight in the local paper, the whole edition would certainly be confiscated. He decided that he must try a more indirect approach. He accordingly phrased it in the form of an official denial, knowing full well that his intelligent readers, accustomed as they were to such methods of outwitting the censorship, would have no difficulty whatever in reading between the lines.

We are asked by a high authority [his story ran] to deny the rumours current in military circles that Colonel Redl, Chief of Staff of the Prague Army Corps who committed suicide yesterday, had betrayed military secrets and spied for Russia. The commission of inquiry sent to Prague, composed of a colonel and a major who in the presence of the Corps Commander Baron Giesl, opened up Colonel Redl's official residence and searched his drawers, were investigating shortcomings of quite a different kind.

In this form the story got through uncensored and was at once picked up by the Vienna papers and the entire provincial press. Meanwhile the journalist, as Prague correspondent of a German newspaper, had also cabled it to Berlin as it stood.

The fat was now well and truly in the fire. The story (which General Conrad had withheld even from the Emperor) was picked up and embroidered by every newspaper in Europe. In Austria itself the authorities were obliged to confirm officially that Redl had been both a traitor and a homosexual. There was an immediate outcry in Parliament and throughout the country at the way in which the case had been handled.

Meanwhile the Army, for its part, had finally decided, on the authority of the Chief of the Imperial and Royal General Staff, to cancel the elaborate military funeral which it had planned for Colonel Redl. Instead, his body, in an ordinary pine coffin, was quietly consigned to Grave 38, Row 29, Group 79 in Vienna's Central Cemetery. But despite the clearly expressed wishes of the dead man, not before yet another post-mortem had been carried out on it. A post-mortem, incidentally, which in the opinion of the medical officer who performed it, showed that the deceased had long been so riddled with disease – with syphilis, to be more specific – as to be no longer in full control of his mental processes.

For the next twelve months or so speculation and controversy continued to rage over the Redl affair. As far as General Conrad von Hötzendörf and the Imperial and Royal General Staff were concerned, their chief objective was to play down its importance, in the hope that with any luck the whole embarrassing business would before long be forgotten. But the case possessed a number of awkward features which made this difficult.

Neither the old Emperor nor the Heir Apparent seem to have been officially informed of the true facts of the case until 28 May, by when, thanks to the press, it had become impossible to conceal them any longer. It was now duly explained to them in simple language that Colonel Redl's homosexual activities had laid him open to blackmail and brought him into financial difficulties; that, as a result of this, he had sold official secrets to a foreign power; and finally that, to escape the consequences of his action, he had committed suicide. Even then the full extent and duration of Colonel Redl's treasonable activities and the exact circumstances of his death were as far as possible slurred over. In this respect General Conrad's report to Franz Josef and Franz Ferdinand seems to have served as a pattern for the statements made later in Parliament by the Minister of Defence, General of Infantry Baron von Georgi.

After sixty-five mainly unhappy years on the throne the old Emperor was accustomed to unpleasant facts being distorted and slurred over. But Franz Ferdinand, who in any case had no great liking for General Conrad, was harder to satisfy. 'How lucky,' he said to him maliciously, remembering his liking for preventive wars, 'that we didn't go to war against Russia with a traitor in our rear!' Nor were some of the members of the ramshackle Imperial Parliament any better pleased. As the *Neue Freie Presse* put it, 'the statement made by the Minister on 5 June 1913 exercised no very calming effect . . . the overall impression was one of dissatisfaction.'

Meanwhile Franz Ferdinand continued to complain and ask awkward questions. Why, he inquired, had no one noticed Colonel Redl's extravagant way of life? And then there was the manner in which Redl had met his end; the fact, above all, that the Browning with which he took his life had been left with him on the express, or at any rate the implicit, instructions of the Chief of the General Staff. Like most Austrians, Franz Ferdinand was a devout Roman Catholic and firmly believed that by forcing Redl to commit suicide, the four members of the Commission of Arrest, like avenging angels in bottle-green uniform, had condemned him to an eternity of damnation.

There was also the purely practical consideration that by eliminating him at such an early stage of the proceedings they had given themselves no chance of interrogating him in depth and so discovering the full extent of his treachery and perhaps some particulars of his Russian and other connections.

Consciously or subconsciously, they may even have had a purpose in this particular sin of ommission – a desire to get the whole unpleasant business over and done with as quickly as possible. Certainly, as so often happens in such cases, the authorities concerned were reluctant to admit that this particular traitor could have had, and almost certainly did have, access to a very wide range of secret information. What they were inclined to leave out of account was that a man in almost any of the various posts which Redl had held over the past twelve or thirteen years, a man of his authority and with his wide official contacts and connections, would have had no difficulty whatever in gaining access to almost any information he wanted and would in his particular circumstances, have had the strongest personal and financial motives for doing so. The more realistic German General Staff, who remembered all too well their full and frank discussions with Redl not many years before and the high decoration they had awarded him, were most painfully aware of this. Though they accepted General Conrad's embarrassed explanations with reasonably good grace, there can be no doubt that from that time onwards their confidence in their Austrian ally was seriously shaken.

One would have thought that, as far as the Army was concerned, there was nothing more left to go wrong. But one would have been mistaken. Some time after Redl's death his remaining personal belongings were sold in Prague. They included a camera containing, as it turned out, an exposed film, which the purchaser duly had developed by a student friend of his. It bore the photograph of a highly secret official document. Six more films found at the same time yielded equally interesting results. Again the story was picked up by the press. Immediately the Heir Apparent was on the telephone to Colonel Urbanski screaming at him for not having had the camera looked at. 'I was,' wrote Urbanski afterwards, 'extremely upset at the prospect of future unpleasantness.' He had every reason to be. Not many months later he was prematurely retired from the Army at the insistence of the Heir Apparent.

Just how much material damage Alfred Redl's treachery did to Austria will probably never be known any more than it is possible to estimate its effect on the morale of the Bottle-Green Corps and on Austrian morale in general. Barely a year after his death the Heir Apparent's assassination at Sarajevo set Europe ablaze and General Conrad von Hötzendörf found himself fighting the war he had so long looked forward to. It was a war which started, continued and ended disastrously for Austria. It is difficult to say whether the various misfortunes which overtook her armies in Galicia and Serbia were due to the enemy's foreknowledge of her war-plans, which no one had bothered to change, or to the incompetence of her generals and the half-heartedness of her troops, or to a mixture of the two.

What, ironically enough, the war did bring was any amount of hard evidence as to the extent of Redl's involvement with the Russians. When the German Army overran Warsaw in 1915, they captured the entire archives of Russia's Intelligence Centre West and an Austrian officer attached to German intelligence was given the opportunity of reading the whole of the correspondence between Alfred Redl and Colonel Nikolai

Stepanovich Batyushin, the Russian Staff officer in charge of the Centre. He was also able to study a goodly stock of secret Austrian and German documents of which it was all too easy to guess the provenance. From the Redl–Batyushin correspondence (since apparently, lost) a number of things were made clear. To get Redl into his power Batyushin had evidently used both the threat of exposure as a homosexual and the stranglehold which his victim's taste for high living afforded him. The intermediary between them seems to have been a Russian agent known amongst other things as Pratt, a strange, insubstantial character who some years later in a prisoner-of-war camp, was in a moment of expansiveness, nostalgically to describe his recruitment of Alfred Redl as 'my most beautiful success'. Once in Batyushin's power (where he had evidently been for a dozen years or more), Redl had sent him as many secret Austrian documents as he could. He had also engaged with him in a regular traffic in spies, every now and then betraying an Austrian spy to the Russians in return for a Russian spy betrayed to him by Batyushin. Besides bringing in financial rewards on both sides, this had the effect of greatly enhancing their personal prestige as spy-catchers with their respective official superiors. Moreover every case of espionage which Colonel Redl had investigated gave him direct access to more and more secret information which he could then pass on to Batyushin.

This was the explanation of much that had hitherto been obscure in the Hekailo case. In this confusing affair Redl had played a highly intricate double game. It was now evident that he himself had sold the Northern Deployment Plans to the Russians in the first place. On learning that the betrayal of the plans had come to the knowledge of the Austrians, probably as the result of a leak by an indiscreet or treacherous Russian, Redl had hastily made contact with Colonel Batyushin and insisted that, in order to save him from discovery, the latter should now sacrifice another of his agents who could then be saddled with the blame. Though Colonel Hekailo had not been involved in this particular piece of espionage, he had done a number of other odd jobs for Batyushin. Moreover he had since fled the country, so that his usefulness to the Russians had been exhausted and he could properly be regarded as expendable.

In these circumstances, Batyushin, reluctant to lose Redl, had provided him with the necessary evidence against Hekailo (which Redl had promptly sold to his own superiors for twenty thousand crowns, later shared with Batyushin) and also told him where his prey could be found in Brazil. After that it had at first been relatively plain sailing, though Redl had had an uneasy moment when Hekailo pointed out that only an officer of the General Staff could have had access to the Northern Deployment Plans, a remark that struck far too near the bone for comfort, but which fortunately for him had not been pursued further. Redl had been in rather worse trouble when Hekailo, under interrogation, had given away the names of his accomplices. Wieckowski and Acht were, as it happened, two of Batyushin's best agents. Batyushin accordingly instructed Redl to save them at all costs, but his sudden volte face was too much for Major Haberditz and once again things looked like going wrong. In the end Wieckowski and Acht had to be sacrificed, but Batyushin demanded an Austrian agent in return and Redl had finally concluded this complicated deal by betraying to him the Russian staff-major working for the Austrians in Warsaw, whom he ruefully described as one of his most valuable agents.

Nor, quite certainly, was this unfortunate Russian staff-major the only Austrian agent that Colonel Redl betrayed to Batyushin. It was Redl in all probability who had betrayed Colonel Laikov and Colonel Grimm back in 1902, and many others besides.

Count Adalbert Sternberg, at one time a member of the Imperial Parliament and a friend of the Archduke Franz Ferdinand, carried this theory further still. 'This rascal,' he said, 'gave the name of every single Austrian spy to the Russians. What happened in the case of the Russian colonels was repeated over and over again. Redl betrayed our secrets to the Russians and stopped us from learning their secrets by espionage. The result was that in 1914 we entirely ignored the existence of seventy-five Russian divisions – more than the whole Austro–Hungarian Army. Hence our anxiety to go to war and hence our defeat. If we had had a clearer view of things, our Generals would never have succeeded in pushing the Court into war.'

Another interesting theory came from the Vatican. 'I have recently,' reported the Austro–Hungarian Military Attaché in Rome in July 1913, 'had a chance of talking to a senior Prince of the Church who is very close to the Pope. He was much interested in the Redl affair and struck me as being extremely well informed about it. He said that what had happened in this case, as in the Dreyfus case, was directly attributable to the internationalist tendencies of the Jews, who never have possessed and never will possess any feeling of patriotism. He went on to say that Redl was a Jew on both sides. He had been into it most carefully and had definite proof . . .'

Thus, if the high ecclesiastic in question was to be believed, it was not an Austrian and a Catholic who had let down the Bottle-Green Corps and whom the Bottle-Green Corps had forced to commit suicide and thus condemned to eternal damnation, but a Jew. Which simplified things for all concerned.

This bright idea, needless to say, was revived a quarter of a century later in 1938, after the Anschluss, when this time no less a person than Herr Julius Streicher wrote from the editorial offices of *Der Stürmer* to ask the Austrian authorities whether Alfred Redl had in fact been a Jew. He was, he said, very much interested to know. After careful inquiries, however, the

Austrian authorities replied that to the best of their knowledge he was not. For Julius Streicher, no doubt, a most disappointing answer.

Looking back two world wars, three or four generation-gaps and several revolutions later, what can we make of Alfred Redl? What, one can't help wondering, did he make of himself, as he looked at his reflection in the gilt-edged mirror and put the barrel of the borrowed Browning into his mouth?

The latter question is perhaps the more relevant. The hardest thing at this distance in time is to find a standpoint, indeed a standard, by which to judge the case. The standards by which Colonel Redl's contemporaries judged him have long since been swept away. No serious person, it will probably be said, could really have felt any loyalty for the Austro-Hungarian Empire, or for its Imperial and Royal Army and General Staff. Anyone, it will also be said, can be born a homosexual; can fall desperately in love; can acquire a taste for high living, if only to impress, and so keep hold of the loved one; can yield under unbearable pressures to overwhelming temptation. *'Tout comprendre'* it will be said, *'c' est tout pardonner.'*

Alfred Redl, as he looked at himself in the mirror of room No. 1 at the Hotel Klomser, took a less lenient view of his own actions. *'Leichtsinn und Leidenschaft haben mich vernichtet,'* he wrote. *'Betet für mich. Ich büsse mein irren mit dem Tode. Alfred.'* Which at that moment was in all probability how he felt. Nor, even if we chose to regard Alfred Redl as having been largely the victim of circumstances, of passion and of unbearable pressures, does this get us very much further. It is true that homosexuality is no longer considered in any way abnormal or reprehensible and that Alfred's relationship with Stefan (once the latter had reached the statutory age) would now be regarded as perfectly acceptable in most civilized countries. It is true also that to many of us now the Austro–Hungarian Empire is no more than a historical concept and a rather improbable one at that.

Even so, when we come to Colonel Redl's dealings with Colonel Batyushin we are on more debatable ground. To us the Austro–Hungarian Empire may not, by present-day standards, seem very real, let alone very progressive, even though, as a place to live in, it certainly possessed advantages which a number of more up-to-date countries seem to lack. To Alfred Redl, on the other hand, it was the world in which he lived and had his being, which had offered him, the son of a minor railway official, the possibility of a brilliant career and with it the *dolce vita* he loved so dearly, Nor, like some spies, did he betray his country on principle, out of loyalty to any other country or political system or idea. He betrayed it because, having become addicted to Stefan, he simply had to have the money to keep him. And also, no doubt, because, even if he had wished to, he could not cease his treachery without bringing down on himself the vengeance of Colonel Batyushin. And from his past dealings with that gentleman, he must have realized that this was not a risk to be taken lightly.

It is, however you look at it, a sad story, typical of the whole murky underworld of espionage and blackmail and, therefore, unfortunately, as likely to recur today in our own enlightened society as in the tinselly, comic-opera world of Franz Joseph and Franz Lehar.

As Alfred Redl himself put it so clearly, frivolity and passion – *Leichtsinn und Leidenschaft* – (both still prevalent) had destroyed him; he was about to pay for, perhaps even expiate his sins by death, and all he could ask his friends to do in that final extremity was to pray for him.

Never having found ourselves in such a situation, it is hard for most of us to grasp its full horror. It should therefore be even harder for us to sit in judgement on Alfred Redl or indeed on any of those concerned. Least of all, of course, on Colonel Nikolai Stepanovich Batyushin, who, as an able intelligence officer, was clearly doing a first-class job for the Allied cause.

Three

DANGEROUS EDGE

Our interest's on the dangerous edge of things . . .
The giddy line midway.

ROBERT BROWNING

In the spring of the year 1892 Yevgeni or Yevno Azef, a young travelling salesman of Jewish extraction, received a consignment of butter from a merchant in the town of Rostov on Don and successfully sold it for eight hundred roubles. Then, instead of handing the eight hundred roubles over to the merchant, he absconded with it to Karlsruhe in Germany, where he entered the local Polytechnic. It was the beginning of a remarkable career.

Yevno had been born twenty-three years earlier, in the little town of Lyskovo in the province of Grodno, the second of the seven children of Fischel Azef, a poor tailor. When Yevno was five, his father had managed to move from Lyskovo to Rostov on the Don. Rostov was outside the confines still imposed on Jews in Russia and seemed to offer better prospects of making a living. In Rostov Fischel opened a drapery shop, but still did not prosper. He succeeded, however, in sending his three sons to the local secondary school. The education he received there fitted Yevno for a variety of small jobs. He gave lessons, worked as a reporter on the local newspaper, as a clerk in an office and finally as a travelling salesman.

In the 1890s Russia was seething with revolutionary feeling. Early in 1892 young Azef was suspected by the police, rightly or wrongly, of distributing a subversive manifesto. Several of his acquaintances had already been arrested for such activities. Yevno, who had always wanted to travel, decided to go abroad. His only difficulty was lack of money. This he solved by selling the butter and keeping the proceeds.

At the Karlsruhe Polytechnic Yevno studied electro-statics. There were a number of other Russian students there and he shared rooms with one of them on the fourth floor of a house in the Wertherstrasse. Like most

Russian students at this time, those studying at Karlsruhe were of the Left. Before he had been there long, he joined the Social Democrats.

The eight hundred roubles which had brought Yevno to Karlsruhe did not last long. To an acquaintance he gave at the time the impression of someone 'literally suffering from hunger and cold'. The problem, once again, was where to get money. It did not take him long to find a solution. On 4 April 1893, within a year of his arrival, he wrote a letter to the Police Department in St Petersburg. 'I have the honour,' it began, 'to inform Your Excellency that two months ago a circle of revolutionaries was formed here whose aim is . . .' There followed a list of names and a number of facts, calculated to show that the writer (who did not reveal his real name) was in a position to provide information about the mood of Russian students abroad and, more specifically, about current revolutionary activities in Rostov on the Don. The writer made no firm proposals, but simply suggested that a registered letter should be sent to him at a given address if the police were interested.

When it reached St Petersburg, Azef's letter was laid before the Deputy Director of the Police Department, who passed it on to the head of the branch concerned. The recruitment of a police spy was a complicated business. Minutes were written, consultations held, information collected. On 16 May a reply was despatched to the address indicated. In it the police were careful not to display undue eagerness. 'We know,' they wrote, 'of the Karlsruhe group and are not very much interested in it. You would therefore not be of great value to us. Nevertheless we are prepared to pay you – on condition, however, that you disclose your name, for we have strict principles and are not prepared to have dealings with certain people.'

Azef replied by return, suggesting the 'delightfully low' price of fifty roubles a month, but still not revealing his name. By now however, the St Petersburg police had discovered who he was. Simultaneously with his letter to them he had written in much the same terms to the Rostov Gendarmerie. There were not many Russians from Rostov living in Karlsruhe. Yevno's handwriting was known to them. The Gendarmerie and Police Department compared notes and identification became an easy matter.

Once he had been identified, it became clear to the Police Department that Yevno would fit the bill. 'Yevno Azef,' the Rostov Gendarmerie had reported, 'is intelligent and a clever intriguer; he is in close touch with the young Jewish students living abroad and he could thus be of real use as an agent. It can also be assumed that his greed for money and his present state of need would make him zealous in his duties.' On receipt of their report, a departmental memorandum was drawn up pointing out that Azef could be 'very useful' and that the price he was asking was not excessive. The assistant to the Minister of the Interior countersigned the memorandum and in June 1893 Yevno received his first month's salary. Being prudent by nature and a born dissimulator, he was careful not to change his way of life or do anything that would arouse the suspicions of his fellow students. On the contrary he continued to send out as before appeals to every charitable institution he could think of, especially Jewish ones, and to show these to his friends who, on the strength of them, not unnaturally assumed that he was as hard-up as ever.

Azef's change in circumstances led, curiously enough, to a change in his political attitude. When he first arrived at Karlsruhe, he had taken a moderate line, siding with the milder Marxists and opposing extreme revolutionary methods. But on entering the employment of the Police Department, he swung sharply to the Left and had soon become known as a leading advocate of terrorism. He was, he explained, no theorist but a man of action. Speaking at meetings was something he avoided, preferring technical and administrative tasks. Meanwhile he took steps to widen his circle of acquaintances, travelling to near-by towns in Germany to attend revolutionary meetings and gatherings of one kind or another. In August 1893 he attended the International Socialist Congress in Zurich. In 1894 he went to Berne, where he met the Zhitlovskis, a Russian couple, who gladly welcomed him to their recently founded Union of Russian Social Revolutionaries Abroad. His membership of this body, as he well realized, would give him the *entrée* to corresponding organizations at home.

While at Berne, Azef also met his future wife, a convinced and dedicated Jewish girl-revolutionary named Menkina then studying at Berne University. From the first she saw in him a fighter for the same ideals as herself, freedom, equality and social justice. They were married almost immediately, their first child, a son, being born in 1895. In her eyes, we may assume, their supposed similarity of aims, and perhaps also the charming love letters he wrote her, made up for any physical shortcomings on his part.

Certainly, as seen by a contemporary, Yevno was not particularly pre-possessing. Quite tall, heavily built, with a puffy yellow face, large sticking-out ears and small feet and hands, a low forehead narrowing at the top, thick lips barely concealed by a straggling moustache and a flattened nose gave him a definitely Kalmuck cast of countenance. His voice was inclined to be squeaky.

But whatever his appearance (and some people even found it repellent), there could be no denying his dynamism, the strength of his personality, his personal powers of attraction or the conviction he carried in revolutionary circles. So much so that when a certain Korobochkin, who had heard stories of revolutionaries being arrested in Rostov on the strength of information obtained from abroad, publicly accused him of being a police spy, Korobochkin was angrily denounced by all and sundry and forthwith expelled from the group as a slanderer. Already his friends' letters refer to Yevno as a 'leading personality' and speak of his utter devotion to the Revolution and its ideals.

A photograph taken at about this time shows him in the middle of a group of students, weightier than his companions, a trifle toad-like even, leaning with total assurance on a conveniently placed coffee-table. The alert look in his eyes and the confidence of his whole demeanour leave one in no doubt whatever that here is a natural leader.

In 1899 Yevno Azef, who was by now thirty, was awarded a diploma as an electrical engineer at Darmstadt, where he had gone from Karlsruhe to continue his studies. Meanwhile the Police Department, delighted at the information which he was sending them, had doubled his salary, raising it to a hundred roubles a month, and also awarded him a special bonus at Easter and the New Year. At one time he thought of settling in Germany, but his friends in the police had other plans for him, suggesting that he should now go to Moscow, where they would help him to find a suitable post as an engineer. And so in the autumn of 1899 Azef left for Russia, warmly recommended by the Zhitlovskis to the Moscow Union of Social Revolutionaries and by the police to S. V. Zubatov, Chief of the Moscow Okhrana, as the current successor to the notorious Third Section was now called.

S. V. Zubatov was in manner and appearance a typical Russian intellectual, with his brown hair brushed straight back, a little beard and tinted spectacles. His small stature, precise manner and rather dim, commonplace appearance presented a marked contrast to the brightly-uniformed and star-bedizened Generals and State Councillors amongst whom he worked. But his influence and power were at least as great as theirs.

Like Azef, Zubatov had started life as a police spy. Though not himself an active revolutionary, he had, while still at school in the 1880s freely consorted with revolutionaries, had almost at once started to inform on them and so had without much difficulty found his way into the service of the Okhrana, rising in barely ten years to be its head.

For this task he was in many ways ideally suited: a good organizer, able to grasp the essentials of a problem, however complicated, and quickly draw the necessary conclusions, possessing great patience and a devious, penetrating mind, Zubatov loved his work for its own sake. A strong upholder of autocracy, he was not content with simply catching revolutionaries. The right policy for the government, he believed, was to seek to drive a wedge between the revolutionary intelligentsia and the working class, who, realistic as usual, were only interested in revolutionaries in so far as they thought they might help them to improve their own material conditions.

Zubatov sought to achieve his aim in two ways: first by promoting labour legislation designed to protect the workers' economic interests and so give them less cause for complaint, helping them, even, to form what were really government-sponsored trade unions; and secondly by deliberately fostering extremist tendencies on the part of the revolutionaries. With these objects in view he now set out to build up within the various revolutionary organizations a Secret Agency of his own, urging his subordinates to handle their relations with their spies and informers 'with the same delicacy as they would a clandestine love-affair'. This was the kind of thing he really enjoyed. 'My connection with the Secret Agency,' he wrote long afterwards, 'is my most precious remembrance.'

In Yevno Azef, Zubatov found a disciple after his own heart. With Zubatov's help Azef quickly found employment as an engineer with the Moscow branch of the General Electrical Company and at the same time became a member of the so-called Intellectual Aid Society, a body whose members were drawn from the flower of the Moscow intelligentsia. Thanks to his friendship with the Zhitlovskis in Berne, Azef was also welcomed with open arms by the Social Revolutionaries.

Yevno's first encounter with the revolutionary intelligentsia of the old capital was at a soirée given by E. A. Nemchinova, a woman writer whose salon was one of their regular meeting places. Here, contrary to his usual practice, he joined vigorously in the discussion, strongly upholding the extreme theories of the Populists and Social Revolutionaries against the attacks of the more moderate Marxists. 'He spoke,' wrote one of his fellow guests afterwards, 'at some length and impressed all present by his sincerity and his knowledge of the subject.' A few days later he called on A. A. Argunov, the founder and head of the Moscow Union of Social Revolutionaries, who had already heard about him from the Zhitlovskis.

At Zubatov's suggestion, however, he did not rush things with the Social Revolutionaries, declaring himself a sympathizer with their cause, but being careful not to cross-question them about the details of their organization and simply picking up such information as came his way. In general he showed himself sceptical about the feasibility under the circumstances then obtaining of setting up large-scale revolutionary organizations or of publishing much revolutionary literature in Russia itself. Terror, he told the Social Revolutionaries was the thing. But, though terrorists in theory, they were not convinced that the time for it had arrived. By comparison Azef believed all other forms of revolutionary activity were 'trifling'. 'Terror,' he declared, 'is the only way.' And when in the spring of 1901 a revolutionary called Karpovich succeeded in murdering the Minister of Education, he was overjoyed. 'The terror,' he declared, 'has begun.' Meanwhile to Zubatov, who shared his enthusiasm for terror, he was careful to pass on all the information he accumulated with special reference to the Social Revolutionaries who seemed to both their minds to offer the most promising field.

Zubatov, for his part, had never been interested in arresting individual revolutionaries. He believed rather in giving revolutionary organizations time to build themselves up and mature, in first familiarizing himself with their ramifications and then, in the fulness of time taking action against them, being particularly careful meanwhile to do nothing that could possibly compromise his own agents.

Though not a member of their union, Azef, as a sympathizer and a practical man, was always ready to help the Social Revolutionaries. By the beginning of 1901 the latter had begun to publish their own paper, *Revolutsionaya Rossiya*, secretly printed in the Grand Duchy of Finland on the estate of a woman sympathizer. To Azef Argunov confided the printers' urgent need for a 'solid but not unwieldy roller'. Azef at once replied that he had a reliable friend who could make one for him. He then quickly arranged, through Zubatov, for the roller to be made in the workshops of Okhrana, who were thus provided with a ready-made piece of evidence for use as and when the situation might demand it.

As yet, Zubatov felt no particular inclination to close down the Social Revolutionaries' printing press, especially as its presence in Finland helped him to keep track of the stream of zealous revolutionaries who flocked across the frontier to attend to its needs. It was some months before he arrived at the conclusion that the moment had perhaps come to give its proprietors a fright. Surveillance was accordingly intensified and suddenly made more obvious. Fearing that a raid might be impending, Argunov decided to move his press to Siberia, where his brother-in-law happened to be in charge of a government emigration centre in the woods near Tomsk, almost entirely staffed by revolutionaries. It was hard to imagine a better place for it. The press was accordingly dismantled and, with due precautions, transported in parts to Siberia, where in September 1901 it was carefully reassembled and work started on the third issue of *Revolutsionaya Rossiya*. It was now that Zubatov decided to act. After consulting Azef, he sent instructions to the Tomsk police to raid the press and arrest the revolutionaries in charge of it.

To Argunov and the other Social Revolutionaries back in Moscow, the Tomsk raid was a blow. It was also a warning. They were not particularly concerned at the prospect of being arrested themselves. This was something they had long expected. What worried them far more was the lack, in case they were arrested, of anyone capable of maintaining the organization of the union and carrying on its work while they were in jail. And now, as though by a miracle, the very man they needed had, as it were, swum into their ken.

By this time a much closer relationship had grown up between Argunov and Azef. 'Azef,' Argunov wrote afterwards, 'wholeheartedly shared our sorrow. It might have been his own grief. His attitude changed. From a passive collaborator, he became an active member of our union. There was no formal entry into the union; it all happened quite naturally.' It was not long before Argunov made it clear that he had picked Azef as his successor.

In Argunov's eyes, one of Azef's many advantages as a future leader of the Social Revolutionaries was the fact that he was not compromised or under police surveillance and therefore at present in no danger of arrest. When they met, the two of them took the greatest care not to give any chance onlooker the slightest indication of what their business was. One of their first meetings took place in the Sundanovski Public Baths, where they exchanged ideas and plans for the future while busily soaping themselves. Zubatov was delighted once he knew that Argunov intended Azef to succeed him as leader. He even gave orders for police surveillance to be relaxed so that the two conspirators could meet more freely.

At about this time Zubatov came to the conclusion that Azef, with whom he was better pleased than ever, could be more useful to the Department abroad. On his instructions the latter accordingly announced to Argunov that he was going abroad for personal reasons and asked whether he could do anything for him while he was away. Argunov accepted his offer enthusiastically, saying that he would send a woman revolutionary, a certain Maria Selyuk, on ahead of him as a kind of courier.

'Like someone on his deathbed,' wrote Argunov afterwards, 'I entrusted everything to Azef. We told him all our passwords, all our connections (literary and organizational) and the names and addresses of our associates. And we recommended him warmly to all our friends. He was to arrive together with Selyuk, enjoying our full confidence as the representative of the union. We looked upon him as a comrade, as a friend, even. In those days of misfortune his active participation brought him closer to us than ever.' Azef left Russia with his family towards the end of November 1901, having been preceded a week or two earlier by Maria Selyuk, whose presence both he and Zubatov felt would be of the greatest use to him as representative of the union.

All things considered, Zubatov had every reason to feel satisfied with the results of his policy up to date. He had by now gained a comprehensive knowledge of the union's working and ramifications and, had he wished, could easily have mopped up various Social Revolutionary groups all over the country. But this was not his purpose. Instead, his intention was that Yevno Azef should negotiate with the revolutionaries he met abroad towards the unification of all the different populist and revolutionary groups in Russia into one nationwide Social Revolutionary Party, of which Yevno would then become to all intents and purposes the leader.

Meanwhile, allowing Azef plenty of time to leave the country, he gave orders for the arrest of Argunov, who was sentenced to several years' imprisonment and a further period of exile. He also gave orders for Azef's salary to be raised to the unheard of sum of five hundred roubles a month, partly as a reward for the success of the Tomsk raid and partly to ensure that he was properly provided for while abroad.

The negotiations for the fusion of the various Russian populist and revolutionary groups into one large Social Revolutionary Party were already well advanced when Azef went abroad in November 1901. The first two issues of *Revolutsionaya Rossiya* had, it seemed, been so favourably received by the various populist and revolutionary groups throughout the country as already to provide a useful basis for agreement. For Azef it now only remained to preside over the actual process of unification and arrange for the future publication abroad of *Revolutsionaya Rossiya*, which was to be the new party's official organ.

In this he and Maria Selyuk, as representatives of the Moscow organization, enjoyed the help of a certain G. A. Gershuni, a young Jewish scientist who was already an experienced revolutionary and represented the organizations of the south and north-west. In the course of the next couple of months the negotiations conducted in Berlin, Berne and Paris were duly brought to a successful conclusion and agreement reached in regard to the new party's programme and tactics. *Revolutsionaya Rossiya*, it was decided, would in future be published in Switzerland.

'In Berlin and Paris,' wrote Azef in a letter to the Police Department, 'I penetrated into the heart of things.' In a relatively short time an important new revolutionary party had been brought into being with the knowledge and to some extent under the auspices of the Okhrana, while henceforth a highly professional police spy would be closely associated with its leadership. When all was said and done, it was an achievement of which Zubatov could well be proud.

During the next couple of years few people played a livelier part in Social Revolutionary affairs than Catherine Breshkovskaya, the so-called Grandmother of the Party. Familiarly known as the Holy Ghost of the Revolution, this aged female firebrand, after several long spells in Siberia, still flitted tirelessly round Russia, inciting the youth of the country to rebellion and stirring up enthusiasm for the revolutionary cause. After her came Gershuni, now in practice the Party's chief organizer, who, following conscientiously in her footsteps, took endless pains to consolidate her successes and turn them to good account.

A dedicated revolutionary with a strongly dramatic side to his character and possessing in no small degree the gift of imparting to others his own overpowering strength of feeling, Gershuni shared to the full Yevno Azef's constantly declared enthusiasm for terrorism. The two had already worked together closely for the unification of the Social Revolutionary movement and this was another bond between them. The essential thing, they agreed, was to commit a terrorist act of the first importance. The Party would then publicly assume responsibility for what had been done and the groups that had committed the act would henceforth be officially entitled the Combat Section. What Gershuni had in mind, he told Azef, was an attempt on the life of Sipyagin, the Minister of the Interior. He had plenty of willing volunteers and would himself undertake all the arrangements.

In January 1902 Gershuni returned to Russia from Germany for the purpose of undertaking a tour of party groups throughout Russia. Azef duly informed the Department of the date of his departure from Berlin and of his intended itinerary, but accompanied the information with the strongest possible plea that he should not be arrested. 'He must not be arrested yet under any circumstances,' he wrote. 'Bear this in mind.' The Department took Azef's advice. 'Gershuni will not escape us now,' they wrote in a memorandum to Zubatov. 'Since he is in such close contact with our agent, his immediate arrest would leave us in the dark as to his plans and furthermore might compromise the agent.' And so Gershuni was allowed to set out on his 'very interesting trip', as the Department called it. They would, of course, take a careful note of anyone he met.

As for Gershuni, since returning to Russia, he had continued to concentrate all his attentions on the assassination of Sipyagin. The attempt on the Minister's life, it was decided, would be carried out by a young student from Kiev called Balmashev. On 15 April 1902 Balmashev, duly briefed, set out from Finland wearing an officer's uniform. In the train, he remembered that he had left his sword behind, but a new one was bought and, complete with sword, he continued the journey to St Petersburg. On arriving at the Ministry of the Interior Balmashev had himself announced as the aide-de-camp of the Grand Duke Sergei. A little surprised, Sipyagin came out into his ante-room to see what message this unexpected emissary had brought him. Whereupon Balmashev, handing him a sealed packet containing the death sentence passed on him by the Combat Section, shot him dead. For which he himself was tried by court martial, condemned to death and hanged a month later.

Sipyagin's assassination caused a considerable stir in Russia and Gershuni was naturally overjoyed at the success of his project. 'He was cheerful and gay,' wrote a friend who happened to run into him at a railway station, 'and full of his first important success.' 'It's only the beginning,' he said, 'the Gordian knot has been cut; the terror has justified itself. A beginning has been made. All discussion is now superfluous . . . It is time for the youth to come forward. Time does not wait. We must act at once.'

The Combat Section was now well and truly in existence and had already drawn blood. Meanwhile Azef, on orders from the Police Department, had remained in Berlin. On paper he now identified himself more explicitly than ever with the police. 'My trip to Paris and Switzerland,' he wrote, 'was very useful to us.' But by now he was beginning to withhold more and more important information from the Department, in particular, information with a bearing on Gershuni's terrorist activities. Already there was more than a hint of ambiguity in his attitude. There can, for example, be no doubt that Azef knew of the plan to murder Sipyagin, but for reasons of his own preferred to say nothing about it to the police, whom he kept urging not to arrest Gershuni, even after Sipyagin had been shot.

His reasons are not difficult to understand. Gershuni was important to him. His position in the Party depended after all on his friendship with Gershuni. Gershuni's arrest would have deprived him of a valuable friend and might even have focused suspicion on him. Far better, therefore, to afford him such protection as he could, at any rate for the time being. As for members of the government and any other target the terrorists might have in mind, they would have to take their chance.

During the first half of June, Azef had several meetings with Gershuni in Switzerland, where the Combat Section were planning, amongst other things, to set up a dynamite factory. He found him in fine fettle, delighted by his success, full of daring new projects, and above all insistent that his old friend Azef should play an increasingly active part in the Combat Section.

Azef, a prudent man by nature, passed on some of the information he collected from Gershuni to the police. But not all. 'We must have a personal conversation about my further work,' he wrote. 'My position has become somewhat dangerous. I am now playing a very active part among the revolutionaries. It would be unprofitable to retreat now, but any action to be undertaken calls for the greatest care.' The Department agreed with his proposal and in July 1902 Azef arrived back in St Petersburg to report in person.

There he found a number of changes. Sipyagin's place as Minister of the Interior had been taken by Vyacheslav Konstantinovich Plehve, a burly, bemedalled, rather Teutonic figure with a big moustache, who in turn had appointed Alexei Alexandrovich Lopukhin, the thirty-eight-year-old scion of an ancient Russian family, to be director of the Police Department. The Lopukhins claimed descent from Rededy, a half-mythical Kassog prince (Peter the Great's first wife, Evookia, had been a Lopukhin). Alexei Alexandrovich had himself inherited a sizeable estate near Smolensk. But for all this, having entered the government service immediately on graduating from Moscow University, he was first and foremost a civil servant, a true functionary, with his gold-rimmed glasses, his stiff white collar and cuffs, discreet necktie, neat button-boots, smooth dark hair neatly parted in the middle, moustache neatly waxed and brushed upwards and an air, one would say, of meticulous reliability.

Lopukhin concentrated the all-important work of the Department in the capable hands of Zubatov and his closer collaborators. At the same time he decided to devote more attention than ever to the development of a regular network of undercover agents. Azef, by this time on the point of being admitted to the very heart of the Social Revolutionaries' Combat Section, was at once much in demand as a key figure, being immediately brought to the notice of the new Minister, who without hesitation gave it as his personal ruling that Azef should henceforth leave no stone unturned in his efforts to penetrate the Party leadership and, more especially, the Combat Section.

Azef's first move on being given permission, indeed encouragement, to join the Combat Section, was to persuade Gershuni to call a meeting of its principal members, which he himself would attend. The meeting was held in Kiev in October 1902 under the close surveillance of the police, who at Azef's request however, made no arrests. The principal item on the agenda was the proposed assassination of the Minister of the Interior, namely Plehve. This was to be carried out by two cavalry officers, one of whom would kill the Minister's carriage horses and the other the Minister himself. This time, on due consideration, Azef thought it advisable to give the names of the two cavalry officers to the police, with the result that they were kept under close observation and given no opportunity to put their plan into execution.

Though Azef had managed to persuade the police that the part Gershuni played in it was only secondary, the Combat Section had by now become an almost completely independent body under Gershuni's personal control. In Zubatov's half-admiring phrase, he was 'an artist in terror'. His method was to recruit volunteers for future terrorist acts in the course of his travels round the country on Party business and then keep them in reserve for future use. He made no elaborate plans in advance but relied on improvisation, acting, as one of his associates put it, 'by inspiration'. It was a system which, for a professional terrorist, possessed the enormous advantage of unpredictability.

On Azef's recommendation, several less important members of the organization were now arrested, but not Gershuni, the most dangerous conspirator of all. Azef was for the time being based in St Petersburg. Here he was more active than ever, controlling the St Petersburg Party

Committee, arranging for revolutionary literature to be smuggled in from Finland, maintaining contact with potential contributors to *Revolutsionaya Rossiya*, keeping in touch with revolutionary students who wanted to stir up the working classes and also, incidentally, finding out all he could about the new Minister of the Interior's habits and way of life.

One of the students whom Azef encountered in the course of his work was a certain Kristianinov, a romantic young man without much experience of life, who pictured revolutionaries as 'elegant young people with pale, noble faces'. Azef's appearance came as rather a shock to him and he has left a description of the pointed, unintelligently shaped head, covered with dark closely-cropped hair coming down low on a narrow forehead above large, protruding, impenetrable eyes that glided from face to face. 'But,' he wrote, 'from this ponderous figure, sitting heavily on a chair, with its dark, immobile face, radiated startling strength and will power.'

Of Azef's force of character Kristianinov was soon to have plentiful proof. Like so many of his fellow intellectuals, he was anxious to engage in subversive activity among the workers. Here Azef was more than ready to be of assistance. At his suggestion, the police had helped him to set up various groups of workers in their own pay to whom the Social Revolutionaries could distribute revolutionary propaganda to their hearts' content, the arrangement, no doubt satisfactory to both parties, being that they should then hand it over to the police unread.

It was to one of these groups that Azef now directed Kristianinov. For once, however, things went wrong. One of the workers in the group happened to have had his feelings hurt by the chief police spy in his group. He had also become tired of working for the police and had taken rather a liking to Kristianinov. Explaining to him that he himself was a police spy, he went on to say that for a variety of reasons he was by now convinced that one of the leaders of the Social Revolutionary Party must also be in the pay of the police.

Putting two and two together, Kristianinov quickly came to the conclusion that the spy must be Azef. The thought appalled him. He fell ill and was tormented by nightmares. Those he consulted treated his stories as the ravings of a neurasthenic. In the end, however, feeling that it was his duty to do something, he insisted on putting his views to a small committee specially formed for the purpose of investigating his complaint.

For Kristianinov it was to prove a most embarrassing occasion. His long, confused, rambling account of his doubts and suspicions was followed by a short, sharp intervention from Azef, in his shrill, rather squeaky voice. On the strength of this the Party executive had no difficulty in at once concluding that Azef 'stood above suspicion'. It was then that Azef, his eyes flashing, as they did when he was roused, turned on his judges. 'This young

72

man,' he began reproachfully, 'may be forgiven for making a mistake, but you, men of experience . . .' And he turned away as though in disgust without finishing his sentence, leaving the members of the committee feeling guilty of something very like *lèse-majesté*. He was fortunately a superb actor, but it had, all the same, been a close-run thing.

Misfortunes never come singly. On 21 February 1903 the Tsar was to review some of his troops. Amongst these were the two young cavalry officers who the previous October had volunteered to assassinate the Minister of the Interior on behalf of the Combat Section and whose names Azef had thought it advisable to give to the police. Feeling that it would perhaps be rather risky to let them take part in a review at which the Tsar himself was to be present, the police, who had been watching them closely but unavailingly for the past four months, decided to pull them in and interrogate them, at the same time making it abundantly clear to them that they were fully informed about the plot to murder Plehve.

The two officers, realizing that only a mere handful of people besides themselves had been aware of the plot, were not unnaturally much taken aback and promptly made a full confession, giving the names and particulars of all concerned. On the strength of this the police then arrested as many of the other conspirators as they could, though naturally leaving Azef himself at liberty. This in itself was embarrassing for Azef. No less embarrassing was the fact that from the officers' confession the police now knew that he had been withholding a great deal of information from them, notably the truth as to Gershuni's real role in the Combat Section and his own relationship with him.

To complicate things still further, the Tsar himself now promised a 'handsome reward' to anyone who succeeded in arresting Gershuni (who, needless to say, had lost no time in making himself scarce). At this Plehve, in a rage, sent for Zubatov and told him that he personally would keep Gershuni's index card on his desk until Gershuni was arrested. Gershuni's description was circulated all over the country. There was talk of fifteen thousand roubles being offered for his capture and a regular man-hunt began. But although a number of people who looked rather like Gershuni were arrested, he himself somehow always succeeded in escaping.

Knowing that Azef could easily help him to find Gershuni if he wanted to, Zubatov, in his turn, now brought all the pressure he could to bear on him, even going so far as to confront him with Lopukhin, the new director of the Police Department. But Azef (who later admitted that he would have been prepared to betray Gershuni for fifty thousand roubles, which was his idea of a handsome reward, but not for less) stood firm, boldly claiming that he had done his best, but that the Department had simply misused the information he had passed to them. With the result that in the end the

73

Department, in the face of such obstinacy, simply gave in and told Azef that he had better go abroad again.

But before leaving Russia Azef had some important business to transact. He wanted, amongst other things, to have a long, quiet talk to Gershuni. Accordingly in March he set out in the greatest secrecy for Moscow, where he spent the next three days in conference with Gershuni at the house of a mutual friend called Zauer, the assistant chief of the Moscow power station, not leaving the house from the moment of his arrival until he finally left and thus successfully escaping the attention of the police.

It was by now clear to Gershuni that he himself could not hope to avoid arrest for very much longer. He therefore took the opportunity to appoint Azef his successor in all Party matters and to entrust to him in particular the control of the Combat Section. He had, however, one more project to carry out while he still could and to this the two of them now put the finishing touches.

Bogdanovich, the Governor of Ufa, had recently caused some unarmed workers to be shot down in the course of a demonstration. The decision was accordingly taken to assassinate him and Azef was given the task of establishing contact with the necessary volunteers and despatching them to Ufa, a little provincial capital due south of Ekaterinburg and just west of the Ural mountains. This assignment he duly fulfilled.

In the event, however, Gershuni resorted yet again to last minute improvisation. On reaching Ufa, he found that the local Social Revolutionaries were not only keeping a close watch on the Governor but had two volunteers of their own ready to assassinate him, a young workman called Dulebov and a young intellectual known only as The Apostle. It would clearly have been unfair to deprive them of this pleasure and, having talked things over with them, Gershuni at once gave them authority to proceed with their plan.

On 13 May 1903 Bogdanovich was taking his usual midday stroll in the Cathedral Garden near his house when two young men accosted him, thrust the Combat Section's sentence of death into his hands, pulled out their Brownings and shot him dead. After which they jumped the fence and, scrambling through a deep ravine, disappeared down the side of the hill towards the river. Neither of them was ever caught.

Gershuni, still the object of a nationwide search, also made good his escape from Ufa. Having written and despatched abroad a full account of the assassination and also published an official bulletin about it on behalf of the Combat Section, he next went to Saratov to visit the Party group there. His plan now was to go abroad again. At the last moment he decided to stop off in Kiev on the way. By mischance the telegram he sent announcing his arrival fell into the hands of a student called Rosenberg, who happened to be a minor police spy, and when Gershuni got out of the train at Kiev, smartly dressed, carrying a briefcase and wearing a civil engineer's uniform cap, he immediately saw that the railway-station was alive with detectives.

The situation was not an easy one. Gershuni accordingly walked up and down the train, looking carefully at the wheels and wondering what to do until in the end the train gave a whistle and steamed out of the station. He then stooped down, as though to tie his bootlace, at the same time watching the detectives out of the corner of his eye. It was this that gave him away. 'That's our man,' said one of the detectives to a companion. 'He's got slanting eyes.' Gershuni next went up to a fruit-stall and asked for a glass of lemonade. But the detectives, their attention now thoroughly aroused, noticed that his hand was shaking so much that he could hardly hold the glass. It was then that they pounced. A minute or two later he was arrested and then chained hand and foot. The opportunity for a dramatic gesture was more than he could resist. Bending down, he silently kissed the iron chains. It made, we are told, an unforgettable impression on all present, gendarmes, detectives and prison guards alike.

Taken by train to St Petersburg, Gershuni was tried by court martial and condemned to death, his sentence being subsequently commuted to penal servitude for life. Azef, who in the meantime had gone abroad, sending the police a carefully-timed telegram on his way through Berlin to absolve him of complicity in the assassination of Bogdanovich, now became undisputed chief of the Combat Section. On his arrival at Geneva in June, he was greeted with enthusiasm by those of its members who were assembled there and who had previously learned from Gershuni of his wishes in this respect. As usual, he set about his important new task in an orderly, methodical, well thought-out way.

A couple of months earlier, on 19 and 20 April 1903, what appeared to be a carefully planned pogrom had taken place at Kishinev, a medium-sized town not far from Odessa with a population that was almost fifty per cent Jewish. Anti-Jewish feeling has to some extent always been endemic in Russia and for two days on end a savage, drunken crowd had pillaged Jewish houses and shops, raped Jewish girls and women, beaten and murdered any Jews they could get hold of without regard for age or sex and bashed out the brains of Jewish babies against walls. The Police for their part, had made no attempt to check the crowd. Indeed, if anything, they had encouraged the rioters. But where Jews resisted, they had intervened vigorously, making arrests and even using firearms to disperse them.

Rightly or wrongly, there were those who felt that a measure of responsibility for what had happened attached to Plehve, who as Minister of the

75

Interior with responsibility for the police, was known to regard anti-Jewish pogroms as a useful means of getting the working class to let off steam and consequently as a convenient antidote to revolution – 'drowning the revolution in Jewish blood', he called it.

Amongst these, as it happened, was Yevno Azef. Not, as the reader will have observed, a man of overwhelmingly strong moral or other convictions except where his own immediate interests were concerned, he was nevertheless outraged by the accounts he had heard of the pogrom. Jewish babies had been brutally murdered and he remembered that three decades or so earlier he himself had been a Jewish baby. Zubatov of the Police Department was later to recall that in April or May 1903, before his departure abroad, he 'shook with fury and hate when he spoke of Plehve, whom he considered responsible'. These feelings may well have weighed with him during the weeks and months that followed.

There were other considerations, too. Money was something he minded about acutely. Until recently the Police Department had served as his principal source of income. Now, as acknowledged head of the Combat Section, he found himself in possession of very substantial funds indeed, infinitely more than the five hundred roubles a month he received from the Police Department, the relative importance of which had now greatly diminished in his eyes. If he was to remain in possession of these funds (and he had every intention of doing so), it was essential that the Combat Section should distinguish itself and that he should be seen to have made an outstanding success of things as its head. The last thing he wanted, even on purely financial grounds, was to be superseded in the leadership and one or two spectacularly successful acts of terrorism were the best way of ensuring that this did not happen. Since the spring of 1903, there had been a perceptible shift in his allegiance away from the police and towards the cause of Revolution. As a fellow Social Revolutionary was to put it thirty years late, 'a peculiarly favourable situation allowed economics to ally themselves with his own inclination'.

When Azef assumed the leadership of the Combat Section in June 1903 he found, as the foremost item on that body's agenda, an attempt on the life of the Minister of the Interior, V. K. Plehve. He kept it there, immediately turning his methodical and resourceful mind to the congenial task of working out a really first-class plan for Plehve's assassination.

It was known that every day the Minister drove in his carriage to the Winter Palace to make his report to the Tsar. The route or routes he followed were known and the times when he took them were also known. It was simply a question of having one or more competent terrorists armed with bombs strategically placed along whichever route it might be on the appointed day.

Most of those who took part in the plot were a good deal younger than Azef, students or former students who had been expelled from the universities for revolutionary activities, men such as Boris Savinkov and Igor Sazonov, both dedicated young revolutionaries. Azef provided the organizing ability, the practical experience. Soon a whole complex organization started to come into being: specialists were to prepare the explosives, revolutionaries disguised as cabmen or newsvendors were to keep watch. 'If there is no traitor among us,' Azef would say reassuringly as he allotted them their respective tasks, 'Plehve will be killed.' By the late autumn of 1903 a well thought-out plot had begun to take shape.

Azef was still out of the country. On leaving Russia earlier that year, he had been put under the orders of Ratayev, whose headquarters, as the newly appointed chief of the Russian Political Police Abroad, were in Paris. Though he had twenty years' police service to his credit, Ratayev, inclined to be a social butterfly, was regarded by his colleagues as a light-weight, a dilettante, whom Plehve openly called a blot on the Department and who had in fact only been sent abroad to get him out of the way. As an immediate superior he suited Azef ideally. For the first three or four months after his arrival Azef sent him no information whatever, on the grounds that he needed time to look around and 'consolidate his position'. In the late autumn, having despatched his team of terrorists to Russia, he showed himself 'a little more lively' and, arriving in Paris, called in person on Ratayev. The latter found him 'sprightly, energetic and talkative'. Though talkative, he said nothing about the proposed attempt on Plehve, but rather made it his business to find out from Ratayev, for his own satisfaction, just how well the police were informed on the subject. The answer, as far as he could judge, was that they were aware of the existence of a plot to kill Plehve, but had no idea of its details. Did Azef know Igor Sazonov, Ratayev asked. No, said Azef, who only a few days earlier had himself sent Igor off to St Petersburg; but he had a feeling he had once met his brother. Meanwhile Plehve, for his part, did not think he had anything to worry about. 'I shall know about all their plans in good time,' he said confidently when a friend, meeting him out by himself for a morning walk on Apothecary's Island, asked him whether it was wise to take such risks.

Not long after his conversation with Ratayev, Azef decided to return to St Petersburg himself, first to put the finishing touches to his own plan for Plehve's assassination and, secondly, to make sure that he was not assassinated by someone else. The competition came in this instance from a woman Social Revolutionary terrorist called Klitchoglu who had arrived in St Petersburg from the south not long before with the firm intention of making an attempt of her own on Plehve. This Azef could not tolerate. At long last he had some hard information to feed to Ratayev. Calling to see

77

him, he told him everything he knew about Klitchoglu's plot and suggested that they should now both go to St Petersburg to present this information to the Police Department. The idea appealed strongly to Ratayev, who saw in it a chance of regaining the Minister's favour. Azef was also pleased as he himself happened to be smuggling a load of dynamite into Russia and felt that Ratayev would provide the best possible cover.

With the help of the information provided by Azef, it did not take the Department long to track down Klitchoglu and her group. Having insisted, however, that Azef must first go and see her, they then arrested her immediately afterwards in spite of his earnest appeal to allow a decent interval to elapse between the two events. Though infuriating, this at least gave Azef a convenient grievance for use against the Department. If this sort of thing happened, he said, he would find it 'difficult to go on working for the police'. And Ratayev whole-heartedly supported him. Both now had ready-made excuses for withholding any information they chose from the Department or from the Okhrana. Meanwhile, in his reports to the Department, Azef, without really ever giving anything away, mingled fact with fiction in such a way as to be able to justify himself whatever the outcome of his plot.

All this time the preparations for Plehve's assassination were going ahead. By the second half of February 1904 the members of the Combat Section had begun to assemble in St Petersburg and a watch was again kept on the Minister's movements. Owing to the impatience of the younger revolutionaries it was now decided, rather against Azef's better judgement, not to delay things any longer, but to make the attempt on 31 March. On that date six young revolutionaries, three of whom, including Igor Sazonov, carried bombs, and Savinkov, who was in overall command, took up their positions in the street between the Department building and the Neva. When it came to the point, however, one of the bomb-throwers lost his nerve and the attempt had to be abandoned.

Azef who, after passing some more information to the police, had very sensibly gone abroad just before the date fixed for the attempt on Plehve's life, returned soon after its failure to find his fellow conspirators in a state of some disarray. Another attempt had been fixed for 14 April, but the terrorist who was to make it had blown himself up with his own bomb. Two successive failures were bad for morale. Azef found that in the Party there was a certain amount of murmuring against the Combat Section and against himself.

Seeing that his position in the Party was threatened, he decided that it was more important than ever to have Plehve assassinated quickly and efficiently. Sending for Boris Savinkov, he gave him a thorough dressing-down and ended by telling him that next time their plan must at all costs succeed. 'Azef's insistence, his coolness and assurance restored the spirit of the terrorists,' wrote Savinkov afterwards. 'It can be said without exaggeration that Azef recreated the organization. We went back to our task with faith and the determination to kill Plehve at any cost.'

At the beginning of May the terrorists' advance-guard re-assembled in St Petersburg. They had taken an appartment at 31 Zhukovski Street where they could hold their meetings undisturbed. Boris Savinkov, as tenant, played the part of Mr McCullough, a rich Scotsman, with Dora V. Brilliant, the revolutionary daughter of a prosperous Jewish merchant, in the role of his rather flashy mistress. The couple lived in some style: Igor Sazonov was the butler and Ivanovskaya, an elderly woman revolutionary, who had taken part in an attempt on the Tsar's life more than twenty years before, made a thoroughly convincing cook.

Azef arrived in St Petersburg in the middle of June. He had spent the last six weeks travelling round Russia, taking his old mother to the watering places of the Northern Caucasus and visiting Samara, while all the time he passed to Ratayev a stream of confusing half-facts (including – rather belatedly – the name of the unfortunate terrorist who had blown himself up with his own bomb). He had even gone to Ufa, ostensibly to ask Igor Sazonov's brother if he knew where Igor was.

Now he spent a week *chez* McCullough, at the apartment in Zhukovski Street, going over the plans, inspecting the watchers along Plehve's route, lecturing the conspirators on security and making arrangements before he left for a meeting to be held in Moscow in early July, when the finishing touches would be put to the plot.

The Moscow meeting was duly held, the various roles assigned and the date for the assassination fixed. Taking old Ivanovskaya with him, Azef went to Vilna to await the result. But when the day came, there was no telegram. Azef showed signs of extreme agitation. 'This,' he said with a scowl, 'means either complete failure or treachery.' In fact, he had some reason to feel agitated. For once he had done little or nothing to safeguard his own position, expressly informing Ratayev that the Social Revolutionaries had decided to postpone the attempt on Plehve.

In fact, as he discovered next day, when the would-be terrorists joined him in Vilna, all that had happened was that Igor Sazonov, the chief bomb-thrower, had arrived late on the proposed scene of the assassination and the whole thing had had to be abandoned.

The conspirators spent the next week in Vilna with Azef and Ivanovskaya. It was decided that a fresh attempt should be made on 18 July. Before their return to St Petersburg, they sat up all night together in a gloomy tavern. 'In a small, dimly lit room,' wrote Ivanovskaya, 'sat thoughtful men, whose fate was already sealed, exchanging trivialities. Azef alone seemed calm, attentive and unusually kind. When the time came for them to leave, he kissed them all farewell.' (It was not,' said Azef some years later, 'a Judas kiss.')

At the appointed time on 18 July the conspirators advanced up the Izmailovski Prospekt to meet Plehve's carriage on its way to the Winter Palace. The first was to let the carriage pass and only throw his bomb if things went wrong. Next came Igor Sazonov, the chief bomb-thrower carrying his twelve pound bomb. He was to throw this as soon as the carriage came within range. Two more terrorists followed, carrying bombs which they were only to throw if Sazonov missed. It was a fine, sunny day.

Punctual to the minute, Plehve's carriage appeared. As it came abreast of Sazonov, it slowed down to pass a slow-moving *droshky*. Stepping quickly into the street, Sazonov, slim and dark, ran across the intervening space towards the carriage. Through the carriage-window he saw the burly Plehve with his heavy moustache start back in momentary alarm at the sight of him. Then he threw his bomb and in the thunder of the explosion Plehve and the carriage disintegrated, while he himself was seriously wounded.

Dr E. J. Dillon, the correspondent of the London *Daily Telegraph*, who happened to be driving by (evidently in the very *droshky* that held up the Minister's carriage), has left a vivid account of the scene. 'My *droshsky* was in the street leading to the Warsaw railway station,' he wrote, 'when two men on bicycles glided past, followed by a closed carriage, which I recognized as that of the all-powerful Minister. Suddenly the ground before me quivered, a tremendous sound of thunder deafened me, the windows on both sides of the broad street rattled and the glass of the panes was hurled on to the stone pavement. A dead horse, a pool of blood, fragments of a carriage and a hole in the ground were part of my rapid impression. My driver was on his knees devoutly praying and saying that the end of the world had come. I got down from my seat and moved towards the hole, but a police officer ordered me back and to my question replied that Minister Plehve had been blown to fragments.'

From Vilna Azef had gone to Warsaw to await news of the attempt, taking old Ivanovskaya with him. On the morning of 18 July they were walking together down the Marshalovskaya when, not far from the Vienskaya Station, they met a cloud of running newsboys carrying special editions announcing that a bomb had been thrown at Plehve – and that was all. 'Can it have failed?' cried Azef in alarm. After a few minutes came more newsboys with later editions. 'Azef,' Ivanovskaya reported, 'seized the new editions with trembling hands. "Plehve Assassinated", he read out and then went all limp, letting his arms hang loosely by his sides. "I feel faint," he said.'

It had been arranged that as soon as possible after the assassination Azef should meet Boris Savinkov in Warsaw, where they would jointly discuss the Combat Section's next moves. But when Savinkov arrived, Azef was no longer there. Without a word to Ivanovskaya, he had caught the first fast train to Vienna and from Vienna he had, immediately on arrival, sent an urgent telegram to Ratayev. The purpose of this was to give the impression that he had only heard the news of Plehve's assassination in Vienna and that it had been as much of a surprise to him as to anyone else. He was in the clear with the revolutionaries; it was now essential for him to do everything he could to put things right with the police. As a first step, he had established what might with any luck serve as an alibi.

From Vienna Azef now made his way to Geneva, where a Congress of Social Revolutionaries was being held and where such members of the Combat Section as were able to assembled a few days after the assassination. He received a hero's welcome. Plehve's assassination had made a tremendous impact, being welcomed even by the opponents of terrorist methods as a blow for freedom. It had been the Combat Section's crowning glory and Azef, as its undisputed leader, was given a tremendous reception. Even old Breshkovskaya, the Grandmother of the Party, who instinctively disliked him, greeted him in the old Russian fashion by bowing almost to the ground. 'The terror,' wrote one Social Revolutionary, 'now became the Holy of Holies and Azef, as its High Priest, was placed on an even higher pedestal than the greatest terrorists of the past.' 'Formerly,' said another, comparing him to Gershuni, 'we were led by a romantic, now we have a realist. He is not a talker, but he will carry out his plans with a ruthless energy which nothing can withstand.' It was a description which would have given Azef himself nothing but pleasure. His position as chief of the Combat Section was now assured.

Azef's relations with the police were rather more precarious. The Minister's assassination had not unnaturally shaken the Department to the core. 'Things must be in a bad way if Azef knew nothing about it,' said one official a trifle ingenuously. It had been Plehve, after all, who had insisted that Azef should join the Combat Section – a gamble that had certainly not paid off as far as he himself was concerned.

The Department now summoned Ratayev from Paris to give an explanation and Ratayev in his turn consulted Azef. Azef, needless to say, had his answer ready. 'Azef,' writes Lopukhin, 'explained his own lack of information in this particular case by the fact that the Police Department had not paid sufficient attention to the information he had given them in the past, often making unwise use of it and then putting the Social Revolutionaries on their guard and in this way cutting off his sources of information at a critical time.'

Ratayev, whom Azef by now could and did twist round his little finger, seems to have swallowed his explanation whole. Lopukhin and the Department followed suit and Azef emerged unscathed from what could have been a very awkward predicament, especially when it is considered that the police by now knew that the conspirators had met in Vilna immediately before the assassination and that Azef had been there at the same time. Obviously their investigation of his activities had been slipshod in the extreme and obviously he was well aware of this.

Soon the police were once again delighted with Azef's work. 'Immediately after the assassination,' said Plehve's successor, Stolypin, 'Azef sent in extremely important and valuable reports which led to the discovery of a whole series of criminal plots.' In fact, he was using his position as a police spy first and foremost to cover up the activities of the Combat Section.

For him it was still as important as ever to consolidate his hold on that body and, more especially, on its funds, now swollen by generous contributions from all kinds of quarters. Though never much interested in political theory or politics as such, he had now become a member of the Central Committee of the Social Revolutionary Party. Even so, he never had much use for Socialism. 'It's necessary, of course, for youth and for the workers,' he said to a friend. 'But not for you or me.' A Liberal Terrorist was perhaps the description which fitted him best. It was one which he himself quite readily accepted.

And in the autumn of 1904 the Combat Section, strengthened by large numbers of new recruits, was ready for a fresh campaign of terror. At a joint meeting in Paris with the Central Committee it was decided that a suitable target would be the Court Party, led by the Tsar's somewhat reactionary uncles, the Grand Duke Sergei, Governor General of Moscow, and the Grand Duke Vladimir. Small parties of terrorists were accordingly told off to assassinate the Grand Duke Sergei in Moscow and, in St Petersburg the Grand Duke Vladimir, with the new Minister of the Interior and the Governor General of St Petersburg thrown in as supplementary targets, while a third detachment struck simultaneously at the Governor General of Kiev. If any or all of these attempts were successful, it would, the Combat Section reckoned, have a salutary effect on the Tsar.

In Paris Azef was in charge, planning the operations, selecting the men for each job and allotting them their respective tasks, setting up a dynamite factory and arranging for the dynamite to be smuggled into Russia. In November the terrorists, whom he had duly provided with forged passports, left for Russia. He himself would follow later in order to put the finishing touches to their plans. It was essential, he felt, that as head of the Combat Section he should run no unnecessary risks.

Nor was Azef neglecting his duties to the police, who found the reports he sent them via Ratayev during the second half of 1904 particularly interesting. But, though interesting, they were far from accurate. The Combat Section, he told them, were planning to assassinate the Tsar. Their headquarters were in Odessa. The most dangerous terrorists were a certain Sletov and Maria Selyuk. By this means he successfully diverted their attention from the true aims and activities of the Combat Section, who had no intention of murdering the Tsar and no organization in Odessa, while, by causing Sletov and Maria Selyuk to be arrested, he got rid of two awkward political opponents.

Meanwhile in Russia and in the world events had taken a new and dramatic turn. Since February 1904 Russia had been at war with Japan. From the first things had gone badly for Russia, catastrophe succeeding catastrophe in the Far East. Instead of distracting attention from the Government's shortcomings at home, as they had hoped, the war had had the opposite effect, aggravating popular discontent and giving rise to a fresh wave of demonstrations, peasant riots and industrial unrest.

Things came to a head on Sunday, 22 January 1905 (to be known thereafter as Bloody Sunday), when, following a general strike in St Petersburg, a vast crowd of workers, carrying holy icons and singing the national anthem, converged on the Winter Palace to petition the Tsar in person. They were led by an Orthodox priest, a certain Father Gapon, a histrionic, equivocal figure, associated alike with the revolutionaries and the police. The authorities had taken steps to control the demonstration, but when it came to the point, panic set in and the order was given to fire on the crowd. The Cossacks charged, several hundred people were killed and the Government found themselves facing a revolutionary situation. Strikes, riots, demonstrations and mutinies continued during the months that followed until in October 1905 the Tsar was reluctantly obliged to authorize the election by popular franchise of a *Duma* or National Assembly.

For the Combat Section Bloody Sunday and the events that followed it naturally served as an encouragement to action. They were full of plans. There was even talk of killing the Tsar. To put their plans into effect, they needed Azef. Urgent appeals were sent to him. But for once he was not very sure of himself or of his ability to repeat his recent success and above all was feeling distinctly nervous at the thought of returning to Russia. Indeed, when that old war-horse Ivanovskaya, happening to be in Paris, called to visit his wife, she was disturbed to find him lying on a couch, trembling like an autumn leaf and with eyes as pitiful as those of a beaten dog.

And so, when the time came, the young terrorists were left to work things out for themselves. They were only partly successful. In Moscow, Kalayev, a former student who had taken a leading part in Plehve's assassination, succeeded in killing the Grand Duke Sergei with a bomb on 17 February. The attempt on the Governor General of Kiev was abandoned as not being worthwhile. In St Petersburg, where a memorial service to commemorate the assassination of Tsar Alexander II was being held on 14 March in the Cathedral of St Peter and St Paul, it had been hoped that this would provide an occasion to assassinate the Grand Duke Vladimir, the new Minister of the Interior and the Governor-General simultaneously with three well-directed bombs. But on 11 March, three days before the attempt, Marc Schweitzer, the leader of the team, a trained chemist who had also undertaken the task of making and distributing the bombs, blew himself up in his room at the Hotel Bristol while putting the finishing touches to the bombs. Nor was this all. The police had got on to the trail of the terrorists. On 29 and 30 March, while they were wondering what to do next and wishing that Azef were with them, their store of dynamite was discovered and all the remaining members of the St Petersburg detachment were arrested except for Dora Brilliant, the Jewish merchant's daughter, who somehow managed to get away. Azef was still in Paris.

The arrests of 29 and 30 March 1905 represented a serious setback for the Social Revolutionaries. At the very moment when a genuine revolutionary situation presented itself, they found themselves hamstrung. Nor was this the only disquieting feature of the situation. To Azef it had begun to look very much as if there was another traitor in the Party besides himself.

Whatever the risks involved, Azef could not afford to remain in Paris. With the emergence of a mass revolutionary movement, the influence of the terrorists had begun to decline. The Party was now organizing a series of peasant risings for the summer and most of its more active members were working among the masses. There was a serious danger that, unless something was done soon, the Combat Section, which for the first time in its history was short of volunteers, would simply fade away from lack of funds and interest. Allowing a decent interval to elapse after the St Petersburg arrests and screwing up his courage to face both the Party and the police, Azef set out for Russia in the early summer of 1905, with the object of drumming up support for the Combat Section, resuming direct contact with the Party in the country and planning a series of terrorist acts for the future.

He had not been in Russia long before he noticed that he and some friends who had planned to meet at Nizhni Novgorod were under police surveillance. Moreover, as he himself had not informed the police of the proposed meeting, it was clear that their plans had been betrayed by someone else with access to inner Party circles.

Some quick thinking was called for on Azef's part. First he had to safeguard the existence of the newly revived Combat Section and secondly he needed to clear himself in the eyes of the police. He accordingly at once informed the police of the proposed meeting at Nizhni Novgorod (of which they knew already), adding for good measure that the terrorists were planning to assassinate the Governor (which was simply not true). At the same time he gave them the name of A. V. Yakimova, a middle-aged woman terrorist who, having escaped from Siberia after serving a twenty years' sentence there for trying to assassinate the last Tsar but one, was proposing to attend the meeting at Nizhni Novgorod and who, he knew, had in any case already been betrayed. He then warned the more important members of his group to keep away from Nizhni Novgorod. Thus, by sacrificing one not very important woman, who was going to jail anyway, he successfully safeguarded his own position and that of the Combat Section. Once again, with consummate skill, he emerged from what could have been an awkward situation and at the same time contrived to keep the Combat Section in being.

But there was worse trouble to come. Immediately after the murder of the Grand Duke Sergei there had been a major upheaval in the Police Department. Lopukhin, its aristocratic director, whom the Governor General of St Petersburg had called a murderer to his face, and with whom the Tsar had declared himself thoroughly dissatisfied, had been forced to resign, making way for his bitterest enemy, Pyotr Ivanovich Rachkovski, a resourceful but thoroughly unscrupulous old man who, starting as a police spy, had attained his present position (and also amassed a considerable fortune) by every kind of disreputable stratagem and subterfuge at home and abroad, notably by gambling on the Paris Stock Exchange with police funds and giving, when he felt like it, useful tips to his superiors.

Having immediately dismissed the ineffectual Ratayev, Rachkovski's next move was to assume personal control of all the Department's secret agents, including Azef, to whom this change, now that he was so well accustomed to Ratayev, was anything but welcome. What seems to have been their first encounter took place in St Petersburg on 21 August 1905.

Nor was the change in police personnel Azef's only worry. He was by now virtually certain that there was another police spy high up in the Social Revolutionary Party and that Rachkovski therefore had his own means of checking the truth and accuracy of his reports. It was clearly essential for him to make a favourable impression on him from the very beginning. He accordingly at once undertook to betray his close associate Boris Savinkov, old Breshkovskaya, the Holy Ghost of the Revolution, and a great many other well-known terrorists. In return for this, his salary and expense-allowance were at once increased and he was given an advance of several thousand roubles. After which he set out with a detective to see if they could not catch Savinkov and Breshkovskaya, both of whom, however, for one reason or another, succeeded in escaping.

No sooner had Azef managed to clear himself with the police than he found himself in trouble with the Party. What, for all his alertness, he had not realized was that a high police official, a certain Captain Menshikov, had had a sudden change of heart and decided to expose as many police agents as he could to the Social Revolutionaries. On 8 September 1905 a mysterious veiled lady, sent by Menshikov, slipped into the house of an important Party member in St Petersburg and, leaving a letter with him, vanished as mysteriously as she had come. The letter she had left contained a startling piece of information. The party, it declared, was being betrayed by two spies, 'an ex-convict called T . . . and Engineer Azef, a Jew who recently returned from abroad.' Later that day Azef happened to call on the recipient of the letter, who at once showed it to him. 'T,' said Azef calmly looking at it, 'that can only be Tartarov. And Engineer Azef, that must be me. My name's Azef.' Then he walked out.

Once again some quick thinking was called for. At least Azef now knew who his fellow spy was: Tartarov, a relatively new recruit to the Party. But that his own connection with the police had been given away was decidedly inconvenient. That same evening he called on Rachkovski to complain in the strongest possible terms of his Department's poor security. Then he went to Moscow to see a leading member of the Central Committee and after that to Geneva.

The leaders of the Social Revolutionary Party now knew for certain that there was at least one spy in their midst, but, when it came to the point, they utterly rejected the charge against Azef. To them it was inconceivable that the organizer of Plehve's assassination could be a traitor. The accusation, they decided, was not even worth investigating.

The case of Tartarov was rather different. Tartarov was the son of the Archpriest of the Orthodox Cathedral in Warsaw. After engaging in various revolutionary activities, he had been sent to Eastern Siberia in 1901. There he had joined the Social Revolutionaries, but this had not prevented him from being recruited as an *agent provocateur* by the Governor-General, who happened to be a friend of his father. In this dual role he had arrived in St Petersburg in February 1905 and had actually been admitted to the Central Committee just as the Social Revolutionaries were planning their triple event in the Cathedral of St Peter and St Paul.

Some Social Revolutionaries had had doubts about Tartarov even before the veiled lady delivered her letter. There had been treachery in St Petersburg and treachery over the meeting at Nizhni Novgorod and in both instances Tartarov had been amongst those involved. A Committee of the Party was accordingly now set up in Geneva to investigate his case. They came to the conclusion that he was in some way connected with the police, though there was not enough evidence to show how. The decision was accordingly taken not to kill him, as had been originally proposed, but to suspend him from Party work and allow him to return to Russia on condition that he kept the Party informed of his movements. Azef was away from Geneva, recuperating in the mountains at the time of the investigation. On his return he was indignant to find that Tartarov had not been executed. 'Is there ever more definite proof in such cases?' he asked.

As usual, he knew what he was talking about, especially where treachery was concerned. That same October, as it happened, an amnesty was declared, under which large numbers of political prisoners were released from jail. Amongst these were the revolutionaries who had been arrested in St Petersburg in March. What they had to say left no doubt whatever as to Tartarov's guilt. It was certainly he who had betrayed them to the police, just as it had been he who had given the Okhrana the names of those attending the meeting at Nizhni Novgorod. Even now some of his friends were reluctant to believe the worst of him and one of them went to Kiev to confront him with the facts and ask him for an explanation. But all that he could think of to say in his defence was that the real spy was Azef; he had been told this, he kept repeating, by a relation of his in the Petersburg police.

This was the last straw. As usual, any imputation against Yevno Azef was received by the Social Revolutionaries with the utmost indignation. In order to save himself, they said, Tartarov was deliberately calumniating Azef, whom the police had for so long been seeking to destroy. He most certainly deserved to die.

The plans for his execution were made by Boris Savinkov and the Combat Section. 'We wanted,' wrote Savinkov afterwards, 'to spare Azef all the worries involved in killing this *agent provocateur*.' But Azef brushed their scruples aside as 'sentimentality' and insisted on taking an active part in planning the execution. From his point of view, after all, it was even more important than from theirs that Tartarov should be liquidated without delay. There was no room, as far as he was concerned, for two police spies in the Social Revolutionary Party.

Meanwhile Tartarov, no doubt suspecting what was afoot, had moved to Warsaw, where he had gone to ground in his father's house, hardly ever venturing outside it. He was followed there some weeks later by a detachment of killers from the Combat Section, led by Boris Savinkov. On 4 April 1906 one Nazarov, a working-class member of the Party, called at the Archpriest's residence and asked to see his son. Sensing the purpose of Nazarov's visit, the old Archpriest demurred. But at this moment Tartarov himself, hearing voices, came into the hall. Whereupon Nazarov at once pulled out his revolver and opened fire. With considerable presence of mind, the Archpriest knocked his hand up. The shots went wide and the Archpriest, his wife and son then grappled with the assassin. The latter, however, was not so easily put off. Drawing a dagger, he first managed to wound Tartarov's mother with it and then, driving it deep into her son's left side, killed him instantly, subsequently making good his escape in the confusion that ensued. The police records show that during the relatively short period in 1905 when he was acting as a police spy Tartarov had received no less than sixteen thousand roubles, a substantial sum, for which, however, he paid in the end with his life.

Tartarov's timely execution took a considerable weight off Azef's mind. But only temporarily. The events of 1905 had had an unsettling effect on government and opposition alike. Among the Social Revolutionaries the debate continued between those who now believed in mass movements and those, like Savinkov, who still favoured action by individual terrorists. Azef had a more personal problem. He had to decide whether in the long run the Revolution was not perhaps going to triumph and whether, if this was so, the time had not come for him to sever his connection with the Okhrana and finally throw his lot in with the revolutionaries. On the other hand, the chances of the present régime surviving might still be good enough to make it advisable for him to continue to keep in with the police.

Since the amnesty of October 1905 and the introduction of something approaching constitutional government, many opponents of the régime who had been living abroad had returned to Russia. Azef, never in a hurry to take unnecessary risks, had followed at his leisure, arriving in time for a meeting of the Central Committee which was held in Moscow that November.

What he saw in Russia failed to convince him that the Revolution was likely to triumph in the foreseeable future. The risings that took place that winter all over the country were vigorously suppressed and the revolutionaries once again driven underground. He himself also received what he took to be a reminder of his obligations towards the police. One dark night he was set upon and stabbed in a lonely alley by two members of the Black Band, a right-wing terrorist group generally thought to be under police control.

Fortunately for Azef the fur coat he was wearing was so thick that the knife failed to penetrate it and he was not even wounded. He was nevertheless very much upset. 'His face,' wrote an eye witness, 'was covered with purple blotches and his lips quivered nervously.' Nor was his fear purely physical. Rightly or wrongly, he interpreted this attack on him as Rachkovski's way of telling him not to commit himself too wholeheartedly to the Revolutionary cause. His reaction was at once to resume contact with the police and provide Rachkovski with a judicious amount of information concerning Social Revolutionary activities.

Meanwhile in the new, more repressive political climate, the upholders of terrorist action in the Party had won the day over those who put their faith in mass movements; the Combat Section had been revived and Azef once again put in charge of it. And once more there was a traitor to be liquidated.

Bloody Sunday had made a popular hero of Father Gapon. His picture was everywhere, with his beard and his pectoral cross and the dual appeal of the priest turned revolutionary. A publisher paid him a large sum for his autobiography. Funds flowed in from all sides. Everybody wanted to meet him. He was acclaimed by the Left. First he joined the Social Democrats, then the Social Revolutionaries, then, aspiring to personal leadership, formed a new political party of his own. He was prodigiously vain. He liked the good things of life. He had plenty of money. He spent it lavishly on wine and women in the best restaurants and cabarets of Paris and St Petersburg and even on the tables at Monte Carlo. Soon his revolutionary ideals, if he had ever had any, had gone by the board. It would have been better for the Revolution, remarked the Austrian Socialist Adler, a trifly sourly, if things had gone otherwise on 22 January and it had been able to reckon Father Gapon among its dead rather than its living heroes.

Rachkovski was not the man to miss such an obvious opportunity. Over a series of expensive dinners at some of the best restaurants of St Petersburg, notably the Café de Paris, with the wine flowing freely, he had outlined to Father Gapon the role he had in mind for him: first to help direct the Russian labour movement along peaceful lines and secondly to keep the police informed about the terrorists and revolutionaries.

To these approaches Gapon had responded with alacrity. He had, he said, a friend who was in close touch with the Combat Section of the Social Revolutionaries, an engineer called Peter Rutenberg. Through him he would be able to find out all he wanted to know about the terrorists' plans.

It was, as it happened, quite true that Rutenberg and Father Gapon were friends. Together they had drawn up the famous petition to the Tsar. Together they had marched to the Winter Palace on 22 January. Together they had lain in the snow under a hail of bullets. And after it was all over, it was Rutenberg who had helped Father Gapon escape to Geneva. At the moment, Gapon discovered, Rutenberg was in Moscow, hiding from the police. Having obtained his address from a mutual friend, he called on him on 19 February 1906.

Father Gapon's manner, even more shifty than usual, soon put Rutenberg on his guard. He noticed that he kept looking away while he was speaking. However Rutenberg listened quietly to what he had to say and after some preliminary remarks about revolutionary aims, was in due course regaled with an enthusiastic account of the vast sums of money the two of them could make by selling the secrets of the Combat Section to the police. Rutenberg still did not demur.

Convinced that he had won him over, Gapon went straight back to Rachkovski to report his success. One hundred thousand roubles, he suggested, would be adequate reward for the work he had in mind. Even Rachkovski was surprised at such effrontery and made a counter-offer of twenty-five thousand, but on referring the matter to higher authority was advised not to bargain unduly.

Rutenberg, for his part, had at once informed the Social Revolutionary leaders of Gapon's approach to him, Azef amongst them. Azef's reaction to this tale of treachery and double-dealing had been immediate and characteristic. 'He thought,' Rutenberg recalled later, 'that Gapon should be killed like a snake.' Rutenberg, he said, should arrange an interview with him, take him out to dinner and after dinner, while driving back through a wood in a sledge that belonged to the Combat Section, stab him and throw his body out into the snow.

The issue was not, however, quite as simple as that. There were other considerations to be borne in mind. To the Russian people Gapon was still the hero of Bloody Sunday. In order to demonstrate his connection with the police, the decision was therefore now taken to kill Gapon and Rachkovski together, and the task entrusted to Rutenberg who, with this object in view, was to continue to play along with Father Gapon and the police.

In the event the plan failed. With Rutenberg's help, an appointment was duly made for Rachkovski to meet Gapon and Rutenberg in order to discuss their plans for the future. But, when the time came, Rachkovski did not keep it, the reason being that Azef, while loudly insisting that Rachkovski must be killed, had already warned him of the impending attempt on his life and suggested that he should not come to the meeting with Rutenberg and Gapon.

In the end, when it became clear that it was not going to be possible to kill Gapon and Rachkovski together, the decision was taken to kill Gapon alone. Arrangements were accordingly made for Rutenberg and Gapon to meet on 10 April 1906 at a lonely *dacha* in the country outside St Petersburg at Ozerki, near the Finnish frontier, for the purpose of discussing the terms of their joint betrayal of the Combat Section. Having arrived at the *dacha*, Gapon, greedy for the money he had been promised, chided Rutenberg for his dilatoriness. 'What are you waiting for?' he said. 'Twenty-five thousand is good money.' Rutenberg said he was afraid that, if caught, the terrorists might be hung. 'Well, what of it?' said Gapon. 'It's a pity of course, but we can't help that. You can't cut down a tree without sending the splinters flying.' In any case, he said, no one would ever know anything about it. Rachkovski would see to that.

Father Gapon did not realize that while they were speaking, in an adjoining room on the other side of a thin partition, a group of specially selected working-class Social Revolutionaries were listening to every word they said. After a time Rutenberg found it impossible to keep up the pretence any longer. Throwing open the door, he stood aside as his infuriated comrades burst in.

Gapon was thunderstruck. 'Brothers,' he said, falling on his knees, 'forgive me for old times' sake.' 'We are not your brothers,' came the answer. 'Rachkovski is your brother.' Knowing what was coming next, Rutenberg's nerve suddenly failed him. 'He was once my friend,' he said, turning away with a sob, and went out of the room. His comrades, however, felt no such scruples. A rope was put round the priest's neck and looped over a handy iron hook. Several sturdy revolutionaries pulled on the rope, Gapon's feet left the floor, the noose tightened and not many minutes later he was dead. After which they locked up the house and returned whence they had come. The body was not found by the police or anyone else for several weeks.

For the over-sensitive Peter Rutenberg, by this time in Finland, another shock was in store. Azef, who, as we know, had himself warned Rachkovski to keep away, now utterly denied that he had ever authorized the assassination of Father Gapon alone or had known anything about it. It had, he maintained, been a purely personal undertaking of Rutenberg's. The latter accordingly now found himself accused of violating Party discipline and, worse still, of misrepresenting Azef, while the press started to hint that he had killed Gapon at the instigation of the political police or simply to get rid of an embarrassing rival. Disillusioned by this somewhat unedifying experience of revolutionary tactics, he resigned from the movement and returned to engineering.

It was, it must be admitted, not altogether easy, even for the most experienced revolutionary or policeman, to hold his own with Yevno Azef.

91

Not more than a few days after Father Gapon had been disposed of, he was to cross swords not unsuccessfully with the redoubtable Rachkovski himself.

Simultaneously with their plot to assassinate Rachkovski and Father Gapon, the Combat Section were contemplating an attempt on the life of P. N. Durnovo, the new Minister of the Interior. With this in view they kept a close watch on his movements, disguising three or four of their members as cab drivers so as to keep track of him without attracting undue attention. However, it was soon noticed by the police that the cab driver outside Durnovo's house stayed there for hours on end, refusing all fares. After watching him for a time, they discovered that he was in touch with two other fake cab drivers and with a fourth rather burly individual who seemed to be in charge of all three of them. What is more, the detective watching them quickly recognized the fourth man as someone who had been pointed out to him some years previously as an important police spy, known apparently as 'Filipovski', for the simple reason that he frequented the Café Filipov at the corner of the Nevski Prospekt and the Troitskaya, an establishment famous for its pastries and pies.

After a certain amount of discussion within the Department, the decision was taken to arrest Filipovski and on about 15 April he was duly picked up by detectives in a deserted side-street near the Summer Garden, as he was walking back at dusk after a talk with one of the three cab-drivers. At this he protested vigorously, producing papers to show that he was Engineer Cherkass. However the police firmly locked him up, explaining that they knew that he was or had been one of their own agents. At this he quietened down and two days later announced that he was ready to speak, but only in the presence of his former Chief, Pyotr Ivanovich Rachkovski.

The confrontation took place in the office of Colonel Alexander Vasilevich Gerasimov, the recently appointed chief of the Petersburg Okhrana, a compact, rather crafty-looking man with slanting eyes, a well-waxed brown moustache and a small pointed beard. Rachkovski had no difficulty in recognizing the prisoner. 'Ah, my dear Yevgeni Filipovich,' he said with a charming smile, addressing Azef by his first name and patronymic, 'we haven't seen each other for some time.' After two days in solitary confinement on prison fare, Azef was not in the best of tempers and responded with a torrent of abuse. But this did not worry Rachkovski. 'Don't get excited, my dear Azef,' he said. 'Keep calm.' And after a little friendly wrangling as to which of them had let the other down and how they had managed to lose touch with each other and after Rachkovski had finally admitted that he had really been at fault, it was agreed that Azef should formally re-enter the service of the Police Department. Which, as it happened, was exactly what he wanted to do.

There was, it is true, still one small point to clear up. Why had Azef been taking such a leading part in the plot to murder the Minister of the Interior? Azef had no difficulty in answering this question. Since Rachkovski had left him in the lurch, he said, he no longer regarded himself as being in the employment of the Department and therefore felt free to continue his professional Party work as a member of the Central Committee and Combat Section. In fact, the least the Department could do was to compensate him for his losses and refund his back pay and expenses for the past six months. And so in the end he went off richer by five thousand roubles, having first, as a gesture of goodwill, given the police some items of rather stale information which they either had already or were bound sooner or later to find out for themselves.

One such bonus, which he threw in with particular glee, was a detailed account of what had happened to Father Gapon, of whom the police still had no definite news. 'So,' he said to Rachkovski, 'you succeeded in buying Rutenberg. And in penetrating the Combat Section. A fine job you made of that, and no mistake!' And he went on to tell them, while they listened aghast, of the kangaroo court and how Gapon's body was at that moment hanging in an empty *dacha* somewhere near the Finnish frontier. He had forgotten exactly where, he said, quite untruly. With the result that the police spent the next four or five weeks searching the woods on both sides of the border until they finally found the empty house with its grisly inmate in priest's robes and pectoral cross dangling disconsolately from a hook.

From his reconciliation with Rachkovski Azef brought away another important concession. In order that he should not be compromised, none of the terrorists working with him was to be arrested, but simply 'frightened' by carefully spread rumours that the police were after them. The terms of his future employment were then submitted to and approved by Durnovo, the Minister of the Interior, until a few days before Azef's intended victim, who, as he signed the order for five thousand roubles, remarked, with scarcely justified confidence, 'It's his risk not ours. If he's ready and willing, why should we worry?'

Azef explained his absence in prison to his fellow-revolutionaries by saying that he had been hiding from the police, which they readily accepted. They then got down to work again, though that spring the apparently firm prospect of democratic government offered by the elections to the Duma had deflected interest from terrorism as a means to the same end. Various plans were put forward and discarded. (Some because the police, through one agency or another, quite clearly knew about them in advance.) In particular, the plan to murder Durnovo was revived and Boris Savinkov put in charge of it. But by now the Minister was so closely guarded that the terrorists found they could get nowhere near him.

A more likely target was Admiral Dubasov, the Governor-General of

Moscow, whom Azef picked as his personal victim. The 6th of May was the Empress's birthday. As Governor-General, Dubasov would be attending the service held in her honour in the Kremlin. Sending the bomb-throwers and technicians on ahead, Azef, who was in Finland, remained there until the last moment. A week before the attempt, he received the infuriating news that once again his technicians had blown themselves up by mistake, destroying not only themselves, but almost the whole of his precious store of dynamite in the process. A lesser man might have let this set-back deter him. But not Azef. Fresh volunteers were found and thrown into the breach and barely twenty-four hours before the appointed day, he himself arrived in Moscow, having first explained to Rachkovski and Colonel Gerasimov that he needed to go there for what he called personal reasons.

On the appointed day, the Governor-General's carriage had no sooner left his massive classical palace on the Tverskaya and started downhill in the direction of the Kremlin, than Azef's chief bomb-thrower broke through the line of sentries and, with deadly accuracy, threw his bomb so that it exploded immediately under the carriage, permanently disabling the Governor-General and killing his aide-de-camp and, as it happened, the terrorist who had thrown it. Meanwhile a few hundred yards up the Tverskaya at the Café Filipov, the Moscow branch of the establishment he so frequently favoured in St Petersburg, Azef was as usual regaling himself on pastries. The noise of the explosion had scarcely died away when the café was surrounded by police on the lookout for terrorists. With them, as it happened, was an old detective who, recognizing Azef as a colleague, immediately told his subordinates to let him go.

One of Azef's motives in planning Admiral Dubasov's assassination had been to put the Combat Section back on the map and clear himself of any suspicion in the eyes of his revolutionary friends. Though only partly successful, it had achieved both these objects. But it had also raised serious doubts in the minds of Colonel Gerasimov and P. I. Rachkovski, which were strongly reinforced when a report came in from Zinaida Zuchenko, a highly reliable woman spy planted on the terrorists by the Moscow Okhrana, saying that Azef had himself organized the whole operation.

Azef's next interview with Pyotr Ivanovich Rachkovski and the Colonel showed signs of being a difficult one. 'That affair in Moscow was *your* doing!' shouted Pyotr Ivanovich, pointing an accusing finger at him. But Azef as usual was not at a loss for an answer. 'If it was my doing,' he replied boldly, 'why don't you arrest me?' And he went on to say that he had every reason to believe that the attempt had been planned by a dangerous, ruthless woman called Zinaida Zuchenko.

As Azef well knew, the police were in a quandary whatever they did. If they arrested either Azef or Zinaida, if it were even suggested that the attempt on the life of the Governor-General had been made by a police spy, there would be an appalling scandal. Nor were they in any case anxious to lose one or both of their best agents. Bewildered, they decided to do nothing, with the result that yet again Azef got away with murder.

Even so, he was well aware that he had run a considerable risk. As a token of his good faith he accordingly undertook to betray his friend Boris Savinkov to the police, at the same time giving them a somewhat exaggerated idea of his importance in the movement. After the mutinies which had taken place the year before in the Black Sea Fleet, notably on board the battleship *Potyomkin*, the unrest in the Imperial Navy had been ruthlessly suppressed by Admiral Chuknin, who thereby automatically made himself a suitable target for terrorists. Azef now sent Savinkov to Sebastopol with instructions to murder the Admiral, at the same time informing the police and providing them with evidence which would make a death sentence inevitable. This plan had the added advantage that the action involved would take place in the Crimea and would not therefore be connected with Azef, who would remain safely in St Petersburg.

In the event, as so often happens, things turned out differently. Soon after reaching Sebastopol Savinkov was arrested, not for his plot against the Admiral, but for his alleged part in an attempt on the life of the general commanding the local garrison, which happened to have been made by some local revolutionaries immediately after his arrival and of which he had no previous knowledge. This, no less than his proposed attempt on the Admiral, meant a death sentence but, fortunately for him, Savinkov was saved by the timely arrival of a rescue group from St Petersburg, who successfully smuggled him out of jail in a soldier's uniform. With the help of a friendly young naval officer called Nikitenko, he was put on board a sailing boat and safely conveyed to Roumania where he spent a few months to rest and give things time to blow over before duly making his way back to Russia to rejoin the ranks of the Combat Section.

The events of 1905 had, as was to be expected, brought considerable changes in the Police Department. At the Ministry of the Interior Durnovo had been succeeded by P. A. Stolypin, a newcomer to the official life of the capital who looked rather like a French provincial doctor, with a bald head and large black beard, a sad-looking wife, an infant son and half a dozen daughters between the ages of six and sixteen. The British Ambassador, who knew him well, called Stolypin 'a great man ... the most notable figure in Europe.' One of the new Minister's first moves, taken on the advice of his former school friend Lopukhin, was to get rid of Rachkovski, who was formally dismissed in June 1906. From this point onwards the effective force in the Political Police was Colonel Alexander Vasilievich Gerasimov, he of the well-waxed moustache, slanting eyes and small pointed beard, who since February 1905 had been chief of the Petersburg Okhrana. Unlike most officers of the Gendarmerie, Colonel Gerasimov, now in his mid-forties, was of peasant origin and had a peasant's slyness, tenacity and singleness of purpose. His purpose at that moment was the suppression of the Revolution and more especially of the Petersburg Council (or Soviet) of Workers' Deputies which he had effectively put out of action in December 1905. Gerasimov had found it difficult to get the decisions he needed from Durnovo or for that matter from his immediate superiors in the Police Department. But Stolypin quickly grasped his potentialities and fully realizing the importance to him, as Minister, of having the chief of the Political Police entirely on his side, gave him the strongest support, by-passing the Police Department and allowing Gerasimov direct access to himself. It was the beginning of a period of mutually beneficial collaboration between them. Soon Gerasimov's influence (and with it that of Stolypin, who was shortly to become Prime Minister) spread far beyond St Petersburg and was extended to the remotest provinces of the Empire.

One of Gerasimov's most important tasks was, of course, the penetration of the various revolutionary parties and organizations. In this connection Azef soon became his right-hand man and, surprising as it may seem, won his complete confidence. 'As a result of the honesty, zeal and precision with which he carried out his duties,' wrote Gerasimov later, 'all doubts about him were quickly dispelled.'

Azef, for his part was fully conscious of the importance of gaining and keeping Gerasimov's good will. Realizing his dislike of the Police Department, he played on this for all he was worth, sniping, whenever the opportunity offered, at 'their empty-headed Excellencies' and hinting that things would go much better now that he was under Gerasimov's direct orders. 'He complained,' wrote Gerasimov, 'that his chiefs took little care of him and expressed surprise at being able to retain the confidence of the revolutionaries in spite of the rumours of treachery circulated against him.' To make up for this, Gerasimov doubled his salary, bringing it up to a thousand roubles a month. 'I advised him,' says Gerasimov, 'not to spend his salary, but to put it in a bank, for he had enough money from the Party for his living expenses. He followed this advice and drew up a will, which is still in my possession, under which this money was to go to his wife on his death.'

Needless to say, Azef did not tell Gerasimov everything. It would have been unlike him to do so. But the carefully selected information which he did pass to him at this time, covering as it did a wide range of political and semi-political subjects, was interesting, accurate and well presented and was avidly read by the Minister as well as by Gerasimov, who actually consulted him on Stolypin's behalf as to the advisability of introducing some moderate Liberals into the Government. It is thus scarcely surprising to find that one official report of the time specifically refers to him, not as a police spy, but as an 'adviser to the Government'.

Realizing that, on a rather different level, Azef was chief of the Combat Section, Gerasimov made him directly responsible to him for its activities. In return he undertook to keep the information he was given on the subject to himself and take no action against the terrorists concerned without first consulting Azef.

For some months past the Combat Section had, by a decision of the Central Committee, been quiescent. With the steady aggravation of the political situation, it was decided that the time was ripe for it to resume its terrorist activities, with Azef once again as its leader. Its first success was in the Crimea. Savinkov had had to leave Sebastopol without assassinating Admiral Chuknin. His omission was now made good by a sailor called Akimov who killed the Admiral and got clean away.

But the Section's main target was once again the Minister of the Interior. Azef had not thought it necessary to warn Gerasimov of the attempt on Chuknin on the grounds that this was no more than a fringe activity. The plot against Stolypin, on the other hand, gave him and Gerasimov an opportunity to try out a new policy which they had jointly evolved and which, for want of a better word, might be termed a policy of frustration. From the start Azef had kept Gerasimov fully informed of the Combat Section's plans, including the names and roles of its various members. But under the terms of their initial agreement, no arrests were made. The plans for Stolypin's murder accordingly went ahead with the full knowledge of everyone concerned including, of course, Stolypin himself, who studied them in detail.

The terrorists' aim was as usual to keep a close watch on the Minister's movements in order to discover the best moment to strike. But Azef had arranged beforehand with Gerasimov that he would regularly send the terrorists out on a false lead so that they never even caught sight of the Minister. What is more, he now encouraged them to intensify their efforts with more secret meeting places and more terrorists disguised as cab-drivers, messenger boys and street-vendors and increasingly lavish expenditure of funds. But all to no purpose. Rarely did they catch as much as a glimpse of the Minister. What unnervingly, they did see in the most unexpected places were groups of Okhrana agents.

Carried to its logical conclusion, this policy should have led to complete deadlock: no arrests, no murders, and everyone kept usefully employed.

But in Russia logic does not always prevail. The irrational is liable to intervene. It was not long before the terrorists, finding their best efforts continually frustrated, showed signs of discarding the carefully laid plans that were given them and branching out on their own, improvising, using their own initiative.

Quite clearly they needed watching. Azef, to whom they trustingly confided their plans, and who had told them that, while far from perfect, these were well worth trying out made it his business to see that they were watched and knew they were watched. With his approval, Gerasimov combed the whole police force for the clumsiest detectives in the business, men who could be seen coming a mile off. 'We had some real specialists in this sort of thing,' wrote Gerasimov afterwards. 'When they were following anyone, they almost breathed down the back of his neck. Only a blind man could fail to notice them. No self-respecting detective would accept such a mission . . .'

Heartbroken, the keen young volunteers would come back to Azef, who would first cross-question them closely, to make sure that all this surveillance was not simply a figment of their overheated imaginations, and then reluctantly come to the conclusion that the Minister was just too well guarded. They would, he said, have to try new methods. The police had got to know the old techniques too well. After which he would painstakingly arrange the escape of each one of them abroad, something which, thanks to Gerasimov, he was exceptionally well placed to do. All of which enormously enhanced his personal prestige and authority. Had he not, after all, said that their plans were not up to much? And sure enough they had failed. And then, with his usual thoughtfulness and foresight he had successfully organized their escape. There was, they all agreed, no one quite like him.

What none of those concerned had foreseen was the likelihood of outside competition. Stolypin, who towards the end of July became Prime Minister, had put down the revolutionary outbreaks of the past few months with considerable firmness and as a result was far from popular. Some time before, a splinter-group, calling themselves the Maximalists, had broken away from the Social Revolutionaries and set up as terrorists on their own, relying on last-minute improvisation and hit-and-run tactics rather than elaborate advance planning. On 25 August 1906 three of their members, carrying bombs, called at Stolypin's house on Apothecary's Island at a time when he was officially available to visitors. Their suspicions aroused, the guards in the hall refused to let them go any further. They accordingly did not wait, but threw their bombs in the hall, killing themselves and thirty other people as well. The explosion demolished a large part of the building and severely injured two of the Minister's children. Their effect was however, hardly felt in the study where the Prime Minister happened to be sitting at the time.

Immediately after the attempt Stolypin received an invitation from the Tsar to come and live in the Winter Palace, which he gladly accepted, henceforth hardly ever leaving the building. Even when he visited the Tsar at Peterhof he went by boat and when Boris Savinkov, as keen as ever, looked into the idea of dropping a bomb on him from a bridge across the Neva, it was only to find that on these occasions the bridges were heavily guarded and that his steam-launch shot under them at high speed.

No one was more deeply disturbed by the news of the attempt on Stolypin than Yevno Azef, who at the time was in Finland. 'He was,' wrote Popova, a woman member of the Combat Section then working in its Finnish bomb factory, 'deeply agitated. He also seemed depressed and distraught. He sat for a time in silence, nervously turning the pages of a railway timetable. At first he wanted to spend the night with us. Then he thought better of it and went off to the station.'

The reasons for his agitation are not far to seek. He had told Gerasimov that he would answer for the Prime Minister's safety with his head. Coming on top of the Dubasov episode, this unfortunate affair would not be easy to explain. To get into trouble for an attempted assassination in which he had had no part would be the ultimate injustice. There was also the danger that, knowing the whereabouts of those members of the Combat Section who were supposed to be plotting against Stolypin, the Okhrana would arrest the lot, thereby ruining his reputation for ever with the revolutionaries. Little wonder that, in preference to spending the night with Popova, he took the first train back to St Petersburg.

Fortunately for him he found that he still enjoyed Colonel Gerasimov's complete confidence. Gerasimov had arrested no one and in the end Azef contented himself with getting the Social Revolutionaries to issue, albeit rather reluctantly, a communiqué denying all responsibility for the attempt and deploring the terrorists' slap-dash approach. He also had an important score to pay off. Quickly collecting all the information he could about the Maximalists, he passed it on to the police for appropriate action.

The weeks and months that followed were taken up with prolonged and highly confused discussions among the members of the Combat Section, the Central Committee and the Party as a whole as to the future of the Combat Section and the practicability and desirability of employing terrorist methods. Yevno Azef was by this time, for reasons of his own, in favour of temporarily abandoning terror and suspending the work of the Combat Section. Their methods, he said, were out of date. They must look for new ones. A lot, he believed, could be done by the skilful use of mines. And he suggested that he and Boris Savinkov should be sent abroad to study the latest technical advances in this field. But Savinkov, for so long the keenest bomber of them all, was by this time deeply depressed by their lack of success and most of all by his recent discovery that it was impracticable to bomb the Prime Minister on his way to Peterhof by boat. In the end he announced that he agreed with Azef (who, though he was not aware of it, had only a few months earlier betrayed him to the police), and shoulder to shoulder the two offered their resignation from the Combat Section, of which they had for so long been the mainstay. In the end, a compromise solution was arrived at, unsatisfactory to everybody, by which the Combat Section was temporarily suspended, but in fact carried on in a somewhat diminished form.

Azef, who for some time had not been feeling well, was found to be suffering from a severe abscess in the throat and soon became too ill to take an active part in the Party's latest discussions which were held in a tourist hotel near a famous Finnish waterfall. His illness, which seems to have been quite serious, made even those who had previously disagreed with him feel guilty and they treated him with even greater respect and consideration than before. But he continued to bear them a grudge, and having provided all of them including Popova the bomb-maker with forged passports, handed a complete list of their assumed names to the police.

Nothing seems to have come of Yevno Azef's proposal that he should be sent abroad to study the laying and setting of mines. But late in 1906 or early in 1907, not long after the Party had concluded its deliberations in Finland, he and his wife left for the pleasant little seaside town of Alassio on the Italian Riviera. 'I have been in terror since the days of Gershuni,' he said. 'And I have a right to rest.' At Alassio his wife, who still believed that he was in constant danger from the Okhrana, gave him her devoted care as usual. As a well-known terrorist, he was also treated with the greatest respect by the other members of the Russian colony there, most of them seasoned revolutionaries like himself. From time to time, when in need of a change, he would go off on his own to Monte Carlo, only a few miles away along that sunlit coast, on what he described as 'urgent Party business'.

Though he did not, while abroad, explore the possible use of mines as a weapon for terrorists, he gave serious consideration to the potentialities of a new kind of heavier-than-air flying-machine at that time being worked on by an anarchist called Buchallo who, it transpired, was ready to place it at the disposal of anyone who would use it to assassinate the Tsar. Having gone all the way to Munich to see Buchallo, Azef returned convinced, as an engineer, that the idea had possibilities and even persuaded the Party to contribute twenty thousand roubles for its development. What happened next is not recorded, though in reporting on Buchallo's invention to Gerasimov, he hinted that it might provide a convenient way of exhausting the financial resources of the Social Revolutionary Party. Unfortunately for the inquisitive researcher both Buchallo and his revolutionary flying-machine seem to have disappeared without trace into the mists of history.

Since Azef's departure abroad and the partial closing-down of the original Combat Section, several new terrorist groups had started to operate in St Petersburg with a considerable measure of success. This was disconcerting for Colonel Gerasimov who, in Azef's absence, had no reliable source of information on terrorist activities. But, when he again made contact with Azef, he found him tired of doing nothing and ready enough to come back to St Petersburg and to all that that city had to offer.

At about the time of Azef's return, another leading terrorist also came back to Russia, G. A. Gershuni, his predecessor as chief of the Combat Section. After more than three years in jail, Gershuni had been smuggled out of prison in Siberia in a barrel of sauerkraut, thereafter assuming the pseudonym Kapustin, *Kapusta* being the Russian for cabbage. From Siberia he had made his way to Japan and thence to the United States, where he had been given a triumphal reception. He returned to his own country with a large sum of money for the most part subscribed by American sympathizers. Soon he and Azef were once again working together, while Azef also resumed his detailed reports to Gerasimov.

A useful new recruit to the recently revived Combat Section was Lieutenant Nikitenko, the young naval officer who had helped smuggle Boris Savinkov out of the country a year or so earlier after his betrayal by Azef. Having resigned his commission in the Imperial Navy in disgust at the vigorous repression of the mutinies in the Black Sea Fleet, he was living in St Petersburg and towards the end of 1906 made contact with the Combat Section and volunteered for terrorist work.

Nikitenko was by any standards a valuable recruit. For one thing, he had a clear record with the police. He also moved in quite different circles from most revolutionaries and as a member of the socially exclusive English Club was in an excellent position to assassinate his fellow member, the Grand Duke Nicholas, who happened to be high up on the Combat Section's list of prospective victims. Indeed he had already volunteered to do so. It was felt, however, that other, more important tasks lay ahead of him. Though still only twenty-two or three, he had in practice already become leader of the Combat Section.

Back in 1902 the Central Committee of the Party had, after a certain amount of discussion, expressly forbidden the Combat Section to try to assassinate the Tsar. The reason for this was the affection and veneration which the Russian peasant still felt for the Tsar as a father figure, reserving his resentment for ministers and bureaucrats. But the events of the years 1905 and 1906 and the Tsar's involvement in them had changed all this. Now the possibility of an attempt was once more under discussion and under Nihitenko's auspices the Combat Section had already started to collect information about the Tsar's day to day movements.

No sooner had Azef returned from abroad than Nikitenko made contact with him. They met in Finland early in 1907, when Nikitenko informed Azef of the details of the plot against the Tsar and even suggested that he should resume the leadership of the Combat Section. This offer Azef declined, giving as a reason his fear that the Section might have been infiltrated by police spies in his absence. The details of the plot and the names of all concerned he immediately communicated to Colonel Gerasimov.

The police, as it happened, were shortly to receive confirmation of the plot from another source. A friend of the plotters, whose father happened to be in charge of the palace telegraph office at Peterhof, had put them in touch with a Cossack of the Imperial Guard called Ratimov as being a man of alleged revolutionary sympathies who might be able to help. But having listened to what the revolutionaries had to say to him, Ratimov like a good guardsman had gone straight to his military superiors and given them a full account of the proposals made to him. This they passed on to the Palace Police, who in due course communicated it to the Okhrana.

It was thus that within a fairly short time of its inception, Gerasimov, thanks to the good services of Yevno Azef and Guardsman Ratimov, found himself in possession of full details of the plot. If the information was welcome to Gerasimov, it was doubly welcome to Stolypin. Politically things were as difficult as ever for the Imperial Government. In the recently elected second Duma, which was just about to meet, the Social Revolutionaries had more than thirty deputies. From the Government's point of view, such proof of their Party's direct involvement in a conspiracy against the Tsar would provide a most welcome diversion.

On 14 April 1907 some twenty-eight members of the Combat Section and their associates were arrested. In the Duma Stolypin made a statement on the conspiracy against the Tsar, asserting that the plot had the approval of the Social Revolutionary Party. The half-hearted denials of the Social Revolutionary Deputies carried little conviction. Eighteen of the conspirators were tried by court martial at the end of August, three including Nikitenko being condemned to death. A few days after their execution, Colonel Gerasimov was promoted general on the Tsar's personal initiative.

In April 1907, shortly before the arrests, Yevno Azef had gone to the Crimea – for his health, he explained. In fact he did not waste his time there. As a holiday task, he collected for Gerasimov some useful information about a local Social Revolutionary plot against the Grand Duke Nicholas, which made possible large-scale arrests in the spring of 1907.

Great care had been taken by all concerned to cover up Azef's betrayal of Nikitenko, none of the information he had provided being used at the trial. Nevertheless, the danger of exposure (and ultimate retribution) was becoming daily more real. The events of 1905 and 1906 had not only shaken the Tsarist Government; they had shaken the Secret Police. More and more police officials, taking note of the way things seemed to be going, were seeking to re-insure with the revolutionaries by betraying official secrets to them. And more and more evidence was building up of the presence of a traitor in the leadership of the Social Revolutionary Party.

Already there had been Captain Menshikov, whose denunciation of Azef, delivered by the veiled lady, had cut so little ice. Other warnings addressed to the Central Committee had had equally little effect. 'My confidence in Azef,' said Savinkov, 'was so great that, even if I had seen it stated in his own handwriting, I should not have believed in his guilt.'

But the members of the Central Committee were not the only people who were interested. There was, for example, Vladimir Lvovich Burtsev, the editor of an historical review entitled *Biloye* (*The Past*), a thin, solemn, narrow-faced, bearded character of noble birth and professorial appearance, wearing steel-rimmed spectacles and stiff, uncomfortable collars. A leading expert on the revolutionary movement in Russia and indeed something of a revolutionary himself, Burtsev was as much concerned with the present as with the past and, more especially, with the penetration of the revolutionary movement by agents of the political police. Over a couple of years he had made a number of useful contacts with various police officials and through them had gathered a great deal of interesting information, all of which pointed to the presence of a strategically-placed traitor at the heart of the Social Revolutionary Party, indeed at the heart of the Combat Section.

One of Burtsev's contacts was a certain Bakay, a somewhat unsavoury character who started as a revolutionary but, when arrested, quickly betrayed his associates and became an agent of the Political Police. By now he had risen to a position of considerable responsibility in the Okhrana, but he explained to Burtsev that he so hated the government that his one object was to help the revolutionaries. What is more, the information he passed to Burtsev was always accurate. It included the story of a police agent at the nerve-centre of the Social Revolutionaries who went by the pseudonym of Raskin.

Burtsev had been turning over in his mind various possibilities in his efforts to identify Raskin, when one day in the late autumn of 1906 he happened to see Azef driving through the streets of St Petersburg in an open *droshki*. It was a time when the police were arresting people right and left and most revolutionaries were keeping their heads down. Knowing of Azef's position in the Combat Section, Burtsev could not help wondering how he could afford to show himself so openly in public. Could it be that he enjoyed some sort of special protection, that he had some kind of arrangement with the police? It was surely inconceivable that so vital a part of the revolutionary movement could be in the hands of a police spy.

And yet it would explain a lot . . . 'To my own surprise,' wrote Burtsev, 'I suddenly found myself wondering whether Raskin and Azef were not the same person . . . and I was forced to admit that the more I weighed this suggestion, the more plausible it became.' And so Burtsev, who combined the persistence of a scholar with the zeal of a revolutionary, embarked on a private investigation of his own.

Aware of Burtsev's suspicions, Azef, who had again returned to Russia in February 1907, used them as an excuse for not telling Colonel Gerasimov everything he knew and Gerasimov, more anxious than ever that so valuable a source should not be compromised, readily accepted this. Politically, meanwhile, things were going badly for the revolutionaries. In June 1907 Nikitenko's conspiracy against the Tsar was used as a reason for dissolving the second Duma. The electoral law was changed and repressive measures intensified.

Since his escape from prison G. A. Gershuni had once more been playing an active part in the Party's deliberations. He was now more than ever convinced of the need for a revival of the terror and of the absolute necessity of assassinating the Tsar. What he said carried conviction and no sooner had such a suggestion arisen than all eyes turned on Azef, as the obvious leader for an enterprise of this kind. Gershuni in particular pressed him to assume the leadership. By blowing up the Tsar, he said, he would at once put an end to all doubts as to his loyalty.

At long last Azef was at the parting of the ways. If he successfully organized the Tsar's assassination, he would clearly be in the worst kind of trouble with the police. If, on the other hand, the attempt failed, any doubts his revolutionary comrades had about him would be confirmed. In this dilemma Colonel Gerasimov's advice to him, for what it was worth, was to try to stall, to prevent any final decision from being reached. If he failed in this, however, Gerasimov said, he should boldly assume full responsibility for the attempt, with the ultimate object of frustrating it from within.

At a meeting of the Central Committee held in late June, soon after the dissolution of the Duma, it was unanimously decided that the time was indeed ripe for the Tsar's assassination and that the necessary steps for it should now be put in hand. Clearly the Combat Section would need to be reorganized and a good deal of preparatory work done.

In July, soon after the meeting of the Central Committee, Azef and Gershuni went abroad, returning in late September or early October. During the months that followed they worked closely together, concentrating all their energies on what was now the principal, indeed the only, task of the Combat Section, namely to murder the Tsar. But towards the end of the year 1907 Gershuni's health, which had suffered during his long imprisonment in Siberia, finally gave way and he was once more obliged to go abroad, where he died a few weeks later, leaving Azef now in sole charge of the project.

For the revolutionaries the autumn of 1907 was a depressing one. The government had once more gained control of the situation. The mass movement had been crushed. There were no more strikes and no more demonstrations. In town and country alike peace of a kind prevailed.

This did not mean, however, that there was a complete cessation of terrorist activities. While Azef concentrated on what he intended to be the culmination of his career, individual terrorists, more or less loosely linked with the Combat Section, carried out individual acts of terrorism. A leading part in these was played by Karl Trauberg, an enterprising Lett who, as leader of a group which became known as Karl's Flying Squad, had of recent years made himself a considerable reputation as a terrorist. One of his men had shot General Pavlov, the Chief Prosecutor, as he was taking his daily walk in the gardens of the Military Tribunal. Another assassinated Borodulin, the governor of the Algachinski Prison, while a third accounted for Maximovski, the chief of the Central Prison Administration.

Although aware of these projects, Azef had not thought it worthwhile to inform Gerasimov of them. He did however suggest to him that he would do well to have Karl arrested. ('You will never have any peace,' he said, 'while he is at liberty.') He also mentioned to him that Karl and his group, whom he despised as provincials, were planning to blow up the entire State Council, using press cards to gain admission and carrying bombs in their briefcases. The result was that security measures were intensified and the attempt rendered in practice impossible. In the end it was largely due to hints dropped by Azef to Gerasimov that early in 1908 Karl and his group, three of them women who were now planning to assassinate the Grand Duke Nicholas and the Minister of Justice, were finally rounded up, condemned to death and executed. Their plots had gone far enough for the police to take them seriously.

Gerasimov had played an active part in tracking down Karl's Flying Squad, personally directing operations from a café in Mihailovski Square, which was a favourite rendezvous of the terrorists across the way from the

Grand Duke's palace. It was only during her subsequent interrogation by Gerasimov that one of the terrorists involved, a pretty young girl called Lydia, realized that she had been sitting bomb-in-hand at the next table to the chief of the Petersburg Okhrana. 'But, General,' she said with a charming smile, 'we've already met. Don't you remember, on New Year's Day, we sat next to each other at the Mihailovski Café? What a pity I didn't know who my neighbour was . . .' But it was Gerasimov who had the last word, for Lydia, with six of her fellow conspirators, was hanged the following week, going to the gallows with a smile on her lips.

Karl, like the Grand Dukes and Ministers he had been planning to murder, was of secondary importance to Yevno Azef. What mattered to Asef in his present frame of mind was his own personal project: the assassination of the Tsar. This, he would tell his friends, was to be his final revolutionary act. This would crown his career.

At the moment he was busily collecting money (it was likely to cost a lot in one way or another) and examining a number of different plans. One useful recent addition to party funds had been three hundred thousand roubles taken in a raid on a bank at Charjui in Turkmenistan, of which he managed to appropriate a hundred thousand for his own use. He believed in doing things well. 'When it's a question of men's lives,' he would say with an air of benevolent wisdom, 'it's not the moment to count the kopeks.'

Of the various plans considered, one was somehow to secure the inclusion of a terrorist in one of the many loyal delegations visiting the Tsar. Once in the Imperial presence, he would know what to do. Another idea for which Azef showed particular enthusiasm was put forward by an enterprising Social Revolutionary who had recently taken holy orders. This promising young priest hoped with the help of his family to get himself appointed to a church literally within striking distance of Tsarskoye Selo, the Tsar's fantastic complex of palaces and pleasure gardens outside St Petersburg. It would then once again simply be a question of awaiting for a suitable opportunity. For Azef the idea of an Orthodox priest assassinating the Tsar Tsar had a special appeal. He was, the priest recalled years afterwards, simply delighted with it. Indeed he advised him to drop all other revolutionary work and devote himself exclusively to this worthwhile project.

Another plan was to assassinate the Tsar while he was on a shooting expedition. With this object in view an elderly terrorist, posing as an enthusiastic monarchist, opened a teashop not far from Tsarskoye Selo, near the Imperial preserves. Yet another proposal was to blow up the Tsar while he was on a visit to Reval in Estonia, either in the Imperial train or when driving through the streets.

All this time Azef remained on the best of terms with Gerasimov whom

he kept informed in outline of most of the plots that were being hatched by
the terrorists on the general understanding that there should be no arrests.
He even told him about the windfall of three hundred thousand roubles
from Charjui, which the authorities were making frantic efforts to recover.
And Gerasimov once more respected his confidence, knowing that a large
part of this sum would find its way into Azef's pocket and so save the police
increasing his salary. Through Gerasimov Azef also discovered the names
of any other police spies there might be within the party, essential information as far as he was concerned, especially when he happened to be
double-crossing the police.

Such was Gerasimov's confidence in Azef that he was one of the very
few people to whom he confided his own private address. For by this time
the Chief of the Okhrana had, as it were, assumed protective colouring and
was himself living like a conspirator under an assumed name in two
furnished rooms at an address which he kept secret even from his own
officials. There, at Italyanskaya 15, Azef would visit him a couple of times
a week; the widow he lodged with would bring in the samovar and the two
of them would sit over it for hours, drinking tea and talking of this and that.
The better Gerasimov got to know him, the more impressed he was by
Azef's knowledge of human nature and grasp of the overall situation and by
the soundness of his views. How, he would ask him, had he, a liberal at
heart, ever come to join the revolutionaries? 'It just happened that way . . .'
Azef would answer, and then change the subject. He was, the General
rightly concluded, inclined to despise his fellow men.

For reasons of his own Azef had emphasized to Gerasimov that the proposed attempt on the Tsar's life at Reval was to be on a considerable scale,
involving a team of from ten to fifteen terrorists. They agreed that it should
be prevented, but without the police making any arrests. This suited
Gerasimov and Stolypin as well as it suited Azef. One purpose of the Tsar's
visit to Reval was to meet the King of England there and from the Government's point of view, it was therefore desirable that it should go off
smoothly.

In discussing the Tsar's proposed itinerary with him, Gerasimov was
repeatedly struck by Azef's extraordinary knowledge of the Tsar's intended
movements. Any proposed changes were immediately known to Azef, on
several occasions before they were known to Gerasimov himself. 'This
latest change has evidently not reached you yet,' Azef would say patroniz-
ingly. 'You will probably hear about it tomorrow or the day after.' And,
sure enough, a day or two later, Gerasimov would receive notification of
the proposed change of plan in a secret, sealed envelope. 'You see,' Azef
would say, 'I was right all along,' and then remind him how lucky he was
that Azef, and no one else, happened to be head of the Combat Section.

Gerasimov did everything to get Azef to give away his source. But nothing would induce him to reveal it. 'You know,' he replied, 'that I am taking every means to thwart this attempt and that I guarantee to be successful. But I cannot give you the name of my informant, because he is very highly placed and only two or three people know of the connection between us.'

According to Azef, the Combat Section had a number of alternative plans which could be varied according to which route the Tsar took and where he stayed. What Azef, as head of the Combat Section and Gerasimov, as head of the Okhrana had to do was arrange the Tsar's itinerary in such a way that he would not be assassinated, while the terrorists, for their part, would be left thinking that their failure had only been due to bad luck.

In this they were brilliantly successful. A terrorist travelling by train missed his connection. (The instructions he was expecting from Azef had, for one reason or another never reached him.) The Tsar did not in the end stay as had been planned at the house of Count Benckendorf, and when, on 9 June 1908 the time came for the meeting of the two monarchs, it went off without an incident of any kind and with no attendant arrests.

It was not until later that for his own satisfaction the chief of the Petersburg Okhrana made further discreet inquiries as to Azef's highly placed informant. 'The result,' in the words of a contemporary, 'made Gerasimov doubt his own senses.' There could be no doubt about it. This informant, this active participant in a plot against the Tsar, was indeed highly placed. So highly placed that there was nothing that he or even Stolypin could do about it. 'The scandal,' said Stolypin, when consulted, 'would be too great ... We had better leave the matter alone.' There was of course another consideration. Neither of them was prepared to take a step which might in any way compromise the invaluable Azef. The identity of Azef's high-placed informant has, so far as I know, never been revealed. It is interesting to speculate who it could have been.

Meanwhile a sudden, startling change had come over Yevno Azef's life. On the evening of 26 December 1907, having nothing better to do, he had gone to a then famous Petersburg *café chantant*, the Aquarium. There he had admired and later entertained to supper one of the stars of that establishment, a lady already well known in the *cafés chantants* of the capital who went by the improbable name of Heddy de Hero. After supper he had returned with Heddy to her apartment. From that moment they had become inseparable.

Heddy was German. Of solid middle-class origin, she had come to Russia four years earlier to try her luck as a cabaret singer and had met with considerable success. Her face and figure, rather than her voice, had been her fortune. Exceptionally well-built, with fine eyes, a generous mouth and a friendly, forthcoming expression, she had arrived in St Petersburg just before the outbreak of the Russo-Japanese War. The war, as wars do, had given the capital a kind of feverish gaiety. Big fortunes were being made by one means or another, money was plentiful and the frenzied nightlife of St Petersburg offered boundless scope for an attractive and enterprising *demi-mondaine*. Heddy was much in demand. Soon she had managed to attract the favourable attention of the Grand Duke Cyril and his pleasure-loving brother Boris, both in uniform and both leaders of a set notorious, even in St Petersburg, for its debauchery. In their company she toured Russia until finally the Commander-in-Chief, General Kuropatkin, was obliged to ask for the early removal of their Imperial Highnesses from the military scene on the ground that their behaviour was demoralizing his already deeply unsettled troops. 'It was all great fun,' said Heddy, looking back twenty years later. It also brought in quite a lot of money. Indeed by the time the war was over, Heddy had accumulated fifty thousand roubles which she rashly invested in a gold-mine in Siberia.

Now she was looking for something more solid. She found it, or thought she had found it, in Yevno Azef, who gave every appearance of being what he said he was, namely a prosperous merchant with his cheque-book always at the ready. He too was on the look out for a liaison that would last. He was now thirty-nine, on the threshold of middle-age – a little old, perhaps, to go to quite as many brothels as he had done in the past. He still enjoyed the reputation of a devoted husband and father. But his wife regarded him as a dedicated revolutionary in constant danger of arrest and there could be little doubt that if, as now seemed all too possible, she made the discovery that he was in fact a police agent, she would turn from him in horror and disgust. He needed not just a woman but a safeguard, a guarantee against loneliness, the occupational hazard of the spy. His liaison with Heddy came at exactly the right moment. From the first it was a tremendous success. He was in love with her and she with him or at any rate with the security he seemed to offer her and which more than made up for any other apparent disadvantages.

A dissimulator in every other context, Yevno now threw caution to the winds, spending all his spare-time with Heddy, taking her to smart restaurants and to the best boxes in the theatre and buying her expensive jewellery. Soon disturbing reports of his new way of life reached both the Party and the police. Both hastened to reprimand him for his frivolity and lack of discretion. To Gerasimov he replied that he had worked long enough for the police; he needed to relax; it was time he retired. To the revolutionaries, he explained that the contacts he was making in the theatrical world would be of the greatest value to him in planning his attempt on the Tsar's life. Both reluctantly accepted his explanations – there was nothing else they could do. And indeed there was an element of truth in what he said to both. It was true, now that he had Heddy, that he wanted to settle down. It was also true that, before settling down, he wanted to crown his career as a revolutionary by successfully arranging for the assassination of the Tsar.

In June 1908, immediately after the Tsar's visit to Reval and successful meeting with King Edward VII, (who, portly and majestic as he was, had, it appears, some difficulty in squeezing into his uniform as Colonel-in-Chief of the Kiev Dragoons and had to have it hastily let out), Azef, now more popular with the police than ever, went to see General Gerasimov. He told him that he was going abroad. In future, he said, he would no longer be taking an active part in Party affairs. He also wanted to give up his work for the police. Gerasimov, realizing what a strain the past fifteen years must have been for him, accepted this, only asking him as a personal favour to pass on to him any useful information that might happen to come his way, especially news of any proposed attempts on the Tsar's life. He also told him that for the time being at any rate he would continue to receive his salary from the Police Department as a kind of pension in recognition of past services. The two men then took an affectionate farewell of each other and a few days later Azef left Russia, taking Heddy with him. After leaving Heddy in Germany to visit her family, he himself went on to Paris and thence, towards the middle of July, to Glasgow, where he had important business to attend to, the nature of which he had disclosed neither to Heddy nor to General Gerasimov.

Azef's business in Glasgow took him to the shipyard of Messrs Vickers, where a skeleton crew of Russian sailors were watching the progress of a new Russian cruiser, the *Rurik*, then being built on the Clyde as a replacement for the battleships so disastrously lost three years earlier in the Straits of Tsushima.

The *Rurik* was to be inspected by the Tsar on her arrival at Kronstadt and a naval engineer called Kostenko, who had come over with the skeleton crew and happened to be a Social Revolutionary, had conceived the idea of taking this opportunity to assassinate him. There were, it was decided, two ways in which this could be done. The Tsar could either be shot by a member of the crew, or failing that by a member of the Combat Section who could be smuggled on board in Glasgow and kept hidden until the Imperial inspection took place.

On Azef's arrival in Glasgow, Kostenko immediately arranged for him to see over the ship and examine possible hiding places, but none of these struck him as suitable, with the result that the idea of hiding a terrorist on board was discarded and it was decided to try and find a volunteer from among the crew.

In the end two volunteers were found, a sailor called Avdeyev, described by a fellow Party member as 'a very daring, energetic and most revolutionary-minded man', and a signaller called Kaptelovich. Each was provided with a revolver by the Combat Section, after which they both wrote farewell letters, duly explaining their motives. They then entrusted the letters to Azef together with photographs of themselves for publicity purposes once the assassination had taken place. In August Azef left to attend a Party meeting in London, having first put the finishing touches to a plan which to him seemed bound to succeed and about which he had for once said nothing to the police. It was after all to be the crowning glory of his career as a revolutionary – something to which he had of recent years devoted considerable thought and which, when the Revolution triumphed, would ensure him a not insignificant place in the pantheon of the new regime.

The *Rurik* sailed for Russia in mid-August 1908. The journey gave Able Seaman Avdeyev time to think things over. This further strengthened his resolve. 'Only now,' he wrote in a letter to Boris Savinkov, 'do I begin to understand myself . . . I can now realize the significance of the task entrusted to me . . . One minute will decide more than whole months.'

The inspection by the Tsar duly took place at Kronstadt on 7 October. In the course of the ceremonies both Avdeyev and Kaptelovich came face to face with the Tsar. Indeed His Imperial Majesty even asked Avdeyev to get him a glass of champagne. But neither did anything and the Tsar continued his inspection unscathed. Some said that Avdeyev and Kaptelovich had simply lost their nerve. According to the engineer Kostenko, however, they had another reason for doing nothing. The crew, it appeared, egged on by believers in mass action rather than isolated acts of terrorism, were planning to mutiny on arrival and seize the fortress of Kronstadt. Clearly their plans would be thrown out if two of their number had already assassinated the Tsar. Accordingly, when it came to the point, they took no action. (Nor, for that matter, did the *Rurik*'s crew ever mutiny or seize Kronstadt.) Whatever the explanation, the plan had failed, but through no fault of Yevno Azef's, who, disappointed, but not discouraged, once more directed his lively, inventive mind to the discovery of a new means of eliminating Nicholas II.

During the next six months, however, Azef was to have other, even more serious preoccupations. For the past two years Vladimir Lvovich Burtsev, painstakingly assembling every scrap of available evidence from every conceivable source, had continued his relentless pursuit of 'Raskin', the traitor whom he firmly believed to be operating at the heart of the Social Revolutionary Party and whom in his own mind he had already identified as Azef. Fanatically, unremittingly, he pursued his end, resisting all attempts to deter him. Nor, though the leaders of the Social Revolutionary Party still stoutly rejected any such suggestions, was he any longer alone in this. With time, others had come to share his suspicions.

It was thus in the autumn of 1908 that Burtsev decided to take a bold new initiative. As editor of *Byloye*, he had on occasion come into contact with Alexei Alexandrovich Lopukhin, the former head of the Police Department, since his enforced retirement a somewhat disgruntled private citizen. Indeed, he had even asked him to contribute some reminiscences of his police work to his periodical, now appearing in Paris and consequently free from the shackles of censorship. He also happened to know that on a certain date in September 1908 Lopukhin would be travelling by the Ost-Express from Cologne to Berlin.

It was thus that soon after the long train had pulled out of Cologne Station, Lopukhin, looking up, caught sight of Burtsev standing in the doorway of his compartment, thin, tense, bespectacled, austerely fanatical, as a friend described him: 'a typical Russian nihilist of the old school, both in dress and manner' and, like himself, nobly born. After the usual polite exchanges, Burtsev came in and sat down and soon the two were deep in conversation. Their talk turned first to Burtsev's review and his plans for the future now that he was free to publish anything he liked.

Something he hoped to publish in the near future, he said, was an article disclosing the activities of an important police agent who was also head of the Social Revolutionaries' Combat Section. To this Burtsev, who was watching Lopukhin closely as he said it, got no reaction, but thought he noticed a sudden wariness in his companion's manner. Now, as the Ost-Express ran smoothly through the autumnal countryside, he put a direct question to him.

'Will you allow me, Alexei Alexandrovich,' he asked, 'to tell you everything I know about this *agent provocateur*, about his activities in revolutionary and in police circles? I shall give you proofs of the double role he is playing. I shall tell you the name by which he is known to the Okhrana and also his true name. I know everything about him.'

'Please go on, Vladimir Lvovich,' said Lopukhin. 'I am listening.'

Whereupon Burtsev began his story, referring to Azef, not by that name, but by the cover-name given him by the police – Raskin. And Lopukhin, without saying anything or showing any signs of emotion, sat and listened; listened, as Burtsev talked with surprising accuracy, of Raskin's meetings with the police, giving the dates and times and places and the names of the officials he had met, and then went on to speak of his revolutionary activities, of his role, as it were, on the other side of the hill, in the Combat Section and on the Central Committee, once again giving names and dates with, it could only be assumed, no less accuracy than when speaking of his dealings with the police. Though clearly not missing a word, Lopukhin, combining the calmness of the trained civil servant with the slight aloofness of his class, had hitherto not reacted in any way to what had been said to him. His eyes meanwhile, which through his gold-rimmed glasses had, when you looked at them, an almost Mongol slant, derived no doubt from the remote Kassog strain in his ancestry, he kept constantly fixed on Burtsev.

In due course Burtsev came to the assassination of Plehve. To Lopukhin, who had been Plehve's protégé, who with Plehve had encouraged Azef to enter the Combat Section, this part of the narrative was bound to be disturbing. To be told that Azef, whom he and Plehve thought they could control, had actually been privy to the plan for Plehve's murder, was bound to come as a shock to him. Quite apart from any feelings he might have had for his benefactor, Plehve's assassination, quickly followed by that of the Grand Duke Sergei, had marked the end of his own career. ('You murderer,' the Governor-General of St Petersberg had shouted at him.) And all because of Azef, whose real name had not yet been mentioned, though by now both knew all too well to whom Burtsev was referring.

For the first time in their conversation, Lopukhin showed some signs of emotion. 'Are you *sure*,' he said, 'that this agent knew of the plans to assassinate Plehve?' To which Burtsev replied that Raskin not only knew of them, but was their author, and he proceeded to give full details of the plan and preparations, adding that he had reason to believe that Raskin was now planning to assassinate the Tsar himself. The game he was playing, he said, was a double one; he would double-cross and betray the police as readily as he would double-cross and betray the terrorists.

As his story progressed, Burtsev had become increasingly excited, shifting in his seat, gesticulating, stressing significant points, repeating himself and all the time waiting, watching for some kind of reaction from Lopukhin. He now reached the end of his narrative. 'As Director of the Department,' he concluded, you must have been aware of the existence of this *agent provocateur*. As you see, I now have all the evidence I need to expose him completely and I want to ask you once more, Alexei Alexandrovich, to let me tell you who it is that hides under the name of Raskin. Then all you will have to do is to say whether I am right or wrong.'

Now, at long last, came the reaction Burtsev had been looking for. 'I know nobody of the name of Raskin,' said Lopukhin as calmly and collectedly as ever. 'But I have seen Engineer Yevno Azef several times.'

It was the first time in the whole of their long conversation that Azef's name had been mentioned. In this context and coming from such a source, its significance was immeasurable. 'The name, of course,' wrote Burtsev later, 'did not come as a surprise to me. For over a year it had been reverberating through my brain at every moment of the day. But coming from Lopukhin's lips, it struck me like a thunderbolt.'

Up to now the suggestion that Azef was anything but a dedicated terrorist had been indignantly rejected by the leaders of the party. 'My confidence in Azef was so great,' Savinkov had said, 'that I should not have believed his guilt even if I had seen it stated in his own handwriting.' But now, for anyone prepared to face the facts, there could no longer be any doubt about it. Azef, on the evidence of a former director of the Police Department was a police spy. Even his strongest supporters among the revolutionaries would find this hard to laugh off.

Until this point in the conversation Lopukhin had for hour after hour let Burtsev do all the talking. He himself simply listened. But having once, as it were, crossed the Rubicon by admitting his connection with Azef, he dropped his reserve and let himself go, talking far more than Burtsev, trying to work out the reasons for Azef's behaviour, trying to find an explanation for his double duplicity, wondering even, if behind Azef there might not perhaps be someone far more important than any of them, someone perfectly well aware of both sides of Azef's game.

Lopukhin could recall, for example, something that had happened when he was still in charge of the Police Department. At that time, three years or so before, he had been sent for by Sergei Yulyevich Witte, the President of the Council of Ministers, in fact, the Prime Minister. The ensuing conversation had been so intrinsically improbable that even he, with his wide experience of such things, could hardly believe it had happened.

It was well known that Witte disliked and distrusted Plehve. Wanting to get rid of him, he had, it seemed, enlisted the Tsar's help. Somewhat characteristically, Nicholas II had promised to see what he could do and then let him down. This had enraged Witte and what he had put to Lopukhin, as Director of the Police Department, was nothing less than the suggestion that he should, through his contacts with the revolutionaries, arrange for the Tsar's assassination. Nicholas could then be succeeded by his more amenable brother Michael. Lopukhin, needless to say, would be suitably rewarded.

In the event nothing had come of this particular proposal. But Plehve had not survived for long and after his talk with Burtsev Lopukhin was left wondering whether things did not sometimes happen in high places of which even the head of the Police Department had little conception. Might not his interview with Witte, for example, be simply the continuation of earlier conversations on the same theme between Witte and his colleague Zubatov of which he had not been informed? Wondering, indeed, about such things as loyalty and the duties of the individual towards society, whatever that in all the circumstances might mean.

One thing at any rate was certain. By telling a man of Burtsev's views of his connection with Azef, Lopukhin, as a former high official, had done a great deal more than commit an indiscretion. He had, with his eyes wide open, betrayed an official secret. This, even for a retired and disgruntled civil servant, was a serious step and, before parting company with Burtsev in Berlin, he obtained from him, as they shook hands, a promise that in making use of the information he had given him, he would not, if possible, disclose its source.

Having at last obtained definite proof of Azef's guilt, Burtsev now decided to force the issue. On his return to Paris he accordingly wrote an open letter to the members of the Social Revolutionary Party repeating his accusations against Azef and had it set up in type. He then circulated it in proof to the members of the Central Committee.

There had already been talk in the Central Committee that summer of bringing Burtsev to trial for libelling Azef. But in the end its members had chosen to regard him as a sincere man labouring under a dangerous delusion and the idea had been dropped. His letter, with the threat of publication, effectively brought matters to a head and the Central Committee to a decision. There was now no other way out. Three venerable revolutionaries were asked to act as judges: Vera Figner, Herman Lopatin and Prince Peter Kropotkin, the well known anarchist. 'We have got to take measures to pacify Burtsev, who is spreading rumours right and left that Azef is an *agent provocateur*,' said a member of the Central Committee in approaching one of them. For that, as he saw it, must be the object of the exercise. The Court of Honour, it was decided, would sit in Paris – in Boris Savinkov's rather austere little apartment with Lopatin presiding. Judges, prosecutors and accused would all sit together.

Azef, for his part, having helped the Central Committee draw up the order of the Court's proceedings, announced with due dignity that he would not himself be present at the trial. He was, he said, 'too disgusted to wallow in the mud stirred up by Burtsev' and readily entrusted his friends with the defence of his honour. He then left for a small resort near Biarritz, where his wife and two children happened to be staying. It was important for his image that at this critical moment he should appear in the role of the loyal comrade and good family man labouring under a monstrous injustice. Heddy, for the time being, was sent elsewhere.

The trial was to last for over a month. The proceedings opened in a relatively relaxed atmosphere. It did not remain so for long. At first things went badly for Burtsev. Inhibited by his promise to Lopukhin, he based his case on the information he had obtained from Bakay, mostly second-hand and depending on the evidence of a notoriously tricky and unreliable witness. Against this the prosecution marshalled Azef's indisputable services to the revolutionary cause. Boris Savinkov was particularly eloquent. 'Now that we have told you of Azef's achievements,' he said to Burtsev, 'I beg you, Vladimir Lvovich, as a historian of the Russian revolutionary movement, to tell us whether there exists in the whole history of the Russian revolutionary movement or in that of any other country, a more brilliant name than that of Azef.'

'Do you know,' asked Vera Figner, still elegant and beautiful despite her long years in prison, 'what you will have to do if your accusations are proved groundless? You will,' she went on, her great eyes opened wide in horror, 'simply have to shoot yourself for all the harm you have done to the Revolution.'

It was at this stage that Burtsev, finding that the trial was not taking the course he had hoped for, decided to break the promise he had given to Lopukhin. 'I have,' he said, 'the evidence of one more witness.' And, while they listened spell-bound, he told them straight out of his conversation with Lopukhin.

When he came to Lopukhin's statement that he had seen Azef several times, pandemonium broke out. 'Give me your word of honour as a revolutionary,' said Lopatin, the presiding judge to Burtsev with tears in his eyes, 'that you heard these words from Lopukhin.' But then, just as Burtsev was about to answer, he turned away with a gesture of despair. 'But what's the use of talking?' he said. 'It's all clear now.'

So clear that in place of trying Burtsev for libel, the next step could only be a full and formal investigation of Azef's activities over the last ten years.

Meanwhile Azef, in his remote resort near Biarritz, had begun to find family life with Madame Azef and the little Azefs unusually hard to endure. Every one of his letters to Heddy during their separation reflected the yearning he felt for her. Fortunately the children's holidays were quickly over and he had been able to send them back to Paris with his wife. He had then telegraphed to Heddy to join him in Biarritz. From Biarritz, when the weather grew colder, he took her towards the end of October for a little tour in Spain, where they visited Madrid and saw some bullfights in San Sebastian.

At first Azef had hardly given the trial a thought. His friends sounded confident of the result. It was, everyone was agreed, simply a question of getting 'this dirty business' finished with as quickly and as painlessly as possible; in other words a question of pacifying Burtsev. In any case he was expecting from day to day a telegram announcing that the sailor Avdeyev had done his revolutionary duty and murdered the Tsar. But, as we have seen, when it came to the point, the sailor Avdeyev had, for reasons best known to himself, simply handed His Imperial Majesty a glass of champagne and loyally watched him drink it. With the result that October went by and there was no cheering message from Kronstadt or anywhere else. On the contrary, the trial dragged on and the messages that now reached him from Paris were far from encouraging. 'It is time to have done with this farce,' he wrote angrily to Savinkov from San Sebastian.

But this was easier said than done. The 'farce', he now learned, had taken a turn which rendered it imperative for him to return to Paris at once in a desperate attempt to save the situation while he still could. A score of years later Heddy was still to remember his receiving some letters which suddenly caused him to tell her that they must part for the time being, as he had to go back to Paris on urgent commercial business.

In Paris he found the situation even worse than he had expected. Nor did he improve matters by the action he now took. Rushing to St Petersburg, he did everything he could jointly with General Gerasimov to induce Lopukhin to take back what he had said. But the effect on Lopukhin was the opposite of what they had hoped. The descendant of those far-off Mongol princes was not as mild as he looked. In the words of a contemporary, he decided to burn his boats. After Burtsev's trial, Argunov, still a loyal supporter of Azef's, had been sent to St Petersburg by the Central Committee to collect evidence about Lopukhin. Making contact with him, Lopukhin now told him all about his dealings with Azef. These revelations came as a considerable shock to him. 'The tale he told,' said Argunov afterwards, 'had a shattering effect on me . . . It breathed of truth.' Nor was this all. Lopukhin now agreed to go to London and there tell his story to the other members of the Central Committee who were at that time meeting there. And, when Azef tried to disprove the statements he had made, he was found to be lying, while the documentary evidence he produced in support of his assertions turned out to be forgeries – forged, moreover, with the help of the police.

On 5 January 1909 the Central Committee met to decide on a course of action and more specifically, to decide whether or not Azef, whom they had formally denounced as a *provocateur* ten days earlier, should now be put to death. Such was his hold over them that even now, when it came to the point, only Savinkov and three others out of the fifteen or eighteen present voted for immediate execution, while one worthy old terrorist from St Petersburg wrote in specially to say that he would 'shoot the whole Central Committee' if they dared lay hands on his old friend Yevno Azef.

In the end, in order to avoid further unpleasantness, a compromise was arrived at. It was decided to lure Azef to an isolated villa outside Paris on the pretext of giving him a formal trial and there do away with him as quickly and discreetly as possible so as not to attract the attention of the French police. Meanwhile, as a first step, Savinkov and two other delegates were sent by the Central Committee that very same day to call at Azef's apartment for a talk. On due consideration however, it was agreed that they should go unarmed, in case one of them lost his head and murdered him on the spot.

From the opening remarks of his former comrades Azef at once sensed that things had gone badly for him at the meeting of the Central Committee. It was an uneasy moment. Once he realized, however, that his visitors were unarmed, he quickly recovered his confidence and, sturdily denying every charge that had been brought against him, agreed with the best will in the world to meet them again at midday the following day.

No sooner were they out of the door than Azef started packing his bags, stopping from time to time to look out of the window in case any of his former comrades should be keeping a watch on the house. But there was no one to be seen. Before setting out he destroyed some of his papers and packed others. In a prominent position on his desk he left the sailor Avdeyev's farewell letter, giving his view of life and the reasons for which he proposed to assassinate the Tsar. To leave this letter where he did for all the world to see was in a sense Yevno Azef's political testament, a gesture designed to show that in the ultimate analysis his sympathies were with the revolutionaries or at any rate that he believed they were going to win.

To his wife, who still had faith in him, he explained that his life was in danger, that it was all a mistake and that he was now going away to collect even more proof of his innocence. At three-thirty in the morning of 6 January 1909, the two of them left their apartment by cab for the Gare de l'Est. There she left him while he caught the first train to Germany, where Heddy, he knew, was awaiting him. Next day he wrote his last report to General Gerasimov from Germany, drawing attention to the part played by Lopukhin and to all the damage he had done.

For Yevno Azef his flight from Paris marked, quite literally, the beginning of a new life. He was just forty. Punctually General Gerasimov had paid him his salary up to 31 December 1908 together with a cash bonus and, better still, had given him a selection of safe passports. In addition to what he had received from the police, he had undoubtedly made ample provision for the future from other sources, notably the funds of the Social Revolutionary Party. And now the future was about to begin.

Having collected Heddy from her mother's home in Germany, he first set out with her on a prolonged honeymoon, travelling first class and stopping, under one name or another, at the very best hotels. It was something he had always wanted to do.

The first half of 1909 they spent in Italy, Greece and Egypt, looking at the Coliseum, visiting the Aegean Islands, scrambling up the Pyramids, pausing at Luxor. Then as the weather grew hotter, they turned northwards and toured Sweden, Norway and Denmark, stopping for a time at Vesterfelde on the North Sea. But as a general rule they did not stay anywhere for long and the first thing Yevno invariably did when they arrived at a new hotel was to scan the guest list for signs of other Russians. They also varied the names they were using until Heddy could often not remember under what name she was travelling.

Yevno had every reason for taking these precautions. His last report to General Gerasimov had brought down on Lopukhin the vengeance of all concerned. Neither his old schoolfriend Stolypin nor Gerasimov could forgive Lopukhin for wantonly depriving them of the services of their most valuable agent and in February 1909 he had been brought to trial with the Tsar's express approval on a charge of betraying official secrets to the enemies of the regime. Though Lopukhin had been restrained from ventilating some of his more dramatic theories, notably those concerning Azef's exact motivation, the trial had been sensational enough and had made headline news in almost every country in the world. It had ended with Lopukhin being sent to Siberia. For months on end the *Affaire Azef*, with its undertones of terrorism, mystery and intrigue and the lurid light it threw on the activities of the Russian Secret Police, was a favourite topic with the world press and Azef's name quickly became a household word. For Yevno the danger of recognition was thus very real and he could never forget that, once recognized, it could only be a question of time before the executioners of the Combat Section caught up with him.

Towards the end of 1909 Azef decided that it was time for him and Heddy to settle down. Becoming Herr and Frau Alexander Neumayer, they made their home in Wilmersdorf, a relatively elegant quarter of Berlin, where they took a large apartment at No. 21 Leopoldstrasse. This they furnished in style, buying a grand piano and much cut glass and silver, while for Heddy, Alexander, as he had now become, bought large quantities of jewellery.

When they had first met barely two years before, Heddy had been on the lookout for a man of substance and this is precisely what Yevno now was. In the course of the fifteen years during which he worked for the police he had accumulated, from them and from the Social Revolutionary Party, a sum approaching a quarter of a million marks. Nor did he leave his money idle. Becoming an active member of the Berlin Stock Exchange, he proceeded to do business on quite a considerable scale. Money was something which had always interested him. From now onwards his life, in marked contrast to his earlier existence, became that of a respectable man of affairs living with Heddy in happy domesticity and entertaining his prosperous new German friends in the style to which they were accustomed. Any yearning for the tension and excitement of his former life he satisfied by occasional visits to Monte Carlo, which as often as not left him without the ready cash to pay his fare home.

But despite all the precautions he took, it was not quite so simple to disappear completely, to sever all connection with his revolutionary past. In the summer of 1912, by one means or another, his address and new identity became known to that paragon of pertinacity, Burtsev, the Sherlock Holmes of the Revolution, as he was known. For years Burtsev had, as a historian, wanted to meet Azef. He accordingly now wrote to him suggesting a meeting, assuring him that there was no question of a trap and only as the merest afterthought adding that if Azef refused to meet him there might be other people who would be glad to be informed of his address.

Azef agreed to the meeting. 'Your suggestion that we should meet,' he replied, 'coincides with my own long-standing desire that the truth about me should be told.' He then disposed of his flat in the Leopoldstrasse, stored the furniture, sent Heddy off to her mother and made a will by which he left everything he had to her.

Azef's meeting with Burtsev took place on 15 and 16 August in Frankfurt at the Café Bristol. For two days the two of them talked almost without drawing breath. Azef's story was that, having as a young man mistakenly made contact with the police, he had never had the strength of mind to admit this to his friends, but rather had sought to use his connection with the police to benefit the revolution in the hope of thus eventually atoning for his original error. It was with this object in view that he had planned the terrorist acts for which he was famous. His ultimate aim, he declared, had been the assassination of the Tsar. After that he would have felt he was in a strong enough position to disclose his connection with the police. But Burtsev, by his untimely intervention, had made this impossible. 'If it hadn't been for you,' he said reproachfully, 'I would have killed him.'

Surely, Azef continued, Burtsev must admit that on balance what he had done for the Revolution more than outweighed any little services he had done the police, with whom he had long since severed all connection. And he held up his two hands in front of him as though they were scales. 'What did I do?' he asked. 'I organized the assassination of Plehve, of the Grand Duke Sergei . . .' And down went his right hand, like a heavily laden scale, to show the weight of his achievement. 'And whom did I hand over to the police? Sletov, Lornov, Vedenyapin.' And his left hand hardly moved or, if anything, lifted slightly upwards, as though to indicate how unimportant to the revolutionary cause these few victims really were.

Burtsev broke in, unable to restrain himself any longer: 'But it's not just a question of that. Basically it's a matter of principle . . .' But then, seeing a look of total incomprehension come into Azef's eyes, he did not pursue his point further. Clearly this was a concept which conveyed nothing to Yevno Azef.

Before taking leave of Burtsev, who undertook not to betray his whereabouts to the revolutionaries, Azef professed himself ready to be tried by his former comrades and abide by their verdict even if it should prove to be a sentence of death. From what we know of Azef, one is inclined to take this statement with a pinch of salt, though Burtsev, who published a lengthy account of his interview in the press, seems to have taken it quite seriously. But the question did not in fact arise, as by this time his former comrades could no longer bring themselves to have anything to do with him and, knowing he no longer had any connection with the police, had in fact lost interest in tracking him down and killing him.

For all this, Azef did not believe in offering more of a target to any potential ill-wishers than was necessary. From Frankfurt he first made his way to Deauville to refresh himself by a flutter on the tables, first losing all his money and then winning it all back again. After which he travelled round Germany for some months and did not re-establish himself in Berlin on a permanent basis until towards the end of 1913.

Many less resourceful or resilient men made a good thing out of the 1914 war. For Azef it spelt disaster. He had kept most of his money in Russian bonds and on the outbreak of war Russian bonds at once ceased to be quoted on the Berlin Stock Exchange, which meant that he had at a stroke lost the greater part of his fortune. But he did not give in. Selling some of Heddy's jewellery, he opened a corset shop in her name and, what is more, made a success of it.

But there was worse to come. In June 1915 he was suddenly arrested and imprisoned. For five months after his arrest he was unable to discover why. Could it be that he was being held as an agent of the Russian Government, which for the last eleven months had been at war with Germany? It was not until November that he discovered the real reason. He had, it was explained to him by the German bureaucrats concerned, been arrested as a dangerous terrorist and revolutionary under an International Police Convention, to which Russia and Germany were both signatories and would, once the war was over, be duly handed over to the appropriate Russian authorities.

For the next two years he remained in prison, complaining of the conditions, worrying about the corset shop, worrying above all about Heddy, whom he was no longer able to support and who he quite unjustly feared might now abandon him. 'I have already been without you for two years,' he wrote. 'It's too horrible for words.'

The event which, finally procured his release was, ironically enough, the Russian Revolution, a revolution, incidentally, which in the end brought power, not to the Social Revolutionaries, who were quickly eliminated and driven into opposition, but to the better-led and better-organized Bolshevik section of the Social-Democratic party. Thanks to the armistice with Germany which followed the Revolution and a subsequent agreement providing for the exchange of civilian prisoners, Azef was allowed to leave prison shortly before Christmas 1917 and not long after that given some kind of employment in the German Foreign Office. The fact that he had once been a famous terrorist seemed somehow to have lost its relevance.

But the two and a half years he had spent in prison had undermined his health. Now, he never felt well. In mid-April 1918 he went into hospital suffering from a serious kidney complaint. A few days after that he sent a letter to Heddy to say that he was feeling very ill and could hardly write. A week later he was dead. On 26 April he was buried in Wilmersdorf Cemetery, with Heddy de Hero as his only mourner.

Over the years there has been much speculation as to the motives underlying Yevno Azef's conduct and his basic loyalties and allegiance. What made him behave as he did? Was he at heart on the side of the revolutionaries or of the police? Of both or of neither?

Without wishing in any way to curtail an enjoyable and potentially endless controversy, I would hazard a guess that he was first and foremost loyal to himself and that one of his chief aims in life was to improve his own financial position.

If his social, racial and economic background and the conditions under which he grew up are taken into account, it will be seen that he had in effect little cause to be loyal to anyone. He might, it is true, like many of his contemporaries, have developed a profound loyalty to some kind of revolutionary ideal. But for that he was too hard-headed. 'Socialism,' he said quite frankly, 'is necessary for youth and for the workers. But not for you and me.'

That he genuinely wished to see the Tsar assassinated and worked to the best of his ability to procure this end, seems probable. Why, is less clear. Possibly because he believed that the Revolution would triumph in the end and wanted to be on the winning side. Or possibly just out of plain professional pride and for the pleasure it would give him to see a difficult job well done.

Of greater interest than Azef's personal motives are the circumstances which made a career such as his possible. Was it simply a byproduct of the Tsarist regime? Was it perhaps due to some special ingredient endemic in the Russian character? Burtsev evidently thought so. '*Il faut être Russe*,' he wrote, '*vivre dans les conditions terribles de la vie russe, pour bien comprendre le sens et la portée de l'affaire Azef.*'

In considering Azef's case one soon realizes that, though probably supreme in this particular field, he was far from being alone in it. For better or for worse, Russian history is littered with similar equivocal characters working away at every level of society.

It could of course be argued that the Anglo-Saxons, Scandinavians, Teutons and even in some respects the Latins place an exaggerated value on what they call straightforwardness. Other races, the Slavs and the Celts for example, not to mention any number of reputedly wily orientals, take a different view of the matter, favouring a subtler and more indirect approach.

Even so, one cannot help feeling that in nineteenth and early twentieth-century Russia this addiction to ambiguity was carried too far, not only for personal comfort, but for administrative convenience. Supposing that there is at any rate an element of truth in Lopukhin's story, admittedly published after the Revolution, that Count Witte sought, when Prime Minister, to enlist his help as head of the Police Department in arranging for the assassination of their imperial master, and supposing, as in view of what we know, we are surely entitled to suppose, that this sort of thing went on all down the scale, and that everyone concerned, from the Tsar downwards, was more or less aware of it, one is left wondering how the machinery of government worked at all. Politics are notoriously a rough profession, but how much rougher if your colleagues, indeed your own Ministers, are actually plotting with their political enemies and yours to have you murdered?

For the revolutionaries, too, the knowledge that they were as often as not being used by the government for purposes of their own must have been equally disconcerting. 'My impression,' said one dedicated terrorist gloomily, after a tour of clandestine revolutionary cells, 'was that even if the Party had succeeded in assassinating the Tsar himself, most of its members would have suspected that this was only an act of provocation.' And, as we know, they could well have been right.

Provocation, '*provokatsia*', the word was to linger on long after the Revolution. It was still in everyday use in the late 1930s, when once again *provokatsia* was said to be rampant and scores of leading Old Bolsheviks, many of them Lenin's close friends and collaborators, were brought to trial as traitors. Some of these, it was suggested, had betrayed the Party and worked for the Tsarist secret police long before the Revolution. Others were accused of spying for capitalist countries or of sabotage. All had at one time or another held high office, most of them quite recently, in the Soviet government. And so, under the Bolsheviks as under the Tsars, there was apparently still this same undercurrent of treachery.

Treachery real or imaginary? If real, one was confronted with the bewildering phenomenon of a great country riddled with treason from top to bottom. If imaginary, with the no less bewildering phenomenon of a government suffering from self-induced hallucinations. In either event a disturbing state of affairs for everyone concerned.

Since then Russia has evolved in a variety of ways. Today there is less talk of traitors and counter-revolutionaries, more of dissidents. There may well be, indeed there almost certainly are, undercover agents of the KGB among the dissidents. There may even be a few hidden dissidents in the ranks of the KGB. But with the increase there has been in Soviet self-confidence and the gradual relaxation of tension and stabilization of the social system, there must on the whole be less scope in the Soviet Union today for two-way operations of the kind once so successfully conducted by Yevno Azef. Which, one is bound in all seriousness to admit, are something that Russia or any other country can very well do without.

Four

SOLDIER STILL AT WAR

Sorge, who grew up in a season of war and died
in a season of war, carried on his bones even
in his final resting place the marks of the
battlefield.

OZAKI HOTSUMI

In the autumn of 1933 the foreign colony in Tokyo received an interesting
new addition in the person of a German newspaper correspondent called
Dr Richard Sorge. When Dr Sorge arrived in Japan in early September he
already possessed something of a reputation as a Far Eastern expert, having
recently spent three years in China, during which he had travelled widely
and contributed a number of important articles on Chinese agriculture to
the *Getreidezeitung*, a German agricultural newspaper of good standing, as
well as writing for a number of other German papers.

Richard Sorge, the son of an oil engineer who had ended his career as a
prosperous Berlin banker, was endowed with a strong and, to most people,
attractive personality. He was now in his late thirties, a tall, loose-
limbed, athletically-built man with high cheek bones, slightly slanting blue
eyes, light brown hair and a sometimes rather arrogant and uncompromis-
ing manner. In August 1914, barely nineteen and as patriotic as most of his
contemporaries, he had left school to volunteer for the army and a month
later had found himself in action in Flanders with a student battalion of the
3rd Guards Field Artillery. In November he had fought at Dixemude,
where the young German volunteers, singing patriotic songs, had overrun
the French machine-gun positions (and suffered appalling losses in the
process) before settling down later that winter to the horrors of trench
warfare. In June 1915 Richard Sorge's battalion had been transferred to the
eastern front to help defend the Galician frontier fortresses against the
Russian onslaught. In July he had been badly wounded and brought back
to hospital in Berlin. Having spent his convalescence working for (and
brilliantly securing) his School Certificate, he had in March 1916 been

125

posted back to the Eastern Front. Within a month he had again been wounded, this time both his legs being broken by shrapnel. For his gallantry in action he had been made a non-commissioned officer and awarded the Iron Cross. But his wounds had left him with a permanent limp and he had spent the rest of the war studying economics first at Berlin and then at Kiel and Hamburg Universities.

The war had had an unsettling effect on Richard Sorge, as on so many of his generation, bringing him to maturity before his time and causing him to question many existing standards and values. His radical, unorthodox approach, good brain, remarkably quick perceptions and rather Bohemian attitude to life made him a stimulating companion and he was to prove a welcome addition to the little world of diplomats, businessmen and newspaper correspondents who made up the foreign community in Japan. The women found him attractive, while the men were impressed by his war record, his ready wit and his ability to drink them under the table.

Before setting out for Tokyo, he had, during two months spent in Berlin in the summer of 1932, arranged with a couple of German newspapers, the *Börsenzeitung* and the *Tägliche Rundschau*, as well as the *Algemeen Handelsblad* of Amsterdam to take any articles he might send them from Japan. He had also provided himself with plenty of introductions, always valuable for a newspaper man. From Dr Zeller, the chief leader-writer of the *Tägliche Rundschau*, who had also fought in the war, he brought a letter of introduction which spoke of him in the warmest terms, addressed to an old friend of Zeller's, Lieutenant-Colonel Eugen Ott, a regular artillery officer now holding the post of Assistant Military Attaché at the German Embassy and at present attached to a Japanese artillery regiment at Nagoya. From various other friends, with business and other connections with Japan, he brought a number of other introductions. In particular Dr Sorge was provided with letters to the German Ambassador, Dr Voretzch, and to various members of the Embassy staff from Karl Haushofer, the founder and Dr Vorwinckel, the editor, of *Geopolitik*, a theoretical journal closely connected with Hitler's National-Socialist party, who, it will be recalled, had come to power in Germany a few months earlier. Karl Haushofer had also given him a letter to Mr Debuchi, the Japanese Ambassador in Washington, on whom he called on his way to the Far East and who, in his turn, furnished him with an introduction to Amau Eiji, the head of the Information Department and official spokesman of the Japanese Foreign Ministry.

On reaching Tokyo Sorge took a room at a hotel, the Sanno, and then called at the Embassy. Dr Voretzch had by this time left Tokyo and his successor had not yet arrived, but the members of the Embassy Staff were much impressed, on offering to put him in touch with the Japanese Foreign Ministry, to be told that he already had an introduction to Amau

Eiji. Next day Sorge called on Amau who, he found, carried considerable weight in Tokyo and who at once introduced him to a number of Japanese journalists.

Among these was Mitsukado Aritomi of the *Jiji Shimpo*. Mitsukado, who already had many friends at the German Embassy, made himself particularly useful to Sorge, recommending a more suitable hotel and helping him in his search for a permanent home. Indeed he showed himself so helpful that Sorge soon began to wonder whether, besides being a journalist he was not perhaps also working for the police who, he did not need to be told, made it their business to keep the closest possible watch on all foreigners living in Japan. This suspicion was strengthened when Mitsukado introduced him to a former Japanese socialist, who for no apparent reason suddenly addressed him in Russian, forcing Sorge to explain that this was a language with which he did not happen to be familiar.

Not long after this Sorge, with Mitsukado's help, moved out of his hotel room and into more permanent quarters in the shape of a *bunka jutaku*, meaning a 'cultured' or up to date residence, at No. 30 Nagasaka-cho in the agreeable and pleasantly secluded district of Azabu. This, according to one frequent visitor there, was 'little more than a summer house in a small garden'. Its upper room, which Sorge used as his study, was in a state of perpetual chaos, perennially piled high with books and papers. Sorge was determined to make himself an expert on Japan and he had no sooner arrived than he started to build up a comprehensive library on every aspect of Japanese life, which, with the rest of his books, left barely enough room for a desk, some chairs and a couch. To these he added in due course some fine Japanese prints and some bronzes and pieces of china, as well as a gramophone and a pet owl in a cage. The floors were covered with matting in the Japanese style and Sorge, who slept on a mattress laid on the matting, followed the local custom of invariably taking off his shoes at the front door. The bathroom was also typically Japanese and Sorge, by nature compulsively clean, would, in the Japanese manner, first scrub himself all over and then soak himself thoroughly in a wooden tub filled with hot water. At six every morning a middle-aged Japanese woman would arrive to attend to the housework and prepare his breakfast and lunch, leaving soon after four. For dinner he usually went out.

Thus installed, Richard Sorge was soon to become a well-known figure in Tokyo society. Most people liked him. There were, it is true, those who found his provocative attitude, his Bohemian approach to life and periodic aggressiveness and intolerance when drunk (which was quite often) rather hard to take. But no one could help being impressed by his intelligence, his ability as a journalist, his expert knowledge of China and his manifest determination to acquire an equal understanding of Japan, where he had quickly made a large number of valuable contacts.

Sorge had come well provided with introductions to the German Embassy and the Embassy, for their part, found his knowledge of China and daily increasing knowledge of Japan of considerable use to them. Towards the end of 1933 Dr Herbert von Dirksen, previously German Ambassador in Moscow, had arrived in Tokyo as successor to Dr Voretch and it was not long before Sorge had established a close and friendly relationship with him. But perhaps the most productive of the letters of introduction he had brought with him was that addressed by Dr Zeller of the *Tägliche Rundschau* to Lieutenant Colonel Eugen Ott, who after a spell as Assistant Military Attaché to the 3rd Artillery Regiment at Nagoya, was in February 1934 appointed Military Attaché in Tokyo.

Before coming to Japan in 1933, Colonel Ott had held an important post at the Ministry of Defence and had been particularly close to General Kurt von Schleicher, who, with Army support, had in December briefly held office as Chancellor immediately before Hitler's accession to power in January 1933 and who was shortly to meet his end in the Rohm purges of June 1934. Slightly older than Sorge, Ott had served as a young artillery officer in the same division as he had during the war. Almost twenty years later this shared experience brought the two middle-aged men together and it was not long before the newspaper correspondent in his late thirties and the Military Attaché in his early forties had become close friends. In the late spring of 1934 Colonel Ott chose Dr Sorge to accompany him on a long tour he made of Manchuria and in Tokyo Sorge was a frequent guest at the Otts' house. Frau Ott, as it happened, was an intelligent and perceptive woman who was prepared to put up with Sorge's Bohemian manners and dislike of social conventions and, when he felt the need for it, she and her husband readily provided their often unorthodox compatriot with a welcome and congenial refuge from official and diplomatic society. Possibly in return for this, Frau Ott is said to have been the only hostess in Tokyo who, when she tried, could persuade Dr Sorge to put on a dinner-jacket in the evening.

Another friend was Captain Paul Wenneker, or Paulchen, as Sorge called him, who was posted to Tokyo as Naval Attaché in 1934. Like Sorge, Paulchen was a bachelor and the two soon became boon companions. Politically, this simple sailor often found himself out of his depth and here Sorge, already quite an expert in his way, could often be of considerable use to him in filling in the Japanese political background.

Then there was Prince Albert von Urach, the son of a famous German general from Württemberg, in whose division Colonel Ott had served during the war. He had come to Tokyo as correspondent of the *Völkischer*

Beobachter, the official organ of the National-Socialist party. Young and easy-going, he took to Sorge immediately, finding him an agreeable companion and a man of refreshingly original views. They were to spend many convivial evenings together.

Though he occasionally spoke critically of Germany's new regime (as of most other human and divine institutions), Richard Sorge had decided not many months after it came to power to apply for membership of the National-Socialist Party and in the autumn of 1934 was duly informed that his application had been accepted. Though he might hold radical and unorthodox views, no one could question the patriotism of a man with his war record. In any case, was not the National-Socialist movement itself revolutionary in character and determined to destroy much of what had gone before? Whatever the rights and wrongs of the matter, there could by now be little doubt that the Nazis were there to stay and that for a German who wanted to succeed in journalism or any other walk of life membership of the party was a useful, indeed an almost indispensable, asset.

In addition to his contacts with the German Embassy Sorge naturally also saw a large number of Japanese. Amongst these was Ozaki Hotsumi of the conservative *Asahi Shimbun*, an extremely able young journalist whom he had already met in China and who in September 1934 was transferred to his paper's Tokyo office. Ozaki had been a most useful source of information to Sorge in China and they now met again regularly, for the most part in restaurants and *geisha* clubs. A significant feature of Japanese political life at this time was the rapid growth of Japanese nationalism, actively promoted and exploited by the army, who saw in it a means of gaining absolute control of the country. On this subject Ozaki was particularly knowledgeable and the information he was able to pass on to Sorge during the winter of 1934–5, with its important bearing on Japan's international relationships, including the very real possibility of war with the Soviet Union, proved of great value not only to him, but to his friends at the German Embassy. For Sorge an indirect source of information on the same subject was Ozaki's friend Kawai Teikichi, a fellow journalist with extensive right-wing connections, whom Ozaki had known in China where he had for a time run a bookshop in Tientsin.

Another friend of Sorge's was a young painter called Miyagi Yotoku, a Japanese from California who had recently returned to Japan. He too was a source of much interesting information, which in one form or another Sorge used for his own purposes or passed on to the Germany Embassy. Miyagi also knew Ozaki, who in turn introduced him to Kawai at a convivial dinner party in May 1935 when the two got drunk together and became firm friends.

Besides his German and Japanese connections, Sorge had also befriended a young Jugoslav, Branko Vukelić, who had arrived in Tokyo in 1933 as correspondent for the Belgrade newspaper *Politika* and for the French illustrated magazine *Vu*. Vukelić, who was not strong and was accompanied by his Danish wife Edith and their little son, did not find life in Tokyo easy. He was short of cash and knew very few people, but Sorge had most generously come to his rescue, advancing him money, helping him to find a house and introducing him to his already wide circle of friends.

Outside his more immediate circle of friends and associates, Sorge shared the day-to-day life of most foreign correspondents in Tokyo. Three times a week he attended the Foreign Ministry's press conferences, at the same time keeping in touch with the press departments of the War Ministry and Ministry of Marine and with the Rengo (later Domei) News Agency. He would also dine periodically at Lohmeyer's excellent German restaurant near the Ginza and frequently drop in for a drink or a chat in the bar or lobby of the sprawling yellow-brick Imperial Hotel.

Among his favourites were two other German-owned establishments, both in the Ginza district, the Fledermaus and the Rheingold. The first of these was a small, rather dingy café or bar, served by two or three giggling and not particularly prepossessing waitresses, who, without much encouragement, would sit themselves next to a customer and put their arms round his neck. Here Sorge came, alone or with friends, to get drunk, passing in turn, as his friend Prince Urach describes it, through 'all the stages of intoxication: high spirits, tearful misery, megalomania, delirium, semi-consciousness and the dreary solitude of a hang-over that can only be cleared away by more alcohol'.

The Rheingold, on the other hand, was a much larger and brighter establishment, boasting a restaurant in addition to a bar and patronized by Japanese as well as foreigners. Here the pay was better and the waitresses attractive and intelligent.

To these and to various other bars, cafés and hotels Sorge, when he had nothing better to do, would regularly go to carouse either on his own or else with a group of hard-drinking cronies, who in time became known somewhat disparagingly as The Balkan Club.

Towards the end of June 1935, Richard Sorge sailed from Yokohama for the United States, not returning to Tokyo until the following September. He was in his fortieth year. A German friend, Hede Massing, who had not seen him for some time and who met him again in New York, was struck by the change that had come over him in the past ten years. 'He had,' she wrote, 'become a violent man, a heavy drinker. Little was left of the charm of the romantic, idealistic student, although he was still remarkably good-looking. His cold, rather slanting blue eyes with their heavy eyebrows had kept their capacity for self-mockery, even when there was no reason for it, and his hair was still thick and brown. But his cheeks and sad-looking mouth were sunken and his nose was pointed, changing him completely.' And certainly surviving photographs taken at the two periods of his life, bear witness to such a transformation.

From the United States Dr Sorge did not return directly to Japan. Instead he sailed from New York to Cherbourg and thence made his way to Paris. From Paris, having first obtained an entry visa from the Soviet Consulate there, he travelled on by way of Austria, Czechoslovakia and Poland to Moscow.

As it happened, the passport on which he travelled and to which the Soviet Consul in Paris had affixed an entry visa was not his own. Nor did it bear his name. It was an Austrian passport bearing, we are told, 'a long and outlandish name'. This he had obtained from a man whom he had met by assignation in New York. His immediate reason for travelling on a forged passport was that he did not wish his own passport to show that he had been to the Soviet Union. The ultimate reason was that Richard Sorge was very far from being what most people took him for.

It was of course quite true that he was the son of Wilhelm Sorge, the prosperous Berlin banker, that he had had a happy and privileged childhood, had fought with great gallantry in the war, been twice wounded and received the Iron Cross. What his new friends in Tokyo could not realize was the full extent of the change which had come over him after that or the line of personal conduct which that change had imposed on him. 'I was,' he said of this period in his life, 'plunged into an intense confusion of the soul.' It was an inner change which had taken possession of him completely and was no doubt to some extent reflected in the outward and visible change which so forcibly struck his friends who saw him in New York.

When Corporal Richard Sorge came out of hospital in 1916 with the black and white ribbon of the Iron Cross on his field-grey tunic and a permanent limp to remind him of Galicia, he was already a very different man from the cheerful, blue-eyed, fair-haired, patriotic youth who had so readily joined up in 1914. His experiences during those two years of war caused him not only to question existing standards and institutions, but to decide that they must at all costs be swept away and replaced by something different.

At the universities in Berlin, Kiel and Hamburg, he had found many others who thought as he did. By the end of 1918 the defeat of Germany's armies in the field, coming on top of four long years of war, had produced what looked like a revolutionary situation. At the time there seemed every

131

chance that in Germany things would go the way they had gone in Russia twelve months earlier. No one strove more vigorously to achieve this end than Richard Sorge. When in 1918 a German Communist Party was finally formed, he at once became a loyal and active member of it.

Although the German Communist Revolution, on which Lenin amongst others had counted with such certainty, came to nothing and although subsequent attempted risings were no more successful, the German Communist Party was to remain an important political force for another fifteen years. At Hamburg Sorge had taken his doctor's degree in political science *summa cum laude* and the Party took full advantage of his talents, using him to organize Party cells and cadres and study-groups, help edit Party newspapers and so on.

At Kiel University an important influence on Richard Sorge's political thinking had been Professor Kurt Gerlach, an enthusiastic and inspiring exponent of Socialist and Communist theory. Professor Gerlach, who was probably also a Party member, was quick to appreciate the younger man's intellectual quality and when in 1919 he was appointed to the chair of economics at Aachen, he took Sorge with him as his assistant.

Sorge stayed at Aachen for less than a year, long enough, even so, for the mutual sympathy which had sprung up between him and Professor Gerlach's young wife Christiane, a distinguished-looking girl with reddish-blonde hair, to ripen into a much closer attachment. For Christiane the appeal of those slanting blue eyes under their heavy brows, the thatch of light brown hair, the lanky, loose-limbed body and above all the restless questing spirit, was irresistible. 'He did not need to pay court to people,' she wrote long afterwards, 'they came flocking to him, both men and women.' True to his progressive principles, her husband made no difficulties. A divorce was granted. And in May 1921 Richard, or Ika as she called him, and Christiane became man and wife, setting up house together at Solingen in North Rhine-Westphalia. Here Christiane continued to study for her doctorate, while Richard, in addition to other less admissible activities, wrote for the local Party periodical, *The Voice of the Mineworkers*.

One item of news which Dr Sorge covered for his paper was the 7th Congress of the German Communist Party, which was held at Jena in May 1921 and which he attended as an official delegate from Rhine-Westphalia. Though his wife apparently had no knowledge of it, Richard was by this time combining his work as a lecturer or journalist with that of a trained underground Party worker.

In October 1922, after first visiting Berlin for discussions with the Central Committee of the Party, Sorge moved to Frankfurt-on-Main for a fresh assignment. As well as being important economically, Frankfurt was at this time very much a centre of artistic and intellectual life. Here he once more found his old friend Professor Gerlach, who apparently bearing him no ill-will for having stolen his wife, helped to find him a somewhat ill-defined job with the newly founded Society for Social Research, a forward-looking, left-inclined body financed by Hermann Weil, one of the city's leading Jewish millionaires. This provided him with congenial company and not very exacting employment as well as excellent cover for his clandestine activities, while Christiane found work in the Society's library.

It was to be Professor Gerlach's last act of kindness to the young couple. Shortly afterwards he died of diabetes, just too soon to become the first director of the Institute for Social Research, which he had helped to plan and which opened a few weeks after his death. Meanwhile Richard and Christiane had installed themselves in what had once been the coach-house of a large mansion. Brightly decorated with the help of a friend who was an artist, it quickly became a centre for highly unconventional gatherings of painters, writers and musicians, who spent happy evenings there in convivial discussions lasting far into the night. Less happy was Christiane who, with her solid bourgeois background, found these occasions 'lacking in light and lustre'. Meanwhile Sorge, who by now had risen to a position of some responsibility in the hierarchy of the Party, spent much of his time travelling about Germany on clandestine missions of one kind or another.

For Moscow, where the doctrine of world revolution had not yet been jettisoned, Germany was still a most important target. In October 1923 a Soviet plan to instigate an armed rising throughout the country was successfully frustrated by the prompt action of the German Government, who used troops to forestall attempts at armed revolt in Saxony and elsewhere. What part, if any, Sorge played in all this is not known.

Apart from provoking a crisis in the German Party, which had as a result been temporarily outlawed by the Government, the failure of the October rising had placed a serious strain on relations between the leaders of the Soviet and German Parties and a number of somewhat acrimonious exchanges between them ensued. One Russian visitor to Germany towards the end of 1923 was D. B. Riazanov, Head of the Marx–Lenin Institute in Moscow, who amongst other things, had come on the lookout for original documents with a bearing on the history of Marxism. As it happened, young Richard Sorge was able to provide him with several such documents, letters written by Karl Marx to his close friend and associate, Friedrich Albert Sorge who, Richard proudly claimed, was his grandfather, though on the evidence available it seems more probable that he was in fact his great-uncle. (It was a family connection of which his father, as a strong supporter of the right, had been anything but proud.)

But the meeting between the famous Soviet scholar and the keen young German Communist was important for another reason: though Sorge may

133

well have had dealings with Russian agents at a lower level, this was his first direct encounter with a leading Soviet personality. What is more, before leaving, Riazanov actually invited him to come to the Marx–Engels Institute in Moscow to join him in the production of the forthcoming new standard edition of Karl Marx's collected works, an invitation which he would have accepted with alacrity, had he not been prevented from doing so by the leaders of his own Party, who were anxious to keep him in Germany.

However, another such opportunity was soon to present itself. The 9th Congress of the German Party was held in Frankfurt in April 1924, the main subject for discussion being the failure of the attempted rising six months earlier. The Congress was attended by a strong fraternal delegation from Moscow, including Stalin's henchman D. Z. Manuilski and several other leading members of the Executive Committee of the Moscow-based Comintern or Communist International. Their primary mission was to strengthen Comintern control over the German Party, a design, incidentally, in which they were largely unsuccessful. But the Soviet delegation had (as their senior German comrades noticed without pleasure) another task besides this: to recruit any likely Germans for the Soviet Intelligence Service. In this they met with a greater measure of success.

Amongst the German Party members directed to look after the Russians was Richard Sorge, whose duty it was to find accommodation for them and act as their bodyguard and guide and who himself accommodated at least two of them in his converted coach-house. Though Sorge was not, so far as we know, directly involved in his Party's discussions with the Soviet delegates, his charm, enthusiasm and manifest intelligence did not escape their attention and before leaving Frankfurt they asked him to come and work for them in Moscow. This time Berlin agreed, and in October 1924 Richard and Christiane set out for Moscow, travelling as students on passports made out in their own names.

It was not the first time Richard Sorge had been in Russia. He had, as it happened, been born there, at Adjikent near Baku, twenty-nine years before in October 1895, when his father Wilhelm had been working as a mining engineer in the Caucasian oil-fields, and had spent the first three years of his life there before moving with his family at the turn of the century, to the agreeable Berlin suburb of Lichterfelde. Moreover, though he could as yet speak no Russian, his mother, the former Nina Kobeleva, was herself a Russian who had married Wilhelm when still in her teens and since borne him nine children, of whom Richard was the youngest. Thus in returning to Russia, now for him, as for every true Communist, the Country of the Revolution and as such his spiritual home, he was also in another sense going back to his native land, to Mother Russia, which has always exercised so strong an attraction on those with any trace of Russian blood in their veins.

What is certain is that for him from now onwards any possible conflict of loyalties was at an end. Private Sorge, who ten years earlier had marched singing towards the French machine-guns positions at Dixemude, might never have existed. His place, after various permutations, had finally been taken by Comrade Sorge, who in March 1925, at Party Headquarters for the Khamovniki District of Moscow was issued with Party Card No. 0049927 of the Soviet Communist Party, which for him obliterated and superseded all previous loyalties or obligations to any other country or party.

Early in 1925 Sorge started work at Comintern Headquarters, a rather dingy nineteenth-century building on the Makhovaya across the way from the Kremlin. Meanwhile accommodation had been found for him and for Christiane at the Hotel Lux, a musty old rabbit-warren of a hotel on the Ulitsa Gorkovo under Comintern management (and surveillance) and strictly reserved for foreign Communists.

Like other government departments (and by 1925 it was in effect little more than a department of the Soviet Government) the Comintern was divided up into a number of different sections, some corresponding to the geographical areas they covered and some to the functions they fulfilled. Of these by far the most powerful was the Orgburo or Organization Bureau set up in 1922 and made responsible for all clandestine activities abroad under the immediate control of the Central Committee. To help direct subversive and other illegal operations abroad and provide a secret link with the local Communist parties in the various countries concerned, a special and highly secret section of the Orgburo had been established, known as the OMS or International Communications Section. It was in all probability to this most important section that Richard Sorge was posted after his arrival in Moscow.

Christiane, meanwhile, was employed at Riazanov's Marx–Lenin Institute, working on Marx's manuscripts. She was not particularly happy. There were many things about Moscow she did not like and she found that Richard, having brought her there, was now inclined to neglect her for his work, for drinking and for other women. She was not greatly interested in politics. Her loyalty was to him and not to the Communist cause. People called her *burzhoika*, the little bourgeoise. In Moscow, with Stalin's rapid rise to power, the atmosphere was by this time beginning to become oppressive. Already foreigners were regarded with suspicion. She felt uncomfortably isolated. In October 1926, after two far from happy years in the Soviet metropolis, she decided to go back to Germany. Richard went to the station to see her off.

From Moscow in 1927 and 1928 Richard Sorge is known to have undertaken a mission on behalf of the Comintern to Norway, Sweden and Denmark. There are also indications that he may again have been active in Germany during this period. In July 1928 he returned to Moscow for the 6th World Congress of the Comintern which was to drag on into September. This in practice marked the abandonment of Trotski's doctrine of World Revolution and victory for Stalin's policy of Socialism in One Country. As Sorge himself put it, 'hopes of imminent World Revolution were put aside'. It was also to mark a tightening of Soviet control over the world Communist movement, corresponding to the simultaneous tightening of the Kremlin's control over every aspect of Soviet life. More than ever had the Comintern become a Soviet government department, designed first and foremost to further Soviet national interests.

Towards the end of 1928 after the Congress was over, Richard Sorge returned for a time to Scandinavia on Comintern business. In the spring of 1929 he was sent to Great Britain for a couple of months to study conditions there, look into the likelihood of a general strike and possibly also engage in espionage and subversive activities. It was a risky undertaking which involved all kinds of precautions and cramped his style in other directions, as he implied in passing with a nostalgic reference to 'those slim, long-legged English girls'.

From England Sorge returned to Moscow, stopping off in Berlin on the way. Friends who saw him on his way through Berlin found him for once depressed and disillusioned. He was short of cash and the strain of prolonged undercover work combined with the frustrations of coping with the soulless bureaucracy of the Comintern was beginning to tell. 'For a long time,' he said to one old friend, 'no one has read my reports.' And to another: 'Those swine! How I hate them! This disregard for human suffering and feeling . . . At least they must give me proper notice. And they have not paid me for months.' 'The Comintern,' he said later, 'had no interest in my political reports.'

Meanwhile in Moscow the process which had begun with Lenin's death five years earlier had reached completion. Stalin was now in control. With Trotski's expulsion from the Soviet Union in 1929 began the elimination of all Stalin's actual or potential rivals and the further consolidation and extension of power in the hands of a single man. From a body which for a time after its foundation in 1919 had retained some vestiges of independence, the Comintern had become no more than a *lavochka*, a grocer's shop, as Stalin (who disliked foreigners) contemptuously called it. From the evidence available it seems safe to assume that, when later in 1929 the time came for Sorge to leave its employment and move to other work, the change was not an unwelcome one.

The work to which he was now transferred was with the Fourth Bureau, one of the six sections of the Red Army's Directorate of Military Intelligence. Presided over since 1920 by the legendary General Yan Karlovich Berzin, a famous figure in the Bolshevik Revolution with a considerable flair for intelligence operations, the Fourth Bureau was responsible for organizing a network of agents and spies beyond the frontiers of the Soviet Union.

Having by this time abandoned any real hope of revolution in western Europe, the Russians, despite the serious setback recently inflicted on the Chinese Communists by General Chiang Kai-shek, recently established as head of the Nanking government, were now directing their attention more and more to the Far East and in particular to China. If they could only provoke a Communist revolution in China, it would, they calculated, radically alter the balance of world power to Russia's advantage.

China had accordingly become a primary target for General Berzin's Fourth Bureau and it was to China that Richard Sorge, after detailed briefing by his new chief, was now assigned. The Soviet Union no longer possessed any diplomatic or consular posts in China and contacts with the Chinese Communists had been seriously disrupted by the setback of 1927. Sorge's directive was to discover all he could about Chiang Kai-shek's newly formed government, its policy and resources, with special reference to its military potential; to investigate the prevailing social and economic conditions; to find out everything possible about the factions opposing Chiang; and to make a study of British and American policy towards China.

When he left for China Sorge travelled legally on his own German passport, which described him as a writer. To provide additional cover, he stopped off in Berlin on his way and there made arrangements to write articles for the *Getreidezeitung* and for a German sociological magazine. Through the Editor of the *Getreidezeitung* he obtained an introduction from the press department of the German Foreign Office to the German Consul-General in Shanghai. In Berlin he also made contact with Seber Weingarten, a Moscow trained radio-operator on an assignment there for the Fourth Bureau. Weingarten, he was told, would go with him to China and would, it was hoped, be able to maintain the necessary wireless contact with Russia.

Richard Sorge left for China in December 1929, having booked a passage from Marseilles to Shanghai on board a Japanese ship. Weingarten, in the guise of a sales agent for patent automatic cookers, had already joined the same ship at Hamburg. With them went a third rather shadowy emissary of the Fourth Bureau, known as Alex, who was nominally senior to Sorge and disguised as a Czech arms-merchant. They arrived at their destination on 10 January 1930. Shanghai with its flourishing trade and industry, its port, its foreign concessions, its large mixed foreign colony and cosmopolitan atmosphere offered an ideal centre for espionage, indeed, despite its admirable international police force, for almost any nefarious or semi-nefarious activity. It had also been picked by the Communists as the most probable focus for an urban revolution.

Soon after reaching Shanghai Dr Sorge took a room in a modest apart-ment-house and duly delivered his letter of introduction to the German Consulate-General, at the same time explaining that he was anxious to make a study of agricultural conditions in China, a grasp of which was essential to any real understanding of Chinese Communism and its aims. After they had provided him with further introductions, the Consulate-General heard little more of him for the time being beyond the fact that his travels took him far and wide in the hinterland of China and that he was said to have left-wing connections. In May he moved to Canton where for the next six months he lived quietly in a boarding-house in the inter-national settlement, improving his contacts and his knowledge of the coun-try and its people and making long journeys into southern China. In mid-November he returned to Shanghai.

There he found that 'Alex', learning that the Shanghai police were after him, had taken the next ship back to Europe, leaving Sorge in charge of the group. Meanwhile their mission had been joined by a second wireless-operator, Max Klausen, a Communist merchant-seaman from Hamburg who had been sent out from Moscow by the Fourth Bureau a year or two earlier. Klausen had already managed to establish a direct secret wireless link with Vladivostok, though during the years that followed radio contact with the Fourth Bureau was to be neither easy nor continuous and the mission was obliged to rely largely on clandestine couriers.

In November 1930, after his return from Canton, Sorge had met a Miss Agnes Smedley, an enthusiastic American left-winger of about the same age as himself with a stormy career as a militant in various revolutionary causes, who, amongst other things, was now the Shanghai correspondent of the *Frankfurter Zeitung*. Knowing, presumably from Moscow, that he could count on her, he asked her to help him establish his group in Shanghai and also to bring him together with potential Chinese 'helpers and supporters' from among her many younger Chinese friends. In this she proved most helpful. She also put him in touch with a young Japanese friend of hers, Ozaki Hotsumi, the *Asahi Shimbun*'s special correspondent in Shanghai.

This, in the long run, was to be the most valuable introduction of all.

Though it was not until considerably later that he was to learn his real name, Ozaki at once took to 'Johnson' (as he had been told to call him) and was soon meeting him at least once a month either in Chinese restaurants or in Agnes Smedley's flat, where they could safely exchange views and information in an atmosphere of mutual confidence. In particular Ozaki was able to provide Sorge with much valuable information concerning the Chinese Communists, with whom Moscow had of recent years been increasingly out of touch.

In September 1931 came the Japanese invasion of Manchuria. This drastically transformed the situation in the Far East, at the same time posing a number of urgent questions. Did the Japanese intend to advance further in North China? How would the rival political and military groupings in China react to the Japanese attack? And finally, did this increase the likelihood of hostilities between the Soviet Union and Japan? 'The Japanese have taken Mukden,' said Sorge one day to Klausen. 'This will complicate our task in China.'

Sorge had been expressly asked by Moscow to give his estimate of Japanese designs on China. He accordingly invited a certain Kawai Teikichi, whom he had met through Ozaki and who was at this time working for the *Shanghai Weekly*, to visit North China and Manchuria on his behalf and let him have a report on Manchukuo, the puppet state set up by the Japanese in Manchuria, giving his comments on the present frame of mind of the Japanese army of occupation, of the various minorities in the area and in particular, of the mood in the northern frontier areas towards the Soviet Union. After he had come back and made his report to Sorge, Kawai was arrested, held for three weeks and closely interrogated by the Japanese police in Shanghai, without however giving any information about the true nature of his mission or its originator.

The questions of Japan's ultimate aims in China, of the relative military strengths of the Nationalist regime and the Communists and the probable reactions of Great Britain and America, were again raised in acute form when on 28 January 1932 fighting broke out in Shanghai between the Japanese and the 19th Chinese Route Army. On the strength of 'very useful information' obtained from Ozaki and based on interviews with the Japanese Service Attachés in Shanghai and of his own direct experience (for he was present during some of the fighting), Sorge wrote a long report, which he later took to Max Klausen for onward transmission to Moscow. What he wrote was naturally of the greatest interest to the Russians, then engaged in trying to decide on their attitude to the Chinese Communists and Chiang Kai-shek respectively.

Early in 1932 Ozaki, Sorge's most valuable contact, was recalled to Japan by his newspaper. But by this time he had numerous other sources of information. As a reputable journalist he was on excellent terms with the German Consulate-General and the members of the German Military Mission to Chiang Kai-shek who, as his grasp of the situation increased, found him as useful as he found them and often invited him to visit them in Nanking or accompany them on trips to Hankow and elsewhere. On one of his visits to Nanking he obtained a map and blueprints of the Chinese military arsenal by the simple and pleasant expedient of seducing a beautiful Chinese girl who had access to them and let him keep them long enough to photograph them. It was all grist to his mill. The Shanghai police who, noting his left-wing contacts, had decided shortly after his arrival that he was probably a Soviet agent, now came to the conclusion that he was working for German intelligence. But on neither score do they ever seem to have thought of arresting him as in the summer of 1931 they had arrested a number of other Communist agents, notably the senior Comintern representative in Shanghai, Hilaire Noulens.

In December 1932, after handing over to a colonel from the Baltic, called Paul, who had been sent out by the Fourth Bureau to replace him, Richard Sorge left Shanghai for Moscow. The three years he had spent in China had been useful ones. He had established a reputation as a competent journalist and expert on the Far East and had gained much valuable first-hand experience of clandestine work there. He had also successfully fulfilled the task which had been set him by furnishing the Fourth Bureau with an accurate estimate of the situation in China, of Japanese intentions and of the military and political potentialities of Chiang Kai-shek's government, all subjects on which Moscow had up to then been inadequately informed and which had a direct and vital bearing on Soviet prospects in the Far East. Finally, in Ozaki Hotsumi he had encountered a kindred spirit with whom it was easy to work and communicate and with whom he had quickly established a relationship of mutual confidence and respect. It was a relationship which, for all anyone knew, might again have its uses in the future.

On his return to Moscow in January 1933 Sorge was enthusiastically received by his superiors and told that his work had given every satisfaction. Asked what he had in mind for the future, he replied that, before undertaking another mission, he would like time to finish the book he was writing on Chinese agriculture. Meanwhile, during the weeks that followed, he was from time to time asked to call at the Fourth Bureau and even entertained by General Berzin at his own home. He also had discussions with the People's Commissariat for Foreign Affairs and with the OGPU, or Political Police, now beginning to play an increasingly active and sinister role in Soviet life. Finally, as a member of the Soviet Communist Party returned from abroad, he reported to the Central Committee, where he was told that his standing in the Party was high. As far as his domestic life was concerned, Christiane's place had now been taken by a Russian girl, called Yekaterina Maximova, whom he seems to have married soon after his return from China. He was not, however, to enjoy this fresh instalment of connubial bliss for long.

In April 1933, after he had been in Moscow for no more than a couple of months, Richard Sorge was summoned to the Fourth Bureau and told by General Berzin that, book or no book, it was time he went on another mission abroad. Did he have any ideas? To this he replied that he would like to go back to Asia, preferably North China or Manchuria. Then, remembering a brief but agreeable holiday he had spent not long before at the Imperial Hotel in Tokyo, he added half jokingly: 'Or what about Japan?'

As so often happens in life, a chance remark had more effect than a considered proposal. A few days later Sorge was once more summoned by General Berzin and informed that the Central Committee of the Party were definitely interested in a possible mission to Japan. From subsequent discussions emerged the idea of a tentative mission for the purpose of finding out how easily Japan could be entered legally, what contacts could be made there with Japanese and foreigners, what could be arranged in the way of communications and finally, what could be discovered about Japanese policy towards the Soviet Union. This last was to be the mission's essential task: 'to study very carefully' as Sorge said afterwards, 'the question of whether or not Japan was planning to attack the Soviet Union. This was for many years the most important duty assigned to me and my group; it would not be far wrong to say that it was the sole object of my mission to Japan.'

In the course of subsequent briefings at which, in addition to the Fourth Bureau, the Comintern, the Party, the Commissariat for Foreign Affairs and the OGPU were all represented, Sorge's terms of reference were further elaborated. In the first instance he would spend two years in Japan, simply to find out whether espionage was in fact feasible there amid the extremely spy-conscious Japanese. He would have three men to work with him, a Japanese, another European and a wireless-operator. He was to have no contacts with the illegal Japanese Communist Party or with the Soviet Embassy. His cover would again be that of a newspaper man. His code-name would be 'Ramsay'. Thus briefed, he left Moscow for Berlin on 7 May 1933.

In Germany, where Dr Sorge spent about eight weeks before continuing his journey to Japan, Adolf Hitler had come to power only a few months earlier. The police records kept under the Weimar Republic had by this time passed into the hands of the Gestapo. For Sorge, well known to a number of people as an early and active member of the German Communist

Party, the prevailing political climate was far from reassuring. 'The situation is not very attractive for me here,' ran one of his messages to the Fourth Bureau. 'I shall be glad when I can disappear from this place.' And again, three weeks later: 'With things livening up in these parts, interest in my person could become much more intensive.'

But, if he was to enter Japan legally as a German newspaper correspondent, he had to have a genuine passport in his own name and a press card. He applied for the passport on 1 June, attaching the most impressive possible character references in the hope that these would render a thorough search into his antecedents less likely. He was also careful not to reveal in his curriculum vitae that he had just returned from China via Moscow. In due course both passport and press-card were issued to him. At some stage he also applied for membership of the National Socialist Party, to the Tokyo branch of which he was duly admitted in 1934. This, too, might have been expected to involve some research into his past history. But either through the inefficiency of the newly created Gestapo or through someone's deliberate carelessness, his revolutionary past was not held against him and he was able to leave for Japan with both the documents he needed, not to mention a number of most impressive letters of introduction and the agreement of several newspapers and periodicals to take his articles.

While in Berlin, he met Christiane and seems to have taken the opportunity to obtain from her a divorce no doubt as friendly as the divorce Professor Gerlach had granted her a dozen years before. Christiane was later to settle in New York, where Sorge kept in touch with her, occasionally sending her money and greetings by friends who happened to be going there.

Some other friends he met at this time in Berlin noticed how heavily he was drinking. But in spite of everything, he still struck them as 'the old Communist idealist' who 'wanted to free the world from capitalist imperialism and militarism and make wars impossible in future. To him all difficulties, shortages and mistakes in the Soviet Union were simply regrettable transitional phenomena.'

To Comrade Gorev, a fellow agent from the Fourth Bureau, also on his way to the Far East, Sorge spoke forebodingly over a drink in a Berlin café of the massing of hostile forces, of the growing danger of war against the USSR and of the hazards of espionage in Japan. He left him with the impression of a man with a strong sense of purpose – 'the sense of purpose of a Soviet military intelligence officer'.

Armed with this sense of purpose, with his valid passport and with his letters of introduction, Dr Richard Sorge landed in Yokohama on 6 September 1933.

.   .   .   .   .

Sorge's first two years in Tokyo were, as his sponsors had intended, mainly exploratory. He was to spend them feeling his way, establishing himself as a local character, making friends of all kinds and, above all, extending his knowledge of Japan and the Japanese.

Within a few weeks of his arrival he had been ready to make contact with the wireless-operator assigned him by the Fourth Bureau, a rather nervous man and a heavy drinker, whose code name was Bernhardt and who had arrived in Japan a short time before under the guise of a businessman called Wendt. Through him Sorge, exercising due caution, got into touch with the other European involved, a rather frail young Yugoslav named Branko Vukelić, who for some time past had been living in France. There he had recently married a Danish gymnastic instructress called Edith. More recently still, on the strength of his rather vague Marxist views, he had been recruited for the Fourth Bureau by an athletic-looking Comintern agent of indeterminate nationality known as Olga. Vukelić had for reasons which are not clear arrived in Japan as far back as February and by the time Sorge contacted him in October was badly in need of funds. Fortunately for all concerned Sorge not long after this received a substantial sum of money through a secret courier from the Fourth Bureau whom he first met by arrangement in a bedroom in the Imperial Hotel and with whom he later went sightseeing at Nikko, where in the seclusion of the national park his visitor handed him a well-wrapped wad of notes.

It remained to make contact with the fourth member of the ring, Miyagi Yotoku, a young Japanese painter from the United States. But he had also been a member of the American Communist Party and, like Branko Vukelić, had not long before been recruited for the Soviet service and in his turn directed to Tokyo.

Miyagi had arrived from California in October and had since been waiting for a sign from 'Schmidt', the code name used in this connection for Sorge. Since his arrival, he had been careful to take in the *Japan Advertiser*, the local English language newspaper. Around the middle of December, he at last saw in it the classified advertisement he had been waiting for: 'Wanted Ukikoye prints by old master, also English books on same subject urgently. Apply Box 423.' A few days later, after a preliminary encounter with Vukelić at which both carried American dollar bills with consecutive numbers as a means of identification, Sorge was explaining to him sotto voce in a Tokyo art gallery that what he needed from him was information on political and military matters in Japan. Sorge's team was now complete and ready for action. It included, it will be observed, no women. 'Women,' wrote Sorge, 'are absolutely unfit for espionage work. They have no understanding of political and other affairs and I have never received satisfactory information from them.'

143

As a team, it left a good deal to be desired. Though he spoke and read Japanese and could support himself by the sale of his pictures, Miyagi had lived in America since he was sixteen and was therefore completely unfamiliar, except by hearsay, with life in Tokyo. He naturally had no contacts whatever in government or official circles. Nor, at thirty, could he be expected to have great maturity or experience of life. Willing, intelligent and ready to learn, his chief contribution was to pass on to Sorge what he read every day in the Japanese press.

Having set up as a businessman in Yokohama, Bernhardt had established two wireless transmitters, one in his own house in Yokohama and the other in the house which Branko and Edith Vukelić had rented in Tokyo. But, though an adequate technician, he was extremely timid and often drunk, with the result that he did not transmit half the messages which Sorge gave him to send. 'I felt,' he explained later with engaging frankness, 'that the frequent sending and receiving of messages would be tantamount to inviting discovery by the police.' As Sorge ruefully pointed out, 'a man who engages in espionage work must have some courage'. But that was evidently not Bernhardt's view and early in 1935 Sorge simply had him sent back to Moscow.

As for Branko Vukelić, Sorge seems to have employed him largely as a phototechnician, photographing documents and producing micro-films for transmission by courier to Moscow, but also as a source of information collected in the course of his work as a correspondent.

In the circumstances it is scarcely surprising that Richard Sorge, casting around for possible reinforcements, should have remembered his former associate in Shanghai, Ozaki Hotsumi, now working for the *Asahi* in Osaka. Just when the idea came to him is not clear, but in the spring of 1934 he despatched Miyagi to Osaka to sound him out.

Ozaki, who did not know Miyagi, was at first suspicious and feared provocation by the police, but on discovering that he came from his old friend 'Johnson' from Shanghai, agreed to a rendezvous with Sorge in the deer park at Nara under the shadow of Mount Kasuga. There he learned what Sorge required of him and at once declared himself ready to furnish him with information on all aspects of the situation in Japan. He was to become in Sorge's words, 'my first and most important associate'.

Ozaki does not seem to have ever been an actual member of the Communist Party. Nor did he spy for money. Convinced that Japan's policy of frenzied expansion represented a threat to peace and indeed to her own best interests, he felt that by the information he furnished to Sorge he was indirectly furthering the cause of world peace and helping to keep his country out of war.

Thanks to the information he received from Ozaki and to what he gleaned from his contacts with the German Embassy, but thanks also to his own shrewdness and skill in interpreting this material and piecing it together, Sorge seems even at this early stage of his mission to have produced reports which kept the Fourth Bureau happy. At the same time he seems to have satisfied himself that despite the difficulties and dangers involved, espionage in Japan was a feasible proposition. ('I think,' he signalled to Moscow on 1 January 1934, 'that I am managing to lead them all by the nose.') As usual, his attention at this time was concentrated on the danger of war between Japan and the Soviet Union, which had seemed to grow greater during the winter of 1933–4, only to die down again the following summer.

Meanwhile in September 1934 Ozaki had been transferred by the *Asahi* to their Tokyo office. This meant that he would now be at the centre of things and enjoy a far wider range of contacts. In March 1935 Kawai Teikichi, who had valuable right-wing connections and had worked for Ozaki and for Sorge in Shanghai, also returned to Tokyo and on arrival there came to Ozaki and asked him for instructions. Despite his right-wing connections, which he still kept up, Kawai was in fact a convinced Communist who now did some useful work for Miyagi, with whom Ozaki had put him in touch. In particular, working with Miyagi, he now produced for Sorge an invaluable chart illustrating the intricate relationship of the various groupings and factions within the Japanese Army.

When in June 1935 Sorge sailed for America en route for Moscow it was on instructions from the Fourth Bureau, whom he had informed that he wished to be recalled for consultations. Another purpose of his journey was to collect a better wireless-operator to replace Bernhardt whom he had already sent back.

In Moscow, where he spent only three weeks, briefly resuming marital relations with his Soviet wife Yekaterina Maximova, he found a new man in charge of the Fourth Bureau in place of General Berzin, now apparently under suspicion. This was General Semyon Petrovich Uritski, famous for having in March 1921 led the successful cavalry attack across the ice against the mutinous sailors of Kronstadt. Like his predecessor General Berzin, General Uritski, though he did not know it, was now approaching the end of his life, which he was to lose before a firing squad or possibly in the cellars of the Lubyanka in the great *chistka* or purge of 1937. These, it cannot be denied, were unsettling years for the Red Army and for Soviet officialdom. It is pleasant to be able to record however, that Generals Berzin and Uritski, together with many of their brother officers, were both officially rehabilitated in 1964.

How far Sorge himself was conscious of the danger which at this time threatened any member of the Soviet establishment, including himself, is not entirely clear. It would have been strange, however, for so perceptive a man not to be aware of it. Nor did he, in fact, find it necessary to return to Moscow after the summer of 1935.

In reporting to General Uritski, the first point Sorge made was that in his considered opinion the conduct of espionage in Japan was a perfectly feasible proposition. As other ventures of the kind had failed completely, this must have been welcome news. He next asked that Ozaki should be accepted as a member of his ring and that he should be given another wireless-operator in place of Bernhardt. Finally he made the request that he should be allowed 'absolute freedom' in deciding what his relations should be with the German Embassy in Tokyo and what information he should pass to them. For his present purposes, he explained, the best method must be 'discussions, consultation and study: to trade information of minor importance for information of major importance – in other words to set a sprat to catch a mackerel.' To all this General Uritski seems to have agreed.

In August 1935, while Sorge was still in Moscow, the 7th Congress of the Comintern was held in the Kolonnyi Zal, the great blue and white pillared ballroom of the former Nobles' Club, shortly to be the scene of the trial for high treason of two of the Comintern's former General Secretaries, Zinoviev and Bukharin. The 7th Congress marked the appointment of Georgi Dimitrov, the hero of the Reichstag Fire Trial, to the post of General Secretary, with Stalin's henchman Manuilski behind him as its real master. At the same time it set the seal on the Kremlin's interesting new policy of a Popular Front against Fascism. As for World Revolution, once the raison d'être of the Comintern, it had for the time being become a dirty word. 'We have never had such intentions,' said Stalin flatly in answer to a question on the subject put to him six months later by an American journalist.

Richard Sorge had wanted to attend the Congress, but was officially forbidden to do so, presumably on security grounds. It seems in any case doubtful whether he would have found its proceedings very congenial. All in all, he saw few friends during his three weeks in Moscow, social life there being as he put it, 'very restricted'. On the other hand he seems to have spent a good deal of time with Max Klausen, the former merchant-seaman from Hamburg, who had been his wireless-operator in Shanghai and who at his instance was now to join him in Tokyo in place of Bernhardt.

At the suggestion of Seber Weingarten, who had worked with both of them in Shanghai and was himself expecting to go back to China, they met at a bar near the Fourth Bureau's Wireless School. From Shanghai Klausen, a burly, jovial, rather heavy-looking man with no pretensions to being an intellectual, had been sent by the Fourth Bureau to Mukden, where as

146

proprietor of a bicycle shop, he had for eighteen months operated a secret wireless set under the very noses of the Japanese. Thence after eighteen precarious months he had been recalled to Russia and then, presumably as a punishment for not doing better, been sent to work as a mechanic at a tractor station in the Volga–German Republic, only to be suddenly recalled by the Fourth Bureau fifteen months later and informed that he was going on a secret assignment to Nazi Germany. Sorge now told him, however, that he wanted him to join him in Japan and could easily arrange this.

A few days later Klausen was summoned to the Far Eastern Department of the Fourth Bureau and his appointment to Japan confirmed. Having always gathered that the Japanese Government was a bad one, even by capitalist standards, he was glad in his simple way to know that he would be working against it, though, needless to say, for the Japanese people.

Before leaving Moscow, Sorge and Klausen were given a final briefing by General Uritski in person, who again emphasized that what was required of them first and foremost was an accurate analysis of Japan's intentions towards the Soviet Union: were the Japanese planning to attack the Russians or not? This, he stressed, was 'a matter of extreme concern to all quarters in Moscow'. The Soviet Government, he said, were also concerned at the apparent *rapprochement* between Germany and Japan, which they were convinced was chiefly directed against the Soviet Union.

Sorge and Klausen travelled separately to Japan, having first agreed to meet in due course at the Blue Ribbon Bar in Tokyo, where Sorge would wait every Tuesday evening. Klausen, who went by way of Leningrad, Le Havre, New York, San Francisco and Yokohama, probably working his passage across the Atlantic, bought and took with him in his luggage two tubes for the small wireless transmitter he intended to build when he reached his destination. He did not reach Tokyo until 28 November.

Sorge's route is less clear. Leaving after Klausen in September, he seems to have travelled some of the way by air, stopping off briefly in New York, where he once again switched passports and reached Tokyo before the end of the month. As things turned out, their first meeting took place not at the Blue Ribbon, but at the German Club, which Max happened to visit the night after he arrived. But it was impossible to talk there without being overheard and they accordingly agreed to meet at the Blue Ribbon the following evening.

The first thing to be done was to establish a wireless link with the Soviet Union. This was easier said than done. The transmitter which Bernhardt had left behind with Branko Vukelić was bulky, conspicuous and in general unsatisfactory. In addition to the two tubes he had brought with him,

Klausen required ten more. These and the copper wire needed for the tuning coils he managed without too much difficulty to buy in Tokyo, though the Japanese radio industry had not at that time attained its present proportions. Finally, around the middle of February 1936, the new set was assembled and contact made with Vladivostok. This was done, not from Vukelić's home, but from that of Gunther Stein, the Tokyo correspondent of the London *News Chronicle* who was apparently enough of a sympathizer with Sorge's aims to take the risk of letting his home be used for such a purpose. Some weeks later Klausen and Vukelić, dressed as hikers and carrying a heavily laden rucksack each, took a day trip to Lake Yamanaka where they hired a boat, rowed out into the middle of the lake and surreptitiously dumped the component parts of Bernhardt's cumbrous transmitter. 'You should have got rid of it in Tokyo instead of going so far away,' was all Sorge had to say when told of their excursion. 'His manner,' Klausen continued rather revealingly, 'was not so bad, but he always treated me as a sort of errand-boy since he had no one else to help him.'

It was of course also necessary for Klausen to provide himself with adequate cover. For this purpose he later set up a printing and blueprint-duplicating firm, which was soon doing work for various large firms and even for the armed services, and proved surprisingly enough very successful, so successful that within a very few years the Fourth Bureau were instructing him, much to his annoyance, to use part of its profits as funds for the spy-ring.

Sorge's ring had by this time already had one very narrow escape from discovery. At five o'clock on the morning of 21 January 1936 eight detectives burst into Kawai Teikichi's bedroom and told him that he was under arrest. He was then taken by various means of transport to Hsinking in Manchuria and there charged with propaganda activities and espionage on behalf of the Communists. For five days after this he was savagely beaten and interrogated about his associates and the information he had received from them. At the end of five days, however, the police, having failed to find out what they wanted, abandoned the attempt and Kawai was simply given a short prison sentence, which he completed the following June. After his release he remained on the mainland and did not return to Japan or resume his connection with Ozaki and Miyagi for several years.

Meanwhile on 26 February 1936 an event had occurred in Tokyo, to be known as the *Ni Ni Roku Jiken* or the Incident of 26 February, which seemed likely to possess the most profound significance and ultimately give rise to the most far-reaching consequences. Just what significance or what consequences was harder to say, the event being a characteristically Japanese one and as such not readily comprehensible to most foreign observers.

Seven months earlier in July 1935 General Mazaki, a hero of the *Kodo-ha* or Imperial Way Faction, had been removed from the high post which he held in the Army, while a number of other, like-minded officers were also demoted or sent overseas. The *Kodo-ha* were a powerful ultra-nationalist faction who aimed at bringing into being a radically remodelled authoritarian socialist state, controlled by the military and under the direct rule of the Emperor. Shortly after this, one of the other officers affected, a certain Lieutenant-Colonel Aizawa, had called on Major-General Nagata, the Chief of the Military Affairs Bureau or Military Secretary, and invited him to resign. This General Nagata had declined to do. Instead he had given immediate orders for Colonel Aizawa to be posted to Formosa. Two weeks later Colonel Aizawa again called on General Nagata and this time hacked him to pieces with his sword. For this he was not unnaturally tried by court martial. His trial, which dragged on for months and at which he represented himself as a disinterested patriot, was held in the barracks of the 1st Division in Tokyo. This, it soon became clear, was having an unsettling effect on the younger officers of the 1st Division, many of whom strongly sympathized with Colonel Aizawa and the *Kodo-ha*. The 1st Division was accordingly ordered to stand by for a move to Manchuria. Meanwhile Colonel Aizawa's trial continued to drag on in an atmosphere of increasing tension.

It was now that the *Ni Ni Roku Jiken* occurred. Just before dawn on the 26th February, in a blinding snowstorm (which for historical reasons was felt to have a special significance) a force of fourteen hundred soldiers of the 1st Division, led by young officers of the rank of captain and below, emerged from their barracks, seized the Ministry of War, Metropolitan Police Headquarters and Parliament Building and assassinated a number of leading statesmen, narrowly missing the Prime Minister (whose brother-in-law they killed by mistake), not to mention two former prime ministers. From their position of strength their leaders then issued a manifesto in vaguely idealistic terms, declaring that they had done what they had from a sense of duty to the Emperor.

For the remainder of 26 February nothing more happened. The mutineers, still in possession of the buildings they had occupied, appeared to be waiting for someone more senior to follow up their initial success, while the government did no more than put out an anodyne and not very informative communiqué referring to the mutineers not as traitors or insurgents, but simply as 'young regular soldiers'. Clearly everyone directly or indirectly involved was doing some hard thinking.

The next day, 27 February, seems to have been taken up with parleying between the mutineers and a number of generals. Meanwhile, on that and the following day, more troops and armour were brought into the area and a cordon consisting partly of naval ratings, thrown round the buildings held by the rebels, while at the same time the 1st Fleet anchored off the city in Tokyo Bay. After which, on 29 February, the mutineers suddenly surrendered without anyone having fired a shot. Martial law, proclaimed at the time of the mutiny, was retained for many weeks after it. In due course, the ring-leaders were court martialled and many of them executed on charges of attempted insurrection.

Clearly this extraordinary episode was bound to provoke intense and prolonged speculation both in Japan and abroad. What did it mean? What were its causes? And what were its future consequences likely to be? In Tokyo, while the Japanese were trying to work out how they felt about it themselves, every foreign embassy and every foreign newspaper correspondent was being bombarded with urgent requests for their considered views.

Richard Sorge was no exception. His friends at the German Embassy wanted to know what he made of it. The editors of the newspapers he represented were equally insistent. And so, back in Moscow, was the Fourth Bureau, always vitally interested in any indication of which way the Japanese were likely to jump.

In interpreting the incident, which he did at length for the Embassy, for Haushofer's *Geopolitik* and last but not least for the Fourth Bureau, Sorge, who had at once grasped its significance and with the help of Ozaki and Miyagi, collected a mass of material on the subject, particularly stressed its social and economic aspects. 'The deepest causes of these radical political currents in the army,' he wrote in his article for *Geopolitik*, 'lie in the social distress of the Japanese peasantry and the lesser bourgeoisie of the towns. ... Given the peasant's lack of political organization and the purely formal interest taken in them by the two main parties, the army necessarily became a mouthpiece and means of expression for the increasing tension among the urban and rural classes. Herein lies the true significance of the mutiny of the Tokyo Division.'

Meanwhile fresh evidence had reached him from another quarter, from Major Scholl, the newly arrived Assistant Military Attaché at the German Embassy, who had served in the same unit as he had on the Western Front and with whom he quickly established a most friendly relationship, Sorge obtained a particularly illuminating clandestine pamphlet by two of the ringleaders of the mutiny, enumerating the army's grievances and bearing out his own theories on the subject.

Dr von Dirksen, the German Ambassador, and Colonel Ott were both much impressed by what Sorge had to say on the subject and, in his words, 'tried to draw even closer to me', exchanging views and material and showing him the reports they themselves were sending. 'And so,' Sorge said later, 'my opinions easily coloured the view taken by the Embassy.' In the

Mata Hari

Alfred Redl

Yevno Azef

Richard Sorge

Elyeza Bazna

Kim Philby

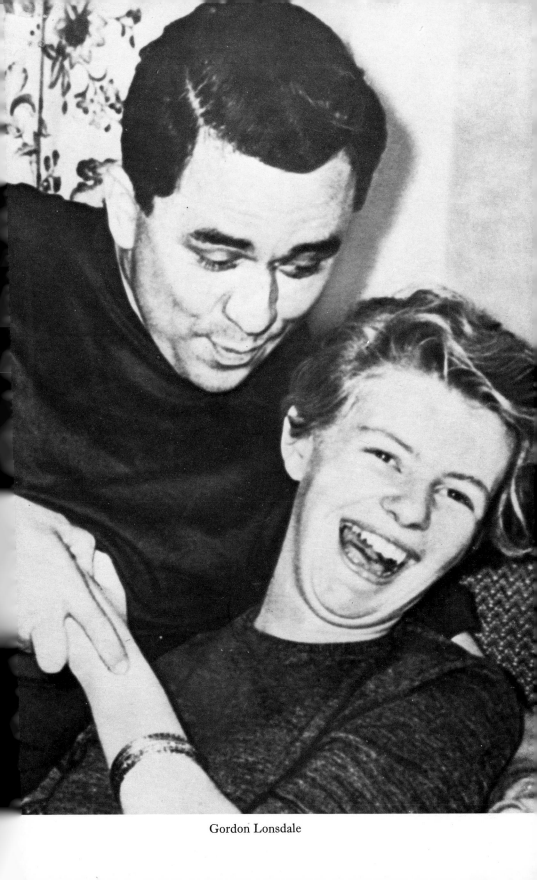

Gordon Lonsdale

Oleg Penkovski

end, although he was not connected with the Embassy, they asked him to write a report on the incident for them to send to Berlin.

From one source or another Sorge, who during the four days of the Incident had seen as much of it as he could at first hand, had soon succeeded in informing himself extremely well on every aspect of the affair. He eventually embodied the results of his investigation in a carefully considered report to the Fourth Bureau. This he sent out in April by courier via Shanghai on microfilm appending for good measure photocopies of the various relevant documents he had been shown at the Embassy. As he himself said afterwards, 'The Moscow Centre was not so much interested in whether the Embassy despatch on the Incident of 26 February was correct or not, as in the attitude of responsible Germans to the Incident.'

How far, the Russians had wanted to know, did the mutiny reflect a wider discontent on the part of the Japanese people as a whole? What were the political and economic aims of the mutineers? Would the result of the Incident be to weaken the power and authority of the Japanese Army? What, above all, would be its effect on Japanese foreign policy? Would it make Japan more anti-Soviet or less?

In his report Sorge, having duly stressed the social and economic origins of the mutiny (which were bound to make welcome reading in Moscow), went on to say that there were two ways in which the Japanese Government could react to the Incident. They could either introduce far-reaching social reforms and at the same time impose strict discipline on the Army. Or, to keep everyone happy, they could simply adopt a policy of what he called 'permanent expansion' (deriving the phrase from Trotski's doctrine of 'permanent revolution'). This, in the light of historical precedents, seemed to him the more probable outcome.

From the Soviet point of view, the next question to be answered was even more important: in which direction would the Japanese seek to expand and at whose expense? And to this his answer was: China. An answer which would be received with relief in Moscow and which, as things turned out, was also to prove correct.

Given his penetrating intelligence and powers of assimilation, there can be no doubt that Sorge's understanding of the Japanese mentality and already profound knowledge of Japanese history, as well as the up-to-date information supplied to him by Ozaki and Miyagi, by now enabled him to analyze and interpret current events with exceptional authority. 'Japan's foreign policy problems,' he wrote. 'could be easily evaluated if one had a knowledge of ancient history.' For him it was not just a question of picking up chance information and passing it on. What he aimed at producing (and did produce) was a scholarly and perceptive interpretation of a constantly shifting and developing situation. 'It has,' he wrote rather engagingly some years later, 'been my personal desire and delight to learn something about the places in which I have found myself, particularly Japan and China. Nor have I ever regarded such study simply as a means to an end. Had I lived under peaceful social conditions and in a period of peaceful political development, I should perhaps have been a scholar – certainly not a spy.'

Richard Sorge's able interpretation of the February Incident did much for his reputation. Soon after he was taken on as a regular contributor by the *Frankfurter Zeitung*, while his views carried more weight than ever with the German Embassy, where a room was put at his disposal as what he called 'unofficial secretary to the Military Attaché' – a facility, incidentally, which made it far easier for him to photograph any official documents he was given to look at. Yet another indication of his standing with the German colony in Tokyo was an invitation which he received to become leader of the local branch of the Nazi Party – an invitation which he declined, but which drew from Colonel Ott, whom he had duly consulted, the rather off-beat comment that perhaps he should after all have accepted the invitation so that the Nazi Party might have at least one sensible Führer.

Meanwhile there were signs of a major new development in Japanese and indeed in German foreign policy. Not long after the February Incident, Colonel Ott told Sorge in the strictest confidence that he and Herr von Dirksen had got wind, not from Berlin, but from contacts of theirs in the Japanese General Staff that German–Japanese negotiations of some kind were in progress in Berlin. These it appeared were being conducted, not through the Wilhelmstrasse, but privately by Ribbentrop (not yet Foreign Secretary), General Oshima, Ott's opposite number in Berlin, and Admiral Canaris, the Head of German Military Intelligence. In order to keep the news secret even from the Embassy staff, Ott now enlisted Sorge's help in encoding a telegram to Berlin asking for more information (only to be referred, for his pains, to the Japanese General Staff). This information, so secret that it could scarcely be imparted to anyone in Tokyo or Berlin, was naturally of the very greatest interest to Moscow, on the lookout for any suggestion of warlike moves on the part of the Japanese.

In the spring of 1936 Sorge was to learn more on the same subject from a certain Dr Hack, a German businessman, who came to Tokyo as a kind of unofficial go-between for Ribbentrop and Canaris with the Japanese. In telling him of the negotiations, Hack went out of his way to impress on Sorge the need for extreme secrecy. It was known, he said, that Soviet agents in Berlin had actually been keeping a watch on the houses of Ribbentrop, General Oshima and Canaris. It was because of this, he explained to Sorge, that he himself had been chosen as an intermediary and sent out to

Tokyo. Strangely enough, when, not long after his conversation with Dr Sorge, Dr Hack returned to Berlin, he, in his turn, was duly placed under Soviet surveillance. 'One should,' was Sorge's ironical comment, 'carefully refrain from careless talk and not reveal secrets to any outsider, even one's most trusted friends.'

Six months or so later in November 1936, after further negotiations through more orthodox channels, the Anti-Comintern Pact was signed between Germany and Japan. Although it contained secret clauses pledging mutual consultation (but nothing else) in the event of a Soviet attack on either country, the pact was mainly a propaganda exercise to which the Russians duly responded with counter-blasts from their own propaganda machine.

More to the point were two despatches sent to Berlin by Ott and Dirksen respectively, stressing Japanese lack of preparation for war against the Soviet Union and the lack of enthusiasm for such a war among leading personalities in Japan. Both despatches were, as it happened, shown by their respective authors to Dr Sorge who, having duly perused them, forwarded a photocopy of each to Moscow.

As Sorge had predicted in the long report he sent to Moscow in April 1936, Japan's policy of permanent expansion was to carry her, not northwards into Siberia, but southwards into China. On 7 July 1937 a clash between Japanese and Chinese troops near the Marco Polo Bridge outside Peking marked the beginning of a war (cheerfully referred to by the Japanese as the China Incident) which was to last without interruption until August 1945, effectively uniting the various hitherto dissenting factions in China in their common resistance to Japanese aggression.

Both Dirksen and Ott (now promoted to Major-General) were convinced that the Japanese would soon attain their objectives and that hostilities would quickly be over. Sorge, on the other hand, with his knowledge of China, correctly foresaw a long drawn-out struggle. Once again he was proved right and, as he himself put it, 'my stock in the Embassy rose accordingly'.

In forming his estimate of events in China, Sorge naturally depended to a considerable extent on the views of Ozaki Hotsumi and on the information which he provided. Asked later what qualities made a good spy, Ozaki replied that in his opinion 'the greatest secret of success is to win the trust of others as a human being and to create situations in which one obtains information naturally. Closely connected with this is preparing oneself by exhaustive study and experience to become a source of information and sound judgement.'

The description exactly fitted Ozaki himself. In the course of 1936, Ozaki's stature had increased considerably. That summer he had, as an authority on China, been a member of the Japanese delegation to the conference held by the Institute of Pacific Relations at Yosemite in California. On this occasion he had made friends with the secretary to the delegation, Saionji Kinkazu, grandson of the greatly revered Prince Saionji and a former undergraduate of New College, Oxford, and with Ushiba Tomohiko, a former schoolfriend of his, also attached to the delegation. Both young men belonged to the entourage of Prince Konoye, a widely respected liberal statesman who in June 1937 was to become prime minister. Yet another link with Prince Konoye was through Kazami Akira, his Chef de Cabinet, whom Ozaki had met through his membership of the Showa Research Department, a body founded in 1936 by supporters of Prince Konoye for the study of current political problems from a liberal point of view. Kazami who was in due course to invite Ozaki to become a temporary Cabinet consultant, was soon seeing him almost daily and gave him free access to all his confidential papers. All the information he acquired in this way he at once passed on to Sorge.

Scarcely less important was Ozaki's membership of the Breakfast Club, founded in November 1937 by some of Prince Konoye's younger supporters as a kind of 'kitchen cabinet' at which questions of policy could be freely and informally discussed and the results transmitted to Konoye. This gave him automatic access to much secret information and frequent opportunities to exert an influence on government policy.

Hitherto throughout their association, Ozaki had always thought of Sorge as 'Johnson'. In September 1936, however, the two met entirely by chance at a tea party in honour of the Japanese delegates to the Yosemite Conference. It was only then, after they had been formally introduced to each other, that he discovered that his old friend Johnson's real name was Sorge.

Miyagi Yotoku was by now also making himself extremely useful assembling material and compiling lengthy reports on a variety of subjects.

A new recruit to Sorge's circle at about this time, though not to his spy-ring (we know his views on women spies), was a pretty young Japanese girl called Miyake Hanako. He had first met her immediately after his return from Moscow on 4 October 1935 at the Rheingold, where he was celebrating his fortieth birthday and where she was employed as a waitress. It was not until a good many months later, after a prolonged and persistent courtship, that she finally became his mistress. From the end of 1936 or beginning of 1937 Hanakosan was to spend a large part of every week at his house in the Azabu and they would also take holidays together at Atami, a seaside resort with hot springs to the south-west of Tokyo. Having left the Rheingold in the early summer of 1937, she occupied herself with the study of music and with learning German. Though she had an idea that her lover had a second occupation besides journalism, it never occurred to her that he was a Soviet agent. As for his occasional affairs with other women, she took these as a matter of course. 'Isn't it natural,' she said later, 'for a famous man to have several mistresses?' But whatever his true feelings towards her may have been, she found him invariably gentle, considerate and generous in his treatment of her, and she was utterly devoted to him.

Towards the end of April 1938 an event occurred which still further strengthened Dr Sorge's position. Dr von Dirksen left Tokyo on his appointment to London and Major-General Ott was appointed German Ambassador in his place. In the years since 1933 what one can only describe as a close friendship had grown up between Richard Sorge and Eugen Ott. It was the kind of relationship which springs up naturally between men of similar background and similar tastes and interests in the narrow little world of foreign diplomats and newspaper correspondents in a place as remote and as exotic as Tokyo. For five years now Sorge and Ott had dined together, talked politics together, exchanged books and ideas, played chess together at weekends and travelled together as far afield as Manchukno and with the Otts Sorge had enjoyed the pleasures of that temporary and vicarious domesticity, which even the most confirmed bachelor occasionally likes to savour. It was the kind of relationship which would naturally in no way be affected by a sudden change in the official status of one or other of the men concerned. The only difference was that instead of being the constant guest and confidant of the German Military Attaché, Dr Sorge was henceforth the constant guest and confidant of the German Ambassador. It was an agreeable relationship which had grown up quite naturally between the two men and which had a number of practical advantages for both – for Sorge the added advantage that in cultivating it, he was carrying out in exemplary fashion the express instructions of the Fourth Bureau.

In May 1938 not long after the new Ambassador's appointment, Dr Sorge found it necessary to visit Hong Kong – for the purpose of delivering a batch of secret material to a fellow Soviet agent whom he was to meet there. At the same time he also acted as a courier for the Embassy, carrying a diplomatic bag with him at General Ott's request – 'a double courier', he called himself with his usual rather sardonic sense of humour.

On his return from Hong Kong, Sorge went to the Rheingold with Prince Albert von Urach to celebrate. When the bar closed at two in the morning, he rode to the Imperial Hotel at high speed on his motor-bicycle with Urach on the pillion. At the Imperial they found a friend with plenty to drink in his bedroom. An hour or two later, having drunk an entire bottle of whisky single-handed, Sorge decided to call it a day and set out for home, this time leaving Urach behind. Suddenly accelerating up a narrow lane near the American Embassy, he lost control of his bicycle and crashed head-first into the Embassy wall.

Drunk and badly injured though he was, Sorge behaved with exemplary presence of mind. The police on duty outside the American Embassy had heard the crash and on his behalf summoned Urach from the Imperial Hotel. To Urach Sorge, who could scarcely speak, whispered, 'Tell Klausen to come at once.' As soon as Klausen arrived. Sorge handed him the secret reports and wad of United States currency which he was carrying in his pocket and which, had they fallen into the wrong hands, would have given the whole thing away. After which, having until then by a superhuman effort somehow retained his senses, he fainted.

Leaving Sorge in hospital, Max Klausen next went to 30 Nagasaka-cho and took away with him everything he could find there that related to their clandestine activities. Not long after Herr Weise, the correspondent of the *Deutsche Nachrichten Büro*, arrived to put seals on everything in the house. 'I shuddered,' said Max afterwards, 'when I thought of how our secret work would have been exposed if Weise had arrived there before me.'

His accident was to leave Sorge with permanent scars which gave his face the look of a Japanese mask – 'an almost demoniacal expression', said one acquaintance. When he came out of hospital, the Ambassador and Ambassadress kindly had him to stay with them until he was quite well again.

Sorge had scarcely recovered from the effects of his crash when a fresh sensation came to flutter the diplomatic dovecotes of Tokyo. In June 1938 General Lyushkov, a senior officer of the green-capped NKVD Frontier Forces guarding the Soviet border with Manchuria, crossed the frontier and gave himself up to the Japanese, bringing with him full details of the Soviet frontier defences, military dispositions and order of battle in Siberia and the Far Eastern Maritime Province. He was also, as his Japanese interrogators soon discovered, prepared to discuss at length the current purge and other connected internal developments in the Soviet Far East and elsewhere, which had no doubt been one of the reasons for his own defection.

Lyushkov, presumably, had not been in the confidence of the Fourth Bureau. Otherwise his defection might have had awkward consequences for Sorge. That, at any rate, was something to be thankful for. By this time the Japanese had passed to the German Embassy full particulars of what Lyushkov had had to say. Sorge's new friend Colonel Scholl, now acting Military Attaché, had shown these to Sorge, who had in turn transmitted a summary of them over Max Klausen's transmitter to the Fourth Bureau, who had maintained a stony silence about the whole distasteful episode.

Meanwhile the German Military Intelligence Service under Admiral Canaris, quickly grasping General Lyushkov's potentialities, had hurriedly sent an expert out to Tokyo to interrogate him in depth on their own behalf. The result was a detailed report some hundred pages in length which Scholl most obligingly lent to Sorge. This he photographed, at the same time asking Moscow by signal whether they would be interested in seeing an actual photostat of the report. His somewhat mischievous enquiry finally stirred the Fourth Bureau out of their sullen, scared silence. 'Do everything possible and use every available means,' they signalled on 5 September, 'to get copies of documents received personally by envoy from Lyushkov. Report at once all such documents obtained.' At last, even in the atmosphere of blind terror prevailing in Moscow that autumn, they had come to realize just what was at stake.

Quite apart from the military secrets he had revealed (and they were of the greatest interest), Lyushkov's description of the state of morale in the Red Army and in the country as a whole following the most recent Soviet purges and his accounts of a strong opposition group in Siberia gave the clear impression that the Soviet Union was in such a state of turmoil and disarray as to have no hope of withstanding a Japanese or indeed any other attack. This of course was precisely what a good number of people in Germany and Japan wanted to hear and would inevitably much increase the likelihood of war. Sorge himself put it in a nutshell: 'One consequence of Lyushkov's report was a danger of joint Japanese–German military action against the Soviet Union.' He could only hope that the recipients of his reports would know what conclusions to draw from the material he sent them.[*]

Meanwhile in discussing the defection with the Germans, Sorge was doing what he could to play down the importance of Lyushkov's revelations: 'It was dangerous to judge Russia's internal situation from statements made by a man like this. Lyushkov's remarks, I said, were just the kind of thing one found in anti-Nazi books written by German refugees. These often suggested that the Nazi regime faced imminent collapse.'

Just what value the Japanese and Germans placed on Lyushkov's disclosures is uncertain. It seems probable, however, that the serious clash between the Japanese and Russians which occurred at Changkufeng, southwest of Vladivostok in July 1938 and the even heavier fighting which broke out a year later at Nomonhan on the frontier between Manchuria and Outer Mongolia were deliberate trials of strength by the Japanese, to enable them to judge for themselves just how strong the Russians were. In any event

---

[*] That it did not cause them to put an immediate end to the purge is evident from the liquidation that summer of Marshal Vasili K. Blyukher, the Soviet Commander in Chief in the Far East, shot a full year after his fellow-Marshals, possibly as a result of some disclosure of Lyushkov's or possibly just because Stalin thought it advisable. Like so many of the *Vozhd's* victims, Marshal Blyukher, who for some years played an important part in the Far East, has since been posthumously rehabilitated.

the Japanese came off worse on both occasions, which presumably cooled their ardour; and Sorge, who at the same time was telling Moscow that there was no danger of the incidents escalating into a full-scale war, made the most of this in talking to General Ott: 'I pointed out that statements by Lyushkov and others about the supposed weakness of the Red Army were now exposed as lies ... Germany ought to study the whole Nomonhan Incident more deeply and should reject the old idea that the Red Army was incapable of putting up serious resistance.'

'I suppose,' said Sorge with a touch of irony as he looked back a good deal later, 'that Germany accepted Lyushkov's ideas rather than my own.' It is also not clear whether the Russians got as much out of his reports as they ought to have done. Certainly the information they contained should have been of the very greatest value, notably the Japanese estimate of Soviet frontier defences in the Far East.

It would have been very strange if the Soviet–German Pact of August 1939 had struck Richard Sorge as being in any way surprising or incongruous. He was too realistic, too experienced and too dedicated an *apparatchik* for that and by now knew instinctively that what mattered in the ultimate analysis was not this or that ideological attitude or gesture, but the supreme, overriding interest of the Soviet Union, the Country of the Revolution.

As it happened, he himself had been directly involved in the manoeuvring for position which had preceded the conclusion of the pact. During the spring and summer of 1939 one of his principal tasks had been to follow as closely as he could the course of the current German–Japanese negotiations for a political and military alliance primarily directed against Great Britain. He was also aware that simultaneously Germany was making top-secret approaches to the Soviet Union. Indeed Ott had hinted to him that 'this approach could lead, not merely to a neutrality pact, but also to a German–Soviet military alliance.'

Through Sorge, who was kept regularly informed by Ott, the Russians had followed the course of the German-Japanese negotiations with some anxiety. Their fear had been that the proposed alliance might turn out to be directed against the Soviet Union. But on this score Sorge was able to set their minds at rest with the information that the enemy envisaged was not the Soviet Union, but Great Britain. It was thus that, when the Germans realized that their negotiations with the Japanese were not going to produce the desired result and turned instead to Russia, they found the Russians entirely reassured and ready and willing to negotiate.

The signature of the Soviet–German Pact made war in Europe certain. It was a war in which Stalin, having taken immediate delivery of numerous assured benefits, hoped in the long run to play the part of *Tertius gaudens.* His mistake, in the circumstances, was understandable.

Once the first shots had been fired, the Fourth Bureau was keener than ever to be kept regularly informed of Japanese intentions. The unfortunate Sorge, who for months and years had been regaling them with a series of unparalleled scoops, was now bombarded with querulous requests for more and better and earlier information. 'Your information,' signalled General Uritski on 1 September, 'has gradually deteriorated . . . My dear Ramsay, I call on you once again to change your method of collecting information . . . Thus and only thus will your residence in Japan be of any value to our work. Director.'

Sorge was continuing to do his best. The Wilhelmstrasse now wanted Ott to take him on as a senior member of the Embassy staff in charge of information and the press. But he declined the offer, feeling that 'official duties would interfere with my work for Moscow' and also preferring not to have his early life examined in too great detail as might have happened had he accepted. Instead, once war had broken out, he took on the task of editing the Embassy's daily news bulletin and for this purpose was allocated a small office of his own in the Embassy. Meanwhile his relations with General Ott and with the senior members of his staff remained as intimate as ever, the Ambassador even showing him his telegrams and despatches in draft and asking him for his views before sending them off. Of particular value to the Embassy, in Ott's opinion, was Sorge's close connection via Ozaki with the entourage of Prince Konoye and also his specialized knowledge of Soviet affairs (acquired, it was assumed, at second hand).

Henceforward the Embassy's main task was to bring Japan into the war against Great Britain, beginning as soon as possible with an all-out assault on Singapore. The closest study was accordingly now devoted to the military capacity and political influence of the Japanese Army in a series of regular discussions in which Sorge usually took part and the conclusions of which he regularly reported to Moscow. Meanwhile the Japanese continued to hang back.

The appointment of Matsuoka as Foreign Minister in Prince Konoye's second cabinet in July 1940 and the signature not long after of a Tripartite Pact with Germany and Italy marked for Japan a move in the direction of a formal alliance against Great Britain, but not against the Soviet Union. In March 1941 at the invitation of Ribbentrop, who since 1938 had been Hitler's Minister for Foreign Affairs, Matsuoka set out for Berlin. He was followed a few days later by General Ott.

By his friend Saionji, who himself accompanied Matsuoka to Europe, Ozaki Hotsumi and, through him, Sorge were at all stages kept fully informed of the purpose, scope and outcome of his mission. Matsuoka's instructions were to listen to what was said to him in Germany and Italy, which he would also visit, but undertake no further commitments on behalf of Japan. On his way back he was to stop off in Moscow and see what could be done to improve Japan's relations with the Soviet Union.

In Berlin and Rome Matsuoka kept strictly to his brief and gave no further undertakings in regard to Singapore or anything else. 'What about Singapore?' Ozaki asked Prince Konoye. 'That,' replied the Prime Minister, 'was Ott's one-man play.' In Moscow, on the other hand, Matsuoka's talks went better than had been expected. Stalin, it appeared, was expecting neither a break with Germany nor any trouble from Japan and on 13 April Matsuoka signed a neutrality pact between Japan and the Soviet Union which he and Molotov had drafted in twenty-four hours and which satisfactorily disposed of a number of frontier problems and other outstanding questions between the two countries. Although Matsuoka seems to have made reassuring noises to General Ott, there can be no doubt that his deal with the Russians came as an unpleasant surprise to the Germans, by now already secretly contemplating an attack on the Soviet Union.

All of which Sorge, kept regularly *au courant* by both Germans and Japanese, reported faithfully to Moscow. Meanwhile Moscow, only partly reassured by the neutrality pact, continued to press for details of Japan's military preparations in the north. For Sorge, helped by Ozaki who since August 1939 had been employed as a consultant by the powerful South Manchurian Railway and by Miyagi, his principal task now became the production of a chart giving in as great detail as possible the Japanese order of battle in Manchuria with the number of divisions, their locations and the names of the divisional commanders. 'Eventually,' said Sorge afterwards, 'we came near to a perfect order of battle, based on the situation in May and June 1941. I photographed it and sent it to Moscow. This chart was the best thing our group produced. I do not think it would have been possible to produce a better one. The Moscow Centre appeared to be satisfied with it,' he added. 'No further instructions on the subject were sent to us.'

In May 1941 General Ott, requiring an informed first-hand account of the attitude of the Japanese military and other authorities in China to a recent Americn offer of mediation with China, decided to send Sorge to Shanghai as an Embassy courier to see what he could find out. His mission proved a useful one. He talked to a number of influential Japanese whom he found ninety per cent against the idea of American mediation and duly reported his conclusions to Ott, who passed them on as they stood to the Wilhelmstrasse, while he for his part transmitted them in similar terms to Moscow.

But by now Richard Sorge had other and more serious preoccupations. Since April, couriers carrying the diplomatic bag to Tokyo from Berlin had been speaking of German troop movements in the general direction of the Soviet frontier. Later Colonel Kretschmer, the new Military Attaché, told Sorge straight out that Germany was massing her forces on the Soviet border and that whether war followed would depend solely on Hitler's whim. Anxiously discussing this news with Ozaki, who gave it as his view that rather than fight, the Soviet Union should if necessary let Hitler have all the oil and grain he wanted, Sorge declared that Stalin would in fact make almost any concessions in order to avoid war. The danger, frankly, lay in a surprise attack, which would leave no opportunity for appeasement.

In May the argument was settled once and for all by a special envoy from the Ministry of War, Colonel Ritter von Niedermayer, who arrived in Tokyo bringing a letter of introduction to Sorge from Dr von Dirksen, the former Ambassador, and the news that Hitler had now definitely decided to attack the Soviet Union. He was followed shortly after by another emissary from Berlin, Sorge's old friend and former comrade Colonel Scholl, bearing top-secret instructions for the Ambassador. From Scholl Sorge learned beyond all doubt that the attack would begin, without any declaration of war, on 20 June or possibly two or three days later and that 170–190 German divisions were now massed ready on the frontier. It was confidently expected in Berlin that the Red Army would give in and the Soviet regime collapse within two months.

Ever since the beginning of March Sorge had been passing on to Moscow by wireless and by secret courier the increasingly detailed information he was receiving on this subject. On 15 May, more than a month before the attack was launched he was able to send a signal giving its exact date: 22 June. Long afterwards Max Klausen was to describe the scene. 'Every hour,' he wrote, 'we were waiting for further information, for confirmation and above all for news of the diplomatic and military reactions of the Soviet Government. We fully understood the importance of the message we had sent. And yet we never got an answer. When the war actually started, Richard was furious. 'Why,' he asked in a dazed kind of way, 'has Stalin not reacted?'

This is a question which historians and others have been asking ever since and which has still not been entirely elucidated. Stalin had received the same information from the British Government, as well as from several other sources, but had apparently preferred to ignore it. Indeed, it seems clear that when the German attack actually materialized, it came as a considerable shock to him. Possibly he suspected that the information had been deliberately planted on him from some ulterior motive. Or possibly he could not bring himself to believe that after two years of friendly cooperation, Hitler was about to double-cross him. For the ordinary person it is not easy to fathom the workings of such an exceptionally devious and by then to some extent unbalanced mind.

To Richard Sorge, although he was clearly prepared for it, the news of the German attack on the Soviet Union, the Country of the Revolution, came as a sad blow. Hanako-san, who had been his constant companion for five or six years, had never seen him so deeply disturbed. That day he wept as though his heart would break.

'Why are you so upset?' she asked.

'Because I am lonely. I have no real friends.'

'But surely you have Ambassador Ott and other good German friends?'

'No, No. They are not my real friends.'

Thus, for a moment, we are vouchsafed a rare glimpse of the unbearable loneliness, the desperate frustrations of even the best and most dedicated of spies.

But however saddened and frustrated, Richard Sorge did not allow his feelings to interfere with his work. Within twenty-four hours he had despatched a signal to Moscow, informing the Fourth Bureau of what was being said at the German Embassy, where the chief topic of conversation was how soon Japan could be brought into the war against Russia. Perhaps the most perceptive comment had been that made by that simple sailor, Captain (now Admiral) Wenneker, namely that Japan would never attack the Soviet Union. For that the interest of the Japanese Navy lay too firmly in the south.

For the Russians, meanwhile, fully extended as they were in the west, the question of if and when the Japanese would attack them had become literally a matter of life or death. It was to the task of answering this question, already the subject of numerous anxious inquiries from Moscow, that all the energies of the spy-ring were henceforth directed.

During the months that followed Hitler's attack on the Soviet Union the information reaching Dr Sorge from different sources was often contradictory or inconclusive. Though some Japanese shared the German view that a rapid defeat of the Red Army would be followed by the early collapse of the Stalin regime, others did not and the general feeling seemed to be that there were strong arguments in favour of playing a waiting game, at any rate for the time being, especially as there was still no means of knowing how things would go with the United States. Thus Ozaki, on the strength of what he had heard from Prince Konoye and his entourage, 'told Sorge soon after the German attack on the Soviet Union that Japan had no intention of attacking Russia. Konoye had said that Japan had its hands full with the China Incident. Since he did not know how negotiations with America would turn out, he did not want a war with Russia.' As for the German service attachés, they were already busy drawing up plans for a Japanese attack on Vladivostok, only to be told rather dishearteningly that it would take the Japanese Army at least two months to mobilize and that they would certainly make no move until the Germans had taken Moscow and reached the Volga.

On 2 July 1941 an Imperial conference was held which was attended by the Emperor in person and at which an overall review of Japanese policy was undertaken and a number of decisions arrived at. According to Ozaki, it was decided that Japan would continue to try for a satisfactory solution of the China Incident, but would at the same time prepare for any emergency in the north or south by carrying out a general mobilization, so as to make possible the despatch of troops in either direction. Meanwhile Japan would remain neutral towards both Russia and Germany. From an account of the conference given him by Matsuoka, General Ott, on the other hand, had derived the impression that Japan's real intention was to mobilize in the north and attack Siberia, while maintaining a holding position in the south. Comparing the two, Sorge preferred Ozaki's version and reported in this sense to Moscow.

Clearly the ultimate answer to the conundrum would lie in a careful analysis and interpretation of the Japanese Army's mobilization plans and it was on this that Sorge and his Japanese associates continued to concentrate. But again the available evidence was not immediately conclusive. What did become clear at once was that mobilization was 'on a very large scale indeed', so large as to surprise Prince Konoye himself. In fact according to Ozaki's friend Kazami, who after being Secretary to the Cabinet had become Minister of Justice, and whom Ozaki had encountered at an eel-party, it affected no less than five million men and a million tons of merchant shipping were being requisitioned to move them. The question was: were they being sent north or south? There were stories of winter clothing being issued to some and tropical clothing and ice-boxes to others.

Meanwhile the Japanese decision to advance into French Indo-China on 24 July and the consequent American and British economic blockade of Japan had led to a sharp deterioration in Japanese–American relations, rendering any prospect of an agreement between the two countries over China less likely than ever. Though Prince Konoye himself was anxious to reach agreement with the Americans, who were pressing for a Japanese withdrawal from Central and Southern China, the Army and Navy took quite a different view and public opinion on the whole was on the side of the Army and Navy. If they had their way, it would be war. And as the likelihood of war with America increased, so the danger of a Japanese attack on the Soviet Union grew less.

Nor were the Germans making quite such rapid progress in Russia as they had expected to. 'The fact that Moscow was not captured last Sunday,' Sorge signalled in early August, 'as promised to Oshima by the highest German authorities, has tended to cool Japanese enthusiasm.' Even General Ott and his staff, under constant pressure from Berlin to produce results, now reluctantly accepted the view that Japan had no immediate intention of coming to Germany's help against Russia. In mid-August came the significant news that only a relatively small proportion of the troops mobilized – some fifteen divisions in all – were being sent north to Manchuria.

Towards the end of August a conference was held by the Japanese High Command to consider the question of war with the Soviet Union. With the help of Ozaki, it did not take Sorge long to find out what decisions had been reached. 'The conference,' he signalled to Moscow, 'decided not to declare war this year against the Soviet Union.' And he went on to say that only in the event of a complete Soviet collapse in Siberia would this decision be reconsidered. Not long after this he was able to report that even General Ott had finally abandoned all hope of a Japanese attack in 1941.

Early in October, after much discussion with Ozaki, Sorge sent off a signal summing up his general conclusions. The first of these was that the state of Japanese–American relations made it safe to assume that there would be war between the two countries 'this month or next month'.* The second that, before even thinking of war against Russia, Japan would quite certainly 'bide her time until next spring'. 'In any event,' he added, 'the American issue and the question of the advance to the south are far more important than the northern problem.' This was as it happened, the last report he ever sent to Moscow.

Over the past six years, but more especially during the past six months, Richard Sorge and his associates had striven unremittingly under perilous conditions and at high pressure to fulfil the tasks allotted to them by the Fourth Bureau. These, it could be said, they had now fulfilled in the most brilliant fashion. They had warned Moscow well in advance of Hitler's impending attack. They had by a remarkable exercise in combined military and political intelligence been able to say with confidence that the Soviet Union need not fear a Japanese attack before the spring of 1942, if then, thereby enabling the Red Army to move more divisions to the German front. They had, to all intents and purposes, foreseen the Japanese attack on Pearl Harbour and the consequent shift southwards of the Japanese war effort.

Whether or not Moscow ever put all this valuable information to good effect is uncertain. According to one account it was filed under the heading

* The Japanese attack on Pearl Harbour took place on 8 December 1941.

164

'Doubtful and Misleading Information'. Certainly there is no indication that Stalin made any particular use of the warnings he was given that Hitler was about to attack him. It is true that a number of Soviet divisions were in the course of 1941 moved westwards from the Far East and Siberia, but whether or not this was on the strength of Sorge's reports, is hard to say. To have his reports ignored or at any rate to get no credit for them is one of the many occupational hazards and frustrations of the spy. As for the other hazards, Richard Sorge was soon to have his full share of those as well.

On 28 September 1941 during a routine investigation of the illegal Japanese Communist Party's not unimportant link with America and more especially with the Japanese section of the American Communist Party, the Japanese police arrested a certain Kitabayashi Tomo, an obscure elderly seamstress then living quietly with her husband in the country in Wakyama Prefecture. Fourteen years before this, in 1927, Mrs Kitabayashi had been living in Los Angeles, where she and her husband occasionally let lodgings to young Japanese, some of them with left-wing views. One of these had been Miyagi Yotoku, then twenty-four, who had moved into her house with the Japanese girl with whom he was then living and four years after that had joined the American Communist Party. Since then Mrs Kitabayashi, who had returned to Japan in 1936, had not seen Miyagi more than a dozen times, but on being hauled off to Tokyo and vigorously interrogated about her contacts in California, she had wrongly assumed that he too must already have been arrested and had unwittingly mentioned his name.

A fortnight later on 11 October the police, continuing their pursuit of suspected Communists and possible links with the American Communist Party, arrested Miyagi Yotoku at his house, which they then proceeded to search. In the course of their search they came on a confidential memorandum from the offices of the South Manchurian Railway by which Ozaki Hotsumi was employed as a senior consultant. It seemed strange that a painter should be in possession of a document of this kind. They continued to interrogate him. Despite severe interrogation, Miyagi refused to admit that he was a spy. But he was in poor health and there was a limit to what he could endure. Picking his opportunity, he threw himself out of a second-floor window. As it happened, there was a tree immediately below it and he merely broke a leg. Next day, after further questioning, he made 'a voluntary statement', admitting that he belonged to a spy-ring comprising Sorge, Vukelić, Klausen, Ozaki and Kawai.

Realizing that they were on to something big, the police referred the case to the Foreign Section of the Tokko or Special Higher Police who, having explained Sorge's connection with the German Ambassador, gave it as their view that he could not be a Soviet spy and pointed out that his arrest would be bound to harm German–Japanese relations. It was accordingly decided for the time being to arrest only the Japanese.

Ozaki was accordingly arrested on the morning of 15 October. By that evening he had made a statement confirming what Miyagi had already said. It was now abundantly clear that both were part of a Soviet spy-ring controlled by Sorge. After they had both been further interrogated, authority was now granted to arrest Sorge.

On the evening of 14 October, Sorge had arranged to meet Ozaki at a restaurant, but he had failed to appear. Two days later on 16 October, Miyagi had been due to come to see him at his house, but had in his turn failed to keep the appointment. On 17 October at about seven in the evening, Klausen and Vukelić called by arrangement at Sorge's house. Sorge was in bed. They opened a bottle of saké. Vukelić had rung up Ozaki's office at the South Manchurian Railway, but had obtained no answer. The atmosphere was tense. 'Neither Joe nor Otto showed up to meet us,' said Sorge heavily, using their code names. 'They must have been arrested by the police.' Not long after they dispersed, feeling deeply uneasy.*

At five o'clock next morning, Saturday 18 October, Detective Ohasi of the Tokko or Special Higher Police, looking out from the near-by police station could see a German Embassy car standing outside Sorge's house a couple of hundred yards away. Wishing to avoid unnecessary embarrassment, he waited until it drove away. Then, accompanied by Yoshikawa Mitsusada, the procurator in charge of the case, and several of his colleagues, he burst into the little house shouting to Sorge as he did so: 'We have come to see you about your recent motor-cycle accident.' Sorge, protesting that his arrest was contrary to the law, was then pushed into a police car in his pyjamas and driven first to the police station and then almost immediately to Sugamo Remand Prison. Simultaneously both Klausen and Vukelić were also picked up.

In spite of their forebodings, none of the three had taken any steps to get rid of such incriminating evidence as they had in their houses, all of which now fell into the hands of the police. Klausen in particular, whose morale was low, had been behindhand with his wireless transmissions and at the time of his arrest no less than ten uncoded messages were found on his desk. In one signal, drafted a couple of days before on 15 October but left unsent, Sorge had inquired of Moscow whether, as there was no longer anything worthwhile for them to do in Japan, he and Klausen could not now 'return home or go to Germany to embark on new activities'. Asked later whether this was because he had sensed the approach of danger, 'Not particularly,' he replied. 'It was rather because I had completed my task in

* For the first time Klausen now realized that 'Joe' and 'Otto', who figured so frequently in the telegrams he sent, were in fact Miyagi and Ozaki.

Japan and wanted to continue my work in Moscow or Europe. When I speak of my task having been completed,' he added, 'I mean that I had confirmed that Japan would not enter the war against the Soviet Union.'

The news of Richard Sorge's arrest, at first in the form of vague, then of less vague, rumours, came as a complete bombshell to the German Embassy and not least to General Ott, whose friend he had been for the past eight years. When as a result of pressing inquiries, the Japanese Foreign Ministry finally spoke of 'treasonable connections', they were even more dumbfounded. In a telegram to the Wilhelmstrasse, where his own close relationship with Sorge was well known, Ott suggested that he might have been the victim of some anti-German intrigue on the part of ill-disposed Japanese politicians who resented his intimate knowledge of their affairs. Meanwhile a hint from the Japanese Ambassador in Berlin, General Oshima, that Sorge might have had Communist connections provoked universal disbelief. It was not for more than a month that the truth of the matter seems finally to have dawned on the Germans.

For the first few days after his arrest, Sorge resolutely refused to admit that he had been working for the Russians. He had, he agreed, been collecting secret information, but for his friend General Ott, whom he absolutely insisted on seeing and who by now was insisting on seeing him.

The judicial authorities, for their part, would sooner have prevented General Ott from seeing Sorge, at any rate until the latter had made a full confession. But General Tojo, who had succeeded Prince Konoye as Prime Minister a few days earlier and was bound to take account of diplomatic considerations, did not feel able to resist the Ambassador's insistent requests for an interview and in the end permission was given, 'as a special and unique favour', for Ott to pay Sorge a purely formal visit in the presence of the procurator and lasting for only a few minutes. During it there was to be no reference to the case under investigation.

Ott's visit, undertaken no doubt with grim forebodings, seems to have taken place on 23 October or possibly earlier. What is not entirely clear from the evidence available is whether it took place before or after Sorge had confessed to being a Communist, which he did at about this time.

According to Yoshikawa, the procurator in charge who was present on both occasions, Sorge had already confessed when he saw the Ambassador. What, after prolonged and intensive interrogation, had finally broken down his resistance was the fact of being confronted with statements from Klausen and the others, admitting everything. He must also have been uncomfortably aware of the undeniable evidence of their guilt lying in all three houses, waiting to be found. Finally Yoshikawa had put the question to him as a moral problem. 'What about your obligations as a human being?' he had asked him, as he might have asked a fellow Japanese. 'Your followers, who have risked their lives to work with you, have confessed . . . are you, as their leader, going to abandon them to their fate?' Whereupon Sorge, calling all at once for paper and a pencil, had written in German: 'I have been an International Communist since 1925.' After which, screwing the paper up and throwing it across the room, he had started striding up and down. Then, suddenly bursting into tears, 'I am defeated,' he said. 'For the first time in my life I am defeated.'

According to Yoshikawa, Sorge, having confessed, seemed reluctant to meet Ott. But Yoshikawa, knowing that they had been friends and again looking at the matter from a Japanese point of view, took it upon himself to suggest that it would be only fitting for him to see him. 'We Japanese,' he said, 'would have a last meeting as human beings, even if ideology made us enemies.' And again Sorge took his advice.

Yoshikawa, who was present and who had by now clearly established some kind of rapport with the accused, later described the encounter:

'When the meeting took place Sorge looked completely exhausted and his expression was one of extreme gravity; and as soon as Ott saw his face he appreciated at once the seriousness of the situation.

Ott said: 'Well, how are you?'

Sorge replied: 'I am well.'

Ott: 'How about the food you are getting?'

Sorge: 'It is sufficient.'

Ott: 'Is there anything you need?'

Sorge: 'No, thank you.'

'Then Sorge said: "This is our last meeting." Whereupon Ott was visibly moved. He was in uniform, and he saluted Sorge in soldierly Prussian style and then left the room.'

Having, within a week of his arrest, obtained from Sorge the admission that he was a Communist spy and not simply an over-enthusiastic German newspaper correspondent or press attaché, the next task for his interrogators was to find out as much as they could about his sponsors, his directives and his methods of operation, as well as about his relationship with the German Embassy and his Japanese political and other contacts, direct or indirect. His interrogation, by the Special Higher Police in the morning and by Procurator Yoshikawa in the afternoon and until late into the night, was to last for eighteen weeks without remission except for 8 December, the day of Japan's attack on Pearl Harbour, and New Year's Day 1942, when even the Special Higher Police allowed themselves the luxury of a holiday. After this Yoshikawa was to continue his interrogation for another three weeks, finally concluding it on 27 March 1942.

As well as answering the questions put to him, Sorge was also required to produce a written statement, part autobiography and part confession, which amounted in the end to some fifty thousand words, the length of a short book. Meanwhile the other members of his group and a number of their associates were also being subjected to a similar examination. It is ultimately on this and connected material, painstakingly amassed and sifted by intelligent, conscientious and often perceptive Japanese officials, that with obvious reservations, we rely for most of our knowledge of Richard Sorge and his career as a spy.

Towards the end of November 1941 the Japanese Foreign Ministry had passed to the German Embassy in strict confidence a memorandum prepared by the Public Prosecutor's Office, giving for the first time some account of Sorge's Communist background and work as a spy. In transmitting this information to Berlin, General Ott said that he was asking to be allowed to see the evidence on which the memorandum was based. He also suggested that steps should be taken in Germany to corroborate the Japanese allegations about Sorge's Communist past. He himself had to face the unpalatable fact that the man who for the past eight years had been one of his closest friends was in all probability a spy and a traitor.

It was not until 17 May 1942, after an advance notice had been given to General Ott, that the Japanese Ministry of Justice issued, to the consternation of Japanese public opinion, their first official announcement concerning the Sorge case. Hitherto there had only been rumours. Now came particulars of the charges together with the names of those charged who included, apart from the foreign members of the ring, not only Ozaki, generally known as an intimate of Prince Konoye, but the latter's extremely well-connected private secretary, Saionji. To many it seemed likely that the former Prime Minister himself would be arrested. To save embarrassment to the Germans, no mention was made of Sorge's membership of the Nazi Party. To avoid a direct confrontation with the Russians, for which the Japanese by now had less desire than ever, it was made to appear that Sorge had been an agent of the theoretically international Comintern, no mention being made of his connection with the Fourth Bureau of the Red Army.

The preliminary judge's examination, held *in camera*, dragged on right through the summer and autumn of 1942 and into the following winter. 'All of us,' the interpreter said afterwards, 'accuser, accused and interpreter, were very exhausted.' For Sorge came some relief from depression with the news, whispered to him by the interpreter, that at Stalingrad the battle was now going against the Germans. At about this time a fellow prisoner, watching through his peephole, saw Sorge, on the receipt of more good news from that far-distant front, literally jump for joy, wave his hat in the air and pat the warder affectionately on the back. Finally on 5 December the preliminary judge concluded his investigation and some days later announced that he had decided on a later formal trial for both Ozaki and Sorge, to be held the following spring.

Ozaki and Sorge each stood his trial separately before the Tokyo District Criminal Court, the hearings beginning in April and May respectively and lasting through August into September. The evidence brought against Sorge by the prosecution was based on his previous interrogations by the procurator and preliminary judge. He was charged with collecting information, including State secrets, and supplying it to a foreign power 'in the knowledge that it might be employed against the interests of our national defence'. The particular state secrets on which the prosecution concentrated were the decisions of the Imperial Conference of 2 July 1941 and the details of subsequent Japanese exchanges with the United States, both obtained from Ozaki and both, needless to say, possessing a direct bearing on the current internal political situation in Japan – not a very happy omen for the accused. Of Sorge's connection with the Fourth Bureau nothing was said.

Both Sorge and Ozaki had hoped to be tried under the Peace Preservation Law as members of an international Communist organization, a charge which rendered them liable to a term of imprisonment. They soon found, however, that they were to be tried under the National Security Law for the betrayal of state secrets, an offence carrying the death penalty.

In his defence Sorge did his best to show that the greater part of the material he had collected and transmitted to Moscow had not really been secret. Most of it, for example everything concerning Japanese–American relations, was a matter of common knowledge, discussed daily in the press. Indeed he himself had sent it in his own cables to the *Frankfurter Zeitung*, none of which had ever been censored. The same was true of the information he had obtained from the German Embassy, which had been given to him voluntarily. Equally Ozaki's information had come to him from his friends in the course of ordinary everyday conversation.

What he said was in many ways convincing. But it did not carry conviction with the Tokyo District Court, who on 29 September 1943 sentenced him to death. The same sentence was passed on Ozaki Hotsumi. Miyagi Yotoku, never very strong, had died in prison a few weeks previously. Of the other accused, Klausen and Vukelić were sentenced to life imprisonment, while Klausen's wife Anna, a Finn with no love whatever for Communism, received three years. As for young Saionji, the former New College undergraduate and Prime Minister's private secretary, he was given a suspended sentence of eighteen months. Both Sorge and Ozaki appealed against their sentences, but both appeals were rejected, Sorge's in January 1944 and Ozaki's in the following April. Nor as the weeks went by was there any sign that the Soviet Government were, as Sorge had half hoped they might, preparing to ransom or exchange their faithful servant.

At about ten on the morning of 7 November 1944, the twenty-seventh anniversary of the Bolshevik Revolution, the door of Sorge's cell in Sugamo Prison opened without previous warning to reveal the Prison Governor who, having formally established Sorge's identity, announced to him that he was to be executed that morning. Having bowed ceremoniously to the Governor and changed into clean clothing provided for the purpose, Sorge was handcuffed and a straw hat placed on his head. He was then escorted by the Governor and other officials across the prison yard to a tall concrete building. Here he was formally received by the prison chaplain who offered him tea and cakes and inquired as to his last wishes. On being asked whether he had anything to say, he replied: 'No, nothing else.' After this he thanked the chaplain and prison staff for their kindness. He was then escorted through an ante-room lit by the candles of a Buddhist altar, to a room beyond, where the gallows had been erected and where, barely half an hour before, his friend Ozaki had preceded him. Calmly and silently, Sorge took his place on the trap and the noose was put round his neck. At twenty minutes past ten the trap was sprung. At ten thirty-six he was pronounced dead.

Of Sorge's associates, Branko Vukelić died in prison in January 1945. Max Klausen was released in September 1945 and having been hurriedly smuggled out of Japan by the Russians, finally settled in East Germany.

In September 1945 when the war was over Hanako-san, who had herself been arrested but eventually released, began her long search for Sorge's body. In the end, after four years, she traced his grave to the corner of a dismal cemetery at Zoshigaya kept for homeless vagrants. In the coffin there was by now only a skeleton. But the size of the skull and bones showed it to be that of a foreigner. Damage to the bones of one leg corresponded to Sorge's war wounds and Hanako could also recognize the gold fillings of the teeth, from which she had a ring made. Ozaki Hotsumi's half-brother Hotsuki, who seems to have been there with her, later wrote a sentence which would have served as a fitting epitaph for Richard Sorge: 'Sorge, who grew up in a season of war and died in a season of war, carried on his bones, even in his final resting place, the marks of the battlefield.' From Zoshigaya Hanako had the coffin removed to another graveyard outside the city where it now lies beside the graves of Ozaki Hotsumi and Miyagi Yotoku.

On 5 November 1964, a couple of days before the forty-seventh anniversary of the Bolshevik Revolution and just on twenty years after Richard Sorge's execution, it was announced in Moscow that Comrade Sorge, who had never before been publicly mentioned there in this or in any other connection, had been posthumously created a Hero of the Soviet Union. At the same time a street in Moscow was called after him, his picture put on a four kopek postage stamp and a play, a book and a number of articles written about him, some of which cautiously put forward the idea that his reports had perhaps not always received the attention they deserved. As *Pravda* put it, 'only after twenty years were there favourable conditions for telling the truth about Sorge'.

Richard Sorge's generation was in many ways a tragic one, not least in Germany. At the end of his preliminary examination the Japanese Public Prosecutor's Office produced their version of his story in a memorandum which they sent to the German Embassy, containing these words: 'The accused, Richard Sorge, after experiencing the horrors of the last war, arrived at the realization that certain self-evident contradictions are inherent in the capitalist system of the present day.' This single sentence, evolved by legal luminaries possessing quite a different background and philosophy of life, in fact contained the essence of his problem. Like countless thousands of hopeful young men from a dozen other countries, he had gone, normal, conformist and full of enthusiasm, straight from school to the front, to fight for what he firmly believed to be a just and also a winning cause. After being wounded, he had gone back to the front, still no doubt moderately full of enthusiasm. Being strong and intelligent, he was a more than adequate soldier and he had gone on fighting bravely and effectively under ever nastier conditions until a second and worse wound had finally put him out of action, with an Iron Cross and the rank of Corporal to show his immediate superiors' appreciation of his services.

In some ways he had been lucky. During the two years that followed, others had worse ends to their war. He, still barely twenty-one, had turned to the study of economics and to those interminable, earnest, forward-looking, iconoclastic discussions with other young men and women and even the occasional professor which flourish in that atmosphere of *akademische Freiheit* by which the Germans traditionally set such store.

Within a year the Russian Revolution, ingeniously promoted by the German General Staff, came to awaken the hopes and expectations of forward-looking young people everywhere. Twelve months later the collapse of Germany's armies in the field put paid to that same German General Staff's dreams of grandeur, at any rate for the time being, while economic collapse, inflation and all that went with it came near to toppling the social and political fabric of a once prosperous and powerful country. Although the Weimar Republic somehow survived for fourteen years, it was, as anyone who knew the Germany of the twenties and thirties will agree, lucky to last that long.

German parliamentary democracy, whether of the moderate left or the moderate right, was a fragile growth. Nor did the Western parliamentary democracies do much to encourage it. For large numbers of young Germans the choice in the inter-war years lay clearly between the revolutionary left and one or other of the nationalist groupings which in 1933 found their focus in Adolf Hitler's National Socialist Movement. Richard Sorge's mind had long since been made up. Having, in the words of the Japanese Public Prosecutor's Office, 'arrived at the realization that certain self-evident contradictions are inherent in the capitalist system of the present day', he had in 1918 plumped firmly for Communism and within a year or two become an integral part of the Party machine.

Everything that followed flows naturally from that first fateful decision of the twenty-three year old ex-soldier. With the benefit of hindsight one could be tempted to wonder, not how Sorge could ever have become a Communist in the first place, but only how this questing, turbulent spirit could have stayed harnessed for so long to Stalin's blood-stained, inefficient, cynically opportunist and generally unprepossessing juggernaut.

Given the complexity, unaccountability and inscrutability of human nature (German no less than any other), it cannot be easy to analyze or interpret the innermost feelings of a man who in any case by virtue of his calling necessarily kept himself to himself. In public Richard Sorge displayed a violent, radical, arrogant, self-assertive character, chasing women, drinking heavily and tearing about on a motor-cycle. In some ways, no doubt, this image appealed to him. It was also up to a point good cover, in no way corresponding to the popular concept of a muffled, muted spy. On the other hand it is conceivable that it masked an inner conflict, a spiritual unease, a difficulty in accepting the revolution he had fought for all his life under its new Stalinist guise.

But this is no more than speculation. Under prolonged Japanese interrogation, Sorge never once betrayed the slightest feelings of disenchantment or disillusion with the cause he had espoused a quarter of a century before. From other sources we know that more than once he expressed impatience, indeed disgust, at the machine's soullessness, incompetence and lack of comprehension. But who, at some time in his life, has not done that?

What seems likely is that, embracing the cause of revolution early on, he stuck to it. Having myself seen Stalin's reign of terror at its peak, I have since sometimes asked survivors of that period whether, even as good Communists, they did not find it and all that went with it disillusioning and hard to take. Their answer (and they include President Tito of Yugoslavia) has generally been that, though appalled by what was happening there,

173

they still saw Soviet Russia as the Country of the Revolution and as such at that time the only hope for the World Communist Movement in which they firmly believed.

This it seems fair to assume, is how Richard Sorge saw it, if he stopped to think. In the 1920s, Moscow, one must remember, was still a very different place from what it was to become ten years later. In the thirties he spent no more than a few weeks there, not long enough to grasp the full horror of it.

Nor was the outside world he contrasted it with all that much more appealing: war-torn China, Hitler's Germany, Japan hell-bent for trouble in one direction or another, the West in his eyes already decadent. Sorge, we know, was a brave and determined man, as disciplined and as dedicated as when he had advanced against those French machine-gun posts at Dixemude in 1914, but in a different cause. Where another might have flinched or taken flight or lost his nerve, he simply soldiered on until the time came to pay the ultimate price demanded of him. It is difficult, all things considered, not to admire such selfless dedication or to grudge our hero the final soldierly salute which his friend General Ott bestowed on him at their last meeting.

Five

SEA CHANGE

Nothing of him that doth fade,
But doth suffer a sea-change
Into something rich and strange.

WILLIAM SHAKESPEARE, *The Tempest*

Early on the morning of 30 April 1943 a member of the crew of a Spanish
fishing-boat, one of a fleet of some fifty such vessels fishing off the mouth
of the Huelva River in south-western Spain, happened to catch sight of
what looked like a dead body floating in the sea. He accordingly hailed a
nearby motor launch which took it on board. It proved on closer inspection
to be the body of a youngish man in British uniform, wearing over his
trench-coat a fully inflated life-jacket or 'Mae West' and clutching in one
hand a black leather official briefcase, which was also attached to the belt
of his trench-coat. Floating upside down in the calm waters of the bay not
far away was an inflatable rubber dinghy of the type carried as a safety
precaution by most aircraft in wartime.

The body was landed by the launch on the nearest beach and handed
over to an officer of the Spanish Army who happened to be there on a
training exercise with a detachment of infantry. This officer summoned a
judicial officer of the Spanish Navy who duly took charge of the briefcase
and also of the personal effects of the dead man. The body was then taken
to the mortuary in the neighbouring town of Huelva for medical examination by a doctor, who certified that the man in question had fallen into the
sea while still alive and that death had been due to drowning. The body,
he said, had been in the sea for five to eight days. It seemed obvious that he
had been travelling in an aircraft which had crashed in the sea but, though
he had managed to get out of it and inflate his Mae West and rubber dinghy,
he had subsequently drowned.

By now the body had been identified by an identity card and other papers
found on it as that of Major William Martin of the Royal Marines, a
slightly-built, not very robust-looking, clean-shaven man of thirty-six. A
pass he was carrying showed him to have been employed as a staff officer at

Combined Operations Headquarters, a body recently set up in London under the command of Vice-Admiral Lord Louis Mountbatten. Anyone who cared to probe further into the rather soggy contents of Major Martin's pocket (and the Spanish authorities certainly did not neglect to do so) would have been able to discover a number of other things about the dead man. He was a temporary member of the Naval and Military Club in Piccadilly. He had an overdraft of £79 19s 2d at Lloyds Bank. He was engaged to a girl called Pam who lived in Wiltshire, who, from the letters she wrote him was evidently very much in love with him and whose photograph showed her to be a young woman of considerable personal attractions. Not long before leaving London, he had bought her from Messrs S. J. Phillips in Bond Street a diamond engagement ring costing £53 0s 6d.

Of considerably more interest were the contents of the black leather briefcase with the royal cipher stamped on it in gold which he was still clutching when he was found. There was first of all a personal letter dated 21 April from Admiral Mountbatten to the Commander in Chief, Mediterranean, Admiral of the Fleet Sir A. B. Cunningham, from which it was clear that Lord Louis was lending him Major Martin as an expert in barges, landing-craft and other equipment required for opposed landings. 'Let me have him back please,' the Chief of Combined Operations had added jocosely. 'He might bring some sardines with him – they are "on points" here!'

In his letter Lord Louis made another request. 'I promised VCIGS,' he had written, 'that Major Martin would arrange with you for the onward transmission of a letter he has with him for General Alexander. It is very urgent and very "hot" and as there are some remarks in it that could not be seen by others in the War Office, it could not go by signal. I feel sure that you will see that it goes on safely and without delay.'

The letter in question, from Major-General A. E. Nye, Vice Chief of the Imperial General Staff, to General Sir Harold Alexander, at this time commanding 18th Army Group in North Africa, ran as follows:

Telephone: Whitehall 9400   War Office
Chief of the Imperial   Whitehall
General Staff   London SW1

PERSONAL AND MOST SECRET   23 April 1943

My dear Alex,

I am taking advantage of sending you a personal letter by hand of one of Mountbatten's officers to give you the inside history of our recent exchange of cables about Mediterranean operations and their attendant cover plans. You may have felt our decisions were somewhat arbitrary, but I can assure you in fact that the COS Committee gave the most careful consideration both to your recommendation and to Jumbo's.

We have had recent information that the Boche have been reinforcing and strengthening their defences in Greece and Crete and CIGS felt that our forces for the assault were insufficient. It was agreed by the Chiefs of Staff that the 5th Division should be reinforced by one Brigade Group for the assault on the beach south of Cape Araxos and that a similar reinforcement should be made for the 56th Division at Kalamata. We are earmarking the necessary forces and shipping.

Jumbo Wilson had proposed to select Sicily as cover target for 'Husky'; but we have already chosen it as cover for operation 'Brimstone'. The COS Committee went into the whole question exhaustively again and came to the conclusion that in view of the preparations in Algeria, the amphibious training which will be taking place on the Tunisian coast and the heavy air bombardment which will be put down to neutralize the Sicilian airfields, we should stick to our plan of making it cover for 'Brimstone' – indeed, we stand a very good chance of making him think we will go for Sicily – it is an obvious objective and one about which he must be nervous. On the other hand, they felt there wasn't much hope of persuading the Boche that the extensive preparations in the Eastern Mediterranean were also directed at Sicily. For this reason they have told Wilson his cover plan should be something nearer the spot, e.g. the Dodecanese. Since our relations with Turkey are now so obviously closer the Italians must be pretty apprehensive about these islands.

I imagine you will agree with these arguments. I know you will have your hands more than full at the moment and you haven't much chance of discussing future operations with Eisenhower. But if by any chance you do want to support Wilson's proposal, I hope you will let us know soon, because we can't delay much longer.

I am very sorry we weren't able to meet your wishes about the new commander of the Guards Brigade. Your own nominee was down with a bad attack of 'flu and not likely to be really fit for another few weeks. No doubt, however, you know Forster personally; he has done extremely well in command of a brigade at home, and is, I think, the best fellow available.

You must be about as fed up as we are with the whole question of war medals and 'Purple Hearts'. We all agree with you that we don't want to offend our American friends, but there is a good deal more to it than that. If our troops who happen to be serving in one particular theatre are to get extra decorations merely because the Americans happen to be serving there too, we will be faced with a good deal of discontent among those troops fighting elsewhere perhaps just as bitterly – or more so. My own feeling is that we should thank the Americans for their kind offer, but say firmly it would cause too many anomalies and we are sorry we can't accept. But it is on the agenda for the next Military Members Meeting and I hope you will have a decision very soon.

Best of luck,
Yours ever,
Archie Nye

General the Hon. Sir Harold R. L. G. Alexander,
GCB, CSI, DSO, MC
Headquarters,
18th Army Group

A third rather bulkier letter in the briefcase, dated 22 April, was from Lord Louis Mountbatten to General Eisenhower, at this time Supreme Allied Commander Mediterranean with his Headquarters at Algiers. This enclosed proofs of a propaganda pamphlet describing the activities of Combined Operations and asked General Eisenhower whether he would provide the pamphlet with a covering message containing, as Lord Louis put it, 'an expression of your invaluable approval'.

Once Major Martin's body had been identified, it was handed over to the British Vice-Consul at Huelva and at noon on the following day was given a proper military funeral in the presence of representatives of the Spanish military and civil authorities. Major Martin being an officer of the Royal Marines, a report was then duly forwarded by the Vice Consul to the British Naval Attaché at Madrid who on 3 May in his turn signalled the news of Major Martin's demise to the Admiralty in London.

By the spring of 1943 the war had reached a critical stage. The whole coast of North Africa from Egypt to Algiers was now in the hands of the Allies. Their next step must clearly be to strike at what Mr Churchill liked to call 'the soft underbelly of Europe'. The question was where? Italy, the Balkans and the South of France were all possibilities. But an opposed landing on such a scale and at such long range would be no easy matter and obviously it was of the greatest importance that the enemy should not have advance warning of where the blow was likely to fall.

Viewed from this angle, the letter from General Nye to General Alexander of which Major Martin had been the bearer was, as Lord Louis Mountbatten had put it, clearly 'very hot' indeed. There was a direct reference to proposed landings by the 5th Division south of Cape Araxos and by the 56th Division at Kalamata, both in south-western Greece, as well as connected references to various cover plans for the landings in question. It was obviously essential to find out what had happened to this letter and to do so without delay and in the discreetest possible manner.

In his signal to the Admiralty announcing Major Martin's death, the Naval Attaché had not mentioned that officer's briefcase or said anything about any official papers. A series of urgent signals were accordingly now sent to Madrid.

The first of these, despatched from the Admiralty on 4 May, informed the Naval Attaché that Major Martin was carrying some very secret and very important papers and instructed him to make a formal request to the Spanish authorities for their return. If this produced no result, he was to make discreet but searching enquiries at Huelva, with the object of finding out whether these papers had been washed ashore and if so what had happened to them. If he succeeded in recovering them, he was at once to send a personal signal to the director of Naval Intelligence saying to whom they were addressed. He should on no account open the envelopes, but return them intact to the DNI.

The Admiralty's first signal was followed by another. This informed the Naval Attaché that it had now been ascertained that Major Martin had been carrying three letters of the utmost importance, probably in a black official briefcase bearing the royal cipher. Once again he was warned to be discreet and to avoid exciting the Spaniards' interest in the documents. He was also instructed to order a wreath from Pam and Major Martin's family and to arrange for a suitable tombstone to be placed on his grave at Huelva.

A day or two later the Admiralty learned from the Naval Attaché's reply to their first signal that the Vice-Consul at Huelva had not been given the briefcase or documents when the body was first brought in, but that he had been informed by the Spanish Minister of Marine that the papers carried by Major Martin were being passed through Naval channels and would eventually reach Madrid by way of the Spanish Naval Headquarters at Cadiz.

A week or so later, on 13 May, came a further signal from the Naval Attaché. This announced that in the absence of the Minister of Marine, who happened to be visiting Valencia, the Chief of the Spanish Naval Staff had now officially handed over to him all Major Martin's effects. These included the black briefcase, open, with a key in the lock. Everything, the Chief of Naval Staff had said, was there. For this the Naval Attaché had thanked him. From their conversation he had gained the distinct impression that the Chief of Naval Staff had at any rate some idea of the contents of the letters, but, he said, he had no reason to believe that he would share this knowledge with others.

In his next signal the Naval Attaché reported that on 15 May he had seen the Minister of Marine, who had at once referred to Major Martin's papers. He had, it appeared, heard, while he was in Valencia, that the papers had arrived in Madrid and had immediately given orders to the Chief of Staff to hand them over at once. He had done this in order to make sure that no one took an unauthorized look at them, which could have had serious consequences. As nothing that had been said to the Minister of Marine by the Naval Attaché could have led him to suppose that the papers carried by Major Martin were of any importance, it looked very much as if he, like his Chief of Staff, had a fairly good idea of their contents.

Not long after this the black briefcase with its contents arrived in

London. The seals on the three envelopes seemed intact, but on closer examination it was found that the letters had in fact been opened.

Up to this time General Franco, despite strong German pressure, had managed to keep out of the war. He had, however, shown his sympathy for the Axis cause by despatching contingents of Spanish volunteers to fight on various fronts and had also allowed the Germans and Italians to use Spanish territory as a base for espionage operations, at the same time passing on to them any useful intelligence material which came his way, notably in regard to the movement of Allied ships through the Straits of Gibraltar. It was therefore fairly safe to assume that if General Nye's letter to General Alexander had been read by the Spaniards it would very soon be read by the Germans as well.

Anyone who made this assumption would in fact have been quite right. German Intelligence had, as it happened, a particularly able and active agent at Huelva, on the best of terms with the local Spanish authorities. He had immediately been informed of the discovery of Major Martin's body and had been able, without too much difficulty, to discover most of the relevant facts about him. He had also been able to discover to whom the three letters in his black briefcase were addressed. After this he had naturally done his best to get copies of all the documents, but had been unsuccessful for the reason that the briefcase, together with all Major Martin's personal effects had already been handed over to the local Spanish Naval Judicial Officer, with whom he did not happen to have a sufficiently close relationship.

However, having once got wind of the tempting prize which the tide had so obligingly deposited on his doorstep, he and his superiors did not give up. If one Spaniard did not show himself amenable, others could certainly be found who would. The powerful intelligence network which the Germans possessed in Spain went into action. An excuse was made to the British Vice-Consul. Before being handed over to the British Naval Attaché, the envelopes were carefully opened, their contents photographed and copies made by the Spanish General Staff both for themselves and for the Germans, who were also actually shown the originals. Early in the first week in May, within a few days of the discovery of Major Martin's body, a summary of the three letters together with an account of how they had been found was duly telegraphed to Berlin by the Senior German intelligence officer in Madrid and subsequently submitted to the German High Command and to the Führer himself. At the same time copies of the intercepted documents were forwarded to Berlin by courier under cover of a written report. This was almost immediately followed by a second and more detailed report, indicating, no doubt in response to a request from Berlin, that still further enquiries were being made into the circumstances of their discovery.

By the middle of May the German Intelligence Service were thus able to submit to Admiral Doenitz, Commander-in-Chief of the German Naval Staff, a translation of General Nye's letter to General Alexander together with a detailed Intelligence appreciation thereof.

Dated 14 May and marked 'FOR PERSONAL INFORMATION ONLY. NOT THROUGH THE REGISTRY', this ran as follows:

SUBJECT: Captured enemy document on Mediterranean operations.
              Attached herewith are:
              (a) Translation of the captured letter from the Imperial Staff to General Alexander.
              (b) Appreciation thereof by the (German) General Staff.

The contents of further captured documents are unimportant. Exhaustive examination by 3Skl. revealed the following:

1. The genuineness of the captured documents is above suspicion. The suggestion that they have intentionally fallen into our hands – of which the probability is slight – and the question whether the enemy is aware of the capture of the documents by us or only of their loss at sea is being followed up. It is possible that the enemy has no knowledge of the capture of the documents.

Against that it is certain that he knows that they did not reach their destination.

2. Whether the enemy will now alter his intended operations or will set an earlier date for their commencement must be taken into consideration, but seems unlikely.

3. *Probable Date of the Operation*

The matter is being treated as urgent; yet there is still time on 23 April to inform General Alexander by air courier of General Wilson's proposal to use Sicily as cover target for the assault in the Eastern Mediterranean, wherein he is requested to reply immediately in the event of his supporting Wilson's opinion, 'as we cannot postpone the matter much longer'. In this case the Imperial General Staff considers altering the planning both in the Eastern and Western Mediterranean, for which there is still time.

4. *Sequence of the Operations*

It is presumed that both operations will take place simultaneously, since Sicily is unsuitable as a cover target simultaneously for both.

5. The Tobruk area comes into consideration as a starting-point for the operations in the Eastern Mediterranean. Alexandria is not considered, as in this case Sicily would have been absurd as a cover target.

6. It is not clear whether the deception worked by the cover target concerns only the period up to the beginning of the operations or whether in fact a cover operation would be used as well as the actual assault.

7. It is *not* clear from the attached whether *only* the 5th and 56th Divisions will

be landed in the Eastern Mediterranean (at Araxos and Kalamata). However *only* these two Divisions are to be reinforced for their assault. It is always possible that all assault troops and targets are included with them.

8. It should be emphasized that it is obvious from this document that big preparations are being made in the Eastern Mediterranean as well. This is important, because considerably less information about preparations has reached us from this area than from Algeria, owing to their geographical situation.

This appreciation was seen and initialled by Admiral Doenitz's Chief of Staff on 15 May and on 18 May by Admiral Doenitz himself, who had just returned from visits to Mussolini and Hitler.

It was followed next day by another memorandum from the German Intelligence Service, reporting in greater detail on the circumstances in which the documents in question had fallen into German hands. This explained that the letters had been found in a briefcase 'clutched in the hand of the corpse' and that the originals had been carefully inspected and bore every sign of being genuine, as did Major Martin's personal papers and the other contents of his pockets. It went on to say that while the Spaniards (and Germans) had been examining the papers, the British Vice Consul had been fobbed off with the story that they had had to be laid before the local legal authorities. It added that they were now being handed back to the British 'and definitely give the impression – as I was able to see for myself – that they had not been opened'.

In an appreciation of probable Allied intentions drafted three months previously in February 1943, the German High Command had given it as their view that the Allies' next move would be against one of the larger islands in the Mediterranean, their first choice in order of probability being Sicily with Crete second and then Sardinia and Corsica. This had remained their view until the beginning of May.

Early in May the signal from Madrid summarizing the contents of Major Martin's briefcase caused them to change their minds completely. This first impression was confirmed when they were able to study the documents themselves. From Lord Louis' somewhat laboured reference to sardines they had even been able to deduce that General Alexander's target in the Western Mediterranean was to be Sardinia.

A landing in the Eastern and Western Mediterranean on a fairly large scale is anticipated [ran a further top-secret appreciation]. Target of the operation in Eastern Mediterranean under General Wilson is the coast near Kalamata and the stretch of coast south of Cape Araxos (both on the west coast of the Peloponnese). The reinforced 56th Infantry Division is detailed for the landing at Kalamata and the reinforced 5th Infantry Division at Cape Araxos.

Target for the operation under General Alexander in the Western Mediterranean is not mentioned. A joking reference in the letter points to Sardinia.

Code-name for this operation is 'Brimstone'. The proposed cover target for operation 'Brimstone' is Sicily. Maintenance of completest secrecy over this discovery and utmost limitation of circulation of this information is essential.

By the middle of May the General Staff of the Army and the High Command of the Navy had thus both come to the conclusion that the documents they had intercepted accurately reflected the intention of the Allies. From now onwards they proceeded on this assumption.

As for the Führer, he had no doubts whatever on the subject. Towards the middle of May, Admiral Doenitz had been sent to Italy in an attempt to stiffen the Duce's morale following the disasters which had overtaken the Axis forces in North Africa. Stopping off on 15 May to see Hitler on his way back, he found him anxious to know what view Mussolini took of 'Anglo-American intentions'. The Duce, Doenitz replied, was convinced that the Allies were going to attack Sicily. But the Führer, on the strength of the first signal from Madrid, was of quite a different opinion. 'The Führer,' wrote Doenitz in his diary, 'does not agree with the Duce that the most likely invasion point is Sicily. Furthermore, he believes that the Anglo-Saxon order which has been discovered confirms the assumption that the planned attack will be against Sardinia and the Peloponnese.'

Doenitz, returning to his Headquarters found copies of the original letters awaiting him, together with the considered opinion of his Intelligence Staff, which he in his turn readily accepted.

It now only remained for those responsible to decide what action should be taken in the new situation which now faced them.

During the next six weeks or so a series of major changes were made in the disposition of the German armed forces in and around the Mediterranean. The bulk of these affected the Eastern Mediterranean, where the main blow was expected to fall. In the German view almost the whole of the Greek coast, as well as the islands, was threatened. Accordingly on 20 May the German Naval High Command gave orders for three new minefields to be laid off Greece, including one off Kalamata itself. At the same time a number of other measures were taken. The German Admiral commanding in the Aegean was ordered to take over the minefields which were being laid by the Italians off the west coast of Greece and instructions were sent for German coastal defence batteries to be set up in territory under Italian control. Orders were also given to establish R-boat bases, command stations and sea patrol services in the areas in question and in early June a whole group of German R-boats was sent from Sicily to the Aegean. There were also consultations with the Luftwaffe with a view to the provision of air support where necessary. Meanwhile from France the 1st Panzer Division was sent right across Europe to Tripolis, a town in the Peloponnese within easy striking distance of both Kalamata and Cape Araxos. In order not to alarm the Turks, still precariously neutral, the German Foreign Office were asked to notify the Turkish Government that German troops and shipping were being moved to Greece but to make it clear that these moves did not imply any hostile designs on Turkey.

At the same time corresponding moves on a rather smaller scale were being made in the Western Mediterranean, where it was expected that, in addition to an Allied assault on Sardinia a diversionary attack might also be made on Sicily as a cover target. On 14 June orders to cover this possibility were issued in Hitler's name by General Keitel, Commander in Chief of the Supreme Command of the German Armed Forces, specifying the requisite measures. Not long after a strong Panzer force with ancillaries and supplies for two months was sent to Corsica and in the weeks that followed further steps were taken to reinforce Sardinia, Corsica and, to a lesser extent, the northern coast of Sicily.

On 9 July General Keitel circulated a lengthy appreciation of the situation by Admiral Doenitz. Doenitz estimated that the Allies had enough troops in North Africa to be able, if they chose, to attack Corsica, Sardinia and Sicily as well as Greece and to follow up their landing in Greece by forming a bridgehead there for further operations in the Balkans. On the other hand he took the view that an Allied landing on the Italian mainland, where the Germans could react fast, was unlikely. His overall conclusion was that the Allies' western assault forces appeared to be ready for an immediate attack which could begin at any time; their eastern forces, on the other hand, 'seemed to be still forming up'.

In appreciating that the Allied forces concentrated at this time at the western end of the Mediterranean were ready for instant action, Admiral Doenitz was abundantly right. Where he had gone wrong was in suggesting that the Allied troops at the eastern end of the Mediterranean were any less ready.

On the morning of 9 July, the very day on which his memorandum was circulated, what Winston Churchill called 'great armadas from east and west', as yet unsighted by the enemy, were already converging south of Malta on their way to invade Sicily in strength. The ensuing invasion was the greatest amphibious operation ever attempted.

Taken by surprise, such Germans as there were in Sicily fought back hard, but just over a month later the island was in Allied hands. 'At 10 am this morning,' General Alexander signalled to the Prime Minister on 17 August, 'the last German soldier was flung out of Sicily and the whole island is now in our hands.' Three weeks later, with Mussolini fallen and Italian capitulation impending, two divisions of the 8th Army had landed in southern Italy and were advancing rapidly through Calabria. Again Admiral Doenitz had been wrong.

Long after the landings in Sicily had actually begun, the Germans still clung to the belief that this was only a diversion and that the real assault was coming somewhere else. Indeed Hitler was so convinced that the main operation was to be the invasion of Greece that as late as 23 July he appointed Rommel, his best general, to command the troops he had so painstakingly assembled there, hurriedly recalling him a few days later to assume command in Italy.

Meanwhile the German Naval Commander-in-Chief in Italy was complaining bitterly to the Naval High Command that the removal of 1st R-boat Group to the Aegean had seriously prejudiced the defence of Sicily, while the Wehrmacht would no doubt have welcomed the support of their thousands of comrades sitting idly in Greece. In the end the Naval High Command grudgingly agreed to allow their unfortunate Commander-in-Chief to keep the R-boats still remaining to him on the grounds that an attack on Greece did not seem likely 'for the time being'. Even now they clearly still found it difficult to accept that they had somehow been fooled.

And fooled they certainly had been. In order to discover just how completely, we need to go back six months or more to the end of 1942 and beginning of 1943. At this stage of the war, Lieutenant-Commander Ewen Montagu of the Admiralty's Naval Intelligence Division happened to be a member of a small inter-service and inter-departmental committee concerned with the security aspects of intended operations, concerned, in other words, to ensure by all possible means that the enemy did not guess Allied intentions in advance. In addition to this negative duty of denying information to the enemy, his committee had a positive duty to confuse and mislead the enemy whenever they possibly could.

Towards the end of 1942 the main problem to which this committee were directing their attention was how to stop the Germans from guessing that the Allies' next target after North Africa, where they had by this time successfully established themselves, was to be Sicily as a stepping stone for the invasion of Italy.

The trouble was that Sicily, commanding as it did the Central Mediterranean, was in many ways the obvious target. As Mr Churchill put it at the time, 'Anybody but a damn fool would know it is Sicily.' And once the Germans had guessed it was Sicily the Allies were going for, they would undoubtedly strengthen that island's defences until its capture became a truly formidable task. What therefore was required was a means of convincing the Germans beyond all reasonable doubt that the expected Allied attack was to be directed elsewhere.

Planting misleading material on the other side is normal practice in war-time and for those concerned with such matters, quite possibly in peace-time as well. The difficulty is to make the material you plant and the circumstances in which it is planted convincing enough to deceive the enemy's normally suspicious intelligence officers, engaged, like you, in seeking by every means in their power to mislead and mystify their opponents.

It was while he and the other members of his committee were puzzling over this particular problem that Commander Montagu hit upon an altogether brilliant idea. 'Why,' he said, 'shouldn't we get a body, disguise it as a staff officer and give him really high level papers which will show clearly that we are going to attack somewhere else? We won't have to drop him on land, as the aircraft might have come down in the sea on the way round to the Med. He would float ashore with the papers either in France or in Spain; it won't matter which. Probably Spain would be best, as the Germans wouldn't have as much chance to examine the body there as if they got it into their own hands, while it's certain that they will get the documents, or at least copies.'

Clearly the idea had great possibilities. But it required some careful working out. First there was the problem of getting possession of a body. Then they had to decide how to deliver it to the Germans so as to convince them that there was nothing suspicious about it. Moreover this would have to be done under conditions of total secrecy. For there could be no doubt that once it got about that a naval officer was trying to borrow a dead body which he intended to dump in the sea somewhere, the news would spread like wildfire.

As a first step, Commander Montagu consulted in the strictest confidence Sir Bernard Spilsbury, the great pathologist. Over a glass of sherry at Sir Bernard's club, he learned that, if the corpse were to be floating in a Mae West when recovered, it would be possible to use for this purpose the body of a man who had either been drowned or had died from quite a wide range of natural causes. Apart from injuries or drowning, the victims of air crashes at sea quite often died from shock or simply from exposure.

This gave Commander Montagu a rather wider choice than he had expected. In the end he was able to find the body of a man who had recently died from pneumonia after exposure and whose relations, on being assured that the body was needed for a really worthwhile purpose and would ultimately receive proper burial, agreed to let him have it on the understanding that the dead man's name would never be revealed.

The body in question was that of a man in his early thirties, not, as far as one could judge, a very fit man. But, as Ewen Montagu rather cynically remarked to someone who pointed this out, 'He doesn't have to look like an officer – only like a staff officer.' Having picked their leading man, Commander Montagu and his team then relegated him to the deep freeze until such time as they were ready for him and embarked enthusiastically on their next task, which was to provide him with a destination, a background and a *raison d'être*.

As a destination, Spain, for the reason given by Commander Montagu, offered certain advantages over France, and in Spain, Huelva seemed the ideal place. For one thing, there was known to be an extremely active German secret agent there, who could be counted on to get his hands on the documents or at any rate ensure that his superiors did so. Moreover the prevailing wind was favourable for an operation of this kind.

As a means of delivering the body there neatly and secretly, a submarine had much to recommend it in preference to a surface craft or an aeroplane. On putting the proposition to the Flag Officer, Submarines, Commander Montagu was glad to find him quite prepared to allow one of his precious craft to be used for the operation, which by this time had been endowed with the somewhat grisly codename of 'Mincemeat'.

Having provided himself with a corpse and decided on its destination and means of transport, Commander Montagu next turned his attention to the most vital problem of all, namely the precise nature of the document to be planted on the Germans. In order to carry conviction with the enemy, he decided it would have to be a communication at the very highest level, passing, not between officers of medium rank, but between the Chief or Vice-Chief of the Imperial General Staff in London and a Commander in Chief in the relevant theatre of war. In the end (and such decisions are not lightly taken) it was agreed that this should be a semi-official letter addressed by General Nye, the Vice-Chief of the Imperial General Staff, to General Alexander, commanding 18th Army Group in Tunisia, both directly concerned at the top level with the conduct of future operations in the Mediterranean and known by the Germans to be so concerned.

It remained to draft the necessary letter. The result, produced jointly by Commander Montagu and General Nye himself, was a masterpiece of ingenuity. The style, not surprisingly, was utterly convincing. Moreover its authors managed to include in it and in the accompanying letter from Admiral Mountbatten to Admiral Cunningham all the misleading information they needed to convey, not necessarily directly, but in such a way that the Germans, when they came to read it, would without too much difficulty be able to draw from it the conclusions they were required to draw, while at the same time congratulating themselves on their own ingenuity and powers of deduction.

In the spring of 1943 the intention of the Allies was to use all their forces from both ends of the North African coastline for a combined assault on Sicily, to be followed immediately by the invasion of Italy. The purpose of Operation Mincemeat was to make the Germans believe that what was intended was not a single massive assault on Sicily, but on the contrary a double operation involving major landings at both ends of the Mediterranean. It was for this reason that General Nye's letter was designed to give the impression that while General Alexander's 18th Army Group and the other forces under General Eisenhower's overall command in Tunis were to attack Sardinia and Corsica, those under General Wilson in Egypt were to attack Greece.

But perhaps the cleverest touch of all was the suggestion it contained that the Allies were hoping to convince the Germans by means of a cover plan that their real intention was to invade Sicily. This would mean that any evidence the Germans obtained from other sources of the actual Allied preparations for the invasion of Sicily would be discounted by them as being simply bluff. In other words they would automatically disbelieve any genuine information that might happen to reach them.

The direct references in General Nye's letter to Cape Araxos and Kalamata made it abundantly clear that Greece was to be General Wilson's target. Commander Montagu, being by this time familiar with the workings of the German military mind, was anxious to include a no less direct reference to Sardinia as the westernmost target. But this the Chiefs of Staff were reluctant to sanction on the grounds that, if the deception failed, a direct reference to Sardinia could pinpoint Sicily more clearly than was desirable as being the true target. He nevertheless managed to include in Admiral Mountbatten's letter the rather far-fetched reference to sardines which, from his knowledge of the German mind, he rightly guessed would produce the desired effect.

The task of creating a staff officer to be the bearer of the letters called for no less ingenuity and attention to detail than the composition of the letters themselves.

For a number of reasons it was thought preferable in the interests of security to make him a marine rather than a soldier or a sailor. Acting major was considered a suitable rank. The Navy List showed that there were several Royal Marine officers of approximately that seniority called Martin – a fact which could prove convenient in case of awkward enquiries. Gradually Major William Martin, Royal Marines, began to take shape. He would need a naval identity card with a photograph. Unflattering as such likenesses usually are, a snapshot of a refrigerated corpse would scarcely answer the purpose. They would have to find a live model. And then, by an extraordinary stroke of luck, Commander Montagu found himself sitting opposite a man at a meeting who, as he put it, 'might have been the twin brother of the corpse'. A plausible pretext was found and the necessary photograph taken.

It remained to find a convincing reason why a relatively junior Royal Marine officer should have been flown to North Africa. He must, Commander Montagu decided, be an expert in the use of barges and other craft likely to be used in a seaborne operation of the kind which all concerned knew to be impending. That this was his role was made clear in Admiral Mountbatten's letter to Admiral Cunningham. In the circumstances it was only natural that he should carry the three important letters with him. The third of these with its bulky enclosures addressed to General Eisenhower, was added to the other two mainly to provide an excuse for the briefcase, as it was felt that, if carried in Major Martin's pocket, two ordinary sized envelopes might conceivably escape the attention of the Spanish authorities.

Would it, they wondered, be enough to close the dead man's fingers round the handle of the briefcase or might it then be carried away by a wave? Safer, they decided, to attach it to a chain which could then be looped through the belt of his trench-coat, even though this might possibly arouse the suspicions of their German opposite numbers. (In fact the chain was to pass unnoticed and uncommented on.)

But Commander Montagu and his team had to do more than give Major Martin official status. He had also to be posthumously endowed with a personality, to be brought, as it were, to life. And, given the meticulous care with which their German opposite numbers could be counted on to examine and probe every aspect of their windfall, it was vital that the personality they gave him should be as plausible and as convincing as possible. With this in mind, they began talking about him among themselves as if he was a friend of all of them. And so, bit by bit, Bill Martin emerged.

He was, they decided an able, reliable officer, though occasionally careless (his naval identity card replaced one he had lost). Fond of a good time (he carried an invitation from the Cabaret Club), he was inclined, as his overdraft showed, to be mildly extravagant. The letters RC on his identity disc and a little silver cross on a chain round his neck indicated that he was a Roman Catholic. As appeared from the letters in his pockets, he had quite recently met and almost immediately become engaged to Pam, the attractive girl whose photograph he carried next his heart.

Nor was this all. Major Martin's rather old-fashioned father, his bank manager and the family lawyer all figured in the miniature dossier contained in his pockets. Letters from them and from Pam, and the bill for Pam's engagement ring from Messrs S. J. Phillips together with the invitation from the night club and the stubs of some theatre tickets were all lovingly prepared and assembled, checked and counter-checked for possible anomalies and then subjected to precisely the right degree of wear and tear to provide them with a convincing patina. By the time the necessary preparations were complete, Major Martin had come to life.

The plans for Operation Mincemeat had been approved by the chiefs of staff and Prime Minister and the time had finally come for Major Martin to start on his long journey to Huelva, where it had been planned that he should arrive on 29 or 30 April.

The submarine allocated for the operation was HM Submarine *Seraph*, commanded by Lieutenant N. A. Jewell. She was due to sail from the Holy Loch for Malta on 19 April, having postponed her regular departure by a fortnight in order to be able to undertake the task.

On the evening of Saturday, 17 April, Commander Montagu and two companions called at the cold storage depot in a Ford 30cwt van to collect Major Martin. A special metal container six feet six inches long and two feet in diameter had been made to take the body and into this Major Martin, who had first been taken out of cold storage, dressed in battle dress and then replaced in cold storage, was now inserted and packed tight in dry ice for the journey.

One problem had been his boots. They were certainly the right size, but to put a pair of boots on to the completely rigid feet of a deep-frozen corpse is, as the team soon found, no easy matter. Nor could they defreeze and refreeze the body without unduly hastening the process of decomposition, which it was essential to avoid. In the end they had simply thawed out the feet with the help of an electric fire, slipped on the boots and put him back to freeze.

Pam's love-letters, his identity card, receipted bills, theatre ticket counterfoils and the rest of the paraphernalia required to establish his personality had all been put into his pockets. On the assumption that the body would be discovered by the Spaniards on about 30 April and working back from then, these were furnished with dates designed to give the impression that Major Martin had left London on about 24 April and that, following an air crash, his body had been in the sea for five or six days before being found, just about sufficient to account for the degree of decomposition which it would in fact by then have attained.

Having loaded the container, which also held the all-important briefcase,

Commander Montagu and his two companions now set out for the north, driving all through the night and taking turns to sleep on the floor of the van side by side with the precious container. Early next morning the canister containing Major Martin and marked 'Optical Instruments - handle with care' was duly stowed away on board HM Submarine *Seraph* which sailed from the Holy Loch on the evening of the following day, Monday, 19 April.

There were still a lot of things that could have gone wrong, but in the event nothing did and ten days later at 4.30 in the morning of 30 April the *Seraph* surfaced in pitch darkness a little less than a mile from the mouth of the River Huelva. The canister was hauled aloft and only then, with the rest of the crew below, did Lieutenant Jewell tell his four officers what it really contained. While the other three kept watch, Lieutenant Jewell and one officer opened up the canister revealing Major Martin, whom they then slid neatly out on to the deck, at the same time removing the blanket in which he had been wrapped. After checking that everything was in place, that Major Martin's hand was gripping the handle of the vital briefcase and that it was properly secured to his belt, Lieutenant Jewell repeated such prayers as he could remember from the burial service. Then, in the words of one of those present: 'A gentle push and the unknown warrior was drifting inshore with the tide on his last momentous journey. Major Martin had gone to war.' He was followed shortly after by his inflated rubber dinghy duly floating upside down. A signal reporting the operation complete was made to the Admiralty at seven fifteen and not long after that passed on to a much relieved Commander Montagu.

By the second half of July it was apparent that the Allied invasion of Sicily had achieved the surprise hoped for by all concerned. How far this was due to operation Mincemeat did not become fully evident until some months after the end of the war in Europe with the discovery of the memoranda already mentioned among some German naval archives captured at Tambach in Thuringia, giving the reactions of the German Intelligence Service, naval staff and High Command to the contents of Major Martin's briefcase and showing quite clearly how completely they had been taken in by them.

For Commander Montagu, summoned by the deputy director of Naval Intelligence to inspect at close quarters the results of his handiwork, this was a moment of supreme satisfaction. Nor was his pleasure in any way diminished when he learned that the British naval officer responsible for sorting the captured papers in question had been so appalled by his discovery that the Germans had managed to get possession of a most secret letter from the VCIGS to General Alexander and by the horrifying breach of security implied that, even now that, it was all over, he had at once brought the file to the director of Naval Intelligence for him to handle personally.

It could be argued that Major Martin was not a spy and should therefore have no place in this book. This is as maybe. But the man who rifled his briefcase was certainly a spy, even though his zeal in the end rebounded on his employers. Nor can it be disputed that, with Commander Montagu's help, the contribution made by Major Martin in the field of military intelligence was infinitely greater than that of most spies or secret agents. It is for this reason and because of the sheer brilliance of the idea which, aided by the wind, the tide and Generalissimo Franco, he helped put into execution, that I was determined at all costs to include him, regardless of whether he could properly be described as a spy or not.

Six

GENTLEMAN'S
GENTLEMAN

Gentlemen do not read each other's mail.

U.S. SECRETARY OF STATE H. L. STIMSON 1929

On the evening of 26 October 1943 Herr L. C. Moyzisch, amongst other things Commercial Attaché at the German Embassy in Ankara, had decided to make an early night of it. It was thus that, when, at about ten that evening, the telephone beside his bed started to ring, he and his wife were already asleep. The caller, when he lifted the receiver, turned out to be Frau Jenke, the Counsellor's wife and also, as it happened, the sister of Hitler's Foreign Minister, Herr von Ribbentrop. 'Would you please come round to our flat at once?' she said. 'My husband wants to see you.'

Without much enthusiasm, Moyzisch agreed, pulled on his clothes, climbed into his car and drove round to the German Embassy compound on the Ataturk Boulevard where the Jenkes had their flat. Frau Jenke herself opened the front door. 'My husband,' she said, 'has gone to bed, but he would like to see you first thing in the morning. There's a funny sort of man in there,' she went on, indicating the drawing-room door, 'who wants to sell us something. You're to talk to him and find out what it's all about.' And she followed her husband to bed.

Not best pleased, Herr Moyzisch went into the drawing-room. A man was sitting in one of the armchairs. His face was in the shadow. He got up. '*Qui êtes vous?*' he asked anxiously. Moyzisch replied that Herr Jenke had asked him to talk to him and this seemed to reassure him. He was a man of fifty or so, not very tall, with thick black hair brushed back from rather a high forehead, shifty dark eyes, a firm chin and a small, shapeless nose. A face Moyzisch thought afterwards, rather like a clown's. Sitting down, Moyzisch motioned to him to resume his seat. Before doing so, the stranger first tiptoed to the door and opened it with a sudden jerk. Then he

193

sat down and, in not very good French, announced that he had a proposal to make to him. 'But,' he said, 'before I tell you what it is, I want you to promise me that, whether you accept it or not, you will never mention it to anyone except your chief. Any indiscretion on your part would make your life worthless as mine. I'd make sure of that if it was the last thing I did.' And as though to emphasize his point, he drew his hand meaningfully across his throat. 'Do you give me your word?' he insisted. 'Of course I do,' said Moyzisch. 'If I couldn't keep a secret, I wouldn't be here. What is it you want?' And he glanced at his watch.

'You'll have plenty of time for me when you know why I'm here,' said the man. 'My proposition is of the greatest possible importance to your government . . . I can get you some top secret papers, the most secret there are . . . straight from the British Embassy. That would interest you, wouldn't it? But I'll want a lot of money for them. My work is dangerous. If I were caught . . .' Again he drew his hand significantly across his throat and then went on: 'You've funds for that sort of thing, haven't you? Or your Ambassador has? I want twenty thousand pounds sterling.'

'Nonsense,' replied Moyzisch, 'out of the question. We don't have that sort of money here. It would have to be something quite exceptionally important to be worth anything like that. And I'd have to see these papers of yours. Have you got them with you?'

For a moment neither of them said anything. Then the stranger spoke again. 'I'll tell you my terms,' he said. 'If you agree, very well. If not, then I'll see if they are interested over there.' And he jerked his thumb in the direction of the Soviet Embassy. 'You see,' he added venomously, 'I hate the British.'

Listening to all this, it occurred to Moyzisch for the first time that the man might be serious, that he might really have something to offer, and as though in confirmation of this, his visitor now began making concrete proposals. 'I'll give you,' he said, 'three days to consider my offer. On 30 October at three in the afternoon, I'll ring you up at your office and ask you if you've received a letter for me. I'll call myself Pierre. If you say no, you'll never see me again. If you say yes, it'll mean you've accepted my offer. In that case, I'll come to see you again at ten o'clock that evening. But not here. We'll have to meet somewhere else. You'll then receive from me two rolls of film containing photographs of secret British documents. And I'll receive from you the sum of twenty thousand pounds in bank notes. You'll be risking twenty thousand pounds. I'll be risking my life. If you like what you get the first time, you can have more. For every roll of film after that, I'll want fifteen thousand pounds. Well?'

Knowing what he did of the German official mind and considering the colossal price asked, Moyzisch thought it most unlikely that he would be authorized to accept this proposition. However, it seemed sensible to carry matters at least one stage further. Before parting, they accordingly agreed that Pierre should ring him up at his office on the afternoon of 30 October as he had suggested and that, if by any chance the offer was accepted, they would meet again that same night near the toolshed at the end of the German Embassy garden.

Before leaving the building Pierre, who had already put on his greatcoat and pulled his hat down over his eyes, insisted on all the lights being switched off so that he might leave under cover of complete darkness. 'You'd like to know who I am?' he whispered, as he slipped through the door. 'I am the British Ambassador's valet.'

Next morning Herr Moyzisch duly informed his Ambassador, Herr Franz von Papen, of his curious encounter and of the proposition that had been made to him. They agreed that Berlin must be consulted and by midday the following personal and most secret telegram had been despatched to the Minister for Foreign Affairs, Herr von Ribbentrop:

To the Reich Foreign Minister. Personal. Most Secret.

We have offer of British Embassy employee alleged to be British Ambassador's valet to procure photographs of top secret original documents. For first delivery on October 30th twenty thousand pounds sterling in bank notes are demanded. Fifteen thousand for any further roll of films. Please advise whether offer can be accepted. If so sum required must be despatched by special courier to arrive here not later than October 30th. Alleged valet was employed several years ago by First Secretary otherwise nothing much known here.
Papen

It would, they knew, reach Ribbentrop within the hour.

The remainder of the 27 October went by and the 28th. The 29 October was the Turkish National Day. Still there was nothing from Berlin. That morning the entire Diplomatic Corps, Germans and British alike, in full dress with decorations, attended the official reception given by the President of Turkey. Herr von Papen was there with his staff. And so was the British Ambassador, Sir Hughe Knatchbull-Hugessen, with his. The two had known each other socially before the outbreak of war between their countries, but now, as the rules of the game demanded, studiously avoided each other.

In the afternoon there was a military parade. On returning from it, Moyzisch found a message asking him to go and see the Ambassador immediately. He went and Herr von Papen at once handed him the answer from Berlin. It ran as follows:

To Ambassador Von Papen. Personal. Most Secret.

British valet's offer to be accepted taking every precaution. Special courier arriving Ankara 30th before noon. Expect immediate report after delivery of documents.

Ribbentrop.

At exactly three o'clock next afternoon the telephone rang in Moyzisch's office. '*Ici Pierre*,' said a distant-sounding voice. '*Bonjour, Monsieur. Est-ce que vous avez mes lettres?*'

'*Oui*,' replied Moyzisch.

'*A ce soir*,' came the answer.

The deal was on.

At ten minutes to ten that evening Herr Moyzisch was at his office in the Embassy. At two minutes to ten he was in the Embassy garden near the toolshed. It was a cold clear night. Almost immediately he saw someone coming towards him through the darkness. '*C'est moi, Pierre*,' said a voice. '*Tout va bien?*' Together they walked in silence to the Embassy, crossed the hall and let themselves into Moyzisch's office.

'Your room looks out on the Ataturk Boulevard,' said his visitor. 'How about drawing the curtains?'

'You are very well informed,' said Moyzisch.

'I have to be,' came the reply.

'Have you the money?' the man asked.

Moyzisch nodded. Putting his hand into his overcoat pocket, his visitor brought out two rolls of 35 mm film. 'First the money,' he said firmly, as Moyzisch tried to take them.

The money, £20,000 in bundles of new ten, twenty and fifty pound notes brought by special messenger from Berlin that morning, was in the safe wrapped in newspaper. While his companion watched him greedily, Moyzisch opened the safe, undid the package and counted the notes in front of him. 'Give me the films,' he said. Handing him the films, the man reached out for the money.

'Not yet,' said Moyzisch. 'You can have it as soon as I know what the films are like. You'll have to wait while they are developed.'

'You are very suspicious,' said his visitor. 'But all right, I'll wait.'

Having put the money back in the safe and given his visitor some cigarettes, he locked him into the office and went down to the Embassy darkroom. There everything was in readiness. Ten minutes later the first film and then the second were ready to be taken from the developing tank and dipped first into the rinsing bath and then into the fixing bath. The negatives looked clear enough. Once they had been through the washing tank, Moyzisch turned on the light and peered through a magnifying glass at the two dripping films. 'Most secret,' he read. 'From Foreign Office to British

Embassy, Ankara' and a very recent date. That was all he needed to know. Going back upstairs, he found his visitor still sitting where he had left him. He looked up as Moyzisch came into the room. '*Eh bien?*' he said. Without a word Moyzisch went over to the safe and, feeling a trifle uneasy as he turned his back to his companion, unlocked it, took out the parcel of notes and handed it to him.

'Please sign the receipt,' he said handing him a piece of paper.

'I'm not such a fool as that,' said his visitor, pushing it away.

'We are so bureaucratic,' said Moyzisch, feeling a trifle foolish. After which the man tucked the bundle of notes under his overcoat, which he had not taken off, turned up his collar, pulled his hat down over his eyes and made off. '*A demain, Monsieur,*' he said, as he disappeared into the darkness. '*A la même heure.*'

That night Herr Moyzisch did not go to bed. The two rolls of film contained photographs of fifty-two different documents. When, several hours later he had finished making the necessary enlargements, he settled down to read them. They were quite clearly of incalculable value. Nor could there to his mind be the slightest doubt that they were genuine.

All were Most Secret or Top Secret telegrams which had passed between the Foreign Office in London and the British Embassy in Ankara. None of them were above a fortnight old and most of them much more recent. They covered the widest possible range of subjects, both political and military, and in addition to the regular correspondence between London and Ankara, also included exchanges of views between London, Washington, Moscow and other important posts.

Moyzisch went on reading till he fell asleep with his head on his desk. Apart from their intrinsic interest, the British telegrams made two things clear to him: first, the Allies' determination to destroy Germany and secondly, the certainty that they would succeed in doing so, and that in the fairly near future. In other words, his country and its leaders were inescapably doomed. What conclusion, he wondered to himself, would those same leaders draw from these documents when they saw them? It was an interesting subject for speculation.

'What about that valet of yours?' asked the Ambassador jocularly of his unshaven, bleary-eyed attaché next morning. 'Did you get rid of the twenty thousand pounds?' In reply, Moyzisch handed him the fifty-two photographs in a folder.

'When I picked up the first one,' Herr von Papen wrote later, 'my surprise was such that I must have given a noticeable start. . . . It needed only one glance to tell me that I was looking at a photograph of a telegram from the British Foreign Office to the Ambassador in Ankara. Form, content and phraseology left no doubt that this was the genuine article.' Soon he was making his way methodically through them. *'Fantastisch!'* he would exclaim from time to time. *'Unglaublich!* When are you seeing him again?' he asked after he had read through all of them.

'Tonight at ten o'clock.'

'I'll have to inform the Foreign Minister about this,' he said after a time. 'For purposes of correspondence we must give the man a code name. Since his documents are so very eloquent, let's call him Cicero.' 'It seemed,' he wrote afterwards, 'a happy nickname.'

Herr von Papen was, of course, no ordinary ambassador. Twenty-five years before as German Military Attaché in Washington, he had, himself briefly dabbled in undercover work. Just over ten years before, during the troubled times which preceded the end of the Weimar Republic, he had, as a conservative politician, briefly held office as Chancellor, quickly making way for General Schleicher, who in his turn made way even quicker for Adolph Hitler. His relationship with the Nazi leaders was an uneasy one. As a founder-member of Count Alversleben's Herrenklub, he had little sympathy with their aims and they, though he had never openly opposed them, disliked and distrusted him. In April 1939 he had accepted the appointment of Ambassador to Turkey without any great enthusiasm in the hope that he might be able to help keep Turkey out of the war which by then seemed inevitable.

Now that he has been given a name, though still only a code name, it is time to turn our attention to the true hero of our story, to Cicero. Who was he? And where did he come from?

According to his own account, he had been born thirty-eight years earlier at Pristina, in what is now southern Yugoslavia, the son of a Moslem religious teacher. His name was Elyeza Bazna. From Pristina his family had made their way to Salonica and thence, as the Ottoman Empire grew still smaller, to Istanbul. After the First World War he had learned to drive a car and worked for a time as a driver. Later he had become a *kavass* or manservant, first at the Yugoslav Embassy, then with the American Military Attaché, Colonel Class, then with Herr Jenke, and then, in April 1943, with Mr Douglas Busk, First Secretary at the British Embassy.

With the years he had acquired a smattering of French, English and German. He had taken singing lessons and conceived the ambition to become an opera singer. And with his savings he had bought a camera and learned how to use it. Somewhere along the line, too, he had got married and fathered four children. His wife lived with the children in Istanbul. He sent her money, occasionally took photographs of the children and in his own words, 'tried not to think about her'. Since entering the employment of Mr Busk he had found other, better things to think about. First of all Mara, the Busks' newly arrived nursemaid, slim, blue-eyed and black-haired, with flashing white teeth, graceful movements and an infectious laugh. And secondly the files of official papers which the industrious Mr Busk would bring back with him of an evening from the Embassy.

In next to no time our hero had had his way with the beautiful Mara. He had also managed to see enough of the Embassy files to acquire an incipient taste for spying. As he himself put it later: 'If you once start snooping, it becomes a passion, a vice.' Before long, having read at length of British plans to bring Turkey into the war, he had, or so he says, even convinced himself that by selling British secrets to the Germans, he would be helping Turkey to maintain her neutrality, and so performing a patriotic duty. But so long as he was only Mr Busk's chauffeur-valet, he calculated, neither Mara nor the top secret Embassy files would be as accessible to him as he would have liked. What he needed was a change of venue, an improved launching-pad for both projects.

It was not long before the opportunity he had been looking for materialized. That autumn, after only five or six months with the Busks, it came to his knowledge that the British Ambassador, Sir Hughe Knatchbull-Hugessen, was himself looking for a valet. It was too good to be true. He at once set to work.

He first convinced Mara, by now 'as inflammable as tinder', that they would be able to see each other much more freely if they were not living in the same house. He then induced her to talk Mrs Busk into persuading her husband to put in a word for him with the Ambassador. Somewhat surprisingly, everything went according to plan. Mr Busk recommended him to Sir Hughe and one fine autumn day, after only a brief interview, Sir Hughe engaged him. Next morning he started work at the Ambassador's residence, an agreeable enough modern building in a commanding position at Cankaya, on the outskirts of the city.

It did not take a man of Cicero's quick perception long to discover that Sir Hughe, an able, conscientious, career diplomat of the old school, was a man of regular habits. Every morning at seven-thirty he was called with a glass of orange juice. By his bed was an official black leather box. After being called, he stayed in bed for half an hour reading. Then he had a bath and dressed. It took him twenty minutes to eat his breakfast, after which he went to his study, preceded by the black box. Luncheon took twenty-five minutes. After luncheon, he would play the piano for an hour and a half. Before changing for dinner, as he always did, he would have another bath. Dinner, when he and Lady Knatchbull-Hugessen were by themselves, took half an hour.

There was also a routine which attached to the red and black official boxes and to the key to the safe which were all kept in the office of the Ambassador's Private Secretary, Louise. During the day Louise was in charge of the key to the safe. At night the Ambassador kept it himself with the keys to the red and black boxes.

For a prospective spy another useful discovery was that, while in the Chancery all official papers were subject to the most stringent security regulations, the often far more important papers which the Ambassador kept back to study personally were simply locked in Louise's old-fashioned safe or left in the black leather box by his bedside.

It was thus that one fine morning towards the end of October 1943, while Sir Hughe was splashing contentedly about in his bath, his valet, while nominally engaged in laying out his suit in the bedroom next door, was able to take a quick impression of all three official keys with the help of some wax which he had especially acquired for this purpose. It was now only a question of getting the necessary keys made and choosing the right moment to abstract and photograph a suitable selection of documents – none of them tasks that presented any serious problems to a man of Elyeza's experience and resourcefulness. After which there could be little doubt that his former employer, Herr Jenke, or one of Jenke's colleagues would provide a ready market for the resulting photographs.

The first meeting between Herr Moyzisch and Cicero had been on 30 October. The next took place, as arranged, on the following evening. When Moyzisch went down to the toolshed at ten, Cicero was already there. They greeted each other like old friends. Had everything been satisfactory? Cicero wanted to know. Moyzisch replied that it certainly had.

Once in Moyzisch's office, Cicero, having once again checked that there were no eavesdroppers, at his host's invitation poured himself a glass of whisky from a bottle obtained by Moyzisch's cook only that afternoon from the British Embassy in exchange for three bottles of hock. He then pushed two rolls of film across the desk. These Moyzisch took but was obliged to explain that he had no sterling available with which to pay for them, though some more was expected from Berlin shortly. '*Ça ne fait rien*,' said Cicero. 'You can give me the thirty thousand for these two rolls next time. I'll be back, *voyez-vous*. And I know that it'll be in your interest to keep me happy. Besides,' he added, 'I trust you.' And they drank to each other's health.

There were a number of things the Germans wanted to know about Cicero; his real name, for one thing, and how he managed to get such good photographs.

'I was amazed last night by the technical quality of your work,' said Moyzisch casually. 'Do you do it alone or have you an assistant?'

'I do everything myself.'

'Where do you do it? In the Embassy or somewhere else?'

'In the Embassy, naturally.'

'But how exactly do you take the photographs? And when? I'm interested.'

'Isn't it enough that I deliver the goods?' said Cicero, suddenly becoming less friendly. And Moyzisch changed the subject.

'You used to be Herr Jenke's servant.'

'If Herr Jenke says so, that is no doubt correct.'

'He can't remember your name.'

'I'm very sorry to hear it.'

'What is your name?'

'When Herr Jenke remembers it, no doubt I shall too.'

Once again he had not got much further.

'When shall I see you again?' asked Moyzisch before Cicero left.

'I'll ring you up when I have some fresh stuff,' he said. 'But I won't come to your office any more. It's too risky. We'll meet in a dark street in the old part of the town. You've got a car, I suppose? We'd better arrange a meeting place tonight, somewhere where you won't have to stop, just drive slowly along with your lights dimmed. When you get there, open the door of the car and I'll jump in. If there's anyone in sight, ignore me. Drive round the block and pick me up when the coast is clear. You'd better drive me into town now and we'll pick a place. There's another thing,' he went on. 'Just in case your telephone is tapped, I'll always give a time twenty-four hours later than I really mean. I'd feel safer that way.'

When Moyzisch brought his car round, Cicero got in behind him and drew the side curtains. From the back seat he then directed him through the dark streets to a part of the old town where there was a piece of waste land between two houses. 'This,' he said, 'will be our meeting place for the time being. And now will you drive me to the British Embassy?'

'Surely not?' said Moyzisch.

'Why not?' said Cicero. 'That's where I live.'

Obediently Moyzisch drove on up the steep hill to where the Embassy residence stands out massively against the skyline.

'Now slow down,' said Cicero as they approached the main gate. 'But don't stop.' Keeping his eye on the road, Moyzisch did as he was told. There was a click behind him as the car door shut. A few minutes later he was back at his own Embassy and hard at work in the dark-room. By six next morning he had forty more enlargements of secret British documents ready to be laid before Herr von Papen. They included the minutes of the Moscow Conference between Stalin, Eden and Cordell Hull.

On 4 November a special courier flew in from Berlin. With him he brought a little suitcase containing £200,000 in British bank notes – enough to keep Cicero going for some weeks.

Next day, 5 November, Herr Moyzisch came back to his office to find that his secretary had a message for him from a gentleman called Pierre, inviting him to a game of bridge at nine o'clock on 6 November. This, according to the arrangement they had made, meant that very evening. When Moyzisch went to get his car out, it would not start and it was not until just before nine that he managed to get it going.

Tossing a brown paper parcel containing thirty thousand pounds on to the seat beside him, he shot off through the darkness arriving at the rendezvous a few minutes late. The flicker of a torch showed that Cicero was waiting for him. Slowing down, he leaned back and opened the back door. Agilely the valet jumped in. 'Make for the new part of the town,' he said. 'I haven't got long.'

As Moyzisch drove, Cicero guided him through the narrow streets. 'Left now ... straight on ... turn right. Have you got my thirty thousand pounds?' he asked.

'Yes.'

'I've brought you another film. You'll like this one,' he said. As he passed him the film, Moyzisch handed over the money, which he tucked under his overcoat, without bothering to count it. He looked pleased with himself.

As they drove on through the streets, some dark and some more brightly lit, Moyzisch returned to the questions he had been instructed to ask. 'Berlin,' he said, 'wants to know your name and identity.'

'My name,' replied Cicero, 'is none of your business or Berlin's either. One thing though you can tell Berlin; I'm not a Turk – I'm an Albanian.'

'You once said you hated the British. Can you tell me why?'

'My father,' came the answer in a voice strangled by emotion, 'was shot by an Englishman.'

'Even after all these years,' wrote Moyzisch long afterwards, indulging in a little retrospective sentiment, 'I can still hear the way he said that. I remember that at that moment I was deeply moved. Perhaps there was a motive here more noble than mere greed for money. For the first time I felt a fleeting sympathy for the man behind me ... I did not put any more questions to him that evening.'

'I played on his credulity,' wrote Cicero no less revealingly many years later. 'What I said burst from me as if I were confiding to him an intolerably painful memory. The lie I told him carried me away completely. The thought that it might conceivably have been true made my voice sound hoarse. Moyzisch started. Now he had what he really wanted most of all – a really satisfactory explanation of my spying.'

'I'm sorry,' said Moyzisch contritely, 'if in the course of my questions I mentioned certain matters which . . .'

At this point he felt a hand on his shoulder.

'Switch off the headlights,' said Cicero. 'Slow down. *Au revoir.*' There was a click and once again Cicero had gone.

'I was left,' he wrote afterwards, 'standing in the dark street. A shudder went through me. I was filled with fear, fear of my father's anger. My father had died peacefully in his bed, and I had misused his memory. The poplars on the hill stood out like threatening shadows. I grinned sheepishly to try and drive away my fear.'

Shortly after eleven next morning Moyzisch delivered to Herr von Papen the enlargements of another twenty British documents, including a full account of the Casablanca Conference. In return the Ambassador handed him a telegram from Herr von Steengracht, Under-Secretary of State at the Foreign Ministry in Berlin. This announced that the Foreign Minister wanted to see Moyzisch in Berlin. He was to bring all the material so far received from Cicero with him. A seat was being kept for him on the Junkers 52 Courier plane leaving Istanbul next morning. To catch it, he would have to take the Anatolian Express to Istanbul that night.

When the Ju 52 landed at Sofia to refuel, Moyzisch was summoned to the information desk and informed that on instructions from SS General Kaltenbrunner a special plane was waiting to take him straight to Berlin. Wondering vaguely what all the hurry was, he climbed on board the military plane that had been sent for him and took off.

It was much colder in Berlin than in Ankara and there was some snow on the ground. At Tempelhof Airport Moyzisch was picked up by a car which took him straight to No. 101 Wilhelmstrasse, the headquarters of the Reichssicherheitshauptamt or Central Security Office, known as the RSHA.

Behind a vast desk in an enormous room sat SS General Kaltenbrunner, who had recently succeeded Himmler as head of the RSHA, a big, formidable-looking man with a booming voice and a face covered in duelling-scars. There were four other men in the room. 'These documents,' he said, coming straight to the point, 'might prove to be of extreme importance if they are genuine. These gentlemen are experts who will examine them from a technical point of view. As for you, you will tell us everything you know about Operation Cicero up to date . . . it's still possible the whole thing might be a cunning trap laid by the enemy.'

One of the four men then plugged in a tape-recorder and they started to cross-question him. The interrogation lasted for more than two hours, every word being recorded. Meanwhile the rolls of film were taken to a laboratory for closer examination, the results of which, however, cast no doubts on the genuineness of the documents themselves.

After this the four experts were sent away, leaving Moyzisch alone with Kaltenbrunner. The two of them moved to more comfortable chairs and the atmosphere became rather more relaxed. 'I had you picked up by special plane at Sofia,' said Kaltenbrunner, once again coming straight to the point, 'because I wanted to see you before Ribbentrop does . . . Ribbentrop is no friend of yours. You're too much one of Papen's men for his taste and you know how he hates Papen. As Foreign Minister, he'll now try and claim all the credit for Operation Cicero. I don't intend to let him. Operation Cicero is exclusively a matter for my department . . . Ribbentrop is still convinced the British sent the valet to you and the whole thing is a plant. Meanwhile incredibly important intelligence material is simply rotting in his desk and being wasted. We can't let that happen . . . I intend to speak to the Führer personally about it and see that in future Cicero is handled exclusively by this department. You are not to accept any more money from the Foreign Office for paying Cicero. By the way, the £200,000 you got the other day came from me.'

Herr Moyzisch's position was a delicate one. While nominally Commercial Attaché at the Embassy, he was in reality an official of the Sicherheitsdienst and therefore responsible not to Papen or the Foreign Office, but to General Kaltenbrunner. Feeling a little bewildered, he now said he very much hoped he could be told quite clearly from whom he was to take his orders. To which Kaltenbrunner replied that he would get the Führer to settle the whole thing once and for all. Then he returned to the subject of Cicero. 'Do you really believe he's being honest with us?' he asked.

'I think he's an adventurer,' said Moyzisch, 'vain, ambitious and intelligent enough to have raised himself out of the class into which he was born . . . he's lost his roots. People like that are always dangerous.'

'Couldn't he still be working for the British?'

'Possibly. But I have no doubt whatever that, if he is, one day he'll give himself away. So far I haven't seen the slightest sign that he's anything but what he says he is. Personally, I'm absolutely convinced the man is genuine. Especially after his chance remark about his father being shot by an Englishman.'

'What?' said Kaltenbrunner. 'Cicero's father shot by an Englishman? Why on earth didn't you report that? It might be the key to the whole thing.'

'But I did. In my last report. It went by diplomatic bag to the Foreign Office.'

'When,' shouted Kaltenbrunner, his features convulsed, 'did that telegram leave Ankara?'

'The day before yesterday.'

'Then Ribbentrop,' he yelled, leaping to his feet, 'has deliberately kept it from me. . . . What about the death of Cicero's father? Go on. Tell me.'

'The last time I saw Cicero on 5 November,' replied Moyzisch, also getting nervously to his feet, 'I asked him why he hated the British. "My father," he replied, "was shot by an Englishman." It sounded like the truth.'

'Did you ask him just how his father was killed?'

'No . . . I thought it better not to insist.'

'Try to find out all you can about his father's death. As for me,' Kaltenbrunner went on, walking over to the window and drumming with his fingers on the pane, 'I'll certainly ask Herr von Ribbentrop what he meant by not sending me your last report.'

Feeling, not without reason, that it might be better if Kaltenbrunner himself informed Ribbentrop of their meeting, Moyzisch asked the General to ring up Ribbentrop and find out from him when he wished to see him. Kaltenbrunner agreed and, having done so, told Moyzisch that the Foreign Minister would see him at seven the following evening. 'Good luck to you,' he said as he saw him to the door. 'You'll need it!'

For security reasons, Moyzisch left his briefcase with Kaltenbrunner. ('I hope you don't have a valet, General!' he said facetiously as he went out, but there was no answering smile.) Next evening it was brought round to his hotel by two important-looking functionaries. 'We come,' they said, 'from S.S. General Kaltenbrunner. We are to accompany you on your visit to the Foreign Minister and be present at your meeting with him.'

But the meeting turned out not to be with Herr von Ribbentrop himself. Instead, Moyzisch was received by two senior Foreign Office officials, Herr von Steengracht and Herr von Altenburg. In turn they examined the one hundred and twelve secret documents he had brought with him. '*Fantastisch!*' they murmured as they looked through them. '*Unglaublich.*'

'They certainly seem genuine enough,' said Herr von Steengracht. 'Look at this one.' And he pointed to the account of the Casablanca Conference, contained in Cicero's latest batch.

'You know, we can confirm this one's accuracy – we happen to be quite well informed about Casablanca. I can't imagine the British putting such an important piece of information into our hands simply as a decoy. And if this document is as genuine as it appears, I see no reason to doubt that your valet has access to his Ambassador's safe. But how does he do it? He must be a remarkable man.'

'He's certainly no ordinary valet,' said Moyzisch. 'Nor indeed an ordinary man.'

'So you believe in him?' said Herr von Altenburg. 'You exclude the possibility that he has been planted on us by the British?'

'I do. But I can't prove it. Not yet, at any rate.'

'There's nothing else you can tell us?'

Moyzisch shook his head and the two high officials got up. 'The Foreign Minister,' said Herr von Steengracht, glancing pointedly in the direction of Kaltenbrunner's two henchmen, 'regrets that he cannot see you himself today. You are to remain at his disposal. I assume we can find you at the Kaiserhof at any time?'

A couple of days later there was an urgent message for Moyzisch from Herr Likus, an older friend of his at the Foreign Office, to come and see him. On arrival Likus told him that the Foreign Minister wanted to see him immediately. He also told him that Ribbentrop was in a filthy temper and furious with Kaltenbrunner. Having himself looked at the Cicero papers, the Foreign Minister, it seemed, was as sure as ever that it was all a British trick. It would, Likus said, be a great mistake for Moyzisch to disagree with him on this or any other point or, if he could possibly avoid it, to mention Herr von Papen, whom he detested.

For some time after Moyzisch had entered the room Ribbentrop said nothing, but stood like Napoleon with folded arms, his cold blue eyes fixed bleakly on his visitor. Then they sat down at a table on which the Cicero papers were spread out. Ribbentrop picked some of them up and fanned them out like a hand of cards.

'So you have met this Cicero,' he said at length. 'What sort of man is he?'

Moyzisch repeated what he had already said and written a dozen times.

'The man's clearly out for money,' interrupted Ribbentrop irritably. 'What I want to know is whether his documents are genuine. What do you think?'

'My personal opinion,' said Moyzisch, 'is . . .'

'I'm not interested in your personal opinion. What does Jenke think?'

'He agrees with me in thinking the documents are genuine and that the man came to us of his own accord. Herr von Papen thinks so too.'

The Ambassador's name was scarcely out of his mouth when he realized what a fatal mistake he had made. Ribbentrop's expression became even more disagreeable. Averting his eyes and speaking slowly and very deliberately, he embarked on a prolonged tirade. What he wanted, he said, was not opinions but facts. If Moyzisch could convince him that the documents were genuine, he might be prepared to forget his past misdeeds. 'Do you,' he concluded, 'feel capable of handling this assignment or shall I send someone else to Ankara?'

Fortunately Likus now came to the rescue by suggesting that, as a first step, Moyzisch might concentrate on finding out whether Cicero had taken the photographs alone or with someone to help him. If the former, it would tend to support the theory that the papers were genuine. Ribbentrop agreed and rose to his feet. 'You are to stay in Berlin for the time being,' he said, 'I may want to see you again.'

'But Herr Reichsminister, Cicero is waiting for me in Ankara, probably with new documents.'

'You will stay in Berlin for the time being.'

And so Moyzisch stayed. During his stay he received invitations to a number of parties, most of which he accepted. At these parties he gained the disturbing impression that he was the centre of attention and that a lot of people knew not only about him, but also about Cicero. Clearly security had been bad. He was thankful when on the morning of 22 November he received instructions to return to Ankara.

By 25 November Moyzisch was back in his office. He told Herr von Papen of his experiences in Berlin. The Ambassador shook his head. 'Believe me, before they've finished, those gossiping idiots will land us in a first class row here.'

Cicero, Moyzisch found on his return, had telephoned a number of times while he had been away. He rang up again that afternoon and they fixed a rendezvous for nine o'clock the same evening. Moyzisch picked him up at the usual place. Where, he wanted to know, had he been all this time? In Berlin, he said. On his account. Which clearly pleased him.

This time Moyzisch took him to a room in a friend's house which he had borrowed for the evening. There were drinks and sandwiches and Cicero smoked a cigar. Moyzisch gave him fifteen thousand pounds for the last roll of film and took delivery of two fresh rolls. Cicero also wanted to be paid for one important film which he had taken but which in Moyzisch's absence he had had to destroy in case it was found on him. Berlin, said Moyzisch, would never pay good money for blank films. Remembering Kaltenbrunner, he then brought the conversation back to the subject that had interested him so much. 'Tell me,' he said, 'about your father's death.'

Cicero looked glum. 'I don't like talking about it,' he said.

'I just wondered what the details were,' said Moyzisch, persisting.

In the end Cicero let himself be persuaded. 'It was an accident,' he said, inventing hard, 'while they were out shooting. My father had been hired as a beater and that silly Englishman's stupidity lost him his life. But,' he went on, warming to his subject and helping himself to some more wine, 'who cares about the life of a poor Albanian? I don't suppose I'd have cared myself if it hadn't happened to be my father. If that fool of an Englishman had learned how to handle a gun properly before going out shooting, my whole life would have been different.' And before once again slipping out into the night, he went on to elaborate still further on his hatred of the British.

Among the latest batch of documents Cicero had managed to photograph were two of the highest importance, both of which made it clear enough that this was the real thing. One, a technical message, concerned the signal traffic between London and Ankara and enabled Berlin to break one of the British ciphers. The other was a comprehensive report, drafted by Knatchbull-Hugessen himself, on the subject of Turkish–British relations and showing clearly that he fully appreciated Herr von Papen's personal influence on Turkish policy. 'A lucid, sober draft, neatly arranged and elegantly formulated,' commented Papen, returning the indirect compliment which had been paid him. At least the enemy appreciated him, even if Herr von Ribbentrop did not. 'Berlin won't enjoy this one very much,' he added maliciously.

In transmitting the latest batch of photographs to Berlin, Moyzisch duly reported Cicero's account of his father's death. In order to annoy Ribbentrop, he was also careful to mention the important film Cicero had been obliged to destroy on account of his own enforced absence in Berlin. But all he got in return was a message to tell Cicero to photograph the documents again.

At about this time Moyzisch encountered what momentarily promised to be an awkward problem. Some time before, as a special favour, Cicero had asked Moyzisch to obtain for him five thousand pounds worth of United States dollars. He had therefore kept back five thousand pounds in bank notes from a consignment sent from Berlin and taken them to the manager of the Embassy's bank in Ankara, who had readily changed them for dollars, explaining that he had an Armenian customer who wanted to buy sterling for dollars. Moyzisch had then duly passed the dollars on to Cicero. Some time later, however, the bank manager had asked him to come and see him and told him that a Swiss who had bought the sterling notes from the Armenian and taken them to England had been told that they were forgeries.

On passing this information back to Berlin he had received an angry telegram from the Wilhelmstrasse, saying that the original notes were perfectly genuine and that the Armenian must have substituted forged ones, but that to avoid any suggestion of scandal the Embassy should reimburse the bank out of its own funds. Still suspicious, Moyzisch now took a selection of British bank notes from his safe to a bank in Istanbul to have them expertly examined. The answer he in due course received was entirely reassuring. The notes were perfectly genuine British bank notes. He heaved a sigh of relief. Even in Berlin they were evidently not foolish enough to imperil the whole project by paying Cicero in forged notes.

Meanwhile an enormous parcel had arrived for Moyzisch by diplomatic bag from Berlin. It contained a large number of books, both fact and fiction, on the subject of spies and espionage. With it came a covering note to say that a thorough study of these works should help him to handle Operation Cicero. To this he replied, as politely as possible, that he had little time for reading fiction and in any case found it hard to detect a parallel between the case he was handling and those of Mata Hari or Captain Dreyfus. What would help him with his work, he repeated, would be to know exactly to whom he was meant to be responsible. In reply he received in due course an unofficial note from a friend, begging him to be patient and implying that Ribbentrop and Kaltenbrunner were still hard at it. Not long after, his patience was rewarded, if that is the word, by a personal and strictly confidential message from Kaltenbrunner, informing him that he was no longer to keep Ambassador von Papen informed about Cicero or show him any of the documents obtained from him. This he decided to ignore. He also showed it to Herr von Papen, who, as can be imagined, was quite considerably incensed. 'Tell your superiors,' he said to Moyzisch, 'that as long as I am Ambassador here, I refuse to tolerate such procedure. You are my subordinate and I require you to show me all the material that passes through your hands.' It was a message which Moyzisch, while observing it in spirit, preferred, in his own interest as well as that of the Ambassador, not to transmit to Berlin.

Meanwhile every meeting with Cicero brought in more secret documents of the highest importance. Only Ribbenrop, consumed with jealousy and spite and apparently still convinced that the whole thing was a trick, maintained his resolutely negative attitude.

Cicero was delighted with himself. His life, when off duty, now left nothing to be desired. He had rented for Mara and himself a country cottage in the hills at Kavaklidere, small but luxuriously furnished with soft carpets, potted plants in every corner, a refrigerator that was always full, a canary singing in a cage, a wireless that played perpetual dance music and a bottle of whisky always handy. Above the door, in tiny letters, he pencilled his private name for it: 'Villa Cicero'.

Nowadays, he always had his hands manicured and a facial massage after being shaved. His suits were well cut and made of the best English cloth. He wore expensive shoes with thick crepe soles. He bought himself a showy gold wristwatch, which Moyzisch noticed with grave misgivings. Mara he drenched in expensive scent and decked out in the smartest clothes and finest underwear money could buy, all from the ABC on Ataturk Boulevard, the smartest and dearest store in town. 'If anyone sees us here,' she whispered, 'they'll wonder how we can afford it.' 'They're too stupid,' said Cicero reassuringly.

Mara enjoyed the whisky and was inclined to drink too much of it, but he liked her husky, whisky-soaked voice and gurgling laugh. He also liked an audience and in a moment of expansiveness told her of his clandestine activities, but let her think he was working for Turkish intelligence, thus making himself appear even more glamorous in her eyes. Once he caught her methodically searching the drawers and cupboards. 'The money's not here,' he said sarcastically, but Mara just laughed lightheartedly and then threw her arms round his neck.

In fact, the money was under the carpet in his room in the servants' quarters of the British Embassy, and multiplying rapidly – £30,000, £45,000, £75,000 – he did not even bother to count it. As he himself put it, he preferred relying on the unsuspecting British to relying on Mara. Besides, he said, he 'enjoyed the sensation of treading on it'.

It was also in his room in the servants' quarters that Cicero photographed the documents with a new Leica straight from Germany, a hundred-watt bulb and a cleverly contrived tripod consisting of a metal ring and metal rods which he normally used for hanging his ties on. From the wax impressions he had taken, he had had duplicate keys made for the official boxes. The documents he scooped up whenever the opportunity offered, tucking them under his jacket or covering them with a duster or a napkin in case he met anyone. Often he skimmed through them before photographing them, thus gaining an unusual insight into the politics and grand strategy of World War II. Several times he was almost caught red-handed with the documents on him but never quite. One night, or so he says, he actually took papers out of the black box by the Ambassador's bedside while Sir Hughe, who had taken a sleeping pill, was asleep and, having read and photographed them, put them back without waking him.

With his employer, meanwhile, he remained on the most amicable terms, bringing him his early-morning orange-juice, running his bath, pressing his trousers, laying out his clothes and in general giving satisfaction in every possible way.

At the same time he was giving even greater satisfaction to Moyzisch. Hardly a day went by without his ringing up to arrange a meeting. The month of December 1943 was to bring in a particularly rich crop of documents including full accounts of the Cairo Conference between Churchill, Roosevelt and Chiang Kai-shek and the Teheran Conference between

Churchill, Roosevelt and Stalin. It also brought the disturbing news that the Turkish President and Foreign Minister had gone to Cairo to meet Churchill and Roosevelt, when, as far as the Germans had known, they had never left Ankara.

One night towards the middle of December a faintly disquieting incident took place. Moyzisch had picked up Cicero in his car, a roll of film and some money had changed hands and they were driving aimlessly through the streets talking, when Moyzisch suddenly noticed a big black limousine some twenty yards behind them. He slowed down. It slowed down. He stopped. It stopped, the glare of its headlights lighting up the inside of his car with Cicero crouched in the back. They were being followed. He tried accelerating. The other car accelerated too. A wild chase ensued through the dark streets and alleyways of the capital. In the end Moyzisch got on to the city's great central boulevard and put his foot right down on the accelerator. The speedometer showed a hundred, a hundred and ten, a hundred and twenty. Looking round he saw that his pursuer was no longer in sight.

'Take me to the British Embassy,' said Cicero from the back seat. A hundred yards short of the Embassy gates he jammed on his brakes and Cicero jumped. Then he accelerated again and disappeared into the darkness. As he disappeared Cicero, from the sidewalk saw, or thought he saw, the other car sweep past in hot pursuit, the driver crouched tensely over the steering wheel. Moyzisch, for his part, though keeping a sharp lookout, did not again catch sight of his pursuer. For both of them, however, the experience had been an unnerving one.

At a dinner party a few days later, Herr Moyzisch found himself talking to a high Turkish official. 'My dear Moyzisch,' he said to him suddenly, 'you seem to be an extraordinarily reckless driver. You ought to be more careful, you know, especially at night.' Once again, Moyzisch was left wondering.

After the nocturnal car chase it was hard for either Moyzisch or Cicero to resist the conclusion that someone was keeping an eye on them. Soon other signs of trouble began to loom up on the horizon.

Shortly before Christmas a document photographed by Cicero made it clear that Turkey was preparing to grant Great Britain facilities for the infiltration into Turkey of military, naval and airforce personnel on a scale hardly compatible with the normal concept of neutrality. Without disclosing his source, Herr von Papen felt bound to make strong representations on this score to Mr Numan Menemencioglu, the Turkish Foreign Minister.

The latter not unnaturally assured him that he must be misinformed and that he had nothing whatever to worry about. But although Herr von

Papen had been careful not to give away his source, Mr Menemencioglu had no difficulty in putting two and two together. As soon as the Ambassador had left, he at once sent for Sir Hughe Knatchbull-Hugessen and gave him a detailed account of what von Papen had said, adding that clearly there must be a leak somewhere. Returning to his Embassy, Sir Hughe immediately reported this disturbing conversation to London. 'Papen,' he concluded, 'evidently knows more than is good for him.'

Barely thirty hours later Moyzisch, thanks to Cicero, had a copy of Sir Hughe's telegram in front of him. He at once realized that he was in the worst kind of trouble. He could not suppress this telegram and yet, when sent to Berlin, it would prove conclusively to Kaltenbrunner that he had deliberately disobeyed his instructions by showing documents obtained from Cicero to Herr von Papen. With a heavy heart, he sent it off. A week or so later came the expected personal letter for him from Kaltenbrunner's office. It said that he was held responsible for a gross breach of discipline and deliberately disobeying orders. Coming from such a source, he could barely bring himself to consider what that was likely to mean.

Cicero, as it happened, had also grasped the telegram's implications and understood that he too was in serious danger. His fears were confirmed when Mara, whom he half suspected of having betrayed him, said that she had heard her employer, Mr Busk, telling his wife that the Germans had a reliable source of information, perhaps in the Embassy itself, and that some British security experts had just arrived from London to investigate. Going to his room, he immediately removed his camera and the money and took them to his country cottage. And sure enough, next time the Ambassador rang for him there were the three experts, ready for a cup of coffee. Before long they were hard at work installing an alarm system and various other up-to-date security devices.

Quite apart from the warning they had received from the Turks, the British had learned of the leak (and of Cicero's existence) from another source, namely from intercepted German telegrams. They had not, however, been able to warn the Ambassador of this by telegram for the simple reason that Cicero, whoever he was, was clearly reading most if not all of their telegrams to Ankara. There was nothing for it but to send someone out to Ankara to deliver the warning in person.

It was thus that, happening to emerge at about this time from Jugoslavia, where I was then employed, the first person I met having dinner at Shepherd's Hotel in Cairo was my old friend, the Vice Marshal of the Diplomatic Corps and Premier Baronet of Great Britain, Sir John Dashwood, a genial, jovial and extremely astute character, on his way, as he put it, to sort things out in Ankara.

But this was to take time. No sooner had Sir John left London than fresh evidence came in with a bearing on the case. Once again it was unsafe for the Foreign Office to communicate with Ankara and so the sorting-out process lasted longer than might have been expected.

As for Mara, she had had no difficulty in working out where the information was coming from. But although Cicero was by now tired of her and letting her see it, and although she had him completely in her power, she did not take advantage of this. Mrs Busk, as it happened, was returning to England with her baby and when she asked Mara to go with her, Mara went, after first taking a tearful farewell of her former lover.

The latter, for his part, lost no time in providing himself with a new mistress in the eye-catching shape of his seventeen-year-old niece, Esra, fair and with a provocative laugh, whom her father had unwisely entrusted to his care, and who in her turn was installed at Kavaklidere and taken to the ABC store to be bought expensive clothes. Soon she, too, like Mara, had become a captive audience and the recipient of what should have been his most closely guarded secrets.

Early in January 1944 there was an addition to the staff of Moyzisch's office. Back in September his regular secretary had slammed her thumb in the door of the safe. This had interfered with her typing. Meanwhile the pressure of work kept growing and for the past three or four months Moyzisch had been trying desperately to find an extra secretary, hitherto without success. In December, however, Herr Seiler, the German Press Attaché in Ankara, happened to visit Sofia. While he was there, there was an American air-raid and in the air-raid shelter of the German Legation he happened to come across Herr Kapp, a senior member of the legation staff and his daughter Cornelia, who was working there as a secretary. Cornelia, blonde and in her early twenties, was, it seemed, highly strung and could not stand air-raids. Her doting father asked Seiler if he could possibly find her a job in Turkey, where there were none. And Seiler, remembering his colleague's problem, had said that he would see what he could do when he got back to Ankara.

Herr Kapp was a career diplomat and extremely well thought of. Until 1841 he had been Consul-General in Cleveland, Ohio, and before that in Bombay. Both his sons were serving as officers on the Russian front. His daughter was a trained secretary and a good linguist. With this background and these qualifications, she seemed just what Moyzisch was looking for. The necessary machinery was put in motion and early in January Cornelia was transferred to Ankara. The next time Cicero rang up Moyzisch at his office a new, rather attractive voice answered the telephone and the following exchange took place:

'Pierre speaking. Herr Moyzisch, please.'

'Pierre? Pierre who?'

Cicero, always on the look-out for fresh conquests, rather fancied her voice, and a little friendly banter followed before she finally put him through.

But Moyzisch found Cornelia less prepossessing than he had expected; listless, grubby, not particularly keen on her work and inclined all too often to be sulky or hysterical. He noticed on the other hand that she had extremely good legs, visible, when he was dictating to her, a long way above the knee.

Though he had by now accumulated well over £200,000, Cicero kept on photographing. A set of keys which Moyzisch had had made for him in Berlin fitted the Ambassador's safe perfectly and he could now do the greater part of his work when Sir Hughe was out. For a time the newly installed electro-magnetic security devices had presented a problem, but he had happened to overhear Sir Hughe discussing them with the experts from London and soon got the measure of them.

Towards the middle of January, on the 14th to be exact, came proof that should have convinced even Berlin that the documents were genuine. The minutes of some staff talks held during the Teheran Conference had revealed that on that date there would be a particularly heavy raid on Sofia by the United States Air Force. On 15 January Moyzisch, to satisfy his curiosity, put through a call to the German Legation there. The raid had indeed taken place the day before. The whole town was on fire and there were four thousand dead.

The end of January brought a disturbing bit of news: Dr Vermehren, an official of the German Consulate-General in Istanbul, holding a key position in the Abwehr and with access to vital information, had defected to the British with his wife, who was a connection by marriage of Herr von Papen. The rats were beginning to leave the sinking ship.

Cornelia, for once rather less lethargic, greeted the news with loud expressions of disgust. How, she asked, could anyone go over to the enemy when his country was struggling against such dreadful odds? What a despicable thing to do. And she went on to speak of her brothers at the front fighting for the Fatherland and later showed Moyzisch a letter she had had from one of them, describing the feelings of a manifestly decent young man, fighting grimly for his life and worrying all the time about the future for his country and those he loved.

Moyzisch felt momentarily encouraged by these signs of life on his secretary's part, but not long after was distressed to find her crying bitterly over her typewriter. He must, he decided, face up to the fact that she was emotionally too unstable and also too scatterbrained for the job she was supposed to be doing. Not long after, at his suggestion, Herr von Papen wrote a tactful letter to her father asking him to pick a suitable occasion to come and fetch her away. Her health, after all, offered a perfectly sufficient pretext.

Early in 1944 Moyzisch began to notice in the documents Cicero brought him references to an impending operation which was evidently both highly secret and of the greatest importance. In one document delivered early in March it was explicitly referred to by the code name Overlord. The documents gave no direct indication of what this represented, but if the name it had been given was any indication, it was clearly very important. There were plenty of other indications besides this that some decisive step on the part of the Allies was imminent. There had, for example, been a telegram from London giving 15 May as the date by which certain negotiations with Turkey must be completed, while from the minutes of the Moscow and Teheran Conferences Moyzisch knew that the British were committed to opening a second front in Europe some time in 1944. Suddenly, in Moyzisch's mind, it all fell into place: Operation Overlord must clearly be the code name for the second front.

Delighted at his discovery, he put this suggestion to Berlin. 'Possible but hardly probable', was the rather discouraging answer he received in return. And there for the next three months the matter rested. Nor was there in the meantime much hope of obtaining any further information on this subject, at any rate from Cicero. At about this time, he suddenly decided to cease deliveries. Whether because the job had become too hazardous for him or because the £300,000 he had already earned, over a million dollars, struck him as being enough, Moyzisch had no means of telling.

From the first Moyzisch had himself handled all the documents he obtained from Cicero and all correspondence relating to them in person. All letters from Berlin referring to them were sent to him in special envelopes marked 'Strictly Confidential – to be opened by Herr Moyzisch in person' and neither his regular secretary nor Cornelia had access to any of them. At the end of March, however, one of his correspondents in Berlin slipped up. A letter which not only referred to Operation Cicero, but also made it quite clear that it concerned something that was happening inside the British Embassy, arrived in an ordinary envelope and was consequently opened by Cornelia. 'Who,' she asked at once, 'is Cicero?' Moyzisch pretended not to hear, but she repeated her question.

'Listen,' he said in the end, 'there are certain matters which I have to deal with entirely on my own. This is one of them. Please don't ask me any more questions about it.'

'Oh, you *are* horrid!' she retorted, with maddening coyness. 'Won't you ever learn to trust little Cornelia?'

'No I won't,' said Moyzisch with a laugh and left it at that, reflecting that with any luck her father would soon come and take her away.

Meanwhile, though it sometimes went against the grain, he continued to try and be as nice to her as he could. A few days later she wanted to go shopping and he therefore gave her a lift into Ankara. When they got there, she asked him to come and help translate for her. She wanted to buy herself some underwear, so they went to ABC. Having turned the whole shop upside down, Cornelia still could not decide what to choose from the great pile of underwear that now lay on the counter. At this moment the door opened and in came Cicero. Marching up to the nearby shirt counter he proceeded to order some extremely expensive silk shirts to be specially made for him. Then, without any indication that he had ever seen Moyzisch before, he went up to Cornelia, who had now decided that she wanted made-to-measure lingerie and was having difficulty in explaining herself, and gallantly offered his services as an interpreter.

This she gladly accepted and soon he was asking her for her exact measurements and draping himself in ladies' underwear, as if he had been doing it all his life. 'I noticed,' he wrote afterwards, 'her auburn hair, her long legs, her eyes – the restless eyes of a woman with a great thirst for life.' Soon they were laughing and joking together as if they had known each other all their lives. Then, having settled his own account from a great roll of bank notes, he left the shop with an exaggerated bow to Cornelia and, when no one was looking, an appallingly knowing wink at Moyzisch. As for Cornelia, she had no means of knowing that this was Cicero, about whom she had been questioning her boss only a few days before. Nor, as they discussed her vital statistics, did Cicero recognize the voice of the secretary who sometimes answered the telephone when he rang up the German Embassy. Only Moyzisch, thoroughly irritated by the whole performance, was in possession of all the facts. Or almost all the facts.

It was some weeks before Herr von Papen received an answer to the carefully worded letter he had written to Cornelia's father. Herr Kapp said that he had not answered sooner because he had been suddenly transferred to Budapest and also because his wife had been ill. This meant that he would not be able to collect Cornelia before Easter.

From Moyzisch's point of view, the great thing was that she was going. He could easily put up with her for another few weeks. In spite of occasional displays of hysteria, her work of late had actually improved and he had even let her inform herself about Operation Cicero, though not about its details.

On 3 April she asked him if she could spend Easter with her parents in Budapest. One of her brothers was coming on leave and he would be there too. She would like to leave on the Thursday.

Disguising his joy with difficulty, he replied that he would see what he could do and went straight off to book her a seat on the train to Istanbul. Once she was in Budapest, he reckoned, her father would be able to keep her there indefinitely.

On the morning of Thursday 6 April she came to the office to say good-bye, announcing that she would be back in a week and bring them all Easter eggs from Hungary. Moyzisch said that he would come to the station that afternoon to see her off and bring her ticket with him. She seemed in the best of spirits.

Moyzisch was at the station half an hour before the train was due to leave. There was no sign of Cornelia. Twenty-five minutes passed and still there was no sign of her. By now he was badly worried. He was even more worried five minutes later when the train left without her. From the station he went straight to the flat she shared with another girl from the Embassy, who assured him that she had left the flat three hours earlier with two big trunks and a suitcase. What, he wondered, could have happened to her? Had she met with an accident? Could she have committed suicide? It did not seem likely. There was, on the other hand, another possibility which scarcely bore thinking about.

Distraught, Moyzisch went back to the Embassy and told the Ambassador, who was far from pleased. 'That,' he said unsympathetically, 'is what comes of employing hysterical women in responsible positions.' More worried than ever, he spent the rest of the day and most of the night scouring the city in his car, going to see anyone he could think of who might know where she was. There was no trace of her anywhere.

Next morning, as soon as the government offices were open, he did the only thing that there remained for him to do and went to see a senior official he knew at the Turkish Ministry of the Interior. He asked him whether the Turkish authorities could make discreet enquiries about the girl and added that the Ambassador was most anxious that nothing should appear in the press. There was a pause. 'I don't believe,' said the Turk at length, 'that there's been an accident or a suicide. I'm afraid I think it far more likely that your secretary has followed the example of the German defectors in Istanbul. In fact there seems to be hardly any doubt that that's what she's done.'

Moyzisch went back to the Embassy deeply distressed. The evil moment could no longer be postponed. Berlin had to be informed. With a heavy heart, he sat down to draft the necessary telegram, reporting Cornelia's disappearance and admitting the possibility of her defection to the enemy. By return came a stream of excited telegrams from Berlin, insisting that she be found at all costs. Then, on 11 April, came the telegram he had been waiting for. It was from General Kaltenbrunner's office ordering him to return to Berlin immediately. The following evening he left by the night express for Istanbul to catch the courier plane to Berlin on the 14th.

At the German Consulate-General in Istanbul Moyzisch found more mail for him that had arrived by the incoming plane: two more messages from Kaltenbrunner and one from the Foreign Office, all blaming him for Cornelia's disappearance and all recalling that it was at his instance that she had been transferred to Ankara from Sofia. There was also a hastily scribbled note for him from a friend of his in the Foreign Office. It warned him that he would be arrested as soon as he set foot on German soil. He was even suspected of having encouraged Cornelia to defect.

The plane was leaving next morning. He had barely twenty-four hours in which to decide what to do. In the end, after walking aimlessly about the streets of Istanbul trying to make up his mind, he sent a telegram to Berlin to say that he had fallen ill and that his doctor had forbidden him to travel by air. This at any rate gave him a respite. Then he went back to his room in the hotel and took a cold shower. As he got out of the shower, the telephone rang. 'I am calling you,' a voice said in English, 'on behalf of the British. If you go to Berlin tomorrow, you will almost certainly be shot. We want to give you a chance. Come over to us and save your life and the lives of your wife and children.'

This was the first of a series of such approaches, some made anonymously over the telephone and some through various intermediaries. Moyzisch rejected them all and simply went back to Ankara. There he found that everybody now knew that Cornelia had gone, but no one yet knew where she was. It was Cicero who provided the answer. They had arranged to meet two days after he came back from Istanbul. Cicero looked nervous. 'Your secretary's with the British,' he said. 'She's still in Ankara. What does she know about me?'

'She knows your code name,' said Moyzisch. 'Perhaps more . . . you had better get out of Ankara as soon as you can.' For the first and last time they shook hands. '*Au revoir, Monsieur*,' said Cicero and slipped back once more into the darkness.

Moyzisch was by now feeling genuinely ill. On Herr von Papen's advice he kept out of the office for the next week or two. Then he went back. Everybody, he felt, was looking at him and whispering about him behind his back. It was a trying time. Approaches direct and indirect continued to be made to him by the British. An anonymous letter delivered at his house contained a single line in German: 'At the British Embassy everything is known about Cicero.' Then, by the next bag, came an official notification from Berlin that an enquiry had been set up to establish how far he was guilty of aiding and abetting his secretary's escape on 6 April.

Not long after this, however, Allied pressure finally produced the desired result and diplomatic relations were broken off between Germany and Turkey. Herr von Papen left at the beginning of August and the Embassy was informed that any German citizens left in Turkey after the end of August would be interned.

During the weeks that followed, all the Embassy staff including Moyzisch were kept frantically busy arranging for their own evacuation and for that of the sizeable German colony in Turkey. Moyzisch and his family were due to leave by train on 31 August. But by then rail communications in the Balkans had been utterly disrupted by Allied action; the train in question never left, and they were interned in the Embassy compound, pending evacuation by sea in a Swedish ship. No Swedish ship materialized, however, until April 1945 and by the time they reached Gibraltar the war was over. By now it was the British who were waiting to intern them. For Moyzisch it had been a difficult and often unpleasant twelve months, but nothing like as difficult or as unpleasant as if he had obeyed General Kaltenbrunner's summons and returned to his own country when told to.

It was not for a good many years that Herr Moyzisch, by then living quietly near Innsbruck in the Tyrol as the export manager of a textile firm, was able to fill in some more of the facts about his one-time secretary, Cornelia Kapp. Though born in Germany, Cornelia had never felt at home there and spoke English as well as her own language, she had, it appeared, left her heart in Cleveland, Ohio, where her father, after a spell in British India, had served as Consul-General right up to America's entry into the war in December 1941. It was there that she had made all her friends and there that she had fallen in love with a good-looking American boy. Already in Sofia she had let herself be recruited by OSS, the American Office of Strategic Services. Her subsequent neurotic behaviour was, in her own phrase, 'all play-acting'. The move to Ankara fitted in perfectly with her plans and those of OSS, especially as the good-looking American boy from Cleveland was now in Ankara and, like her, working for OSS. Nor, from the Allies' point of view, could she have found a better section of the Embassy to infiltrate than Herr Moyzisch's office. Once installed, it only took her a short time to obtain the key to the safe. Once she had it, she copied and passed to her American contact a wide selection of secret documents, including those concerning Cicero. From these it soon became clear that Cicero must be employed at the British Embassy and the midnight car chase through the streets of Ankara represented a sporting, though unsuccessful, attempt on the part of OSS to discover just who he really was.

By the end of March 1944, Cornelia, well aware of the risks she was running, had decided, with the approval of OSS that it would be as well for her to get out. 'It had,' she wrote afterwards, 'become too dangerous. ... I had gained all the information about Cicero that it was possible to

obtain. I knew that he must be an employee of the British Embassy. I did
not remain in danger any longer.'

It had never been her intention to spend Easter with her parents in
Budapest. Instead of going to the railway station on the afternoon of
6 April, she had simply packed her bags and driven round to her American
friend's apartment. Her long fair hair was now cut short and dyed black
and her appearance altered in every possible way. After being smuggled
out of Turkey she was, by her own account, flown to Cairo for interrogation by the British security authorities. After the war, in return for her services to the Allied cause, she was allowed to settle in the United States,
where she married a former agent of the F.B.I.

Let us end, as we began, with Cicero. By April 1944, he, too, had begun to
feel that it was time for a change of scene. Cornelia's disappearance made
him all the more certain of this. He destroyed his camera, put his money
in a safe deposit in the bank, terminated the lease of his country cottage,
moved his mistress into a room in Ankara and on 20 April gave his notice
to Sir Hughe.

According to Sir John Dashwood, whose business it was to investigate
the source of the leak, the moment of truth came for Cicero late one evening
after the Ambassador had gone to bed. Taking a glass of whisky to help
him pass the time, Sir John sat himself down one night in the Ambassador's
study, turned out the light and patiently awaited developments. In due
course his patience was rewarded. The door opened and Cicero crept in,
key in hand. At that moment Sir John turned on the light and their eyes
met. Neither spoke; it was not long after this that Cicero gave in his notice,
thus becoming a gentleman of leisure with £300,000 to spend.

Or so he thought. He had rented a smart flat in the Maltepe quarter. He
had sent his shapely little niece Esra to the university and found himself a
new, more sophisticated mistress in her place. But time hung heavy on his
hands. After a few months he decided to go into business and eventually
used some of his great store of Bank of England notes to settle an outstanding account. In due course, after they had passed through various hands,
someone, feeling doubtful about them, sent some of them to the Bank of
England to be examined. They were pronounced forgeries. So, on examination, were the vast majority of the other notes he had been given. Of the
three hundred thousand pounds he had been paid, only the first thirty or
forty thousand turned out to be genuine. The next quarter of a million and
more were clever forgeries manufactured by the Reichsicherheitshauptamt
who kept a stock of them for their own nefarious purposes. And so, instead
of being a millionaire, Cicero found himself a man of much more modest

means, a change of fortune which by his own account he accepted philosophically, marrying a new wife twenty years younger than himself and fathering four more children before his death in 1971.

His story is by any standards instructive. Instructive, in the first place, to diplomats, sometimes a little remote from the ugly realities of life. Instructive, too, to anyone inclined to take spying seriously. For here, after all, was a spy who really came up with something worth having, who for once really did deliver the goods. But delivered them to customers, for the most part so obsessed with their own personal and interdepartmental jealousies and so reluctant to hear anything that was not to their own immediate advantage, that they largely failed to appreciate what had come their way at its proper value. Instructive, finally, to the spy, whose rewards are so rarely commensurate to the effort expended or the risks taken and who, in this instance, though supremely successful, was left at the end of the day with a vast pile of worthless paper.*

* It has naturally been suggested that Cicero was under British control throughout. On the evidence available this seems unlikely. According to Professor H. R. Trevor-Roper, however, who writes with authority and inside knowledge, Cicero had already been identified before he left the Embassy and for his final period of service there was used by British Intelligence 'to deceive instead of to inform'.

Seven

THIRD MAN

'One does not look twice at an offer of enrolment
in an élite force.'

KIM PHILBY

On 7 June 1951 the London *Daily Express* carried in banner headlines a
news story which was at once picked up by the press of almost every
country in the world. It reported the disappearance almost a fortnight
before of two British diplomats. That afternoon the Foreign Office
reluctantly revealed their names: they were Donald Maclean, head of the
American department of the Foreign Office, and Guy Burgess, who had
recently returned from Washington, where for the last year he had held the
post of Second Secretary at the British Embassy. Speculation as to their
whereabouts and the reason for their sudden departure knew no bounds.
Not only the Foreign Office, which was clearly much embarrassed by the
whole episode, but their families and anyone who had ever known either
of them were immediately besieged by frantic journalists, avid for any
scrap of information about them. Bit by bit, a rather more coherent
story emerged, though one which still left considerable gaps to be filled in.

A glance at the Foreign Office List for 1951 gave the bare outline of
Donald Maclean's career. Born in 1913, he was now thirty-eight, the son
of the late Sir Donald Maclean, a much respected Liberal politician whose
father, the son of a crofter, had moved from the Isle of Tiree to Cardiff.
He had been educated at Gresham's, Holt, and Trinity Hall, Cambridge;
had passed into the Foreign Office in 1935; and had been posted in 1938 to
the British Embassy in Paris, where he had remained until the fall of
France in 1940. Just before leaving Paris he had married an attractive
American girl, Melinda Marling. From 1940 to 1944 he had served in the
Foreign Office. In 1944 he had been sent to Washington as First Secretary.
moving to Cairo in October 1948 as Counsellor and Head of Chancery. In
1950 he had come back to the Foreign Office to be head of the American
department.

It seemed, on the face of it, an eminently satisfactory career. Maclean was able and intelligent and with his good looks and distinguished bearing, closely approximated to the popular idea of a Foreign Office official. Indeed, to those who met them casually, he and his charming wife seemed an altogether ideal young diplomatic couple. If, however, you looked a little closer or if you talked to anyone who had known Maclean at all well, you found that for all its apparent promise, his career had also had its distinctly seamy side. For one thing, he was inclined to drink and in spite of a second child in 1946 his marriage with Melinda had for some time been showing signs of strain.

In Washington the then Ambassador, Lord Inverchapel, himself a strange, flamboyant character, had been loud in his praises of his brilliant First Secretary. 'Donald's a sweetie,' he would say cosily, and to me, a casual visitor, he declared that my name sake was the best Head of Chancery he had ever known. Meanwhile his First Secretary, though no doubt performing his official duties quite adequately, was by now drinking a great deal more than was good for him. And when he had had a drink or two, he was inclined to express himself in the most unflattering terms on the subject of America and the Americans.

To those who knew him well there were other signs of suppressed tension, manifesting itself in a variety of different ways. It was true, of course, that his work at this time was both exacting and highly responsible. In 1947 he had been designated United Kingdom Secretary on the Combined Policy Committee, a body concerned with atomic energy matters and consisting of representatives from the United States, the United Kingdom and Canada. He was also British representative on the Combined Development Agency and as such held a permanent pass to the Headquarters of the Atomic Energy Commission, which he often found convenient to use out of office hours. To help him perform his duties he was naturally kept briefed by the officials of all three bodies in addition to being fully informed from London on his own country's atomic energy programme. It was perhaps only to be expected that after four exhausting years in Washington he should begin to show signs of strain.

For these and for other reasons Melinda, it seemed, had welcomed the move to Cairo, where the Ambassador, Sir Ronald Campbell, was an old friend of Donald's from Paris and Washington. They had an agreeable house and garden in Zamalek, with four Egyptian servants and an English governess. And Donald's promotion to Counsellor at the early age of thirty-five was a notable step forward.

But it was not long before the less reassuring side to Donald's character had broken out again, and broken out, this time a great deal more unmanageably. Soon he was drinking harder than ever and when drunk, would turn increasingly aggressive, denouncing the Egyptian Government and his own indiscriminately and on more than one occasion becoming involved in highly unedifying encounters with the Egyptian police who, until convinced to the contrary, found it hard to believe that the drunken barefoot vagabond they had picked up in some gutter was in fact the Counsellor of the British Embassy.

Matters reached a climax (or what anyone without much experience of these things might have expected to be a climax) in March 1949, when Melinda hit on the promising idea of giving a cocktail party on board a wide-sailed barge. While they and their guests were drinking and admiring the sunset, this would convey them fifteen miles up the Nile to Helouan (with luck no more than a couple of hours' sailing) where some friends had asked them all to dinner.

Unfortunately, however, things did not go according to plan. The wind dropped and it took them nearly eight hours to reach Helouan. Long before they got there, Donald was very drunk indeed and in a furious rage with his wife, whom he made a determined attempt to strangle, being only stopped from doing so by the combined efforts of their guests. After which he sat hunched and glowering on the deck. But this was only a beginning. On their disembarking at Helouan at two in the morning, an American friend who was with them fell on his head and fractured his skull. His attention attracted by the ensuing pandemonium, an aged Egyptian watchman now approached them, carrying an ancient rifle. Furious, Donald threw himself on the old man and, seizing his rifle, proceeded to swing it round his head in a menacing manner. Feeling that it was time to intervene, Lees Mayall, the First Secretary of the Embassy, a close friend, courageously grappled with him and a scuffle ensued in the course of which Mr Mayall's leg was broken, an injury for which Donald, now deeply contrite, prescribed a tumbler of gin as the only possible remedy. Their dinner host, when they finally reached his house, was anything but pleased to see them. It was a sadly battered and bedraggled group that drove back to Cairo in the cold light of dawn.

Although Donald had been in Cairo barely six months, it had already become evident to the Embassy Security Officer (though not apparently to the Ambassador) that it might be better if he were transferred elsewhere and he duly reported in this sense to the Foreign Office. His reports, however, were ignored. The Embassy, it was felt, could not afford to lose a man of Maclean's ability. The Security Officer also suggested that less than proper care was being taken to ensure that Secret telegrams (of which Cairo received a great number) were properly looked after in the Chancery and that none of them were taken out of the building. But once again his recommendations were rejected – as far as Donald was concerned, fairly brusquely.

It was not until May 1950, over a year and a great many more incidents later, that the decision seems finally to have been taken to send Donald home. His last week in Egypt was in many ways the most spectacular of his whole career there. On 10 May Miss Margaret Pope, a British newspaper-woman, was tipped off by a friend in the Egyptian police that a senior British diplomat was in jail in Alexandria. The Embassy strongly denied this. But Miss Pope, her professional instincts aroused, persisted and by a mixture of ingenuity and luck managed to be at the entrance to the British Middle East Office at the exact moment when two security men hauled a familiar figure down the steps and into a waiting car which took him, hotly pursued by Miss Pope, to the airport. After this the truth could no longer be suppressed. Donald, it seemed, had been arrested in Alexandria and thrown into a jail for drunken sailors. It was not until a couple of days later that he had been sober enough to explain who he was, whereupon he had been duly released. Mr Maclean, the Embassy Press Attaché explained diplomatically, was 'suffering from a nervous breakdown'. Miss Pope, who had seen him, knew just what this meant.

But there was more to come. In the course of his last forty-eight hours in Cairo he was continuously drunk and managed, before leaving, to break into and wreck the apartment of the American Ambassador's private secretary, ending up by dumping most of her clothes down the lavatory. 'The bloody girl's an American!' he shouted triumphantly, in explanation of his action.

After this the Foreign Office, who seem to have received favourable reports on his work from Sir Ronald Campbell, gave him six months leave for rest and reappraisal, before appointing him in November 1950 to be head of the American Department, a position of very considerable responsibility and one which automatically afforded him access to a wide range of top secret papers. His friends, meanwhile, were shocked by the speed at which he was obviously going downhill. 'His appearance,' wrote one of them, 'was frightening; he had lost his serenity, his hands would tremble, his face was usually a livid yellow and he looked as if he had spent the night sitting up in a tunnel . . . it was clear to us that he was miserable and in a very bad way. In conversation a kind of shutter would fall as if he had returned to some basic and incommunicable anxiety.'

To some of his friends it seemed that this anxiety might be sexual in origin – even that he might be a supposed or semi-suppressed homosexual. Encouraged by their well-meant speculation and by the advice of a psychiatrist, who urged him to be frank with himself, he fell (or thought he fell) passionately in love with the black commissionaire at a night club called the Moonglow. The latter, however, resented his attentions and made this abundantly clear to him in the ensuing punch-up. Melinda, meanwhile, had spent the summer in Spain with her children and a friendly Egyptian prince, who, however, left her abruptly on discovering that she had returned from a brief visit to England pregnant for the third time by Donald.

Towards the end of 1950 Donald bought a house near Westerham for his wife and children, with the idea, apparently, of returning there every evening. Sometimes he did and sometimes he did not. The next six months showed some slight resolve on his part to pull himself together, but a resolve that was tempered by frequent relapses, beginning with drunken arguments, as often as not ending in scuffles and fist-fights or by Donald simply passing out cold in some friend's flat long after the last train for Sevenoaks had chugged out of Charing Cross. On one particularly deplorable occasion at the Gargoyle Club, he is said to have bitten Rodrigo Moynihan in the knee. And there were other incidents of the kind.

Friday, 25 May 1951 was Donald's thirty-eighth birthday. He celebrated it by having luncheon with two old friends of his, Robin and Mary Campbell, starting with oysters and champagne at Wheeler's in Old Compton Street and continuing more substantially at Schmidt's in Charlotte Street. To the Campbells he seemed in better form, calmer and more confident, talking of Melinda's pregnancy and asking himself to stay with them in the country when she would be in hospital a couple of weeks ahead. To Cyril Connolly, another friend whom they met on their way to Schmidt's, he looked 'creased and yellow, casual but diffident', to become, however, after a brief exchange of pleasantries, 'calm and genial'. After lunch he had a couple of large whiskies at the Travellers Club in Pall Mall, cashed a cheque for five pounds and then went back for what remained of the afternoon to his desk in the American department. At five nineteen he caught his usual train back to Sevenoaks.

Outwardly, at any rate, Donald Maclean had seemed tailor-made for the Foreign Office. It was a good deal more surprising to find Guy Burgess there. Looking back, I recall my own amazement, when visiting Mr Hector McNeil, then Minister of State at the Foreign Office, in 1947, at discovering Guy firmly established in his outer office, apparently as his Private Secretary. Things, I reflected rather pompously, thinking back to before the war, were not what they had been in my day. Though excellent company in a noisy way and highly intelligent, he was by any standards an utterly disreputable character and, to do him justice, made no bones about this whatever. 'At this moment in history,' he would say, 'how is one expected to behave except badly?' Where, I wondered, had this promising young Labour Minister managed to find himself this particular Personal Assistant and what could they have in common? For the two of them were clearly on the friendliest possible terms. Nothing I knew about Guy from an acquaintanceship going back more than twenty years led me to suppose that he could possibly be the right man for this particular job.

Guy Burgess was the son of a naval officer who had died when he was still a child. After a year or two at Eton he had left to go, like his father, into the Navy, but had been rejected on account of poor eyesight and had come back to Eton for another year or two before becoming a scholar of Trinity College, Cambridge.

At Cambridge as at Eton, he was remarkable for his abounding energy, vitality and effrontery, all qualities which in their way contributed to his undeniable charm. Grubby, drunken, obstreperous, bellowing with laughter and bubbling with outrageous ideas, he was, amongst other things, openly and aggressively homosexual, forever boasting of his successes and flaunting his conquests – notably two teenage 'nephews' whom he would proudly parade along the Backs. Though at one time he claimed to have seduced Donald Maclean, who had been a contemporary at Cambridge, he later vigorously denied it. 'That great white body?' he would say. 'Never! It would have been like sleeping with Dame Nellie Melba.' A friend has left a vivid description of him, 'tall, medium in height, with blue eyes, an inquisitive nose, sensual mouth, curly hair and alert fox-terrier expression ... extrovert, exhibitionist, manic, cynical and argumentative, avidly curious', while another has written of his 'bird-bright ragamuffin face'.

In the long vacation of 1934 at the end of his fourth year at Cambridge, he visited Russia accompanied by a Communist friend from Oxford and provided with letters of introduction by a son of Lady Astor's. In Moscow we hear of him lying dead drunk in the Park of Rest and Culture.

After coming down from Trinity, where he took a First in History, Guy started in rather a desultory way to look around for a job. For a time he earned £100 a month advising a friend's mother, Mrs Charles Rothschild, on her quite considerable investments. After that, using to the full such contacts as he had (which were not inconsiderable), he tried the Conservative Party, *The Times* and the BBC. Up to now such views as he expressed had been more or less Left-wing. 'Guy,' said his progressive friends on learning of his latest aspirations, 'has gone fascist.' while one Marxist academic formed the opinion that he had moved so far to the right as by now almost to qualify for membership of the Labour Party.

A first approach to Conservative Central Office was unsuccessful (someone noticed how dirty his fingernails were), but in Captain Jack Macnamara, the ebullient Conservative Member for Chelmsford and, like himself a confirmed bachelor, he found a patron and occasional employer whose ideas, in their own way, were almost as unbalanced as his own and who amongst other things was a leading member of the Anglo-German Fellowship. Under Captain Macnamara's auspices, he paid a number of visits to Nazi Germany, including a particularly enjoyable one to the Nuremberg rally as leader of a group of ideologically-minded schoolboys, whom their parents had imprudently entrusted to his care. On occasion he even expressed admiration for what he saw there. 'A terrible thing had happened,' wrote his friend Cyril Connolly, 'he had become a Fascist! Still sneering at the bourgeois intellectual, he now vaunted the intensely modern realism of the Nazi leaders. His admiration for economic ruthlessness and the short cut to power had swung him to the opposite extreme.'

For some weeks in 1936 Guy was given a trial as sub-editor on *The Times*, but as a contemporary who was to have a distinguished career on the paper later explained: 'he was obviously not quite the thing for *The Times*'. By now he had in any case set his sights on the BBC and in October 1936, with the enthusiastic support of Dr G. M. Trevelyan who had a high opinion of his intellect and gifts as a historian, he was appointed to the Talks Department of the BBC, thereby still further widening his range of contacts.

By this time he had another part-time activity: when the occasion offered, he did odd jobs for the British Secret Intelligence Service. In this connection a valuable and convenient contact was the homosexually inclined Monsieur Edouard Pfeiffer, Chef de Cabinet to Monsieur Daladier, the French Prime Minister, and a man of some importance in the French Boy Scout Movement. Guy was also used by Monsieur Pfeiffer as a courier for confidential letters from Monsieur Daladier to Mr Neville Chamberlain, the then Prime Minister, who preferred whenever possible to conduct his foreign policy himself, thus by-passing the Foreign Office and eventually provoking the resignation of his Foreign Secretary, Mr Anthony Eden. The letters in question did not, however, remain as confidential as they were intended to for the simple reason that Guy was apparently having them photographed for a branch of the Intelligence or Counter-Intelligence Service (and possibly for other customers too) on the way. It seems possible that he was also the bearer of the notorious secret correspondence conducted at this time by Mr Chamberlain with Signor Mussolini.

During this period Guy's private life was as active and varied as ever. He was living in an agreeable but chaotic flat in Chester Square decorated in red, white and blue, which he maintained was the only possible colour-scheme, and sharing it at one time or another with various companions. In addition to the Reform Club in Pall Mall (where a large glass of port soon became known as a double-Burgess) and the Gargoyle, David Tennant's drinking club in Dean Street, he was a frequent visitor to the Bag of Nails, the Nest and many other similar places of entertainment and usually a vigorous participant in any incidents by which the proceedings there were enlivened. One of his most constant companions at this period was a seventeen-year-old dancer from Gateshead called Jack Hewit. In 1938 there was a momentarily embarrassing episode when Guy was arrested for alleged misbehaviour in a public lavatory, but in the end he seems to have cleared himself successfully of this charge.

Meanwhile his occasional work for the Secret Service had evidently proved satisfactory and in December 1938 he was offered a full-time job in a new secret department, which, it appeared, was being set up to handle propaganda and subversion in the all-too-likely event of war. It was exactly the kind of thing he had been looking for. He accepted with alacrity, starting work in January 1939.

Though formed under the relatively respectable auspices of the old-established Secret Intelligence Service, Section D, the department in which Guy Burgess found himself working on the outbreak of war, was at least as chaotic as any of the innumerable other clandestine organizations which sprang up at this time. Largely a product of private initiative and manned for the most part by enterprising individuals, who, foreseeing the war, had been anxious to provide themselves in advance with amusing and picturesque, but not unduly arduous employment, its aim was subversion and sabotage. From the start it was viewed with utter distrust by the Foreign Office and service departments who were expected to work in with it. I recall at about this time attending a meeting of the Chiefs of Staff in the course of which its representative, an undeniably bright but still relatively junior officer, boldly declared that the work in which he was engaged was far too secret to be discussed in the presence of such people as the Chief of the Imperial General Staff, the First Sea Lord and the Chief of the Air Staff. And to my amazement, got away with it. Whether the letter D was simply chosen to distinguish the new Section's head from C, the head of the Secret Intelligence Service, or whether as some people said, it stood for Destruction, we never knew. Not that it mattered much anyway.

Nor was Section D the only such mushroom growth. MI (R) was formed, it was said, for the purpose of supporting resistance movements favourable to the Allied cause or possibly just Revolution. There was also Electra House, the domain of Sir Campbell Stuart, an elderly whizz-kid remaindered from the First World War; not to mention the JBC or Joint Broadcasting Council and the PWE or Political Warfare Executive, all somehow responsible for 'black' propaganda and all lavishly provided with public funds and country houses at a comfortable distance from London and the bombing, which was soon to make work in the metropolis as risky or indeed riskier than most service with the armed forces. For anyone of Guy Burgess's tastes and appetites, these organizations offered almost unlimited opportunities for intrigue, for secret missions, for long unexplained absences from duty, for bright ideas and jolly drunken arguments and interminable discussions in smoke-filled, whisky-sodden rooms. At one time or another Guy seems to have served in most of them. Not long after the beginning of the war, he had moved into a large flat at 5 Bentinck Street. This soon became a meeting place and often an overnight stop for a far-flung assortment of drunks, homosexuals and people working in one secret department or another. As one pillar of MI5 was to observe later in his under-stated Wykehamist way, 'it was a bit of a standing joke in intelligence circles', while another friend describes it as having 'the air of a rather high class disorderly house in which one could not distinguish between the staff, the management and the clients'.

Amongst other more serious events, the summer of 1940 saw the liquidation of Section D and its replacement by a larger, longer-lasting and (improbable as this may seem) even more virulently chaotic organization under the direct responsibility of the Minister of Economic Warfare, Dr Hugh Dalton, and known as the Special Operations Executive or SOE.

With the disappearance of Section D, one might have thought that SOE would have provided the ideal niche for Guy Burgess, as it did for many kindred spirits. Instead he found his way back into the BBC, where for three years from January 1941 until the summer of 1944 he worked for the European Service, being responsible for propaganda to occupied Europe and liaison with SIS and SOE.

Here again, the work suited him. 'Reckless and indiscreet,' wrote a friend, 'he seemed to care for only two things, that, whether he succeeded or failed in the job assigned him, he should preserve his reputation for great ability . . . At the same time he was drinking and living extravagantly. He was fond of luxury and display, of suites at Claridges and fast cars which he drove abominably. He liked to breakfast, unshaven, every morning at the Ritz. He frequented foreign journalists and the correspondent of the Tass agency. He belonged to the febrile war-time café society of the temporary Civil Servant.'

And the friend, Cyril Connolly, goes on to give a vivid sketch of Guy's dream-image of himself:

Brigadier Brilliant, DSO, FRS, the famous historian, with boyish grin and cold blue eyes, seconded now for special duties. With long stride and hunched shoulders, untidy, chain-smoking, he talks – walks and talks – while the whole devilish simplicity of his plan unfolds and the men from MI this and MI that, SIS and SOE, listen dumbfounded. 'My God, Brilliant, I believe you're right –

it could be done,' said the quiet-voiced man with greying hair. The Brigadier looked at his watch and a chilled blue eye fixed the Chief of the Secret Service. 'At this moment, sir,' and there was pack-ice in his voice, 'my chaps are doing it.'

Of one thing there could still be no doubt. Dirty, drunken and disreputable though he was, Guy Burgess had charm, charm deriving from his abounding energy, his intellectual capacity and indeed from his outrageous effrontery. 'He was,' writes another of his many friends (and he had many), 'persistent as a child is persistent, who always knows it will have its own way if it is willing to behave badly enough; and Guy always was willing to behave badly enough.'

Guy might well have stayed in the BBC for the rest of the war. In June 1944 he was offered a temporary job in the News Department of the Foreign Office which he readily accepted. Here, he was even more in his element. His colleagues in the department were sympathetic, entertaining even. He liked the rough and tumble of journalism and the company of hard-drinking, quick-thinking newspapermen. The briefings he gave the press were never dull. What is more, his work was appreciated in official circles. He was promoted and, better still, 'established'. Miraculously he had, amid the turmoil of war somehow become what, strangely enough, he had always wanted to be: a permanent Foreign Office official.

Such, as I was later to discover, had been the processes which led to his appointment in 1946 as personal secretary to Hector McNeil, the Minister of State, a key position at the very centre of government at a critical time in history. With his Minister, whom he had first met when working for the BBC and who had himself been a newspaperman, he was on the best of terms, accompanying him on his trips abroad and seeing to it that his creature comforts and newly developed taste for high living (which his personal secretary certainly shared) were adequately provided for. Indeed, according to one friend, 'McNeil listened to Guy's views with a deference which often seemed as if it were Guy who was his superior, rather than the other way.'

Towards the end of 1947 Hector McNeil, clearly a little dazzled by his Private Secretary's brilliance, conviviality and self-assurance and wishing, in the kindness of his heart, to further his future career in the Foreign Office, arranged for him to be appointed to a political department, the Far Eastern Department, his object being to widen his protégé's experience and fit him for further promotion. For a short time in 1948 he seems also to have served in a new Communist-watching department set up by Christopher Mayhew, the resolutely right-wing Socialist who was then Under-Secretary at the Foreign Office, by whom, however, he was quickly dismissed as 'dirty, drunk and idle'.

Not long after this he was (no doubt justifiably) pushed down the steps of a night club by a friend who was later to become an ambassador. He suffered a cracked skull and severe concussion. Having been given two or three weeks' leave by the Foreign Office in which to recover, he spent these with his mother in Tangier and Gibraltar. While there, he drank as heavily as usual and there were a number of incidents of the kind which inevitably marked his progress wherever he went. 'For God's sake shut up, Guy' shouted an old friend from Eton days, as he disported himself one night at Dean's Bar in Tangier. But nothing did the slightest good. 'Little boys are cheap today,' he kept singing at lunch-time in the Café de Paris, 'cheaper than yesterday.' And when one of a group of respectable British tourists complained, he retorted, no doubt with the feeling that he was neatly hitting the nail on the head, that there was nothing to stop him singing the Eton Boating Song if he felt like it.

But this was not all. In the course of conversation Guy was also guilty of at least one grave breach of security. All of which was investigated locally and then reported back to London, with the result that on his return Guy was very nearly sacked altogether.

But not quite. Once again Hector McNeil seems to have intervened; Burgess's misdemeanours were again overlooked; and in August 1950 he was appointed to Washington as Second Secretary with special responsibility for Far Eastern affairs, at this time a particularly important field, the Korean War having started a couple of months earlier. Before he left to take up his new appointment, his friend Hector, now Secretary of State for Scotland, tried to give him a little guidance, the occasion being a farewell party at a flat Guy had taken in New Bond Street and at once redecorated in the usual red, white and blue. 'Don't,' Hector said, 'be too aggressively left-wing. Don't get involved in race-relations. And, if you can, avoid homosexual incidents.' His well-meant advice gave Guy an opening which he could not resist. 'In other words, Hector,' he retorted with exceptional felicity, 'you mean I mustn't make a pass at Paul Robeson.'

The Secretary of State was right to be nervous. From the Embassy's point of view, Guy was not what was needed in Washington. Soon, disapproving violently of British policy in the Far East, he clashed directly with his own immediate superior Hubert Graves, a distinguished official with immense experience of Far Eastern affairs, whom he scathingly dismissed as 'the wrong type of ex-consul'. It was not long before he was shifted to a section of the Embassy where, though certainly not fully employed, he could at least do less actual harm.

Nor, as can be imagined, was his conduct out of office hours any more satisfactory. Quite apart from his sex-life, he was now drinking, arguing and brawling more than ever. One of his colleagues, Kim Philby, an old friend from Cambridge and Secret Service days, who was working at the time as a liaison officer between the British Secret Service and the American CIA with the rank of First Secretary at the Embassy, had been kind enough to offer to put him up when he arrived and for a time he stayed with him and his attractive wife in their agreeable house on Nebraska Avenue. Though he was good enough to company, Aileen Philby, who was expecting a baby, found him a definite strain as a house-guest, rolling home at all hours and leaving empty bottles all over the place. 'Who do you think has arrived?' she wrote despairingly. 'Guy Burgess. I know him only too well. He will never leave our house.' The four Philby children, on the other hand, Josephine, Miranda, John and Tommy, regarded drunken Uncle Guy with a mixture of awe and delight. Smelling strongly of drink, he was always bringing them presents and, not having much else to do, would spend hours playing with John's electric train in the basement. After a time Kim Philby made it clear to him that he could not stay with them indefinitely and in due course he found himself an apartment of his own, where he soon created the cosy, casual, squalid atmosphere that had come to characterize all his places of residence. But he remained on friendly terms with the Philbys and would often spend the weekend with them.

A first incident of the kind which was apt to mark Guy's social life anywhere came four months after his arrival, in December 1950, when he crashed an evening party given in his beautiful Washington home by Mr Joseph Alsop, the distinguished American columnist, for Mr Michael Berry, the proprietor of the London *Daily Telegraph*, and his wife Pamela, daughter of the great Lord Birkenhead and a famous London political hostess. The party was a formal one to which the beau-monde of Washington (as elegant as ever) had been summoned in strength. Bursting drunk, dirty and, above all uninvited into this select gathering, it took Guy hardly any time at all to become involved in a noisy rampaging argument that threatened almost immediately to become a brawl. For Mr Alsop, who under a calm and elegant exterior, is a man of iron determination, there was nothing for it but to turn him out of the house. Had Guy tried, he could not have found a more certain way of attracting unfavourable attention and getting himself and his shortcomings talked about amongst people who, as the saying is, mattered.

Meanwhile he was beginning to attract attention in other quarters as well. The Embassy Security Officer, for one, was disturbed to find that the new Second Secretary was as often as not drunk in office hours, was extremely careless with classified papers and paid not the slightest attention to the various security regulations which he sought optimistically to introduce. Sooner or later, he decided, Burgess would have to go.

Finally in February 1951 an incident occurred which brought the Ambassador, Sir Oliver Franks, somewhat abruptly to the same conclusion.

Guy was stopped no less than three times in one day for speeding by the Virginia State Police. ('I was doing at least a hundred,' he said angrily when they charged him with driving at eighty miles an hour.) But more disturbing still, in the atmosphere then prevailing, was the fact that accord-to an FBI report, the American who was with him in the car had a record of homosexual offences. For Sir Oliver and his advisers that was enough and at the beginning of May Burgess sailed for London in the *Queen Mary*.

Guy Burgess landed at Southampton on 7 May. Career-wise his prospects were quite clearly not good. Thanks to Hector McNeil, he had survived one disciplinary board. He could scarcely hope to survive another. 'Resign before they sack you and find something else,' was the frank advice of his old friend Harold Nicolson, the writer and former diplomat. He accordingly took a few soundings with likely newspaper proprietors including Michael Berry of the *Daily Telegraph*, and was soon saying that he had the offer of several jobs. A week or two after his return he had lunch at the Royal Automobile Club with Donald Maclean. He wanted, or so he said, to give Donald some messages from his brother in America and to discuss with him a long memorandum he had written on the dangers of the situation in the Far East. But precisely what passed between them on this occasion was to remain for the time being their secret.

On the morning of 25 May, Guy Burgess woke at around nine o'clock in his flat in New Bond Street. His friend of nearly fifteen years, Jack Hewit, the former dancer from Gateshead, brought him a cup of tea in bed and, leaving him to drink it, went off to work.

Guy could afford to take it easy. The Foreign Office showed no signs of wanting to employ him and so far nothing else had materialized. Meanwhile he was proposing to take a short holiday abroad in the agreeable company of Bernard Miller, a progressive young American he had met on the *Queen Mary*, and, with this in view, he had booked a two-berth cabin on the SS *Falaise*, sailing from Southampton at midnight that night for St Malo and (for anyone who cared to make the round trip) returning via the Channel Islands on Monday. But Guy and Bernard were planning to go further afield. From St Malo, if they felt like it, they could take the train to Paris or even to Italy, where they might visit a friend of Guy's, the poet Auden. Just before ten Guy, having completed his toilet, made a telephone call to another acquaintance, Mrs Stephen Spender. He was, he said, trying to get into touch with Auden, who was then in London. He seemed to her entirely relaxed and in no particular hurry.

At ten-thirty Guy was due to meet Bernard Miller in the lobby of the

Green Park Hotel to finalize the plans for their trip. He was there on time, but, unlike Mrs Spender, Miller found him anything but relaxed. On the contrary, he seemed in a state of considerable agitation. He might easily, he said, as they walked together in the nearby Green Park, have to call their trip off. A young friend of his in the Foreign Office was in serious trouble and he was the only one who could help him. He would let him know about the trip one way or another by eight-thirty that evening. And he hurried off to make whatever arrangements he needed to make. Something, evidently, had happened between ten and ten-thirty to necessitate a complete change of plan. One can only surmise what it was.

The arrangements which Guy now proceeded to make were relatively simple. He ordered a self-drive car, a white Austin 70, from a firm in Wigmore Street and collected it a little after two o'clock. From Messrs Gieves in Bond Street he bought a white mackintosh and a new suitcase. In the suitcase he packed some shirts and underwear, a tweed suit and a dinner-jacket, while into his Foreign Office black leather briefcase bearing the royal cipher in gold he crammed nearly £300 in notes and a bundle of Savings Certificates. He was just leaving the flat with his luggage when Jack Hewit came back from work. Guy, he thought, seemed worried and in a hurry. He did not call Bernard Miller back.

Instead, from New Bond Street he now drove down to the Macleans' house at Tatsfield near Westerham. Whether, before doing so, he rang up Donald Maclean at the Foreign Office is not known. What is certain is that, having arrived at Tatsfield, he had dinner there with Donald and Melinda, being introduced to Melinda, or so she said afterwards, as Roger Styles. After dinner the two men walked in the garden. Donald (once again according to Melinda) then said that they had to go and see a friend of Ronald's near Andover and might have to stay the night there. He would, he promised, be back next day. He then took a dressing-gown and his brief-case and got into the car with Guy.

From Tatsfield they drove to Southampton arriving just in time to catch the *Falaise* before she left at midnight. They left the car by the quayside. 'What about the car?' yelled a dockhand. 'Back on Monday,' shouted Burgess.

Burgess and Maclean had left St Malo on a Friday night. The first hint the Foreign Office had of their departure was on the following Monday morning when Maclean failed to show up at his desk in the American Department. Burgess, being on leave, had no work to go to. When Melinda Maclean was asked where her husband was, she replied that she did not know and could think of no reason why he should suddenly want to disappear.

As soon as it became generally known, the disappearance of Guy Burgess and Donald Maclean caused a considerable stir, not only in Great Britain, but in America (where Senator Joseph McCarthy's current witch-hunt had roused public opinion to fever heat), and all over the world. Soon the wildest theories were circulating concerning both the reasons for their sudden departure and their present whereabouts. It became a kind of mad guessing game. Had they, one of their friends asked, 'disappeared on an alcoholic fugue, to wander about like Verlaine and Rimbaud and to start a new life together?' Or had they gone to Russia together 'to make a personal appeal for the ending of the war in Korea?' To those who knew them best anything seemed possible. As someone closely involved was to write afterwards, 'explanations of extraordinary silliness were offered in preference to the obvious, simple truth'.

Meanwhile, immediate steps had of course been taken to try and find out what they had done on reaching France. At Saint Malo, where the *Falaise* had docked at ten next morning, they had, it seemed, remained on board, breakfasting and drinking beer until all the other passengers had gone on shore. Then they too had disembarked just after the Paris express had left the station and, leaving behind Guy's new suitcase, had taken a taxi to Rennes, a railway junction fifty miles away, giving, the driver recalled sourly, no tip on a fare of 4,500 francs. At Rennes they could again have caught the train for Paris, had they wished to. They could also, it was surmised, have travelled as far as Le Mans and there changed trains. But no one had seen them join the train or alight from it either in Paris or at Le Mans. Instead, all trace of them ceased after they had paid off the taxi at Rennes.

On 7 June, however, three telegrams arrived, handed in at ten the night before at an all-night post office in Paris. One was from Guy Burgess to his mother, saying that he was starting on a long Mediterranean holiday. Two were from Donald Maclean: one, signed with a pet name, to his mother and one to Melinda. 'Had to leave unexpectedly,' the latter ran, 'terribly sorry. Am quite well now. Don't worry, darling. I love you. Please don't stop loving me. Donald.'

To most people the likeliest solution of the problem (but also the most shocking) by now seemed to be that the Missing Diplomats, as the newspapers called them, had disappeared behind what had come to be called the Iron Curtain. This was an awkward thought, implying as it did that they had been working for the Russians all along. A trifle belatedly everyone now started to dredge up from their subconscious scraps of evidence to show that both had been Communists, or something very like it, from the start.

The present author for one. My first encounter with Donald Maclean had been eighteen years earlier, in the summer of 1934, at a dance at the

Savoy. I had passed into the Diplomatic Service the year before and was consequently quite pleased with myself – the model, I hoped, of a promising young diplomat. My hostess suggested that I might like to meet a slightly younger namesake of mine who also hoped to become a diplomat. I could think of things I would sooner have done at that particular moment, but agreed politely and for five minutes made conversation with a tall, rather droopy, good-looking, golden-haired young man in faultless white tie and tails who caused me no more than momentary astonishment by announcing (it was almost the first thing he said) that he was a member of the Communist Party. 'Yes,' said his clearly adoring mother, joining in the conversation. 'Donald is even more of a radical than his dear father was.'

Lady Maclean's rather naïve comment illustrates as well as anything most people's attitude at that time towards Communism, particularly those who prided themselves on being progressive. A Communist was simply someone even more progressive than a Liberal or a Socialist. For my part, I assumed that with Donald, as with so many of my contemporaries, it would be no more than a passing phase. I also felt, knowing nothing of his academic qualifications, that it was fairly unlikely that he would get into the Foreign Office.

In this I was wrong. Returning to London on leave three or four years later, the first person I met in the passages of the Foreign Office was Donald, elegant in the black coat and striped trousers which were to earn him in the typing-pool the sobriquet of Fancy-Pants Maclean (to distinguish him, I learned in due course, from Fitz-Whiskers). I had spent part of the intervening period in Paris (where the Front Populaire was in power); I had met such significant Communist leaders as Maurice Thorez, Gabriel Péry and Marcel Cachin; and I was by now at our Embassy in Moscow – Stalin's Moscow, the Moscow of the purge trials. By this time I had a rather better idea of what Communism was about and of what being a Party Member involved. 'Are you,' I asked Donald, for want of anything better to say, 'still a member of the Communist Party?' 'Why do you ask that?' he said, a trifle sharply. 'Because last time we met you said you were.' 'Oh, that,' he said, 'was simply a childish aberration. I can assure you that now I am well to the right of you.' (Which he correctly assumed, was some way to the right of centre.) And he went on to assure me and re-assure me of this at considerable length. At greater length, it seemed to me, than the denial of a childish aberration really warranted. But even so, I had not (as with the hindsight of eighteen years, I realized I perhaps should have done) rushed round to MI5 to denounce him. Rightly or wrongly, that kind of precaution had not yet become normal practice.

Like my own recollections of eighteen years before, much of the evidence which now came pouring in from all quarters concerning the apparent left-wing tendencies of both Burgess and Maclean went back a long way. Donald, it was discovered, had, while at Cambridge, written an article proclaiming that capitalist society was 'doomed to disappear'. He had also announced to anyone who cared to listen that he was a Marxist and, as soon as he came down, would be off to Russia to give a helping hand with the Revolution. Both he and Guy Burgess had taken part in the Cambridge Anti-War Demonstration of November 1933, directed against any attempt at British re-armament in the face of the already emerging Hitlerite menace, and roughly corresponding to the publicly declared determination of the Oxford Union 'in no circumstances to fight for King and Country'. As for Guy Burgess, while lunching every day at the Pitt Club, where the food was a good deal better, he had, it now appeared, even organized a strike of college waiters at Trinity. At a time, of course, when a greater number of other undergraduates at both universities were making a number of equally meaningful (or meaningless) and equally progressive (if that is the word) gestures.

Once safely in the Diplomatic Service, Maclean had on the whole refrained from unduly provocative pronouncements, at any rate in public (his interests, he had remarked jokingly in 1936, now lay 'with the oppressors rather than with the oppressed'). Burgess, on the other hand, a more self-confident, extrovert character, had among friends never really bothered to make a secret of his left-wing ideas, any more than he did of his homosexuality or his drunkenness. Sometimes, especially when he had had a drink or two, he would go further still. 'I am,' he told a friend quite frankly in 1938, 'a Comintern agent.' And the friend, a fairly progressive Fellow of All Souls, though a little surprised, had come to the conclusion that in the circumstances then prevailing, 'it did not seem immoral to work for the Comintern'.

As for Donald Maclean, it had not, it seemed, been until much later, not, in fact, until a short time before their disappearance, that he, in his less guarded moments, had again begun to blurt out what was beginning to look more and more like the truth. To one friend he had spoken of his longing 'for a leap of faith that would convince him that Communism was right'. To a group of cronies at the Gargoyle he had announced dramatically between drinks that he was 'the English Hiss'. 'What would you do,' he had asked a friend, 'if I told you I was working for Uncle Joe?' By this time, moreover, he had begun to show ever increasing signs of almost obsessive anxiety, fear and tension. Fear, in particular, of two real or imaginary men who he thought were always following him. 'There are two men in a car waiting outside,' he had written to a friend. 'They've been there for four hours. Are they after me?' And then he went on to wonder whether these 'men in a car' really existed or whether they were not, perhaps simply the figments of a disturbed mind.

In fact it is quite possible that they did exist and that he had seen them. Since 1949 at least the Security Authorities had, thanks to the revelations of a Soviet defector, come to realize that the Russians had a spy working for them in the Foreign Office. Gradually the field of suspicion had been narrowed down to several suspects of whom Maclean was one. Since then he had been kept under observation (though not, by an odd quirk of the British system, at weekends), and steps had been taken to ensure that he no longer received quite as many secret papers as he would have done normally.

By the beginning of May he was the principal suspect. Finally, on the morning of Friday, 25 May, while Donald was looking forward to his birthday lunch with Robin and Mary Campbell, Mr Herbert Morrison, at the time His Majesty's Principal Secretary of State for Foreign Affairs in Mr Attlee's Government, had actually put his signature to a document authorizing his interrogation at 11 am on the following Monday, 28 May, by Mr William Skardon, one of MI5's toughest and most experienced investigators. But by Monday Donald was elsewhere.

Once the investigation into the disappearance of Burgess and Maclean had got under way, one of the questions which began to be asked most insistently, both in public and in private, was what had made the disappearing diplomats disappear when they did? In other words, how had Donald Maclean discovered that he was seriously suspected of being a Soviet agent; that he was going to have to face Mr William Skardon of MI5 on Monday, 28 May; and that he had therefore better get out of the country as quickly as he could?

In trying to find an answer to this question it was very difficult to avoid the conclusion that someone with the necessary information at his disposal had tipped him off or, rather, in view of the known circumstances of their departure, that someone had tipped off Guy Burgess and that Guy, walking up and down the lawn at Tatsfield on the evening of Friday, 25 May or possibly, for example, over their lunch at the Royal Automobile Club, had in turn passed the information on to Donald and, having done so, had decided to take no further chances and go with him. Indeed a possible pattern of events seemed to be that at the RAC Guy had given Donald a general warning that he was under suspicion, and that it had not been until around ten on the morning of 25 May that he himself had suddenly received the deeply disturbing news of Donald's impending interrogation which had made their immediate departure essential.

Clearly a first step in any such investigation would be to find out, first, exactly who in the Foreign Office and in the other services concerned had known that Maclean was under suspicion and was about to be interrogated and, secondly, who amongst those possessing this information would have had the occasion or opportunity or, indeed, the wish to pass it on to Burgess.

Once again the net was cast as wide as possible. Once again a process of gradual elimination narrowed the number of suspects to a mere handful. And once again, amongst the possible starters, one name began to stand out as at any rate a possibility – the name, this time, of Kim, more officially, Harold Adrian Russell Philby, whom we last saw acting as a link between the CIA and the SIS and offering welcome hospitality to his old friend Guy Burgess after the latter's arrival in Washington.

Let us follow the example of the security authorities and probe some way into his past. Kim Philby had been born thirty-nine years before, on New Year's Day 1912, at Ambala in the Punjab. His father, the famous St John Philby, was by any standards a remarkable and romantic character, an eccentric Englishman in the grand tradition of a kind that seems to gravitate irresistibly to the Near and Middle East. Having started life as an Indian Civil Servant and speaking a wide range of oriental languages, he had on the outbreak of war in 1914 been given an intelligence job with the British forces in Mesopotamia, serving first there and later in Arabia in a variety of seemingly significant roles, quickly discovering a strong affinity for the Arabs and emerging by the end of the war a passionate supporter of the Arab cause.

This he remained for the rest of his life, becoming in the process something of a legend. Leaving (to their mutual satisfaction) the service of the British Government in 1925, he subsequently spent more and more time in Saudi Arabia, undertook some notable journeys in the Empty Quarter, became a Mohammedan and made the pilgrimage to Mecca. At one time he even went into business in Jeddah, dealing in cheap cars, cough mixture and radio-sets.

Politically he was by nature an enthusiastic espouser of causes, many of them lost, none of them particularly worthy and almost all of them highly controversial. His attitude during the Second World War earned him a short period of imprisonment under Regulation 18B. Towards the end of his life he left his British wife to fend for herself and set up house in the Lebanon with a slave-girl called Umferhat given him by Ibn Saud, and the two children he had had by her. Though profoundly unaccountable and clearly not an easy father, he was a sufficiently strong and colourful character to catch his son's imagination and, to this extent, directly or indirectly, to influence him, setting him, above all, an extraordinary example of individual independence and total disregard for established convention. If ever there was a man who followed a different drum, it was St John Philby. In this respect, if in no other, he and his son had something in common.

A scholar of Westminster, where St John had been Head of the School, Kim, continuing to follow in his father's footsteps, went up to Cambridge in 1929, the same woolly-minded, earnestly progressive Cambridge to which Maclean and Burgess and, for that matter, the present author, all went up within a couple of years of each other. At Trinity, where he read History, he was a friend and neighbour of his rather more brilliant fellow historian, Guy Burgess.

After coming down from Cambridge in the autumn of 1933, he went, like so many other young Englishmen in the nineteen-thirties for six months or so to Vienna. There were barely four years to go before the *Anschluss* and Austria was in a state of turmoil, torn apart by internal dissension. Armed clashes between the rival paramilitary forces of left and right were to continue spasmodically until Hitler's storm troops finally marched in in 1938.

Kim Philby's sympathies, like those of many foreign observers, lay with the Left. At Trinity he had been a left-winger ('that nice young Cambridge Communist', Naomi Mitchison called him) and it was with the Left that he associated in Vienna. When in February 1934 the Heimwehr shelled two blocks of workers' tenements, Kim was one of those who tended the wounded and helped smuggle fugitive Communists and Socialists out of the country before the police could catch up with them. One of those he helped leave Austria at this time was his landlady's daughter Alice or Litzi Friedmann, a lively and attractive young Jewish divorcée only two years older than himself, whom he married in February 1934 and not long after took back to England with him. Litzi, as it happened, was an active and dedicated Communist and at least one of Philby's progressive English friends, Hugh Gaitskell, was distinctly worried by his marriage to 'that young Communist girl'. But the marriage, except on paper, was only to last for a couple of years. For Litzi one important consideration had been to provide herself with a British passport in order to get out of her own country.

Back in England with Litzi, Philby, as a start to a career in journalism, got himself a job at four pounds a week as a sub-editor and occasional feature-writer on *The Review of Reviews*, a rather dim liberal monthly with offices in King William Street. To those who dined with him and Litzi at their flat in Hampstead he gave the impression of being a liberal democrat who probably voted Labour, but was certainly not a Communist. For their summer holidays in 1934 and 1935 he and Litzi went to Spain, at that time still a rather unstable left-wing democracy with no very marked ideological overtones. Meanwhile, to supplement his meagre income from *The Review of Reviews* (or so he said), he edited the magazine of the more than slightly suspect Anglo-German Fellowship and even attended its dreary swastika-decked dinners.

In Vienna Kim had had a first taste of the undercurrents of violence which were to run all through the nineteen-thirties. There was more to come. For the more ideologically minded of the generation which reached manhood in the nineteen-twenties and thirties the Civil War which broke out in Spain in the summer of 1936 was an event of immeasurable importance. Representing, in theory at any rate, the inevitable and symbolic clash between Fascism and the forces of the Left in a stylized and idealized form and against a picturesque background of native Spanish heroism and ferocity, it quickly became for many young men and women a kind of emotional and political climacteric, enabling them to overlook with apparent ease, the utter cynicism with which the Great Powers regarded it. To many of the volunteers, mainly of the Left, but also of the Right, who found their way to Spain, the cause which they so enthusiastically espoused seemed to offer something far better worth fighting for than the 'King and Country' of the Oxford Union debate.

To the clearer-sighted supporters of the Republican cause, however, the Communist and more especially the Soviet attitude towards their allies of the Left, followed by the ultimate withdrawal of Soviet support and the signature a few months later of the Soviet-German pact, must have been profoundly disillusioning. In much the same way, it can scarcely have escaped any right-wing Catholic or Monarchist traditionalists who threw themselves into the fight on Franco's side that Spain was simply being used by Hitler and Mussolini as a convenient practice-ground on which to flex their muscles in preparation for the real confrontation to which they were already looking forward.

But that is by the way. At the time, the distinction between Left and Right, between Progress and Reaction seemed clear enough and for a committed young man with nothing better to do Spain was the place to go. With his adventurous nature and impeccably progressive background (if one forgets the Anglo-German Fellowship), Kim Philby might well have gone as a volunteer to the Republican side. In fact, he went in February 1937 as a more or less free-lance reporter to the Nationalist side, already enjoying the enthusiastic support of both Hitler and Mussolini.

Officially accredited to a London news agency, Kim also had a loose arrangement with *The Times*, who in due course published one of his articles. This quickly led to greater things. In May 1937 he was appointed by *The Times* as their special correspondent with General Franco. In this capacity he soon found favour with the Nationalist press officers. 'Philby,' said one of them later, 'was a gentleman. Philby was objective.' *The Times*, too, not at that time unduly progressive, was more than satisfied with what he wrote.

Philby also found favour with Lady Lindsay-Hogg, better known as Frances Doble, a Canadian actress in her mid-thirties, who, dazzled by the dubious glamour of the Nationalist cause, had like a number of other enterprising young women on both sides, progressive or reactionary, fought her way to the front or just behind it. Soon she became his mistress. Years later an inquisitive journalist asked her why. 'It's hard to say why,' she said. 'There was nothing exceptional about him, but he was attractive and above all very sincere.'

On the last day of 1937, Kim Philby was wounded by a splinter from a Russian shell which killed two other journalists travelling in the same car. For this he received a couple of months later the Nationalist Red Cross of Military Merit, which General Franco himself pinned to his chest, at the same time embracing him cordially on both cheeks. On his return from this ceremony, Lady Lindsay-Hogg found him 'exhausted with emotion because of the high honour done him'. Or so it seemed to her. Meanwhile in the House of Commons Mr Willie Gallacher, the Communist member for West Fife, was enquiring angrily of Mr Neville Chamberlain whether he was aware that 'Mr H. A. A. Philpot' had been offered a decoration by General Franco and whether he had been authorized to accept it.

Early in 1939 the Republican stronghold of Barcelona fell to Franco. 'Your correspondent's car,' cabled Philby, 'which was the first to cruise down the Diagonal and enter the Plaza de Cataluna, was surrounded by crowds of madly excited people who, with red and gold bunting in their hands, mounted the mudguards, footboards and bonnet, cheering with arms upraised. Tears mingled with the shouting and laughter. People seemed torn between hysterical abandon and disbelief.' In London the Republican Spanish Embassy protested to *The Times* at its correspondent's undue bias in favour of Franco and *The Times*, with due dignity, replied defending his objectivity.

The Civil War was now as good as over. Let down by the Russians, unable to contend against the Nationalist superiority in arms and equipment, the Republicans were at their last gasp. With the fall of Madrid to Franco, Philby established himself there in the train of the victorious army. 'If Philby is going to be domiciled in Madrid is there any reason why he should still retain a car?' asked *The Times* immediately and cut his pay and allowances by fifty pounds.

He had by now been in Spain for two and a half years and there was nothing to keep him there any longer. Besides, in that long hot summer of 1939 there were signs of trouble elsewhere on an altogether larger scale. Having first informed his parsimoniously-minded paper that the volume of news no longer justified the retention of two correspondents in Madrid, he took a fond farewell of Lady Lindsay-Hogg and reported back to Printing House Square for fresh employment.

By October 1939, Philby was again overseas, in Arras, this time, at the Headquarters of the British Expeditionary Force as Chief War Correspondent for *The Times*. On his war correspondent's tunic he wore General Franco's Red Cross of Military Valour. Like most British war-correspondents (or, for that matter, soldiery), in France, he saw very little of the Germans until the summer of 1940, when he suddenly saw a good deal too much of them, retreating headlong from Amiens to the coast, being hastily evacuated from Boulogne and then, after a brief return visit, no less hastily re-evacuated shortly after. I remember him as a dark, good-looking, rather saturnine young man of twenty-eight, much in demand with London luncheon hostesses longing for a first-hand account of what it had been like in France. He also saw a certain amount of his father, who though as outrageous and outspoken as ever, had as yet not been interned as a Nazi sympathizer.

Meanwhile for Kim Philby a new and interesting job was waiting. Not for the first time in its history, *The Times* had served as a stepping-stone to clandestine employment. There was, it seemed, room for a good man in Section D of the Secret Service. To this he was welcomed by his old friend, Guy Burgess, who offered him occasional hospitality at 5 Bentinck Street.

Section D did not survive the summer of 1940. But by now Philby had his foot in the door. From Section D he moved, with a minimum of difficulty, to the newly established Special Operations Executive and for a year or so he served as an instructor at one of that body's special schools at Beaulieu in Hampshire, where future agents were trained for eventual infiltration into German-occupied Europe. After which, following a well-timed lunch with his father and Colonel Vivian, the Deputy Head of the Secret Service, he moved with equal ease from the elemental chaos of SOE into Section V of the Secret Intelligence Service or SIS. As a friend said to him at about this time: 'If you have to work for a racket, let it be an old-established racket.'

By contrast with SOE and the other mushroom growths that sprang up so suddenly and disconcertingly during the early stages of World War II, the British Secret Intelligence Service (or MI6, as it was sometimes known) was in fact a relatively old-established – its critics might even say old-fashioned – organization, sharing many of the better traditions of the other Whitehall departments and drawing its recruits from much the same social strata as they did.

Discreetly known as the Friends, its members reported the results of their labours through a carefully filtered channel, writing anonymously on sheets of deep blue writing paper of the kind then affected by many society hostesses. A public speech made soon after the beginning of the war by Heinrich Himmler, in which he disclosed the names of all the more important Friends from their Chief downwards came as something of a shock to the SIS, who, however, having classified the text of the offending speech 'Most Secret', seem to have carried on much as before.

Directly responsible to the Prime Minister, the Chief of the SIS, officially known as C, had since 1939 been Brigadier (soon to become Major-General) Stewart Menzies, a quiet, able, friendly man of fifty with blue eyes and sandy hair, who combined an outstanding record as a fighting soldier in World War I with considerable experience of intelligence work.

Abroad, the representatives of MI6, one stage closer to the actual secret agent with his false beard and collapsible camera, were as often as not loosely attached to the local Embassies and Legations, usually somewhat thinly disguised as diplomats or passport control officers. In general they were well known to the corresponding intelligence and counter-intelligence authorities of the host-country, who, depending on their country's relations with Great Britain, either worked with them or else kept a close watch on them.

In addition to collecting secret intelligence from all over the world, the Secret Service was at the same time responsible for the so-called Government Code and Cypher School at Bletchley in Hertfordshire, whose task it was to break cyphers and intercept and read the enemy's (and not only the enemy's) telegrams and signals. This was a most successful undertaking which, as is now well known, did much to win the war for the Allies, thereby greatly enhancing the reputation of the Secret Service as a whole.

Unlike the remainder of SIS, Section V was responsible, not for espionage, but for counter-espionage, its primary function being to keep a watch on espionage operations mounted against Great Britain from abroad; while MI5, another old-established body, sought to counter subversion and espionage within Great Britain.

By this time a high proportion of German intelligence operations against Great Britain were being mounted from the Iberian Peninsula and it was felt that Philby's first-hand experience of Franco's Spain would be invaluable in this connection. Moving from Beaulieu to St Albans, whither Section V had overflowed from SIS Headquarters at 54 Broadway, he took up his new appointment in September 1941. It was to be the beginning of a long and, in more ways than one, remarkably successful career in the Secret Intelligence Service.

This is not the right place, nor am I the right person, to attempt a detailed study of the inner workings of the Secret Service during the war or at any other time. Quite apart from other considerations, such a study would, I think, be about as interesting to the average reader as a parallel account of the wartime workings of the Ministry of Food, Agriculture and Fisheries – in fact probably a good deal less so. Though fascinating to those personally involved, the intrigues and petty jealousies from which no government department is entirely free, have a limited appeal for the uninitiated. Nor, by their very nature, do the corresponding structural and hierarchical problems or the resulting intricacies of the chain of command make for very entertaining reading. What is interesting is Kim Philby's remarkable career.

Philby was able, hard-working, imaginative and possessed of considerable charm. It was not long before his sub-section, up to then a fairly weak one, was more than holding its own against German counter-espionage in Spain and Portugal and the head of Section V, Colonel Felix Cowgill, soon found that he had every reason to be satisfied with his new subordinate. With the approach of the landings in North Africa, Cowgill asked Philby whether he would extend his responsibility to that area. He subsequently asked him to take control of Italy too. There could be no doubt that Philby was beginning to make his way in the Secret Service.

In the summer of 1943 Section V had moved back from St Albans to London, establishing itself in new premises in Ryder Street. For the past three years now Philby had been living with Aileen Furse, a slim girl with auburn hair and blue eyes. She came from a prosperous, upper middle class family in the West Country. Her ideas were vaguely progressive. In the course of the next four years she was to bear Philby no less than three children at their house near St Albans.

It was not long before Philby took an important step forward in his career. By the end of 1943 it had become fairly clear that the Germans were bound to lose the war. Looking ahead, there were those who guessed that Britain's wartime ally, the Soviet Union, might well succeed Germany as a potential menace for the future. At about this time a new section, Section IX, was accordingly set up to counter this possible danger and entrusted with the task of taking on our Soviet allies at their own nefarious game. When it came to finding a head for it, the choice fell not on Felix Cowgill but on Philby, who had gone to great pains to prepare the ground in advance and turn opinion against his superior officer and rival. Nor was this all. Within a year Sections V and IX were united and, Cowgill having by this time resigned, Philby was put in charge of both of them as head of a new department to be known as R5. His position was by this time a highly responsible one.

Having moved from Ryder Street to the seventh floor of SIS

Headquarters at 54 Broadway, a rather nondescript building blandly labelled 'Government Communications Bureau' and situated just opposite the St James's Park Underground Station, he was now at the centre of things. In this connection it is worth noting that early in 1944 a formal approach made by *The Times* via the Foreign Office with the object of securing his release to become a key war correspondent in the forthcoming campaigns was firmly rejected on the grounds that his work was so important and that he was performing it 'with such exceptional ability' that his release simply could not be contemplated.

For a temporary unestablished government servant, he had clearly played his cards well and made a considerable impact in the right quarter. So considerable that we are in no way surprised to find him emerging at the end of the war as an established officer of the Secret Service and even as a member of the Committee on SIS Reorganization which was set up in September 1945 by Major-General Sir Stewart Menzies (as he now was) with the object of placing the whole rather haphazard organization on a sounder and more rational basis.

Meanwhile in the late summer of 1945 a curious incident had occurred, a minor setback which momentarily interrupted the work of the normally smooth-running department over which Kim Philby presided. One August morning soon after he had arrived at the office, Kim was called in by General Menzies and given a letter to look at that had been sent over to him by the Foreign Office. It was from Knox Helm, Minister at the British Embassy in Turkey. In it he enclosed copies of correspondence with the British Consulate General in Istanbul and of Embassy minutes and memoranda concerning this correspondence and asked for instructions.

The matter on which he requested instructions was as follows. One of the British Vice-Consuls in Istanbul, a Mr Page, had, it appeared, suddenly been approached by Konstantin Volkov, his opposite number at the Soviet Consulate, with a request for asylum for himself and his wife. Volkov, who seemed nervous, had gone on to say that, although officially a Vice-Consul, he was in fact an officer of the NKVD, as the Soviet Secret Police were then known. In return for asylum, he would be prepared to give a detailed account of the personnel and operation of NVKD Headquarters in Moscow, where he claimed he had himself worked for years. He could also give details of Soviet spy-rings and agents working abroad, including the names of two Soviet spies at present working in the Foreign Office in London and of one who was head of a British counter-espionage organization. He had gone on to say that he had one absolutely vital request to make, namely that, if his approach were reported to London, this should be done by bag and on no

247

account by telegram, as the Russians had broken most of the British ciphers and were likely to read anything sent in this way. His request had duly been complied with and it was therefore now more than a week since Volkov's visit. What, Knox Helm wanted to know, was the Embassy to do?

After reading the letter and its enclosures through carefully, Kim gave it as his opinion that they were on to something of the very greatest importance and asked for a little time to dig into the background and, in the light of any further information on the subject, make appropriate recommendations for action. To this C agreed, telling him to report back next morning and in the meantime to keep the papers strictly to himself.

Having considered the matter from every possible angle, Kim reported back to General Menzies first thing next morning. He had not, he said, been able to find anything on Volkov. He still considered the matter to be of great potential importance and, in view of the delays attendant on communication by bag, recommended that someone fully briefed should be sent out to Istanbul from London to take charge of the case on the spot. 'Just what I was thinking myself,' replied C. And Kim, who had had himself in mind for this important mission, was delighted.

A trifle prematurely, as it turned out. The night before, it appeared, C had met Douglas Roberts, the Brigadier in charge of Security Intelligence (Middle East), MI5's regional office in Cairo, who happened to be on leave in England, but shortly returning to the Middle East. C had been much impressed by Roberts, who spoke fluent Russian, and he now proposed to ask Sir David Petrie, the Head of MI5, to send him straight out to Istanbul to take charge of the Volkov case. He promised to let Kim know what was happening immediately after lunch.

On coming back from lunch, Kim found a message from C asking him to look in. He found the Chief looking rather depressed. Brigadier Roberts, it seemed, could not bear flying and had already arranged to return to Cairo by boat from Liverpool the following week. What is more, nothing that either General Menzies or Sir David Petrie could say would make him change his plans.

Kim, needless to say, was ready with the answer: might it not be best if he went out in the Brigadier's place? He could easily brief his deputy on any outstanding business. With obvious relief C agreed, the necessary arrangements were made, and clearances obtained. Three full days later, almost a fortnight after Volkov's visit to the Consulate-General, Kim took off for Cairo en route for Istanbul.

His journey, as it turned out, took longer than it should have done. Owing to electric storms over Malta, the aircraft was diverted to Tunis. After spending the night there, they flew on next day to Cairo via Malta. When they reached Cairo, it was already too late to catch the onward flight to Istanbul. Another twenty-four hours had been wasted. Nor did things move much faster when they finally got to Istanbul. The Minister could agree to nothing without consulting the Ambassador. For this another twenty-four hours were needed. Meanwhile the Minister took him home to have a drink. With him he met the Military Attaché who asked him to dinner. Next day was Saturday. Helm had by now spoken to the Ambassador who, it appeared, wanted to discuss the matter personally with Kim and had invited him to spend Sunday with him cruising on the Sea of Marmara in the Embassy yacht *Makouk*. Finally on Sunday afternoon, after an excellent lunch on board, Kim and the Ambassador, Sir Maurice Peterson, had their talk. While the *Makouk* lay at anchor off Prinkipo, Kim put the Ambassador in the picture, mentioning that he had brought with him a letter from the Foreign Office asking that he should be given all reasonable facilities. 'Then,' said Sir Maurice decisively, 'there's no more to be said. Go ahead.'

Philby and Cyril Machray, the head of the SIS Station in Istanbul, spent Sunday evening discussing plans for getting Volkov out of Turkey, with or without Turkish co-operation. Clearly the first thing was to make contact with Volkov himself. This, they decided, could best be done through Page, whom Volkov had approached in the first place.*

Next morning, Page, who had been invited to come and see them, explained that he frequently had routine consular business to discuss with Volkov and that it would be quite normal for him to invite him over to his office for a talk. This seemed a sensible idea and he accordingly picked up the telephone for the purpose of putting it into effect. Having got through to the Soviet Consulate-General, he asked for Volkov. A man's voice answered. They talked in Russian. Page looked puzzled and shook his head.

'He can't come?' asked Philby. 'That's funny.'

'Funnier than you think,' said Page. 'I asked for Volkov and a man came on saying he was Volkov. But it wasn't Volkov. I know Volkov's voice perfectly well. I've spoken to him dozens of times.'

Page then tried again, but could only reach the telephone operator, who this time said that Volkov was out. It was not easy to see what more they could do. In the end they decided to have another try next day.

When the three of them met again next morning, Page once more rang up the Soviet Consulate-General. After he had got through, Philby, listening in, could hear a woman's voice, then a sharp click and then silence. Page put down the receiver. 'What do you make of that?' he said. 'I asked for Volkov and the girl said Volkov was in Moscow. Then there was a sort of scuffle and slam and the line went dead.'

* According to another version, the attempt was made, not by Mr Page, but by one of his colleagues.

Though by now beginning to realize that something must have gone wrong, Philby still persisted. Would Page, he asked, mind calling at the Soviet Consulate-General and asking for Volkov in person? Page agreed but was back within an hour in a state of extreme exasperation. 'It's no bloody good,' he said. 'I can't get any sense out of that madhouse. Nobody'd ever heard of Volkov.'

This, as things turned out, was the last anyone ever did hear of Konstantin Volkov. There were stories later of an inert, heavily bandaged body being carried on board an unscheduled Soviet aircraft at Istanbul Airport. Equally, in Turkish history the Bosphorus has often served as a convenient repository for unwanted bodies, while most Soviet Embassies are reputedly provided with the equipment necessary for their disposal. Clearly there are a number of possibilities. All we know for certain is that at about this time Volkov disappeared and that shortly afterwards his name was removed from the official list of diplomatic and consular personnel resident in Istanbul.

That same Tuesday evening, Kim despatched a signal to C, admitting defeat and asking leave to wind up the case and come home. He expanded on this message in a report, which he drafted while flying back to London. In it he attributed Volkov's disappearance to his refusal to allow the Embassy to communicate with London except by bag. Almost three weeks, he pointed out, had gone by since his first approach. During that time the Russians would have had plenty of chances of getting on to him. Perhaps his living quarters were bugged. Perhaps he had got drunk and talked too much. There were all kinds of possibilities.

There was, it is true, one other possibility which occurred to Kim Philby, but which, on reflection, he decided not to include in his report: the possibility that someone had tipped off the Russians about Volkov's approach to the British. It had, in one way and another, been a curious and disturbing episode.

For Kim Philby the New Year's Honours List for 1946 brought an OBE, a token of official appreciation of his work over the past five years and a first step towards the knighthood to which every established government servant aspires. By the end of September of that year he had taken two other steps in the direction of orthodoxy and respectability. Rather belatedly he had (with the full knowledge of his departmental superiors) obtained a divorce from Litzi, now living with a Communist lover in East Berlin, and on 25 September had no less belatedly married at Chelsea Register Office Aileen Furse (or Philby, as she preferred to be called) now heavily pregnant with her fourth child. After the civil ceremony (Kim, as it happened, was a militant atheist) there was a suitable celebration at 18 Carlyle Square, a fine big house which, with the help of Aileen's rich mother, they had taken on a twenty-one-year lease.

Towards the end of 1946, not much more than a year after his apparently abortive trip to Turkey, Philby, who was by now due for a posting abroad, was sent for by Major-General Sinclair, the new Deputy Chief of the Secret Service, and told that he had been chosen to take charge of the SIS station in Turkey, with his headquarters in Istanbul. He took up this appointment early in 1947, having stopped off in Cairo on his way out and flown thence to Jidda for a visit to his father in Saudi Arabia. But, fond though he was of his father, he soon found that he did not share his passion for Arabia and the Arabs. He did not, he wrote, feel the slightest temptation to follow his example. 'The limitless space, the clear night skies and the rest of the gobbledygook are all right in small doses. But I would find a lifetime in a landscape with majesty but no charm, among a people with neither majesty nor charm, quite unacceptable. Ignorance and arrogance make a bad combination, and the Saudi Arabians have both in generous measure. When an outward show of austerity is thrown in as well, the mixture is intolerable.'

Amid what he calls 'the riotous wonder of Istanbul', on the other hand, he felt much more at home. Soon he had found a charming old Turkish house with its own lobster tank right on the water at Beylerbey on the Asiatic shore of the Bosphorus and there installed his wife Aileen and their four children and travelled to work every day by ferry-boat. Here in 1948 he entertained his old Cambridge friend, Guy Burgess, who, characteristically, found some pretext for visiting him there in an official or semi-official capacity and who, a friend recalls, distinguished himself after a few drinks by diving drunkenly from the top storey of the villa into the Bosphorus and then at once swimming back to do it again.

Though rather more restricted in scope than what he had been doing in London, the work to which Kim now travelled daily on the ferry clearly had its compensations for anyone with a sufficiently keen interest in espionage or counter-espionage. Certainly it did not lack variety. In addition to sharing the Black Sea with the Soviet Union, Bulgaria and Romania, Turkey has a common frontier with both Bulgaria and the Soviet Union; Soviet ships of all kinds are constantly passing through the Bosphorus; Turkish ships ply to Soviet, Bulgarian and Romanian ports; and Istanbul itself, where the representative of the Secret Service has his offices on the ground floor of the former Embassy, possesses a mixed population which includes plentiful samples from the Balkans, Russia, Georgia, Armenia, Azerbaijan and Central Asia. Of these many, with a minimum of encouragement, would, it is safe to say, gladly engage in a little amateur espionage (or counter-espionage) on behalf of almost anyone who made it worth their while, or would at least, if paid enough, produce large quantities of unverifiable intelligence material purporting to come from almost anywhere.

From what I have seen of the frontiers of the Soviet Union, I cannot myself imagine that it would be either very easy or very rewarding to try to send agents across them. However, spies will be spies and from what Kim Philby himself has to say on the subject, it appears that in his day the attempt was occasionally made in both directions, though how many agents returned to tell the tale is another matter. Those Kim sent across seem not to have done, at least one being greeted on arrival with a burst of machine-gun fire. But for that there may well have been a special reason.

A more profitable undertaking from everybody's point of view, and no doubt a more enjoyable one, was a photographic reconnaissance which Kim made in 1948 of part of the frontier with Soviet Transcaucasia. To this he gave the name Operation Spyglass. By means of powerful telescopic lenses he found that you could, for what it was worth, easily photograph whatever there was to be photographed beyond the wire on the Soviet side of the frontier, including, if you got to the top of Mount Ararat, the prosperous city of Erivan twenty miles away through the mist. With Turkish help he was also able to take what he calls a long hard look at the Turkish frontier region – which from his point of view was probably well worth doing and might well come in useful some day.

But in the summer of 1949, before Kim could complete his survey of the frontier, he received a telegram from 54 Broadway offering him the extremely important job of SIS representative in the United States and liaison officer with the FBI and the newly established CIA. This he accepted with alacrity. For one thing, co-operation between the SIS and CIA was now so close at headquarters level that for anyone destined for a top post in the SIS, as he himself quite clearly was, a good knowledge of the American scene was essential. For another, he would once more be at the very centre of things and would be getting a close-up view of the American intelligence organizations which by this time were playing a considerably more important role in their own field than were their British counterparts. Sustained by a case of champagne sent him by a rich friend, he sailed for New York in the SS *Caronia* towards the end of September.

Philby's job in Washington was far from simple. A delicate balance had to be kept in his relations with the tough Bourbon-drinking, all-American FBI under Edgar Hoover and the more sophisticated, more socialite, more cosmopolitan CIA, where not long after his arrival General Bedell-Smith succeeded Admiral Hillenkoetter. Like the corresponding organizations elsewhere, these two bodies were inclined to be jealous of each other. ('What do they teach them in the CIA, son?' one senior FBI operative asked him soon after his arrival. 'Why, how to use knives and forks and how to marry rich wives.') It was also important that he should allow neither the FBI nor the CIA to play him off against the Washington representative of MI5 and vice versa. And then, as always, there were a number of other no less delicate considerations for him to keep in mind. The job was in every sense of the word a demanding as well as a rewarding one. The strain was considerable and Kim sought to relieve this, his friends noticed, by drinking more heavily than usual.

On the whole Kim got on well with his American opposite numbers, who found him quick-witted, convivial and as ready as they were to sit up all night drinking Bourbon or Scotch. Within the CIA, the Office of Strategic Operations or OSO looked after intelligence, while the OPC or Office of Policy Co-ordination was concerned with subversion. Philby dealt with both, discussing in detail their current or projected activities all over the world and, where necessary, making arrangements for joint British and American action or for a mutually satisfactory division of labour.

If anything, his relations with the OPC were more active. Indeed, as soon as he arrived in Washington, he found himself involved in a combined British-American project which had already been under discussion for some years and which was designed to overthrow the Communist government of Albania and so detach that distressing little country from the Soviet bloc. A number of dissident Albanians were to be infiltrated from abroad by land, sea and air in the hope that they would somehow succeed in rallying the resident population in a nation-wide rising against the Communists.

In fact, it did not work out like that. In the spring of 1950 a first batch of dissidents were duly landed and others followed. Weeks passed and in due course a few disillusioned survivors managed to straggle out to Greece. The story they had to tell was uniformly depressing: wherever they landed, the police had been waiting for them. The inhabitants had shown little or no enthusiasm for the idea of a rising. In the end the whole idea was quietly dropped and jobs found with the Forestry Commission for a few of the surviving dissidents. It is hard to resist the impression that the project had from the first been bound to end disastrously, though perhaps not quite as disastrously as it did in the event. As for detaching Albania from the Soviet bloc, the Albanian Government were to do this far more effectively for themselves a few years later.

Another area in which the CIA and the SIS seem to have tried their hand, this time in competition rather than in co-operation, is the Ukraine. Again without any apparent success. Here too dissidents were dropped in by parachute, only to disappear without a trace. 'I do not know,' writes Philby, a trifle cryptically, 'what happened to the parties concerned. But I can make an informed guess.'

With the FBI much of Philby's work concerned Soviet espionage in the United States. In particular joint British-American investigation had discovered some time before a serious leakage from the atomic energy establishment at Los Alamos and this was still being followed up. By the winter of 1949–50 the net had closed on Dr Klaus Fuchs, a German-born, naturalized British scientist from Birmingham University, with known Communist sympathies. On his next visit to London in February 1950 Fuchs was arrested by Superintendent George Smith of Special Branch and, on being skilfully examined by William Skardon of MI5, admitted everything. His confession initiated a chain reaction which led to the rounding up over the next couple of years of a far-flung Soviet spy-ring specializing in atomic secrets and operating on both sides of the Atlantic, and to a series of spectacular spy-trials, culminating in the conviction and execution of Julius and Ethel Rosenberg at Sing Sing in June 1953.

In addition to the leakage at Los Alamos Philby found that the FBI also had evidence which showed that during the years 1944 and 1945 there had been a serious leakage of secret material from the British Embassy itself. This they had been enquiring into painstakingly for a number of years without making much progress. Their investigations so far seemed to point to locally recruited labour, an office-cleaner or someone of the sort, rather than to an actual British diplomat and for this reason they were, as Philby put it, 'still sending us reams about the Embassy charladies'.

But Philby himself took a different view and after a time he decided that the moment had come for him to give the investigations what he has called 'a nudge in the right direction'. In a memorandum to Broadway Buildings, he recalled that as long ago as 1937 Walter Krivitski, a high ranking Soviet intelligence officer who had defected to the West, had spoken of a well-connected young British diplomat who had been recruited by the Russians shortly before. Might this not, he asked, have some bearing on the present case? After this things moved faster. Before long a short list had been drawn up consisting of the names of half a dozen suspects and including, he noticed, that of Donald Maclean.

In the summer of 1950 Kim Philby, who had now been in Washington for almost a year and had moved into a large, comfortable, rather untidy house with room for his growing family at 4100 Nebraska Avenue, found in his mail a letter which he read with mixed feelings. It was from Guy Burgess. 'I have a shock for you,' it began. 'I have been posted to Washington.' And it went on to ask whether Kim would put him up until he had found a flat for himself.

After considering the matter carefully, Kim, who knew Guy well, decided that he might as well have him to stay and wrote to him in this sense. He had hardly done so when the Embassy Security Officer brought him a letter to look at from the head of the Foreign Office Security Branch, warning him about the trouble Burgess was liable to cause, but going on to say, rather optimistically, that his eccentricities would be more easily overlooked in a large embassy than a small one. He next gave some account of his past misdeeds and added that there might be worse in store. 'What does he mean – *worse?*' asked the Security Officer irritably – '*Goats?*' But on learning that Kim was going to have him to stay and would personally keep an eye on him, he seemed considerably relieved.

As we have seen, Guy Burgess's nine months in Washington did not pass smoothly. Nor did the size of the Embassy or Kim Philby's promise to keep an eye on him help very much. When he left at the beginning of May 1951, the Embassy was only too glad to see him go.

Early one morning several weeks later Kim was rung up at home by Geoffrey Patterson, the MI5 representative in Washington. He had, he said, just received a tremendously long and Most Immediate telegram from London. His secretary was on leave. Could he borrow Kim's to help him decipher it? Kim agreed and, later that morning, when he got to the Embassy, looked in on Patterson to see how he was getting on. Patterson looked grey. 'The bird,' he said in a half whisper, 'has flown.' 'What bird?', asked Philby, registering horror – 'not Maclean?' 'Yes,' he answered. 'But there's worse than that. Guy Burgess has gone with him.' At which Philby, thinking of his own long and intimate association with Burgess, looked and felt even more horrified.

In Washington as in London numerous different theories were advanced to explain the disappearance of Burgess and Maclean. To those who knew of the investigations which had been taking place it seemed quite clear that Maclean must have been warned by somebody or something. But how and by whom?

Philby had his own theory and he stuck to it. It ran as follows. Once Maclean had come under serious suspicion, the decision had been taken to withhold certain categories of secret papers from him and to place him under surveillance. A man of his experience (and, according to Krivitski, he had been working for the Russians for sixteen years) could not have failed to notice this and draw the necessary conclusions. Although there had been nothing definite against Burgess, it was surely clear enough by now that he must be a Soviet agent too. To Maclean Burgess's sudden return to England had been a godsend. Not being under surveillance, Guy had been able to make all the necessary arrangements and the two had accordingly left together, Burgess because by now he was pretty near the end of his tether in every way and in any case had nothing to keep him in England.

This theory, which Philby readily expounded to anyone who cared to listen to him, found favour with the FBI. It was also practically impossible to disprove. The CIA, on the other hand, under the hard-headed Bedell-Smith, were less enthusiastic about it. They were also less enthusiastic about Philby. When it came to theories, Philby reflected, he had been one of those who knew Maclean was suspect. He was also an old friend of Burgess's and had actually had him to stay in his house. Inevitably this would be taken into account. Sooner or later, and probably sooner, these unpalatable facts would be cast in his teeth and he would be asked what he had to say for himself. What he was now expecting was a personal telegram from headquarters, summoning him home. And it was therefore no real surprise to him when a few days later such a telegram in fact arrived. After saying goodbye to his friends in the CIA and FBI (who wished him good luck in the friendliest possible way) he booked a flight to London.

On reporting to Broadway Buildings, he was told that Dick White, a senior official of MI5 and an old acquaintance, wanted to see him as soon as possible. With Air Commodore Easton, the Assistant Chief of SIS, he drove across the park to Leconfield House in Curzon Street, where MI5 had their headquarters.

White began by saying in quite a friendly way that he wanted Kim's help in clearing up this appalling affair of Burgess and Maclean. In reply Kim poured out a mass of information about Burgess's past and some general impressions of his personality. To him, he said, it seemed inconceivable that anyone could ever have employed a man of Burgess's character as a secret agent, let alone the Russians, who demanded of their agents the highest standards of behaviour and discretion. As for Maclean, he said, he had certainly heard of him and might even have met him, but offhand could not even put a face on him, which was no more than the truth.

A few days later they met again. This time White wanted Kim to give an account of his relations with Burgess. He also wanted, he said, a detailed account of Kim's own career. Kim gave both. More even than the first, their second meeting had the character of an interrogation and he was therefore not surprised when a few days later C himself sent for him to tell him that he had had a strongly worded letter from General Bedell-Smith, as Head of CIA, which would make it impossible for him to return to Washington. A few days after that C sent for him again. This time it was to tell him, with obvious regret, for they were friends and C had hoped that one day Philby would succeed him, that he must ask for his resignation. He would, he said, receive £4,000 in lieu of pension – £2,000 down and the rest in half-yearly instalments of £500. Taking his two thousand pounds, he spent the rest of the summer looking for somewhere to put his family, finally settling on a small house at Heronsgate near Rickmansworth in Hertfordshire. It bore the optimistic name of Sunbox.

By now the strain on Kim was beginning to tell. He was drinking more heavily than ever and having an affair with a middle-aged female civil servant he had found (or who had found him) in London. Aileen reacted to the situation hysterically, seeing spies everywhere and harping continually on Kim's alleged involvement with Burgess and Maclean. After barely five years their long-delayed marriage was in jeopardy. Life at Sunbox, where Kim spent as little time as possible, was far from happy.

In November there came a fresh summons from C, who explained, when he saw him, that a judicial enquiry had been opened into the escape of Burgess and Maclean. It was in the hands of Mr Helenus Milmo K C, better known as Buster, an extremely able lawyer who had worked in MI5 during the war. C hoped that Kim would have no objection to giving evidence. Together they drove once more across the Park to Leconfield House.

One of the first charges which Milmo, a burly, round-faced, rather florid-looking Irishman with singularly alert eyes, brought against him was that Kim had entrusted to Burgess what he called his 'intimate personal papers'. On his being asked to explain what he meant by this, it appeared that he was talking about Kim's Cambridge degree, which had been found tucked into a book on one of Burgess's shelves. This had not been a very difficult charge to deal with. There were a dozen ways, he said, in which this long forgotten document might have found its way there, especially as Burgess was always helping himself to other people's books and not returning them. Kim, for his part, was as helpful as he could be, going into the greatest detail and offering all kinds of answers and explanations. These took even longer than they might have done because of his stammer, something always slightly disconcerting to the interrogator in anyone who is being cross-examined.

The next point raised by Milmo was of quite a different kind. Two days after the news about Volkov reached London, there had, it seemed, been a marked rise in the volume of NKVD wireless traffic between London and Moscow, followed by a similar rise in the traffic between Moscow and Istanbul. Again, shortly after Kim had been secretly briefed about the Embassy leakage in Washington, there had been another, similar rise. How, Mr Milmo asked incisively, did Mr Philby account for that? To this Kim replied quite calmly that he could not account for it. And there, for the time being at any rate, the matter rested.

The judicial enquiry was over. The prosecution, if that is the right word for it, had failed to pin anything on Philby who, however much he had drunk the night before, had never once let himself become rattled or flustered under interrogation. Milmo was one of the ablest and most experienced cross-examiners at the Bar. 'But,' said another lawyer who was present, 'it began to look like the stupidest man in the world cross-examining the cleverest.'

After the enquiry, one of the MI5 men asked Kim for his passport and, on learning that it was at Rickmansworth, said that they would send

257

someone down with him to collect it. The man they sent was William Skardon, who only a few months before had, as Philby well knew, made his name by obtaining a full confession from Dr Klaus Fuchs, the renegade scientist from Los Alamos. This was clearly not a coincidence. On the way down Skardon dwelt at some length on the advisability of co-operating with the authorities. And Philby listened politely.

During the weeks that followed Skardon came down to Rickmansworth again several times for more questioning. He also asked Kim for written authority to examine his bank account and this was duly given. In the end he stopped coming. After this Kim was once more summoned to Broadway and there subjected to further questioning by Major-General Sinclair and Air-Commodore Easton, but still without any tangible results.

For Kim Philby the next couple of years were an anxious period in more ways than one. He was now forty. He had his two thousand pounds and, he hoped, two thousand more to come. And he had a family to provide for. When he applied for jobs, prospective employers were inclined to ask him why he had left the Foreign Service. The best hope seemed to lie in journalism – he had after all started life as a newspaperman. For a few weeks in 1952 (having recovered his passport from MI5) he went to Spain for a firm of fruit-importers. While he was there, he received a letter offering him a job with a London import-export firm. He accepted and for a year commuted a little unhappily between Liverpool Street and Rickmansworth. After that he reverted to the arduous and precarious life of a free-lance journalist.

By this time Kim had more or less left Aileen, whose mother, once more coming to the rescue, bought her daughter and five grandchildren a large gloomy house at Crowborough in Sussex. Here she was to live from now onwards, coping ever more ineffectually and despairingly with the children (the younger of whom, Harry, suffered from convulsions), the bills, the housekeeping and Kim when he chose to turn up.

Meanwhile there had been a new and not uninteresting development in the case of Burgess and Maclean. In September Melinda Maclean had told the MI5 men who had been in touch with her ever since Donald's disappearance that she wanted to leave England and go to Switzerland in order to start a new life there with her three children. No obstacle was put in her way and she did as she proposed. For the next two years she lived quietly in Switzerland, seeing a few friends and looking after her children, while British Intelligence kept a discreet eye on her. Then on 11 September 1953 she, in her turn, suddenly disappeared taking the children with her. To the old, part-worn mystery of Burgess and Maclean a new mystery had been added, the mystery of Melinda. Where was she?, people began asking. Had she always been a Communist?

In 1954 the spectacular defection of Vladimir Petrov, nominally Third Secretary at the Soviet Embassy in Canberra, but in fact a senior Soviet intelligence operative, and his subsequent revelations concerning Maclean and Burgess, who, he said, had been Soviet agents for the past twenty years, again stirred up public interest in the case and, more particularly, in the third man, who it was claimed must have helped them to escape. In Fleet Street (but not in the newspapers produced there) Philby's name was being freely bandied about in this connection. Just how the leak occurred is not particularly important; the fact was that by the autumn of 1955 the press were buzzing round Philby like bees round a honey-pot, at the same time uncomfortably aware of the risk, should they go too far, of a libel action.

Philby's first reaction in the circumstances was to keep clear of them and get in touch with his friends in the Secret Service. Predictably these urged him most strongly to make no statement before the debate impending in the House of Commons. They also asked him to do two things: to re-surrender his passport and submit to a final interrogation. Kim agreed, again handing over his passport and answering such questions as were put to him. These did not give him the impression that his interrogators had any fresh evidence to work on. After that he made it his business to keep away from the press.

Meanwhile in September 1955 the Government had at long last issued a *White Paper Concerning The Disappearance Of Two Former Foreign Office Officials.* It was not a very informative document. High spots were passages revealing the length of time taken by the security authorities to establish the source of the leak and identify it and the astonishing fact that, having finally identified it, they had not thought it necessary to keep an eye on Maclean when he was at his house in the country. As regards the third man theory, Philby observed with interest that the White Paper followed the line he himself had taken, namely that Maclean had probably been alerted by the decision to place him under surveillance and withhold certain categories of document from him. All in all, it added little to what was already known or surmised. But the British press and British parliamentary democracy being what they are, the matter was not allowed to rest there.

Strap-hanging in the underground towards the end of October and looking over his neighbour's shoulder, Kim Philby suddenly saw his own name in headlines in the *Evening Standard.* A Labour Member of Parliament, Colonel Marcus Lipton, had asked the Prime Minister whether he had 'made up his mind to cover up at all costs the dubious Third Man activities of Mr Harold Philby'. In doing this he himself was of course protected by parliamentary privilege from any legal action.

For the next week or two, after again consulting SIS, Philby took refuge

from the Press in his mother's flat in Drayton Gardens, buried the telephone under a pile of cushions and waited for the long-promised
debate in the House of Commons. It took place on 7 November and in the
course of it the Foreign Secretary, Mr Harold Macmillan, expressly
defended Philby against Colonel Lipton's allegations. 'No evidence,' he
said, speaking with all the authority lent him by his high office and elaborately patrician manner, 'has been found to show that he was responsible for
warning Burgess and Maclean . . . While in Government service he carried
out his duties ably and conscientiously. I have no reason to conclude
that Mr Philby has at any time betrayed the interests of this country or
to identify him with the so-called "Third Man", if indeed there was
one.'

'That statement,' wrote Philby afterwards 'gave me the green light.'
After waiting a couple of days, he removed the cushions from the telephone
and asked his mother to tell anyone who called that he would be available
to visitors at 11 am the next day.

At eleven next day, 10 November, Mrs Philby's flat in Drayton Gardens
was besieged by journalists. Kim was very much at his ease, asking a reporter lolling in an arm-chair if he wouldn't give up his seat to a news-
paperwoman who was standing. Quite clearly, he felt in command of the
situation. Before doing anything else he circulated a type-written statement
explaining that in certain respects reticence was imposed on him by the
Official Secrets Act. Then he said he would answer questions.

The way in which he did so was masterly. One of the first questions put
to him concerned Colonel Lipton. 'Ah, Lipton,' he said at once and then
added allusively: 'That brings me to the heart of the matter.' He then suggested that Colonel Lipton should either produce his evidence for the
security authorities or else repeat his charge outside the House of Commons. Soon four or five reporters left to catch the evening papers. What,
asked those who remained, did Kim think of Burgess? Was he a friend of
Maclean's? How did he account for their disappearance? Where were
they? Was he the Third Man? They were all easy questions to answer. To
any that were not, he returned a firm: No Comment. Then he handed
round beer and sherry and the atmosphere, already friendly, became
friendlier still.

A couple of days later Lipton withdrew his previous statement. 'I
think,' said Kim, 'that Colonel Lipton has done the right thing. So far as
I am concerned, the incident is now closed.' And closed it was, leaving him
with his reputation cleared and the image of a man who had not been
very well treated, but had bravely made the best of it. As for the press, from
now onwards they dropped him, in his own words, like a hot brick.

. . . . .

In February 1956 one more piece in the puzzle fell into place. Guy Burgess, still wearing an Old Etonian tie, and Donald Maclean, still looking every inch a diplomat, gave what purported to be a press conference in Room 101, the nearest thing to a royal suite in the National Hotel in Moscow. They did not in fact say anything at it, but simply handed out without comment a duplicated statement in the third person in Russian together with a rather lame English translation. According to this, they had never been Soviet agents, just honest British officials who had given up all hope of ever guiding British policy into peaceful ways. At long last it had been officially established where they were. It also now became known that Melinda Maclean and her children had in fact joined Donald in Moscow a couple of years earlier.

In the years that followed their defection both Burgess and Maclean seemed to have made lives for themselves in Moscow in quarters provided for them by a more or less benevolent Soviet Government and doing the work apportioned to them by that Government, involving in all probability the interpretation of Western policy, sometimes, in all conscience, not a very easy task even for Western observers. With time, both re-established a measure of contact with their friends and relations in England, while Burgess, who seemed to have more difficulty in adjusting to local conditions, managed to provide himself with a regular supply of Old Etonian ties and other little luxuries from the Old Country.

Meanwhile for Kim Philby, after five years of harassment and anxiety, things were beginning to look a good deal better. With, it was generally believed, government backing, he became in September 1956 the correspondent of *The Observer* and *The Economist* in Beirut, an agreeable town in an interesting part of the world. It seems certain that, at the same time, he also resumed work for the SIS. 'It would have been odd,' he wrote himself, 'if·they had made no use of me at all.' Just what kind of use remains an open question.

Philby, who had left Aileen and their five children in England, was to spend more than five years in Beirut. He put up first at a rather sleazy Arab hotel, moving later to a white stone house in the mountains above Beirut, where old St John, known locally as 'the Hadji', was living with Umferhat, or Rosie, as the family called her, the Baluchi slave-girl given him by Ibn Saud, and their two young sons.

Among the first people he met in Beirut were Sam Brewer, the Middle East correspondent of the *New York Times* whom he had known in Spain, and his wife Eleanor, a tall, dark, slender, quietly attractive woman in her mid-forties. He got on well with both of them and they, in Eleanor's words, 'took him under their wing', and asked him to spend Christmas with them. To this invitation he responded wholeheartedly, making himself useful about the house, going shopping with Eleanor and helping to cook the Christmas dinner and decorate the Christmas tree. There was much about Kim – his stutter, his untidiness, the warmth of his smile – that made people, especially women, feel protective towards him. Soon he had become one of their closest friends.

'He was then,' wrote Eleanor, 'forty-four, of medium height, very lean, with a handsome heavily-lined face. His eyes were an intense blue.'

I thought that here was a man who had seen a lot of the world, who was experienced, and yet who seemed to have suffered. I soon discovered that we had some mutual friends and many common interests, especially music. He had a gift for creating an atmosphere of such intimacy that I found myself talking freely to him. I was very impressed by his beautiful manners. . . . In the spring of 1957 we started seeing each other more frequently. My husband was away from Beirut a great deal of the time and Kim would often meet me in the crowded fruit-market, where I did my daily shopping, or in one of the Arab coffee-houses on the waterfront. It seemed to me that I had never met a kinder, more interesting person in my entire life . . .

Kim had started writing Eleanor letters. It was something he did particularly well. 'Like his beautiful manners,' wrote Eleanor, 'Kim's skill in writing letters was a reminder of a civilized way of living, particularly appealing to an American.' The letters became increasingly affectionate. By June, Kim and Eleanor had become lovers. 'Deeper in love than ever, my darling XXX from your Kim,' Kim would write on a piece of paper and slip it across the table to her as they sat together looking out over the old Phoenician port.

Later that year Eleanor went back to America on a visit. Her ten-year-old marriage to Sam Brewer had not, according to her, been a particularly happy one. Before she left, she promised Kim to get a divorce. After she had been in the States some months, she received a cable and a letter from Kim announcing that his wife had died and asking her to marry him.

Aileen, forty-six and deeply neurotic, had been living at Crowborough alone for much of the time, drinking heavily and coping with life as best she could. On 15 December her daughter Josephine, back for the Christmas holidays, found her mother dead in bed in the empty house. The coroner's verdict was that she had died of heart failure following influenza.

Kim flew back for the funeral, cooked Christmas dinner for his children, put the house up for sale and three weeks later flew back to Beirut. Six months after this, in July 1958, came a cable from Eleanor to say that she had obtained a Mexican divorce. 'CLEVER WONDERFUL YOU FLY HAPPILY SONG IN HEART LIFE IS MIRACULOUS

GREATEST LOVE KIM,' he cabled back and then went to see Sam Brewer.

'I've come to tell you that I've had a cable from Eleanor,' he said. 'She has got her divorce and I want you to be the first person to know that I'm going to marry her.'

'That sounds like the best possible solution,' said Sam. Then, as one newspaperman to another: 'What do you make of the situation in Iraq?'

In the autumn of 1958 Eleanor returned to Beirut where she and Kim set up house together. Not long after they flew to England, where in January 1959 they were married at Holborn Register Office. 'You will never regret marrying an Englishman,' said the registrar to Eleanor.

For Kim the visit marked another stage in his rehabilitation and return to general acceptance by many of his former friends. The same was true in Beirut where he and Eleanor were now living happily together in an agreeable top floor apartment in the rue Kantari with its own terrace and a fine view of the mountains. Everyone accepted them. The story of Kim's alleged involvement with Burgess and Maclean was beginning to be forgotten and certainly never held against him. People regarded him simply as someone who had had bad luck, who had, indeed, been badly treated. 'To me,' wrote Eleanor, 'he was a divine husband. I can still hear his voice calling out in the early morning: "Tea, darling, on the terrace." I used to lie in bed thinking about my past life and feeling this was too good to be true.'

From Beirut Kim travelled all over the Near and Middle East, filing copy from Amman, Riyadh, Damascus, Sharjah, Bahrein, Bagdad, Teheran and Cyprus. Once he even took Eleanor on a trip to the Empty Quarter of Arabia, his father's former stamping ground.

The stories he sent to *The Observer* and *The Economist*, though not very numerous, were well balanced and objective, in every way up to the standard of those excellent periodicals. What other reports he sent and to whom was to remain a matter for speculation. In the middle of 1960 an old friend and former colleague of his had arrived in Beirut as Station Commander for the SIS. Henceforward they were to meet a couple of times a week.

In September 1960 old St John stopped off in Beirut to visit his son and new daughter-in-law on his way back to Riyadh. It was a happy, uproarious reunion. But on 29 September, after an unusually heavy party, St John, who on such occasions did not allow his religious convictions to interfere with his consumption of alcohol, had a heart attack. He died next day and was buried with Moslem rites. 'St John Philby, Greatest of Arabian Explorers' was the inscription a saddened Kim chose for his father's tombstone.

For two years all went well. Then, towards the end of 1962 Kim's friends began to notice signs of deterioration in him. Once again he was drinking heavily. He must, they decided, be worried about something.

He was. On the evening of Wednesday, 23 January 1963, a wild, stormy day, he and Eleanor had accepted an invitation to have dinner with Glen Balfour-Paul, First Secretary at the British Embassy, and his wife Marny. Late that afternoon Kim put on a mackintosh and went out into the downpour, saying he had an appointment, but would be back at about six. At six he telephoned to say that he would meet Eleanor at the Balfour-Pauls' at eight. Eleanor went to the party by herself, telling her host and hostess that Kim would join them later. He never did.

Though public opinion had by now become more used to such shocks, Kim Philby's sudden disappearance caused almost as great a sensation as that twelve years earlier of Burgess and Maclean. Eleanor was immediately besieged by frantic newspapermen. She was also anxiously cross-questioned by the local representative of the SIS. Another visitor was her former husband, Sam Brewer, who came around for coffee. 'What's the old boy up to ?' he said, giving her a funny look.

Early in February, however, two letters from Kim reached Eleanor, giving no indication of his whereabouts, but assuring her that she was constantly in his thoughts, that he loved her deeply and had no intention of disappearing out of her life. On 2 March these were followed by a cable (handed in the day before by an Arab at a Cairo post office). 'ARRANGEMENTS FOR REUNION PROCEEDING,' it said.

On 20 March Mr Edward Heath, Lord Privy Seal in Mr Macmillan's government, when pressed on the subject in the House of Commons, declined to speculate about the reasons for Philby's disappearance, but declared reassuringly that 'since Mr Philby resigned from the Foreign Service twelve years ago, he has had no access of any kind to any official information.'

But the press, especially the American press, would not leave the story alone and in June *Newsweek*, doubtless possessing inside knowledge probably derived from the CIA, announced bluntly that Philby was the Third Man, that he had for many years been a Soviet agent and was now almost certainly safe in Russia, and rather unkindly went on to examine in this light the conduct in the matter of successive British governments.

It had by this time become difficult for Mr Macmillan's government to go on pretending they knew nothing. On 1 July Mr Heath, with the air of a not very expert conjuror finally producing a rather tired rabbit out of his hat, rose in the House of Commons to announce that it now appeared that Philby had been a Soviet agent since before 1946 and had in fact been the Third Man in the affair of Burgess and Maclean.

The mystery, such as it was, was finally cleared up once and for all on

30 July by an announcement in *Izvestia* that by a unanimous vote of the Praesidium of the Supreme Soviet Harold Philby had been afforded political asylum in the Soviet Union and at the same time granted Soviet citizenship. Two years later came the news that, on top of this, he had also been awarded the Order of the Red Banner. At about the same time, once again a little belatedly, the British Government deprived him of his hard-earned OBE.

What was it that caused Kim Philby to disappear so abruptly on the night of Mrs Balfour-Paul's dinner-party? The answer is that he and his Soviet employers had suddenly realized that his former British colleagues had at last caught up with him and that there was now no longer any other course open to him.

Of recent years there had been a number of changes in Whitehall. In 1953 Sir Stewart Menzies had retired and had been succeeded as head of SIS by his former deputy, Major-General Sir John Sinclair. In 1956 Sinclair had in his turn been succeeded by a civilian, Sir Dick White, previously a senior official of MI5, who had brought a new, perhaps rather more professional approach to the whole business of espionage and counter-espionage. The years 1961 and 1962 had in fact brought some notable British successes in this field: the defection, on the Soviet side, of three important intelligence officers, Penkovski, Goleniewski and Dolnytsin, and the arrest of George Blake, a former colleague of Philby's in SIS and like him a Soviet agent of long standing.

With the help of the new material thus made available to them the British had been able to fill in most if not all the missing pieces in this and other puzzles. Dick White had himself been personally involved in the early stages of Philby's investigation. He realized as well as anyone that the outcome of the Volkov case had been highly suspicious and that Philby's relationship to Burgess and Maclean was open to more than one interpretation. And he had made it his business to see that the relevant file was kept open. By the end of 1962 the case against Philby was virtually complete. As Mr Heath was to tell the Commons six months later, it was now clear that he had been working for the Russians since before 1946 and that it was he who had tipped off Burgess and Maclean.

How did Philby learn that the net was at long last closing in on him? The news of the defection of a number of senior Soviet intelligence officers must in itself have been unnerving, both to him and to his employers. According to his own account, the latter, realizing the danger he was in, 'decided to call me to the Soviet Union to ensure my safety'. But it seems in any event probable that he himself by this time realized all too well from his continuing contacts with the British Secret Service that they were not only fully aware of his exact status as a Soviet agent, but were now attempting to turn this knowledge to their own advantage and seeking by one means or another to get him into their power. Whether or not he was afraid of being drugged or made away with he had seen the red light and at once put the appropriate contingency plan into operation.

Once you come to realize, as the British Security Services eventually did, that Kim Philby had been a Soviet agent from the first, much becomes clear and many phases of his life take on a new and altogether different significance. And here his own reminiscences (though clearly to be treated with caution), provide a useful commentary and guide.

Kim Philby had become a Communist when he was at Cambridge, or very soon after. 'It cannot,' he wrote, 'be so very surprising that I adopted a Communist viewpoint in the thirties; so many of my contemporaries made the same choice. But many of those who made that choice in those days changed sides . . . I stayed the course.' And he goes on to explain why. 'How, where and when I became a member of the Soviet Intelligence Service,' he continues with a conspiratorial nudge, 'is a matter for myself and my comrades.' One thing is certain, that when the offer did come, he accepted it with alacrity. 'One does not,' he wrote, 'look twice at an offer of enrolment in an élite force.' In fact he seems to have been recruited in 1934, but merely as a kind of probationer. Only during the Spanish Civil War (though by then he was already carrying a Soviet Secret Service cipher in the ticket pocket of his trousers) was he, to his great delight, finally accepted as a fully fledged agent.

He was never, he rightly insists, a double agent. 'All through my career,' he tells us, 'I have been a straight penetration agent working in the Soviet interest. I had been told in pressing terms by my Soviet friends', he explains, 'that my first priority must be with the British Secret Service.' And so, as we have seen, 'after dropping a few hints here and there,' he joined the British Secret Service with an ease which astonished him and caused his Soviet contact to wonder whether he had really got into the right organization. But this implied no conflict of loyalties. 'The fact that I joined the British Secret Intelligence Service is neither here nor there; I regarded my SIS appointments purely in the light of cover jobs, to be carried out sufficiently well to ensure my attaining positions in which my service to the Soviet Union would be most effective.'

This, clearly stated, is the premise we start from and it is in the light of it that we need to examine all that follows. It is a fascinating exercise. Henceforward every move, every decision is inexorably dictated by the same immutable set of considerations. Indeed one feels as though one were watching the doctrine of predestination work out with the added advantage of an almost divine foreknowledge.

Thus Philby's, at first slightly surprising choice of the Franco side in Spain and his membership of the deplorable Anglo-German Fellowship immediately fall into place. Guy Burgess, whom Kim had by then already recruited for the Russians, and who was himself trying to do the same sort of thing, was naturally quick to understand his motives, though characteristically a good deal less quick to grasp the need for discretion. 'Kim wouldn't have gone to Franco,' he announced portentously to his young friend Jack Hewit, 'unless he had a very good reason.'

But all this, like his spell in France as a war correspondent for *The Times*, had been no more than a preliminary manoeuvring for position and a preparation of the ground. The real moment for which he and his Russian friends had been waiting (though even then they could hardly believe their good luck) came in June 1940 when, apparently at Guy's instigation and after a vague talk with an elderly lady, he received a summons to report for duty to an address in Caxton Street, Westminster, evidently housing some section of the British Secret Service and 'presided over by a colonel in plain clothes looking like a character straight out of William Le Queux', whom the cognoscenti will have no difficulty in recognizing as the mysterious D himself. Little wonder, all considered, that his Soviet guardian angel was momentarily afraid the whole thing might be a joke in poor taste on the part of his British opposite numbers.

In June 1941, within barely a year of his joining the British Secret Service, Kim's personal position underwent an important adjustment, indeed easement. With Hitler's attack on the Soviet Union (which Stalin has so pig-headedly refused to believe in) World War II, from being the Second Imperialist War, became overnight the Great Patriotic War Against Fascism; and from being an adversary, Great Britain became, for the time being at any rate, an ally of the Soviet Union, in some ways quite a useful one. From one day to another Kim's attitude, like that of orthodox Communists everywhere, suffered a sudden change. Henceforward he would be working (within limits) for the British war effort rather than against it.

This simplified things considerably. With whatever mental reservations, he showed himself (as we know from Mr Harold Macmillan) an able and conscientious functionary. Henceforward, for most purposes, there needed to be no serious conflict between the two halves of his superficially and deliberately split personality. All, or almost all his ability and conscientiousness could safely be directed into one channel.

Until, that is, the British planners (in competition, quite certainly, with their Soviet colleagues) started looking, and planning, beyond the end of the war with Germany. This, in a sense, was Philby's finest hour. To have positioned himself, by the simple expedient of eliminating poor Colonel Cowgill, at the head of the department concerned with countering Communism, was nothing less than a masterstroke, meriting, one would have surely thought, something a little better than a belated Order of the Red Banner.

Besides being a masterstroke, it saved his bacon. Had he not been where he was in August 1945, he might have failed to frustrate the knavish tricks of the defector Volkov ('a nasty piece of work'), whose revelations, as he himself says, might well have 'put an end to a promising career'. Little wonder that he was relieved when the task of handling this delicate matter was directly entrusted to him, although by then his friends in Moscow were quite certainly already giving the matter their urgent attention.

As for his subsequent posting to Istanbul as Station Head, this too offered plentiful scope for his special talents and it was of course proof of his undoubted efficiency that the agents he so painstakingly infiltrated into Soviet Georgia should have been punctually greeted with a burst of machine-gun fire on the other side of the frontier. (Though just what they could have achieved, had they ever reached their destination is, to me at any rate, far from clear.) That Kim should, with Turkish help, have used the pretext of taking long-range photographs of the Soviet side of the frontier in order to take close-ups of the no less carefully guarded Turkish side is also a nice touch, although from the ground both sides of the frontier are so alike as to be practically indistinguishable from each other and for good results, should really be (and no doubt regularly are) photographed from the air.

With the advantage of hindsight, old Turkish hands now tell the story that in his office in Istanbul Kim had hanging a photograph of Mount Ararat (which is just in Turkey and usually veiled in mists) taken not from the Turkish, but from the Soviet side and with the two humps of Greater and Lesser Ararat therefore the other way round, symbolizing, presumably, for his own, if for no one else's amusement, the essential ambiguity of his own role.

His appointment to Washington was, as things turned out, the culmination of his career in the British Secret Service. As he himself has said, he was by now well on his way to a knighthood and, had things gone otherwise, might even have ended up as C – a disturbing thought, even for those who are not inclined to take espionage too seriously. As it was, his appointment cost the lives of a lot of no doubt relatively innocent Albanians (although they were probably doomed in any case); did untold damage to British–American relations at a time when a close understanding between the two countries was particularly important; and quite certainly handed to the Russians on a plate a large amount of extremely valuable information. Finally, it enabled Kim to play his most celebrated role of all – that of the Third Man.

For those who enjoy hypothetical history this phase of the story offers a rich field for speculation. From a Soviet point of view, was Maclean really worth rescuing, at such a price? Would it not have been wiser at whatever the cost to keep Philby where he was, clear-headed, resourceful, utterly dependable and with a considerable future potential, and leave Maclean, by now of little use to anyone, to take what was coming to him?

And then of course there was Burgess, the joker in the pack, so unaccountable, so unpredictable, so essentially improbable in the role of a secret agent that even when he stepped on board the *Falaise* at midnight on 25 May 1951, he still had a clean record (in the eyes of the security authorities if in no one else's). Was he used by the Russians to the best advantage? Why was he used at all? His knowledge of people and their habits, his wide range of friends in society and on its fringes, in politics and in Whitehall and not least in MI5 and MI6 must clearly have been of considerable use to the Russians in assessing the facts at their disposal, though just how to employ him must by 1951 have set a pretty problem to the Soviet spymaster concerned (as it did so often to the long-suffering Personnel Department of the Foreign Office).

For Philby the decision he had to take when, in the summer of 1950, he got that letter from Guy (whom he had recruited for the Russians in the first place) announcing his impending arrival and asking to be put up, was not an easy one. 'In normal circumstances,' he says, 'it would have been quite wrong for two secret operatives (meaning, of course, Soviet secret operatives) to occupy the same premises.' But, as he goes on to point out, the circumstances were not normal. The two were old friends and known to be so. And Philby knew from the files (who better?) that as far as MI5 were concerned Guy had a clean record. Moreover, after mature consideration and two lonely motor trips to points outside Washington to consult with his Soviet sponsors, he had come to the conclusion that he might in fact be able to make good use of him.

While Kim was still in Istanbul, his Soviet contact there had asked him if he could find out what the British were doing in a case under investigation by the FBI involving the British Embassy in Washington. Some cross-checking had made it clear to him that this referred to the suspected leakage back in 1944-5, eventually to be pinned on Donald Maclean. At his discussions with his Soviet contacts, the decision was taken that Maclean must at all costs be rescued and that Burgess should be used for this purpose.

If Guy went back to London it would be only natural that he should call on Donald as head of the American Department. He could then, as one

Soviet agent to another, slip a piece of paper across his desk with a warning on it and all would be well, or fairly well.

The question was how to get Burgess back to London without delay, for Philby, who was himself due for posting elsewhere, could not afford to postpone the operation a day longer than necessary. But this presented no real problem. Guy, helpful as always, deliberately got himself booked for speeding three times in one day and was cheeky to the police who booked him. The Governor of Virginia, the State Department and Sir Oliver Franks reacted predictably. And in a very short time Guy was on his way.

On Guy's last evening in Washington the two old friends and comrades had dinner together in a Chinese restaurant with individual music in every booth. Under cover of this personalized cacophony, they went over the plan together. On his arrival in London, Guy was to meet a Soviet contact and give him a full briefing. He was then to call on Maclean at the Foreign Office, with a sheet of paper giving the time and place of a rendezvous and at an appropriate moment slip this across the desk. After this he would arrange a second meeting with Maclean and put him fully in the picture.

Next morning Kim drove a seemingly slightly uneasy Guy to the station. 'Don't you go too,' were his last words to him, spoken, he tells us, only half-jocularly.

Meanwhile, it was clearly desirable that Philby's own position should be safeguarded. If Burgess happened to be seen with Maclean before the latter's departure, further enquiries might lead back to Philby. Hitherto the FBI, in trying to identify the source of the British Embassy leak, had been wading hopefully through reams of material about former Embassy charladies. It was now, with the rescue plan already formulated, that Kim decided to give the enquiry what he called 'a nudge in the right direction', with the object, in the long run, of diverting suspicion from himself.

So far so good. Encouraged by Kim's helpful nudge, the security authorities, progressed beyond the charladies and were working on a list which, in addition to Donald's, contained the names of two future Ambassadors and one future head of the Foreign Office. They were now concentrating on the latter. This was fine as far as it went. But next came the news that Maclean had moved to top of the list. He would, it appeared, not be informed of the charge against him till the case was complete. Meanwhile certain categories of paper were to be withheld from him and he would be placed under surveillance. (Two measures, as Philby at once saw, which would, if necessary, provide a convenient explanation of his escape.)

Even so, time was of the essence. On the pretext of asking him what he wanted done about a car he had left behind, Philby wrote a letter to Burgess discreetly conveying this message. Having done that, he could only wait. MI5's most urgent telegram to Geoffrey Patterson put an end to this painful period of suspense. The latter's announcement that the bird had flown immediately took an enormous weight off Philby's mind. His next sentence: 'Guy Burgess has gone with him,' put it right back there. 'At that,' he tells us, 'my consternation was no pretence.'

He was now quite clearly in the very worse kind of trouble himself. Guy's departure had most definitely not been part of the plan. Inevitably it immediately focused the spotlight of enquiry on Kim himself, who was a friend of Burgess and had also known that Maclean was being investigated. The question was: what ought he to do? With his Soviet friends, he had worked out an escape plan to be put into operation in case of extreme emergency. Just how extreme, he asked himself, was the present emergency?

Before making up his mind, it was worth testing the feeling of the FBI. He did this by taking round to them the telegram from MI5. Greatly to his relief, they received it with remarkable calm, indeed even with a hint of malicious pleasure at the mess their British colleagues had evidently made of things. Having been trained (twice over) to take no risks, the next thing he did was to drive out to Great Falls. He parked his car at a place he had already selected for the purpose on a deserted stretch of road with the Potomac on one side and some thick scrub on the other, then doubled back a couple of hundred yards through the bushes and, using a trowel he had brought with him, dug a hole and buried his camera and the rest of his photographic apparatus, emerging a few minutes later doing up his fly-buttons. As far as inanimate objects were concerned, he was, in his own words, 'as clean as a whistle'.

He next addressed his mind to the question of whether or not he should try to escape. By nightfall he had decided, on various grounds, to stay and see it through. It was a decision that called for steady nerves, but his chances of survival he calculated were considerably better than even. He had worked for eleven years in the Secret Service. 'I knew the enemy well enough,' he writes, 'to foresee in personal terms the moves he was likely to make.' This was an important asset. He also had many important friends at home who would want to see his innocence established. Finally, while a strong presumption of guilt might be enough for an intelligence officer, it would not satisfy a lawyer, who would require hard evidence. And this, with any luck, would not be forthcoming.

His decision proved to be the right one. It meant that he was able to serve his Soviet employers 'in the field' for a dozen more years, before finally coming in from the cold and joining Burgess and Maclean in Moscow, in that far Country of the Revolution which he had served for thirty years and which to him in a sense was home, although as far as is known he had never before set foot there.

Exactly how or where he crossed the Soviet frontier or what escape route he followed to get there is not particularly important. There are plenty of ways of getting from Beirut to Moscow, especially if you have plenty of forged passports and an escape plan prepared in advance. As he himself said, dozens of people cross the Lebanese frontier illegally every month, and if the MVD or KGB have any difficulty in getting one of their own agents out of the Lebanon and into their own counry by land, sea or air, they are not the efficient organization which most of us take them for.

Soon after his arrival in Moscow, Kim lost an old friend. Despite his ideological allegiance, Guy Burgess had never really taken to life in Moscow, resenting the bureaucracy and the surveillance and finding it no easier to conform to Soviet than he had to Western standards of behaviour. Loyal though they usually are to those who have served them well, the patience of the KGB, like that of the British Foreign Office, must at times have been sorely tried by this particular pensioner. In the end he had found himself a companion, a twenty-year-old factory-hand called Tolya, who played the accordion. With him he set up house in a two-room flat agreeably furnished with some fine pieces of old furniture he had sent for from England. But in general he was no Russophile; Slav charm meant little to him; above all he missed England and his friends there. Grubby and unkempt but as usual wearing his Old Etonian tie, he would during his last years hang rather pathetically about the bars and hotels frequented by foreigners in the hope of finding someone out of his past who might be prepared to talk to him.

Prematurely afflicted with hardening of the arteries, he gradually became, with the years, so dependent on drugs and drink that even his former Moscow friends kept out of his way. In August 1963 at the age of fifty-two he died in hospital of arteriosclerosis and was cremated in Moscow, while a brass band played the *Internationale* and Donald Maclean delivered a funeral oration declaring him 'a gifted and courageous man who devoted his life to the cause of making a better world'. To Kim, who arrived in Moscow barely in time to visit him in hospital before he died, he left £2000 and part of the contents of his flat.

A month later, in September 1963, Kim was joined in Moscow by Eleanor who, after a rather ridiculous attempt by the Russians to smuggle her out of Beirut clandestinely, in the end simply flew by the regular BOAC flight to London and thence some four months later by Aeroflot to Moscow.

Until his sudden departure Eleanor had never for a moment suspected that Kim was working for the Russians or indeed that he had any connection with them. But she loved him and the discovery in no way weakened her determination to join him. During the eight months of their separation he had continued to write her those loving, intimate, tender letters which had won her heart in the first place. With Kim to meet her at the airport on her arrival in Moscow, she was, in her own words, 'wildly happy'.

In Moscow she found her husband living in a style suitable to his relatively high rank in the Soviet hierarchy, with a well-furnished four-roomed apartment in a large modern block, a maid to look after him and a chauffeur-driven car. Financially he was also well provided for, even receiving a substantial sterling allowance for the maintenance of his children in England. Meanwhile, she wrote, 'he was still the same lovable, completely charming, sentimental man I adored'.

But now, for the first time, Eleanor gradually became aware of something which in all their years of affectionate intimacy she had never before noticed: the scarcely perceptible barrier between them which was an inevitable consequence of his work and of his all-embracing loyalty to the Party. Suddenly she realized that for all those years she had been completely unaware of what was by far the most important thing in his life. For any woman, however devoted, it was bound to be something of a shock.

For several days after her arrival Kim cross-questioned her minutely about the talks she had had with British Intelligence during the eight months which followed his flight from Beirut, wanting to know everything they had said to her and she to them and learning without pleasure that for the past seven years his friends in the SIS had known that he was a Soviet agent – a fact that cast a new and somewhat disturbing light on his relationship with them during that period.

Eleanor tells us that she soon became bored by what was fast becoming a regular interrogation. But Kim, though patient, was unusually stubborn and insistent. 'What is more important in your life,' she asked him in the end, 'me and the children or the Communist Party?' 'The Party, of course,' he replied. It had, as she immediately realized, been a silly question to ask him.

By the end of her first winter in Moscow, Eleanor, lonely, speaking no Russian and with no one much to talk to except their fellow expatriates Donald and Melinda Maclean, with whom they constantly dined and played bridge, but to whom she did not feel herself immediately drawn, was not entirely happy. Though still deeply in love with Kim, she could not share his enthusiasm for the Soviet scene or adapt herself to Soviet life as readily as he had done. In the end she decided to keep a promise she had made to her daughter and to fly over to America and see her.

Leaving Moscow in late June or early July, she spent the summer peacefully with her daughter in California. Meanwhile from Moscow Kim wrote her his usual long, chatty, affectionate, entertaining letters, telling her how much he missed her, begging her to come back soon and giving her amusing details of his everyday life. They gave her, as always, enormous pleasure. Clearly he was lonely without her, loved her and longed for her to come back. Being lonely, he seemed to be seeing more than usual of Donald and Melinda Maclean, at whose *dacha* outside Moscow he often spent weekends and with whom he would often go to the theatre and restaurants. But that was only natural.

Sometimes when Donald was not available, he would take out Melinda, who evidently welcomed the change. Gradually the references to Melinda in his letters became more frequent. 'Melinda and I had a nice lunch at the Ararat yesterday,' he wrote on 4 September. 'After lunch we visited an exhibition of Russian woodwork . . . After that I walked with her up to the Post Office. Then Melinda came back here. . . .' And again in October: 'I am meeting Melinda today on the steps of the Bolshoi to see what is going on in the way of opera, ballet, etc. She welcomes the chance of getting away from the flat occasionally and it is nice to have someone to take out in default of my own darling.'

A month later, at the end of November, Eleanor retrieved her American passport from the State Department, who had temporarily taken it into safe keeping, and duly obtaining a visa from the Soviet Embassy she flew back to Moscow. While in the States she had provided herself with a good fur-lined coat and boots. She was, she says, determined 'to make a real effort to come to terms with life in Russia'.

She found Kim restless and uneasy. On the night of her return he opened one of the bottles of duty-free whisky she had brought back with her and deliberately drank himself silly. When she asked about the Macleans, he said that he had had a filthy row with Donald who had called him a double agent (to him, the ultimate insult). Melinda, it appeared, was in Leningrad.

On Melinda's return from Leningrad, Eleanor noticed that she was more than usually tense and on edge. Her relations with Donald, never good, were clearly worse than ever. She looked, Eleanor thought, like an unhappy Pekinese. 'Melinda's not well,' said Kim solicitously. 'Don't you think she's on the verge of a nervous breakdown? We must do something to help her.' So the three of them took to going about together. Kim, she noticed, was also tense and on edge. As usual, he sought to relieve the tension by heavy drinking, spending Christmas and New Year in a haze of alcohol.

'I'm worried about Kim,' said Eleanor to Melinda one day. 'He's drinking too much; he's so nervous and depressed that I sometimes think he doesn't love me any more.' 'He did,' replied Melinda with a long hard look, 'until a while ago.'

Finally in April Eleanor asked Kim straight out what was going on. 'Melinda is so unhappy,' he replied. 'Donald is impotent. She's had a miserable time for fifteen years and I feel that it's partly my fault. I must try to make the rest of her life happier.' 'But what about my life?' asked Eleanor. 'I don't want you to leave; of course you can stay on,' replied Kim. 'You know I'm very fond of you and Melinda understands my very special feeling for you.' But Eleanor, wondering vaguely whether Kim was acting from ideological or purely human motives, decided to leave.

Early in May after months of heavy drinking Kim was finally taken off to hospital suffering, Eleanor was told, from pneumonia and tuberculosis. Just before the ambulance came for him, two KGB officials called to inform him officially that he had been awarded the Order of the Red Banner. He was excited and much gratified.

The day before she left, Eleanor went for the last time to see Kim in hospital, where he was making good progress. They took a fond and emotional farewell of each other and as a parting gift Kim gave Eleanor his old Westminster School scarf.

Next morning, 18 May 1965, Eleanor left Moscow and Kim for ever. The junior of the two KGB officials who worked with Kim saw her off at the airport with two dozen tulips. In the aeroplane she read and re-read a farewell letter from Kim, one of those tender, loving, intimate letters which had always meant so much to her. She was later to tell the story of her life with Kim in a surprisingly evocative and moving book. With the proceeds she bought a house in California, only to die there three years later.

Kim's affair with Melinda, which had begun in September after an unusually good lunch at the Aragvi, did not end in marriage. In due course she went back to live, if not with Donald, at any rate in or near the same apartment block, while Kim, his powers of attraction for the opposite sex apparently undiminished, set up house with a rather good-looking and very much younger red-haired Russian girl called Nina, whom he eventually married.

As for his day-to-day life in the Soviet Union, Kim is not very informative, telling us simply that 'like all the other millions of Muscovites', he lives in a flat. Nor does he give many first-hand impressions of the system under which he now lives, a system offering the strongest possible contrast to anything he had ever experienced before and no scope whatever to a potential deviator (though now, he would no doubt contend, he no longer feels any need to deviate).

By rescuing him when in peril, by granting him Soviet citizenship and the Order of the Red Banner, and by pensioning him off under what must to him be agreeable circumstances, the Soviet Government have clearly

275

shown their appreciation of the outstanding work he did for them. And he, in return, makes it equally clear where his loyalty lies and has always lain for the past forty-odd years.

Kim Philby, as one looks back over his life, is an interesting phenomenon, more interesting certainly than those weaker vessels, Burgess and Maclean. His proudest claim is that for more than forty years he 'stayed the course' without wavering, without for a moment allowing himself to be disturbed by the Darkness at Noon of Stalin's purges, by the Soviet-German Pact and all that accompanied it, by the utter cynicism and successive twists and turns of the Party Line, by such interludes as the invasion of Hungary and of Czechoslovakia or even by the revival of a rampant Russian Imperialism which puts Peter and Catherine the Great into the shade. All these, he would no doubt argue, have been necessary stages in the Soviet Union's predestined advance towards world supremacy.

In this he is more orthodox than the Kremlin, more Russian, too, than many Russians, at a time when increasing numbers are at long last beginning to question these antediluvian values and to show, here and there, faint flickerings of independence. Meanwhile, as the century draws to a close, he, for his part, still clings religiously to the tenets in force in the nineteen-thirties, when, with Stalin in control, the young Kim Philby first saw the light.

His steadfastness, his unswerving loyalty and utter devotion to a cause compel recognition, as do the consistency, the self-control and the steady nerves which carried him through four exacting decades. More obscure to non-Communists, though clearly not to him, are the mental and moral processes which brought such an able, intelligent man to his present position and still maintain him there. Shortly before his own departure from England, Donald Maclean, a weaker character under severe stress, about to sacrifice everything for the sake of an idea only half-held, spoke to a friend of the 'leap of faith' needed to convince him that Communism was right. This is the leap which Philby made forty-four years ago and, as far as we know, has never regretted. In this connection Professor Trevor Roper speaks convincingly of a religious conviction of blinding force. This, as he says, is the most probable explanation of a state of mind involving a *sacrificio dell'intelletto* as complete as that made in comparable circumstances by the Jesuits of the sixteenth century. It is a parallel which Mr Graham Greene, another old friend and former colleague of Kim Philby, has, strangely enough, also hit on.

On a rather different, non-ideological level it is possible to identify in Kim Philby another, less dramatic motive, strong in most good public servants: pride in belonging to, in being part of a powerful and efficient machine and love of that machine as such. As he himself puts it: 'One does not look twice at an offer of enrolment in an élite force.' For ten years it was this professional pride in his work that brought him enthusiastic recognition as an apparently loyal and efficient member of the British Secret Service and was, in the long run, to bring him even more enthusiastic recognition for his work on behalf of the Soviet Union.

Eight

ONE FOR THE LADIES

'This case has the characteristics of what is
called a spy-thriller . . . Keep your feet firmly
on the ground and consider only the evidence
before you.'

LORD CHIEF JUSTICE PARKER

In the year 1955 the Royal Navy (and therefore their NATO allies) were
still well ahead of their Soviet counterparts in their methods of tracking
enemy submarines while submerged. This awkward fact clearly to some
extent diminished the value of the Soviet Union's big new submarine
fleet, which by this time had reached an overall strength of seven hundred,
and made it essential for the Russians to find out everything they could
about British underwater detection techniques and how to contend with
them. It was to this all-important task that Soviet Naval Intelligence
experts accordingly now directed their maximum attention.

One morning in February 1955 Dr Leslie Fowden of 18 Penderry Rise,
Catford received a visit from a pleasant-looking Canadian couple in early
middle age, Mr and Mrs Peter Kroger, who had been sent to view the
house by an estate agent. Dr Fowden was leaving shortly with his family for
the United States and had decided to let his house furnished while he was
away. The Krogers wanted somewhere to live temporarily while looking for
something more permanent. The house seemed to suit them and, in due
course, an appropriate rent was agreed.

Peter Kroger, who was a dealer in rare books, had, it seemed, come to
England from Canada a couple of months before partly because of his
health. Once they moved in, he and his wife quickly made friends with
their neighbours and were soon taking an active part in the social life in
the district. By July Peter, a quiet, reserved, grey-haired man, had found
suitable premises for his business in a back room off the Strand, where he
installed part of his stock. Many of his dealings were by post and he spent

278

a lot of time wrapping up books and posting them off to his customers. He also attended most of the big book sales. On the whole the neighbours saw more of his wife Helen than they did of him. She was a friendly, forthcoming woman with rather a loud voice, who talked a lot and enjoyed a glass of gin. Sometimes it would be several glasses of gin. After which Helen would become tearful and bemoan the fact that she and Peter, otherwise so happily married, had never had any children.

But for the Krogers Catford was only a temporary perching place. In October they found the permanent home they had been looking for: a good-sized double-fronted bungalow at a price they could afford in Cranley Drive, Ruislip. Having bought some furniture, they moved into 45 Cranley Drive early in 1956. To their friends from Catford, who came to visit them there, Helen explained that her husband had to have more room for his books. And indeed several of the rooms in their new house were soon completely filled with them. To guard his precious possessions. Peter had the doors and windows of his bungalow fitted with the most elaborate locks and security devices.

At Ruislip, as at Catford, the Krogers, who were naturally gregarious, quickly became popular with their neighbours and spent a good deal of their time entertaining or being entertained. By now they had also made a number of friends in the book trade. Peter clearly had a good grasp of his subject and a real love of books. In 1958 he gave up the premises in the Strand and thereafter ran his business from Ruislip. He was soon well-thought-of amongst his fellow-dealers and in August 1960 was elected a member of the Antiquarian Booksellers' Association. Quite often the Krogers would go abroad on business or pleasure for a month or so at a time, never failing to send numerous picture postcards back to their friends from the places they visited.

One fairly regular visitor at 45 Cranley Drive, who sometimes spent the weekend there, was a compact, well-dressed, confident-looking man of about thirty-four with dark curly hair called Gordon Lonsdale, who had arrived from Canada some months after the Krogers. 'Our young Canadian friend,' Helen Kroger called him when she mentioned him to the neighbours. For all this, she did not go out of her way to introduce him to her many friends.

Gordon Lonsdale had landed in Southampton from New York on 3 March 1955. According to his passport, he had been born at Kirkland Lake near Cobalt, Ontario, on 27 August 1924, of a Canadian father and a Finnish mother. From Southampton he had caught the train to London, where he took a room at a hotel. Like so many Canadian visitors to London, he had joined the Overseas League and made good use of its various facilities. He had then started out to see the sights of London, visiting Buckingham

Palace, the Albert Hall, the Tower of London and the House of Commons and even meeting some Commonwealth-minded Members of Parliament – Tories for the most part.

Like the Krogers, Gordon Lonsdale, who seemed to have plenty of money, was looking for somewhere more permanent to live. In May 1955, on the strength of a reference from the Overseas League, he moved into a flat in the White House, an agreeable apartment building near Regent's Park. He particularly asked for a flat on the top floor. It suited him better, he said. A couple of months after moving in, in July 1955, Gordon, who was clearly out to enjoy himself, went on a fifteen-day coach tour of Scandinavia, followed not long after by a fortnight's tour of Italy. Good-looking, good-humoured, amusing and open-handed, Gordon quickly made friends among his fellow-tourists, notably with a pretty nineteen-year-old Canadian girl with whom he kept in touch for some time after they came back to London.

In October 1955 Lonsdale, who talked of possible business interests in the Far East, enrolled as a full-time student of Chinese at the London School of Oriental and African Studies, following the course for two years and eventually leaving with a reasonably sound knowledge of the language. While at the School he made numerous friends among the students of both sexes and sometimes entertained them at his flat, especially Carla, a good-looking Italian girl with a gift for making omelettes. They found him excellent company, full of entertaining stories about life in Canada. Many of his fellow students were Foreign Office officials or officers of the Army, Navy or Air Force, mostly employed in Intelligence. He also made friends with several officers of the United States Air Force stationed in England and their families.

Meanwhile, though never seemingly short of cash, he had decided that it was time to find ways of making a little money. For him this should clearly present no difficulties. He was persuasive and good at projecting himself. No one could fail to be impressed by his energy and drive. Few could resist his charm. As a first step he bought a couple of juke-boxes, which he immediately sold at a good profit. By the end of 1955 he was also selling bubble-gum machines. Before long he had become a director of the Automatic Merchandizing Company, based at Broadstairs, where the machines were assembled. On his visits to Broadstairs he would usually combine business with pleasure, taking full advantage of whatever night-life the locality offered.

Meanwhile there appeared to be a surprising demand for juke-boxes or bubble-gum machines. Business was flourishing and a subsidiary company was set up in London of which Lonsdale also became a director. In due course it occurred to the partners that there might be a market for their wares abroad. At his own suggestion, Lonsdale made a number of trips to

Europe, where, he told his associates, he had many useful contacts. Accordingly at Broadstairs production was increased, more material ordered, more men taken on and towards the end of 1959 a first large consignment of bubble-gum machines was shipped to Italy. It was only after the machines had reached their destination that it became clear, to everyone's dismay, that there was in fact no demand for them there. Soon the Automatic Merchandizing Company was in serious trouble and early in 1960 it was wound up.

The early part of 1960 was an awkward time for Gordon Lonsdale. For a while he even had to move into a smaller and cheaper flat near Victoria. But Gordon was nothing if not resilient. In February he became a director of the Master-Switch Company, set up to market an ingenious device designed to immobilize cars. Soon his affairs were in better shape and he was able to move back into the White House and start entertaining again. He also now traded in his runabout for a large and impressive white Studebaker.

Gordon Lonsdale did not spend all his time in London or on trips abroad. Nor was his circle of friends by any means limited to the Krogers and his various business associates. He was, for one thing, never short of female company. As Helen Kroger had said early on in their acquaintanceship, he was definitely 'one for the ladies'. There were plenty of successors to the pretty Canadian girl, both blondes and brunettes. There was a Yugoslav called Zlata and a Swede called Ulla, a German called Annemarie, a Chinese girl called Daisy Wong, and a secretary from Luton called Gillian, not to mention Carla, the Italian girl. Gordon was frankly interested in women, and women, for their part, found him attractive, partly for his looks, partly for the attention he paid them and the trouble he took with them, and partly for the stories he told, fascinating stories about every kind of thing, told in an intimate, confidential manner. Some of them no doubt went to bed with him and others did not. Back in Canada, he said, he had a wife. But she, it appeared, had left him. Meanwhile in London he continued to make the most of his reputation as a playboy.

Among Gordon Lonsdale's wide circle of friends and acquaintances were Harry Houghton, a rather jaunty-looking ex-Naval Master-at-Arms living at Broadwey near Weymouth, and his girlfriend, Ethel or 'Bunty' Gee, a brunette in her early forties with a bold eye and a ready smile. Sometimes Gordon would meet Harry and Bunty at Broadwey but usually they met in London.

Like many sailors, Harry Houghton had had a full and interesting life. Joining the Royal Navy at the age of sixteen in 1922, he had served in a gunboat on the Yangtse and then at Singapore and Malta and a number of other stations at sea and on shore. He had married in 1939, just before the outbreak of war. During the war he had served in a large number of ships, from the battleship *Ramillies* to a small armed merchantman. He had been on escort duty in the Arctic and in the Mediterranean, and had been shelled, bombed and torpedoed. More than once the ship in which he was serving had been sunk. All of which gave him plenty to talk about and made him excellent company when he had had a drink or two.

He had left the Navy in 1945 as a full Master-at-Arms, with twenty-three years service to his credit and the pension that went with his rank. He was now thirty-nine. With his record he had no difficulty in getting a job as a clerical officer in the Civil Service at Portsmouth. In 1950 he became an established Civil Servant and a year later, in July 1951, he was appointed Writer to the Naval Attaché in Warsaw. With him to Warsaw went his wife, Peggy. For some time things had not been going well between them. They went no better after their arrival in Warsaw.

For a convivial character like Harry Houghton the job of Writer to the Naval Attaché at a diplomatic post like Warsaw had much to recommend it. The work was interesting and not unduly arduous. Living conditions were good and pay and allowances excellent. There were plenty of parties and plenty of duty-free drink for any one who wanted it – rather too much in Harry's case. And when he got drunk, he took it out on Peggy – or so she said. There were unpleasant scenes in public and even more unpleasant scenes in private.

Drinking was not Harry Houghton's only form of relaxation in Warsaw. He had not been there long before he met a blonde, blue-eyed Polish girl, twenty years younger than he was, called Karytzia, to whom he was immediately attracted and who responded readily to his advances. In her altogether delightful company he sampled Warsaw's night-life, such as it was. There was only one problem – money. But Karytzia had the answer to that: selling duty-free coffee and other imported goods on the black market. Soon he was making an extremely good thing out of it and spending more than ever on drink and other pleasures.

When it becomes known, this kind of thing is frowned on in diplomatic circles, being, it is thought, bad for Britain's image abroad. It is not known whether Harry Houghton's misdemeanours became known or whether his transfer was due to some other reason, but in October 1952, well before the end of his two year tour of duty, he was posted back to Great Britain and there, somewhat surprisingly, given a highly responsible job at the Admiralty Underwater Weapons Establishment at Portland.

At first the Houghtons lived in a house provided by the Admiralty between Weymouth and Portland. Here the rows continued, as the neighbours were quick to notice. Nor was there any improvement when in 1953 they moved to a cottage Harry had bought, overlooking Weymouth Bay.

Harry, meanwhile, had met Bunty Gee, a blacksmith's daughter from

Hamble in Hampshire, who also had a job at the Underwater Weapons Establishment. In 1929, at fifteen, she had gone to work in a confectioner's shop owned by her Uncle John in Portland and had stayed there until the war. After that she had had a succession of not very exciting jobs until October 1950, when she successfully applied for a job at the Admiralty Underwater Detection Establishment, as it was then known. Since her father's death she had lived a very quiet life with her mother, her uncle and her aunt in a terraced house in Hambro Road, Portland. By now all three were in their eighties and Aunt Elizabeth was bedridden.

Soon Harry and Bunty had become inseparable, spending their evenings drinking together and making little attempt to disguise the nature of their relationship. Finally, to make things easier, Harry bought, with money borrowed from Bunty, a caravan which he installed at a mutually convenient site. This was the last straw as far as Peggy was concerned. They had already separated. She now instituted divorce proceedings and in due course the marriage was dissolved. When in 1959 Peggy remarried, Harry moved back into the cottage at Broadwey, which he at once set about improving.

In February 1957 Harry was transferred to the Port Auxiliary Repair Unit. Here he was one of two clerical officers in the unit at a salary of £15 a week, with responsibility for the handling of all papers and drawings and access, in the ordinary way, to classified material. Bunty, meanwhile, was still employed at the Underwater Weapons Establishment.

From 1956 onwards, after Harry had moved into the caravan, he and Bunty saw each other constantly. Sometimes, on their outings together, Bunty would remonstrate with Harry for drinking too much, but without much apparent effect. Once Harry's divorce had gone through, they were free to marry and might well have done so had Bunty not felt that, for the present at any rate, it was her duty to go on living at home and looking after her old mother and her uncle and aunt. 'I would have married him if conditions had been different at home,' she said afterwards.

Sometimes, as a change from Portland and Weymouth, the two of them went to London together for the weekend, though when this happened they had to invent an imaginary couple to chaperone them, so as not to shock Bunty's intensely respectable family. But, if this couple was imaginary, there was another friend they met sometimes in London and sometimes nearer home, who was very real indeed. This was a rather good-looking, dark-haired man of about thirty-five with a good deal of personal charm, a confident manner and an American or possibly Canadian accent, whom Harry introduced to Bunty as Commander Alexander Johnson from the office of the American Naval Attaché in London. Had he been asked to do so, the Commander could have produced a visiting card to confirm his identity, though anyone familiar with the occupant of Flat 634, the White House, Regent's Park could not fail to have been struck by his startling resemblance to Gordon Lonsdale.

Two local hotels at which Harry Houghton and Bunty Gee were regular customers were the New Inn at Longmoor and the Elm Tree at Langton Herring. At the beginning of 1960 another customer at both establishments happened to be a Naval Security Officer who knew Harry Houghton by sight, knew the work he was doing, and could not help wondering how a clerk earning what he was could afford to spend as much as he did on drink. It was not, it is true, much to go on, but even so he thought it worth mentioning to his superiors. On the strength of this, the latter made a few discreet enquiries. From these it emerged that Houghton, whose consumption of alcohol had increased of late, was now spending £20 a week on drink alone and that, on a combined pension and salary amounting to less than £1,000 a year, he had recently somehow managed to buy a new car and an expensive radio-gramophone, not to mention the extensive improvements he had made to his house. Rather belatedly it was also now recalled that back in 1954, when they were still married, Houghton's wife Peggy had come across a batch of Admiralty documents which Harry had left in their bedroom in a brown paper parcel and had told her friends about this. The story had eventually reached his superiors, but even so it had not been thought necessary to investigate the matter. And in 1957 Harry had been moved to the Port Authority Auxilliary Repair Unit.

The enquiries about Houghton began in February 1960. By the end of the month it became clear that something fishy was going on; a full-scale investigation was ordered; MI5 were alerted and from March onwards a watch was kept both on Harry Houghton and Bunty Gee. By April the police had come to know of their meetings with Commander Alexander Johnson of the United States Embassy or rather (for they had little difficulty in discovering his true identity), with Mr Gordon Lonsdale of the White House, Regent's Park. This interested them and, when, on Saturday 9 July, Harry and Bunty again set out for London from Portland in Harry's new Renault Dauphine, they were discreetly followed by a succession of different cars all the way to the Cumberland Hotel, where they booked a double room. When, that afternoon, they took tickets on the underground to Waterloo, two rather nondescript men were just behind them. At Waterloo they went to the main-line station and thence by subway to Waterloo Road. 'This is the way we came last time,' said Harry to Bunty, making for the Old Vic Theatre. There at exactly four o'clock they were joined by Gordon Lonsdale, whom it was clear they already knew quite well.

Together the three walked across the little park opposite the theatre, sat down on a seat and after a few minutes Harry handed Lonsdale a brown paper parcel, receiving a white envelope in exchange. A little later Lonsdale left them, took a turn around the Waterloo area and, coming back in the end to his car, drove away. After they had had a cup of tea, Harry and Bunty went back to the Cumberland Hotel.

Not long before this there had been another significant development at Portland. In June an officer concerned with certain tests on a new piece of equipment had gone to Miss Gee's office to get the reports that had been made on it. They were found to be missing. An enquiry was made into their disappearance, which did not lead to their discovery, but revealed an almost total absence of proper security arrangements in the Underwater Weapons Establishment. Slowly, but, one hopes, surely, steps were taken to put this right.

Between July 1960 and January 1961 five meetings between Lonsdale, Houghton and Gee were observed by MI5 or Special Branch agents. On each occasion either Harry or Bunty was seen to hand over a parcel.

By this time both MI5 and the police had become deeply interested in Gordon Lonsdale, who was henceforth kept under constant observation. The task of watching him was entrusted to Detective Superintendent George Smith of Special Branch, silver-haired, bespectacled and benevolent-looking. Just opposite the office Lonsdale was now using at 19 Wardour Street was a public house, the Falcon. Without too much difficulty two of Smith's officers managed to rent from the landlord an upstairs room with two-porthole-shaped windows giving an excellent view of the office. There, according to the proprietor, they installed two attractive young women – one with binoculars and the other with a radio transmitter – who kept a round-the-clock watch on Lonsdale, reporting all his comings and goings to Scotland Yard. Thence it was at once relayed to other waiting Special Branch officers on foot and in cars who made it their business to follow him wherever he went, keeping him constantly in view. Once, it seems, they followed him right into Scotland Yard, where he tried to sell a switch-lock device to the Transport Department for use on police cars.

As the weeks went by, George Smith, with the help of MI5, was able to piece together a fairly complete picture of the man he was after. Though he did not spend a lot of time at his office, Lonsdale always seemed to have enough money. He went to any number of West End bars and night-clubs and had plenty of girlfriends. But some of his other activities struck Smith as even more interesting.

On 6 August he met Houghton over a pot of tea at Steve's Restaurant in the Lower Marsh. There was, as it happened, a man from MI5 sitting back to back with them.

'You seem to have plenty in your case,' said Lonsdale.

'Yes,' Houghton replied, 'more than just my sleeping and shaving kit.'

'It seems like a lot of work for me tonight,' said Lonsdale.

'Plenty,' said Houghton and they went on to talk about dates for future meetings, and the cost of his room at the hotel – 'That will be taken care of,' said Lonsdale.

On 26 August Lonsdale's followers watched him park his white Studebaker with the registration number ULA 61 in Great Portland Street. Carrying an attaché case in one hand and a deed-box in the other, he then made for the Midland Bank, coming out ten minutes later carrying neither. Two days later he left the country by plane from Heathrow. Some time after this Superintendent Smith, having first obtained the necessary order from a magistrate, himself called at the Midland Bank, leaving shortly after with the deed-box and attaché case which he took to the Special Branch laboratory.

In the attaché case he found an expensive-looking Ronson tablelighter, a Praktina camera with special attachments for photographing documents, a black bag for changing films and a sheet of paper bearing a list of street names with numbers typed opposite them. In the deed-box were Gordon Lonsdale's personal papers, which showed him to be a Canadian by birth and a sales-manager by profession. After the contents of both had been inspected, they were carefully repacked and returned to the bank.

Lonsdale was away for nearly two months, returning to London towards the end of October. On 24 October he was seen to collect the deed-box and attaché case, and take them to his office in Wardour Street. He then walked to Piccadilly Circus and caught the tube to Ruislip Manor. On emerging from the tube at Ruislip Manor Station, he walked around the neighbouring streets for some time, doubled back on his tracks once or twice and finally disappeared near Cranley Drive, having successfully lost the MI5 men who were following him.

This put MI5 and the police on their mettle. For one thing there was an American air base near Ruislip. And for another it was frustrating to have been following the same man for months without finding out any more about him. From now onwards the team of watchers, considerably increased for the occasion, made absolutely certain that Lonsdale was never let out of sight.

Lonsdale's next meeting with Houghton was on the evening of Saturday 5 November. This time Houghton travelled to London by car, stopping at the St Leonard's Hotel at Ringwood for a drink on the way. Looking through the windows of the Renault while he was in the hotel, the MI5 men following him could see a leather briefcase and a cardboard box thrown carelessly on the back seat. From Ringwood Houghton drove to Ditton Road, Kingston, where, just after 6.30 p.m. he picked up Lonsdale, who was also carrying a briefcase. Choosing a dark spot not far away, the two of them then sat in the car and talked for half an hour, after which they drove to a nearby public house, the Maypole, where they sat for a little longer drinking whisky and talking. It was noticed that by the time they left, they had exchanged briefcases. Houghton then took his companion (who had arrived on foot) back to where he had parked his car.

A quarter of an hour later Lonsdale was driving his white Studebaker flat out along the Kingston by-pass, tailed, this time, by no less than three police cars also travelling at high speed. By 9.45 p.m. he had reached Ruislip and parked his car in Willow Gardens, just round the corner from Cranley Drive. Not wanting to alarm their quarry, the watchers did not follow him after he had parked the car, but simply kept a watch on the white Studebaker throughout the night, at the same time patrolling the whole area. Early next afternoon one of them saw him come out of 45 Cranley Drive. Not long after a woman left the house and drove off in a Ford car, then a man left on foot. It did not take the police long to find out that these were its owners, Peter and Helen Kroger, and to fill in their background. Another piece in the puzzle had fallen into place. Its exact significance remained to be seen.

On 10 December Harry Houghton and Bunty Gee once again travelled up to London, this time by rail. Their train was late, and at 3.45 Gordon Lonsdale was seen looking anxiously at the arrivals indicator at Waterloo. But they eventually joined him, as arranged, on the seat in the little park. Later that evening the white Studebaker was again parked in Willow Gardens.

Meanwhile, down at Portland, Harry and Bunty continued to lead their usual pleasant existence. At about 8.30 on every weekday morning Harry would pick Bunty up at the corner of Hambro Road and take her to her office. The evenings they usually spent drinking together in their favourite bars. Christmas passed uneventfully. Immediately after Christmas, however, what seemed to be an emergency meeting took place. On the Tuesday after Christmas Lonsdale rang Houghton up long-distance and said, in suitably guarded language, that he wanted to see him the following evening at Dorchester. And Houghton, leaving Bunty to drink alone at the Elm Tree, climbed into his car and obediently motored over to Dorchester, where he duly met Lonsdale in the bar of the Junction Hotel.

For Detective Superintendent George Smith and the other Special Branch officers assigned to the case, the end of December and the beginning of January were a particularly busy time. A determined effort was now made by George Smith's deputy, Chief Inspector Ferguson Smith,

DFC, a quiet-spoken former fighter pilot from Aberdeen with a fair moustache, who had been put in charge of the undercover investigations, to find out more about the Krogers and their ordinary-looking bungalow in Cranley Drive. One thing he found out almost immediately was that the doors and windows were equipped with just about the best anti-burglar devices he had ever come up against. Meanwhile Lonsdale, Houghton and Bunty Gee were being kept under continuous observation. It began to look at if things might be coming to a climax.

In accordance with what it had become clear was his usual practice, Lonsdale was due for his next meeting with Harry and Bunty at 4.30 p.m. on Saturday 7 January outside the Old Vic. Soon after 6.30 that morning Detective Superintendent George Smith received a message to say that Houghton had taken his car out of the garage. Other messages followed, transmitted by the MI5 and police watchers on the spot and received by Special Branch on their short-wave wireless. At 7.45 a.m., they reported, Houghton had left his house in the Renault Dauphine and was on his way to Portland to collect Miss Gee. By 8.45 a.m. he had picked up Bunty and together they were heading for Salisbury with MI5 and the police, led by Chief Inspector Ferguson Smith, following.

At nine o'clock George Smith moved to Scotland Yard to await further developments. Soon after 10 a.m. came a message to say that they were held up by ice on the roads. Then came another message at about 11 a.m. to say that they were approaching Salisbury. Then another one that they had missed their train. And finally the announcement that they were all aboard the 12.50, due to reach Waterloo at 2.45 p.m.

Wearing a borrowed coat and a beret, George Smith arrived at Waterloo well before 2.45 p.m. to be greeted with the news that there had been a landslide on the line and that the train had been delayed. At 3.20 p.m., as the big Southern Region Atlantic-type locomotive steamed in over half an hour late, he was standing at the barrier of No. 14 platform. Scattered amongst the crowd at the station were a dozen police officers, some wearing pin-stripe suits and bowlers and carrying rolled umbrellas, others shabbily dressed and selling matches or bootlaces, two in porter's uniform and two more dressed as women (which, as it happened, is what they were). From where he stood, George Smith could see Harry and Bunty get off the train and make for the barrier. They were walking arm in arm. Bunty was carrying a shopping-basket with a parcel in it. Behind them came Chief Inspector Ferguson Smith in hot pursuit. Operation Last Act had begun.

After hesitating for a moment, Harry and Bunty walked down the steps into York Road and boarded a No. 68 bus at the stop near the Union Jack Club. This took them to East Street, Walworth. Here on Saturday afternoons there is a busy, rather colourful street-market, where they wandered for a time amongst the various stalls. At 4.15 p.m. they left the market and caught another No. 68 bus back to Waterloo Road. They then took a walk along Lower Marsh, coming back so as to be outside the Old Vic at exactly 4.30 p.m. At this moment Lonsdale appeared, compact and confident-looking, having left his Studebaker parked fifty yards or so away. Seeing Lonsdale, Harry and Bunty strolled off unconcernedly southwards along Waterloo Road. But Lonsdale, catching up with them from behind, affectionately put one arm round Bunty's shoulder and the other round Harry's. He then neatly changed places with Bunty, taking the shopping bag from her as he did so.

It was at this point that George Smith took out his pocket handkerchief and fluttered it behind him as a signal to his followers. He then ran round in front of Lonsdale and his two companions and, turning to face them, said, 'You are all under arrest. I am a police officer.'

'Oh!' said Bunty, turning pale.

'What?' said Harry, also changing colour.

Gordon Lonsdale, for his part, said nothing. Nor did his expression change in any way, as he allowed George Smith to relieve him of Bunty's shopping basket. By now three police cars, bringing the rest of the team, had caught up with them. Lonsdale was pushed into the first ('It's Scotland Yard for you, my boy,' said George Smith). A police-woman pulled Bunty into the second and Harry Houghton was bustled into the third. As they moved off, a short message went out over the radio: '*Lock, stock and barrel!*' – a message which those waiting anxiously at Scotand Yard and in Dorset had no difficulty in interpreting.

On reaching Scotland Yard, the first thing George Smith did was to inspect the contents of Bunty's basket. He found in it four Admiralty files and a tin sealed with adhesive tape containing a quantity of undeveloped film, which, when later developed, revealed over three hundred photographs of highly secret Admiralty material concerning the atomic submarine *Dreadnought* and other Naval vessels and equipment. On the strength of this he now cautioned Lonsdale and told him that he was detaining him on suspicion of offences under the Official Secrets Act. To this Lonsdale calmly replied: 'To any questions you might ask me the answer is: No. So you needn't trouble to ask.'

On being searched, Lonsdale was found to be carrying one envelope containing £125 in five-pound notes, another containing fifteen American twenty-dollar notes and what looked like the key of his flat. As George Smith was leaving the room, Lonsdale said with a smile: 'As I appear to be going to stay here all night, could you find me a good chess player?' 'I'll see what I can do,' said Smith, smiling back. He was as good as his word. Among the police officers assigned to Lonsdale from now on there was usually at least one first class chess player.

'What's he really like, George?' a newspaperman asked Superintendent Smith after he had arrested Lonsdale. 'Like you and me,' was the answer. 'He had a difficult job – so do you and so do I. He did his job well. How can I condemn a man for that?'

It was Harry Houghton's turn next. 'I've been a bloody fool,' he blurted out, when cautioned. Bunty, on the other hand, showed no signs of contrition. 'I've done nothing wrong!' she said.

With Lonsdale, Harry and Bunty safely under lock and key, George Smith next drove out to Ruislip, arriving there at about a quarter past seven. Having left his car some distance away and thrown a cordon of police round the Krogers' bungalow, he walked up to the front door accompanied by Ferguson Smith, and rang the bell. The elaborate bolts were drawn back and Peter Kroger peered warily out into the darkness. 'I' said Smith, putting his foot in the door, 'am a police officer making enquiries about some robberies that have occurred locally. May I come in?'

'Certainly,' said Kroger and took them through the hall into a large comfortably furnished sitting-room at the back of the bungalow. When he asked them to sit down, they remained standing. 'I would like to see your wife as well,' said George Smith. But at that moment Mrs Kroger came into the room.

The Superintendent next explained who he was and asked to be told the name and address of 'the gentleman who comes and stays with you each weekend, particularly on the first Saturday of each month and arrives at about 7.15 p.m.'. At this Mrs Kroger sat down on the corner of the sofa and looked at her husband, who looked back at her. Neither of them said anything.

'Would you care to tell me?' repeated George Smith. 'We have lots of friends,' replied Peter Kroger and on being asked to name some of these friends, mentioned several, but not Lonsdale.

Superintendent Smith now told the Krogers that he would have to arrest them and handed Peter a search warrant, which the latter read out to his wife. He told them that they would be taken to Scotland Yard and asked Mrs Kroger to get ready. Going into her bedroom, Mrs Kroger partly closed the door. But George Smith immediately opened it again. As he did so, he saw her take an overcoat out of a cupboard and put it on and then, keeping her back to him, bend down slightly over a chair. After which she turned round and came back into the hall, holding, George Smith noticed, a bag half-hidden under her coat.

'As I'm going out for some time,' she said, 'may I stoke the boiler in the kitchen?' 'Certainly,' George Smith replied, 'but first let me see what you have in your bag.' And he took the bag from her. In it was an envelope containing a typed sheet of paper, bearing what was evidently a cyphered message; a second sheet of paper giving the names of several streets with typed numbers opposite each name, which he recognized as the one Lonsdale had left with his bank; three microdots mounted between two microscope slides; and a five-page letter in Russian dated that very day, 7 January 1961. These interesting discoveries would have to await expert attention. Meanwhile the Krogers were driven to Scotland Yard and locked up and Chief Inspector Ferguson Smith left in charge of the bungalow.

Taking with him a team of police officers, George Smith now drove to Lonsdale's flat at the White House. Here they found much that was of interest to them. First and foremost, the portable typewriter on which the cyphered messages in Helen Kroger's handbag had been typed. Two ornamental Chinese scrolls, one hanging on the wall in the sitting-room, proved, on inspection, to have hollow ends, one of which contained eighteen hundred dollars. A leather belt contained another three hundred dollars. The deed-box Smith had borrowed from the Midland Bank in September was also there. It contained a valid Canadian passport issued on 21 January 1955 in the name of Gordon Arnold Lonsdale and a birth certificate showing that Gordon Arnold Lonsdale had been born at Kirkland Lake, Cobalt, Temiskaming District on 7 August 1924. The Ronson table-lighter which George Smith had already seen also repaid closer examination. In it was a cypher message, ready for transmission and three one-time cypher pads, printed on inflammable paper of the type regularly used by Soviet agents for sending their messages. When turned the right number of times, the top of a tin of Yardley's Talcum Powder opened to reveal two secret compartments, one of which was found to contain a device for reading microdots and the other three signal plans. The ordinary radio receiver in Lonsdale's sitting-room also turned out to be less ordinary than it seemed at first sight, having been specially adapted to receive fixed-time messages from Moscow, while a closer study of the various codes and cyphers in the flat revealed several Moscow call signs: *Lena ya Amur; Volga ya Azov; Esteo; Rosa ya Fielka*. Not unnaturally, the MI5 communications centre lost no time in trying these call signs out and in each case received a prompt acknowledgement from Moscow. In Gordon's desk were a large number of love-letters, some still unopened, from a variety of young women and also a number of photographs. They left no doubt that Helen Kroger had been right in describing him as 'one for the ladies'.

Returning to Ruislip, George Smith found that the searchers at 45 Cranley Drive were also making good progress. Here, too, a cigarette-lighter and a tin of talcum powder had revealed secret compartments in which were hidden notes of the same Moscow call-signs George Smith had found in Lonsdale's flat. Another tin of talcum powder contained a microdot reader. They had also found Lonsdale's Praktina camera. Tucked behind some books were two valid New Zealand passports in the names of Peter and Helen Kroger. In a writing-case were two forged Canadian passports in the names of James Wilson and Jane Smith. Hidden in the roof of the house was a plastic bag full of dollar bills and British travellers' cheques. More dollars were hidden in two book-ends. The massive radio-set, like that in Lonsdale's flat, was capable of receiving messages from any part of the world.

The searchers' task was an arduous one and lasted for a week or more. Every one of Peter Kroger's hundreds of books had to be gone through page by page. And rightly so. The family Bible was found to contain the specially treated photographic paper used for microdots, while hidden in another book called *Auction Sales* were negatives of signal plans for a wireless transmitter. The only thing missing was the transmitter itself, for clearly the bungalow in Cranley Drive was the spy ring's communications centre from which their wireless messages were regularly transmitted to Moscow.

For a solid week every bit of the bungalow was tapped and sounded and probed, but without result. There was, they found, a sizeable gap between the floor of the bungalow and its concrete base. Access to this space was through a trap-door in the kitchen floor beneath the refrigerator. Crawling about under the floor, they took soundings of every square inch of it. But still without success. Then they tried a more direct approach and tapped it all over with hammers. Finally a vigorous blow cracked the concrete and underneath it they came on a steel box containing a high-powered transmitter. This, they found, was equipped with a special keying device making possible extremely rapid transmission in cypher (no less than 240 words a minute), thus reducing the risk of discovery.

Meanwhile, on receiving the message 'Lock, stock and barrel' from London on the afternoon of 7 January, Detective Superintendent Bert Smith of the Dorset CID had at once started his search of Harry Houghton's bungalow and the house where Bunty Gee lived with her uncle and aunt and her mother. Here again the material found was incriminating. In Bunty's house the police found a list of eighteen Admiralty test pamphlets and a highly compromising questionnaire in her own handwriting – a questionnaire, which, to anyone with a knowledge of the Russian language, was clearly a direct, rather clumsy translation from the Russian. In Harry's bungalow they also discovered a number of Admiralty test pamphlets, some charts of Portland Harbour, a plan showing Admiralty installations there, an Exakta camera and an old paint-tin containing £650 in pound notes. There was also a box of Swan Vestas which on further inspection proved to have a false bottom. Concealed in this was a rough plan of part of London, bearing the word 'Punch' and evidently providing an alternative *rendez-vous* in case of need. When they searched Houghton's car at Salisbury station, the police found a folded copy of *Punch*, no doubt to be carried if necessary as a means of identification.

On 8 January all five prisoners were charged with 'conspiring together and with other persons unknown to commit offences under the Official Secrets Act 1911' and remanded in custody. An order was then made for their finger-prints to be taken. These produced one interesting result: when referred to the American Federal Bureau of Investigation, the Krogers' fingerprints proved them to be an American couple called Morris and Lona Cohen, who ten years before had suddenly disappeared from their luxurious apart-ment on East 71st Street on the very day when Julius and Ethel Rosenberg had been arrested by the F.B.I. The Rosenbergs, as was well known, had belonged to a far-flung Soviet spy-ring set up in America in the 1940s and 1950s, had passed American atomic secrets to the Russians, had been caught and, after a sensational trial, had eventually in June 1953 gone to the electric chair in Sing Sing Jail. The Cohens, on the other hand, who had been closely associated with them, had been warned in time for them to get away.

With the Cohens' identification came their complete dossier. Born in the Bronx in 1910, the son of immigrants from Russia, Morris Cohen was a university graduate. He had become a keen Communist at university and had fought in Spain. In 1941 he had married Lona, born likewise of immi-grant parents and also a Communist, and had then spent three years in the American Army as a GI. They had started spying before the war was over. They were well provided with forged passports and, between the time of their disappearance from New York in 1951 and their arrival in England in 1954, they seemed to have travelled all over the world, eventually some-how assuming the identity of a couple called Peter and Helen Kroger, who, as it happened, had died in New Zealand some time before.

Far harder to identify in the full sense of the word was Gordon Lonsdale. His Canadian passport was genuine. So was his birth certificate. And so was his Canadian (or possibly American) accent. And yet quite clearly he was a Russian. The letters in Russian which the police had taken from Helen Kroger's handbag at 45 Cranley Drive showed that.

First of all, there was a letter in his own handwriting, bearing the date of 7 January, evidently written on the day of his arrest and addressed to 'My beloved Galyusha'. In this he thanked Galyusha, who was clearly his wife, for her letters which had reached him in the form of microdots. There were several of these and one from his daughter Liza, dated a month or two earlier. Galyusha had written on 9 December:

Hello, my darling,

My best wishes on the 43rd anniversary of the October Revolution. We were expecting letters from you but it turned out that they may come at the end of the month. So far as my work is concerned, everything is all right. Among our pupils are two Roumanian girls, aged 7 and 8, and I have taken on the task of teaching them the Russian alphabet. The progress they have made is terrific (thanks to the girls themselves, of course). At the same time as I am teaching them Russian, they are 'teaching' me Roumanian! During a visit of [one word obliterated] with the Central Committee's Commission, they read so well that I really felt happy. And now, every time I come, they keep on asking me whether I'll teach them some more.

On the 3rd of November we had an evening party at the place where I work, and I sang 'The Cranes', etc. It reminded me of our life in Prague, and I felt very, very sad. Whenever you and I meet, we have to rush off, and we are left with so little time. I remembered the day before the last one we spent in Prague. 'The Cranes' in particular upsets me and somehow it has become difficult and sad for me to sing it.

At home everything is as before. Liza has distressed me very much this term. For the first time in her six years at school, she brought home a school report with four 3s [2, 3 and 4 are marks: 2 means bad, 3 means just passed, 4 is good] for geometry, algebra, English and PT. The rest are 4s. You cannot imagine how this upset me, considering that the Institute is now in the offing. Dina brought back even worse marks, particularly for discipline and diligence.

On the 7th I was at Rina and Igor's. We had a nice evening. There were fourteen people, including the Tromkins. We drank your health and everyone asked to be remembered to you. . . . We were all sad you were not with us and I was especially sad. I must have been alone now for seven October Celebrations and six May Days – not to mention family celebrations.

How unjust life is. Of course I understand that this is your work and your duty and that you love it and try to do it as well as you possibly can. But even so, I'm a woman, with a woman's mind, and I suffer dreadfully. When you write, tell me how you feel and say you love me and perhaps that will make me feel better. . . . By the way, if you can possibly manage it, try and let me have 2,500 roubles a month.

In spite of feeling so miserable, Galyusha had written in another of her letters, again passing rapidly from the depths of unhappiness to more mundane considerations, 'I wonder if you could possibly send me a white brocade dress with white shoes.'

Liza's letter was dated 6 November:

Hello, dear Daddy,

I congratulate you on the 43rd anniversary of October. How do you feel? We are all well. We are going tomorrow to Aunt Vera. She has asked mother to come and see her.

The term finished badly: three 3s. I'll try to do better next term. The 3s I got for the subjects for which I had 2s in the last term.

Winter has already started here. Aunt Vera fell and broke a leg. The leg still gives pain. Grandma is well.

Daddy, all of us are expecting you. Come home quickly. Trofim recently wrote a letter to you and kept on dictating to himself 'Dear Daddy, come home quickly'.

Many, many kisses,

Your daughter, Liza

And Trofim had added, as a postscript to his sister's letter: 'PS Daddy, come home quickly. Trofim.'

These were the letters Lonsdale sat down to answer on the day of his arrest, 7 January:

My beloved Galyusha,

I have just been given your letters. I was delighted to get three letters from you at the same time. Many thanks for doing what I asked you to do.

To tell you the truth, the family chronicle is so full I don't know where to start. I will write this very day to V.M. and ask that you are sent 2,500 roubles (or rather 250 roubles). A few days ago I saw pictures of the new currency. I think it's a great improvement.

As for the white brocade dress, this is rather difficult. In 'other countries' brocade is not worn. And then how to send it to you and when. One can't put a dress and a pair of shoes in one's pocket. I will do everything I can to fulfil your first and last requests. The only thing I can't say is when.

Of course I understand how you feel. You say in your letter that you have spent seven anniversaries of the October Revolution without me. I know you have. But I have spent them without you and without the children and away from my own people. When we were at P., I tried to explain things to you. I am not complaining, but even you can't imagine how sad I feel, especially at this moment. I am quite well in myself, though I sleep badly. I live in a new flat consisting of one room of about ten square metres, bathroom and lavatory and a kitchen that's so small there isn't even room for a chair in it. This is the eighth New Year's Day I have celebrated without you. *Such is life* – I know the expression in so many languages, it makes me sick.

I hope you won't think I am hard-hearted and think about no one except myself. All I want to say is this: I have only one life and not an entirely easy one and I want to spend it so that, when the time comes, I shall have nothing to be ashamed of, whatever anyone may say.

I know very well what loneliness is. From the age of ten, for the last twenty-nine years, I have only spent ten years among my own people. I didn't want this and I didn't seek it. It just turned out that way . . .

295

'Many kisses to my beloved wife and children', he had put at the end of his letter and then added gloomily as a postscript: 'I will soon be thirty-nine. Is there much left?'

For a moment or two the letters gave those concerned a fleeting glimpse of ordinary Russian family life some seventeen hundred miles away and of Gordon Lonsdale, in the role, this time, not of the professional ladies' man, nor of the go-getting sales executive, nor indeed of the master-spy, but rather of the devoted husband and father, missing and missed by his family, feeling lonely and sorry for himself, and concerned about Galyusha's brocade dress, little Liza's poor marks, Dina's indiscipline and Aunt Vera's broken leg.

But that was all. All attempts on the parts of the police to probe further were met by Lonsdale with the same bland refusal to answer questions and, wherever else they looked, by the same apparent absence of any supplementary evidence or information.

As for Harry Houghton and Bunty Gee, the police and MI5 already knew most of what they needed to know about them. Nor was it long before Houghton, from his cell in Brixton Jail, sent a message to Superintendent Smith to say that he was prepared to help the police, always provided that they made it worth his while. But Smith, for his part, knowing what he did, showed no inclination to do a deal with him. 'I told him,' he said afterwards, 'I could not have that.'

Gordon Lonsdale, the Krogers, Harry Houghton and Bunty Gee appeared at Bow Street Magistrate's Court before Mr K. J. P. Barraclough on Tuesday 7 February 1961, just a month after their arrest. The hearing lasted for three days. The opening speech for the prosecution was made by the Attorney General, Sir Reginald Manningham Buller in person – a most unusual proceeding in a Magistrate's Court. It lasted two hours and was an impressive performance.

Sir Reginald, large and authoritative as he peered through his spectacles, left nothing to the imagination. Lonsdale, he said quite openly, was a Soviet citizen and the accused were spying for the Soviet Union. The subsequent examination of the witnesses was left to the Senior Treasury Counsel, Mr Mervyn Griffith Jones. From their evidence it was possible to put together a clear enough picture of the activities of the accused. The witnesses included a number of nameless men from MI5, referred to as Mr A, B, C or D. The accused, for their part, showed few signs of emotion, though Lonsdale, listening at one moment to Mr D's description of how he had sat back to back with him in a café, making longhand notes of every word he said, could not, as an expert in this kind of thing, suppress an appreciative grin. On Friday 19 February, all five of the accused were committed for trial at the Central Criminal Court.

The trial of 'Miss Gee and others' opened in No. 1 Court at the Old Bailey on Monday 13 March 1961. The case was heard by the Lord Chief Justice, Lord Parker, and lasted several days. All five of the accused pleaded not guilty. Once again the Attorney General led for the prosecution. And once again witnesses were called who left no doubt as to the type of activities in which the accused had been engaging. In addition to the Special Branch and MI5 agents who had already appeared at Bow Street, there were also a number of technical witnesses, who commented on the various compromising objects which had been found among the belongings of the accused, and others who testified as to the importance of the secret information they had passed to the Russians.

Confronted with the mass of devastating evidence assembled by the Crown, the accused had little to say in their defence – little, that is, that was likely to carry conviction with the jury. Gradually, however, as the case went on, an ever clearer picture of the spy-ring's activities took shape.

Having been caught red-handed with the documents in her shopping basket, Bunty Gee could scarcely deny that she had taken secret material from the Underwater Weapons Establishment and given them to Harry Houghton to pass on to Lonsdale or, as she had thought of him, Commander Alexander Johnson. She claimed, however, that she had been paid nothing for doing this.

Houghton, for his part, had a dramatic story to tell of his love affair in Warsaw with Karytzia or 'Christina', as he now called her, and of its ultimate consequences. In January 1957, some four years after his return to England, a Pole calling himself Tadeusz and claiming to be a friend of hers and a business man had rung him up and arranged to meet him at a public house in Earl's Court. There Tadeusz had explained that he had an attractive business proposition to make him. All Harry had to do was to help him buy British-made penicillin through official channels for eventual sale on the Polish black market, in return for which he would be handsomely rewarded. The venture, as Tadeusz had promised, proved extremely profitable – while it lasted. But, in due course, he was told that there was no longer the same demand for British penicillin in Poland. It was then, just as Harry was wondering where to turn for more money, that Tadeusz came up with a fresh suggestion. He knew of another, even more remunerative line of business. A friend of his would get in touch with him and tell him about it.

Eventually the friend accordingly telephoned Houghton, introducing himself as 'Nikki', and suggested they should meet on the following Sunday outside Dulwich Art Gallery. In order that Nikki might recognize him.

Harry was to have a copy of *The Times* under his arm and be carrying a pair of brown kid gloves.

The meeting took place as arranged. Nikki, who seemed to know everything about Harry's past life and present financial problems, made it clear from the start that he was a Russian. (He was in fact a member of the Soviet Embassy staff.) What he wanted, he said, was secret naval information. For this he was prepared to pay and pay well. If, on the other hand, Harry refused to co-operate, he had plenty of ways of making things unpleasant for him. Houghton agreed and was provided with a camera and £100 for expenses. After that, there had been regular meetings at the Maypole public house off the Kingston by-pass and elsewhere, at which Houghton had handed over batches of documents and received cash payments in return.

In 1960, after Houghton had moved back into his cottage, he had received a visit there from Gordon Lonsdale, curly-haired, smiling and bearing gifts including an expensive gold lighter from Dunhill's. He had introduced himself as a friend (and colleague) of Nikki's. What he wanted, he said, and wanted urgently were test pamphlets on submarine detection. When Houghton explained that he was no longer working in the Underwater Weapons Establishment and therefore could not get the documents he wanted, Lonsdale had all at once become fractionally less friendly. 'It is,' he said curtly, 'an order.' He knew, it seemed, all about Bunty Gee, who was still employed there. She could get what was needed. Houghton, by now on his best behaviour, had suggested that Lonsdale should assume the role of Commander Alec Johnson of the United States Embassy, who, he would explain to Bunty, had a hold on him because he happened to know about his black market dealings in Warsaw. Lonsdale agreed and it was arranged that the three should meet, appropriately enough, at a performance of the Bolshoi Ballet, then visiting London. Bunty took to the alleged Commander Johnson immediately and readily agreed to co-operate. The material was obtained and handed over and Harry was soon richer by several hundred pounds.

Lonsdale, for his part, went out of his way to take the blame himself. The Krogers, he said, were in no way responsible for any of the compromising objects found in their house, which had been put there without their knowledge – including the forged passports. The transmitter in the basement belonged to him and he had installed it while they were away on holiday. 'I accept,' he said, 'full responsibility for my actions, irrespective of the consequences to me personally.'

The Krogers, when their turn came, took the same line. They had first met Lonsdale in 1955, said Peter Kroger, after which he had become a close friend of theirs. Such things as the Ronson lighter and the hollow bookends were all presents from him to them. 'Neither my wife nor I,' he contended, 'engaged in spying or in any activities which may be considered or regarded as irregular.' The envelope found in her handbag, said Helen Kroger, had been given to her that afternoon by Gordon Lonsdale, who had simply said to her, 'Would you please hold these letters until I see you?' To which she had innocently agreed. 'He was the last person,' she added, 'I would have thought to have been in trouble with the police.'

The Lord Chief Justice passed sentence on the prisoners before a crowded court on 22 March, the jury having found all five guilty.

To Lonsdale he said: 'Gordon Arnold Lonsdale, you are clearly a professional spy. It is a dangerous career and one in which you must be prepared, as you no doubt are, to suffer, if and when you are caught. I take the view that in this case, yours was the directing mind. You will go to prison for twenty-five years.' At which Gordon Lonsdale smiled.

Next came the Krogers. 'Peter John Kroger and Helen Joyce Kroger,' said the Lord Chief Justice, looking directly at them, 'you are both in this up to the hilt. You are both professional spies. The only distinction I can see between you and Lonsdale is that, if I am right, yours was not the directing mind or minds and you are older than he is. You will each go to prison for twenty years.' Like Lonsdale, the Krogers took their heavy sentences calmly.

'Harry Frederick Houghton,' said Lord Parker next, 'your conduct was in many ways the most culpable. You betrayed the secrets of your country by communicating secret information about Her Majesty's Navy. I've considered long what to do with you. You are, however, now fifty-six, and not a very young fifty-six, and it is against all our principles that a sentence should be given which might involve your dying in prison. But for that, I would give you a longer sentence. . . . Fifteen years.' And a shattered, sweating Houghton made his way down the steps from the dock.

Last of all came Bunty Gee. 'Ethel Elizabeth Gee,' said Lord Parker, 'you betrayed your trust. I am quite unable to think it is a possibility that you did what you did out of some blind infatuation for Houghton. Having heard you and watched your demeanour in the dock and in the witness box, I am inclined to think that yours was the stronger character of the two. I think you acted from greed. You will go to prison for fifteen years.' And Bunty, grim-faced, thrusting her hands deep in her pockets, disappeared in her turn down the steps.

It was not until almost the end of 1961 that the Federal Bureau of Investigation finally established the identity of Gordon Lonsdale. He was, they discovered, Konon Trofimovich Molodi, born in Russia in 1922, the son of a well-known Soviet scientist. At the age of seven, in 1929, an aunt had taken him to Berkeley, California, where for nine years he had lived with her and received his education. In 1938, when he was sixteen, his aunt had told him that he must decide whether he was going to stay in the United States and become an American citizen or go back to Russia. He decided to go back to Russia. Arriving in time to serve in the Red Army during the war and fight with the partisans behind the German lines, he automatically found his way into military intelligence, received the necessary training and by 1954, at the age of thirty-two, was ready to make the return journey across the Atlantic, this time to Canada.

As for Gordon Arnold Lonsdale, he, too, had been a real man and in due course the Royal Canadian Mounted Police succeeded in finding Dr W. E. Mitchell, the general practitioner who had brought him into the world at Kirkland Lake, near Cobalt, Ontario on 27 August 1924, the son of a Canadian father and a Finnish mother. Thirty-seven years later, in 1961, Dr Mitchell still clearly remembered the event. He also remembered something else. He had circumcised the child in question. But the Gordon Lonsdale who came to Canada in 1954 had not been circumcised.

Further enquiries now led to the discovery of the real Gordon's father, Emanuel Lonsdale, still living at Kirkland Lake. His Finnish wife, Olga, he said, had left him the year after Gordon was born and in 1932 had gone back home to South-Eastern Finland taking her little son with her. After which nothing more had been heard of either of them. But in 1939 had come World War II and the Russo–Finnish War, and by 1945 South-Eastern Finland was part of the Soviet Union. What became of the true Gordon Lonsdale after his return to Finland is anybody's guess. The Russo–Finnish War, World War II, this purge or that could have accounted for him. According to one version, he deserted to the Russians during the Finnish War, joined the Red Army and was killed at Stalingrad.

What we do know is that, by the time Konon Trofimovich Molodi was ready to start for Canada in 1954, the real Gordon's identity, genuinely Canadian and in every way suitable, had most conveniently become available. All that was needed was for Konon Trofimovich to slip into Canada, say as a merchant seaman or on a forged passport, send for a copy of Gordon's birth certificate and then, with the help of two forged letters from sponsors looked up in the telephone book, apply for a passport in Gordon's name, acquire a proper Canadian accent and then start out on his travels again. All this, in fact, he did during the year he spent in Canada, leaving again on 22 February 1955 for New York en route for London and all that awaited him there.

It would somehow have been surprising if the man we have come to think of as Gordon Lonsdale had spent the next twenty-five years in a British prison. Nor, in fact, did he. In 1963 Greville Wynne, a British businessman whom the Russians had accused of spying in the Soviet Union, was sentenced to eight years' imprisonment. Here were the makings of a deal. In due course, the necessary machinery on both sides was put into motion and, after Gordon or Konon had served just over three years of his sentence, it was arranged that the two men should be exchanged for one another. At Checkpoint Heerstrasse, on the border between East and West Berlin, at exactly 4.30 a.m. on 22 April 1964, the East German police halted the East-West traffic waiting to cross the checkpoint, while the West German police did the same on their side. At 5.15 a.m. in the bleak half-light a black Mercedes with Lonsdale sitting in it drove up to the checkpoint from the Western side. Simultaneously a yellow Mercedes halted expectantly on the other side. Two Soviet agents, escorting Greville Wynne, now approached the barrier from the Eastern side and two British agents, escorting Gordon Lonsdale, from the Western. A minute or two later the exchange had been effected. Greville Wynne was a free man. And Molodi or Lonsdale, his experience widened and deepened and still only forty, was once again free to place his indubitable talents at the disposal of a doubtless appreciative Soviet Government.

For the time being he seems to have directed his energies mainly to literary composition. Spy stories are as popular in Russia as they are here. In 1965 his memoirs, written with the help of his colleague Kim Philby, were published in this country under the title *Spy*, in which he gives it as his considered opinion that it was a mistake ever to employ Houghton whom he describes as 'vain as well as shifty'. Three or four years later, for the delectation of Soviet audiences, his adventures were made the subject of a feature film called *The Dead Season*, shot partly in England, in which a resourceful Soviet spy, going by the name of Lonsfield, visited the seaside resort of 'Dorgate' and sold juke-boxes as an ingenious cover for his real activities.

In October 1970 the Soviet press announced that Konon Trofimovich Molodi had died of a heart-attack while picking mushrooms in a field near Moscow. In *Krasnaya Zvezda*, the official Army newspaper, an obituary tribute from a group of former comrades praised the dead man for his great services to his country. He had, it appears, been awarded two high Soviet decorations: the Red Star and the Red Banner. To Superintendent George Smith, by now retired to his native Wiltshire, the news of his death came as a surprise, a shock almost. He had, he said, found him a jovial, likeable chap and he had been in the best of health when released from prison.

Like Lonsdale, the Krogers or Cohens did not serve their full sentence, but were released in October 1969 in exchange for Gerald Brooke, a British lecturer whom the Russians had put in prison in 1965. Though American-born, they showed no desire to return to the United States, where they knew that the Federal Bureau of Investigation would be waiting to settle old scores with them. Just before their release it was suddenly discovered that they were Poles, and by the time they settled into their first-class seats on a Warsaw-bound plane in October 1969, they had been duly provided with Polish passports. 'Hello, sweetie-pie!' said Helen to Peter affectionately as they met after eight years of separation, and they ordered champagne with their lunch. 'Ta ta,' said Peter to the accompanying journalists when they reached Warsaw. 'Say good-bye for me to all the lads in Parkhurst.'

The last of the ring to be released were Harry Houghton and Ethel Gee, who both came out on 12 May 1970. 'My main objective,' said Harry, on being asked what his plans were for the future, 'is to love and cherish Miss Gee,' and he went on to speak of an early marriage. Miss Gee was less forthcoming. 'It takes two to make a wedding,' she said. 'At present I have no plans for the future.' But a year later came the news that on 20 April 1971, the two had been secretly married at Poole Registry Office.

Like his former associate Gordon Lonsdale, Harry Houghton lost no time in trying his hand as an author. In *Operation Portland, the Autobiography of a Spy*, published in 1972, he gives a considerably more dramatic account of his activities than emerged in court. His troubles, he confirms, all came from 'chasing a bit of skirt behind the Iron Curtain'. After this, he says, he was blackmailed into working for the Russians, but working for them on a far more spectacular scale than ever appeared during the trial. According to him, his first meeting at the Dulwich Art Gallery marked the beginning of innumerable contacts with a wide variety of Soviet agents in widely varying locations. These entertained him at the Mirabelle and treated him to holidays in Austria and Ireland, where he had further encounters with more agents, not forgetting 'a striking-looking brunette, probably on the wrong side of forty', who asked him, in accordance with a pre-arranged code, whether he knew what Irish coffee was. They also, it appears, told him the truth about the capture and death of Frogman Crabbe (which they themselves had helped to organize) and, with his assistance, arranged for the landing of still more agents by boat at lonely spots along the Dorset coast. Finally, in his company and with his help, several of them, including Gordon Lonsdale, actually broke into the Portland Underwater Detection Establishment itself in the middle of the night, taking a professional safebreaker with them, and spent more than an hour and a quarter there, making a complete tour of the place and looking at and photographing anything that took their fancy.

As for his eventual discovery and arrest, he insists that this was, not due to the amount he was spending on drink (which he claims was minimal) or on other luxuries, but rather to his being denounced by his first wife, Peggy, or else given away by Michal Goleniewski or some other Soviet defector – both, it must be admitted, very definite possibilities. Finally he claims, perhaps predictably, that the British security authorities were less than efficient and that the real leader of the spy-ring, a well-dressed Russian known to him as 'Roman', got clean away – a somewhat irritating thought to leave us with.

Nine

ALEX

'We all work separately. Each man here is alone.'

OLEG VLADIMIROVICH PENKOVSKI

One day in the summer of 1955 Mr Greville Maynard Wynne, a British electrical engineer and business man who had served in Intelligence during the war, was by his own account approached by a war-time friend of his, now in the British Secret Service, with the suggestion that it might not be a bad thing if he were to extend his business contacts in Eastern Europe. Coming from such a quarter, this suggestion had certainly fairly definite implications. Mr Wynne nevertheless fell in with his friend's suggestion. After visiting the other East European capitals, he went in 1957 to Moscow, returning there in 1958 and 1959, with the object of making contacts and trying to establish a market for British electrical equipment. In November 1960 he made contact, at his friend's suggestion, with the Soviet State Committee for the Co-ordination of Scientific Work, a body with approximately the status of a Ministry, which concerned itself, amongst other things, with visits to the Soviet Union by foreign technologists and engineers. The State Committee has its offices in the middle of Moscow in a handsome new building on Gorki Street. Its Foreign Department, with which Wynne was concerned, was at this time presided over by Dzherman Mikhailovich Gvishiani, an able young Georgian, the son of a KGB general, believed to have been related to Stalin, and himself married to Mr Kosygin's intelligent and attractive daughter, Ludmila. Gvishiani's deputy was Yevgeni Ilich Levin, youngish too, and with a taste for drink, who amongst his other duties was a colonel in the KGB and KGB representative in the State Committee.

In the course of his talks with the officials of the State Committee, Wynne suggested to them that it might help to promote trade between their two countries if he brought to the Soviet Union a delegation of technical specialists from the various companies which he represented. This proposal was accepted and it was agreed that Wynne should return with a suitably qualified delegation before the end of the year.

Among the officials Wynne met in the course of his discussions with the State Committee was a certain Colonel Oleg Vladimirovich Penkovski, a well-dressed, rather distinguished-looking man in his early forties of noticeably military bearing with reddish hair greying at the temples and strongly defined features. When, on his return to London, Wynne, by now busily getting his delegation together, told his friends in Intelligence of his talks with the State Committee, he found them particularly interested in Colonel Penkovski. He was, it seemed, someone with whom they were anxious to make contact.

Not long after this, Wynne returned to Moscow a few days ahead of the other members of his hastily assembled delegation, to find that Colonel Penkovski had been chosen to look after the British party while they were in Moscow. In the course of the delegation's visit he and Penkovski quickly made friends and were soon on first name terms, calling each other 'Grev' and, instead of Oleg, 'Alex', which Penkovski said he preferred. As such visits go, this one had been reasonably successful and, before Wynne went back to London, he discussed with Penkovski the possibility of a return visit to England by a Soviet delegation.

In April 1961 Wynne returned to Moscow for further discussions concerning the proposed visit. In the interval he had learned from his friends in intelligence that Penkovski who, it appeared, had held important appointments in GRU, the Soviet Directorate of Military Intelligence, was known to be anxious – indeed had already tried, though unsuccessfully – to make contact with them or with the CIA. It should simply be a question of gaining his confidence.

Wynne was given a friendly enough reception in Moscow, but, when he was shown the list of Soviet delegates who were to visit England, he found it less than impressive and said as much to Alex, who was going to lead it. This was on Wynne's last evening in Moscow, as he and Penkovski were walking back across Red Square to the National Hotel, where he was staying.

Penkovski clearly found Wynne's comments upsetting and begged him not to object to the delegation. By doing so, he explained, Wynne would be depriving him of any chance he had of getting to London. Then it all came pouring out. Things in the Soviet Union were appalling, he said. He himself was in possession of certain facts which he must at all costs pass on to the appropriate authorities in the West.

After listening to what he had to say, Wynne dropped his objections to the proposed composition of the Soviet delegation and that night, back at his hotel, Alex put into his hands a double-wrapped, double-sealed envelope containing full particulars of himself and enough top-secret material to convince those who read it that they had happened on a quite exceptional source of information.

A couple of weeks later the Soviet delegation, led by Penkovski, landed at London airport. They were staying at the Mount Royal Hotel near Marble Arch. During the daytime Colonel Penkovski was busy looking after his fellow delegates, attending the talks and accompanying them on the visits that had been arranged for them. He was also, needless to say, required by his employers in Soviet Military Intelligence to watch out for anybody or anything that could possibly be of interest or use to them.

But in addition to these, he had a third duty to fulfill. Each night after his Soviet colleagues had gone to bed, Alex (it had become his code name) would slip away to some rooms that had been specially equipped for the purpose and there submit to intensive cross-questioning by a succession of British and American intelligence officers. They could scarcely believe their good fortune. By the end of his first week in England, he had divulged a fantastic amount of vital secret information covering the widest possible field. What is more, his long experience as a high-grade intelligence officer, combined with a remarkable memory, made it all the easier for him to absorb or impart information.

But Alex did not spend all his time working. London night-life, his hosts soon found, had a strong appeal for him, as did the great department stores of the metropolis. When the delegation finally left for Moscow, he went back loaded with luxuries, including a special consignment for the wife and daughter of his own boss, General Ivan Alexandrovich Serov, formerly head of the KGB and now of the GRU – a fortunate connection, which without doubt greatly facilitated his passage through customs. This was just as well, for he also took with him, by courtesy of the British Secret Service, a Minox camera, a good supply of film and specific instructions on how to secure methods of communication with London after his return to Moscow.

What, it may be asked, lay behind Colonel Penkovski's decision to put himself and all the vital information to which he had access at the disposal his country's adversaries? Why should a seemingly patriotic Russian, an active Party member, a high-ranking army officer enjoying the confidence of his superiors, with a good job and reasonable prospects for the future – in short, a prominent and well-connected member of the Soviet ruling class, enjoying all the privileges that this implies – embark on this extraordinary course of action? The question is not an altogether simple one to answer.

Oleg Vladimirovich Penkovski had been born just forty-two years earlier, in April 1919, at Vladikavkaz in the Northern Caucasus. He came of a family who under the Tsars had served as soldiers and senior officials. He could not remember his father, an engineer by profession, who had been killed in the civil war in 1919, fighting (though this was not generally known) against the Bolsheviks. He had subsequently been brought up by his mother and had attended school at Vladikavkaz (or, as it later came to be called, Ordzhonikidze). His grandfather, Florian Antonovich Penkovski, had before the Revolution been a judge. Florian's brother and Oleg's great-uncle, Valentin Antonovich Penkovski, a regular soldier of outstanding ability, was to become a Lieutenant-General in the Soviet Army, eventually succeeding Marshal Malinovski as Commander of the Far Eastern Military District.

On leaving school at eighteen, in 1937, Oleg had entered the 2nd Kiev Artillery School with the object of making the Army his career, at the same time joining the Komsomol or Communist Youth Organization. On passing out from Kiev two years later he was commissioned as a lieutenant in the artillery. At about the same time he was also accepted as a candidate Party member, becoming a full member the following year.

On the strength of this and of his earlier work in the Komsomol he was appointed Politruk or Battery Political Officer, while serving with First Western Army Group during the Soviet invasion of Poland in 1939 and later in the war against Finland, where he had his first experience of heavy fighting. From 1940 to 1942, he held various political and staff appointments in Moscow Military District. Meanwhile, in June 1941, Hitler had launched his surprise attack on the Soviet Union. In November 1943, a major at twenty-four, though without much battle experience, Oleg was sent to First Ukrainian Army Group, where he soon got to know the Artillery Commander of the Army Group, Lieutenant-General Varentsov. In March 1944, on General Varentsov's recommendation, he was given command of a Guards Anti-Tank Regiment, with which he took part in the ensuing spring and summer offensives. In the following June he was badly wounded in the head during a reconnaissance and spent the next two months in hospital and convalescing.

While in Moscow, he looked up an old friend and former commanding officer from his time at Moscow Military District, Major-General Gapanovich, a senior member of the Army Political Directorate. He also visited General Varentsov, who was convalescing in Moscow at the time and who used him as a temporary liaison officer with his headquarters at the front. These were useful contacts,

At the end of 1944, having by now completely recovered from his wound, he was, thanks largely to General Varentsov, appointed to command the

41st Guards Anti-Tank Regiment in time for the forthcoming offensive through Southern Poland into South-Eastern Germany. Between then and the end of the war in May 1945, he and his regiment greatly distinguished themselves during the hard fighting that followed in Poland and Germany. He also invented an ingenious and extremely practical device for the rapid traversing and aiming of anti-tank guns in battle.

Oleg ended his war as a twenty-six-year-old Lieutenant-Colonel with five decorations, including two Orders of the Red Banner and the Order of Alexander Nevski, and six medals. On his last visit to General Gapanovich he had been much taken with the General's pretty teenage daughter, Vera, small and slight with a good figure and hair the colour of burnished copper. It would suit him, he decided, to get a job in Moscow and so see more of her. General Varentsov had by now become a close friend. With his help Oleg obtained a much-coveted posting to the Frunze Military Academy. In the autumn of 1945 he and Vera were married.

In 1946 a daughter, Galina, was born to the young Penkovskis and that same year, with a little help from his father-in-law, Oleg managed to get an apartment in a fine new nine-storey block on the Maxim Gorki Embankment, overlooking the Moscow River. From now onwards this was to be their home. As a prospective graduate of the Military Academy, the protégé of one important General, the great-nephew of another and the son-in-law of a third, with a more than presentable wife and an agreeable apartment, he was starting his post-war career under the best possible auspices.

Having successfully completed his three-year course at the Military Academy in 1948, Oleg first took a couple of staff jobs in Moscow. Towards the end of 1949, by now aged thirty, he was transferred to the GRU or Directorate of Military Intelligence and entered the Military Diplomatic Academy (in practice a school for espionage), where, amongst other things, he took a three-year course in English. In 1950 he was promoted to full Colonel and, on graduating from the Academy in July 1953, was duly posted to the GRU or, to give it its full official name, the Chief Intelligence Directorate of the General Staff of the Soviet Army.

In the summer of 1955, after a couple of years in the Fourth Directorate, responsible for the Near East, he was posted to Ankara as Assistant Military Attaché. Owing to a difference of opinion with his immediate superior, the Military Attaché, he served there for barely a year, but for long enough nevertheless to gain some idea of what the capitalist world outside the Soviet Union had to offer. From 1956 to 1958, he was Senior Officer in the Fifth Directorate of the GRU, responsible for the Middle and Far East in preparation, apparently, for posting as Military Attaché and GRU Resident in India, an appointment which never materialized. Finally, after taking a nine-month course on missiles at the Dzerzhinski Military Artillery

Engineering Academy and passing out first, he was, after a further brief stint in the Fourth Directorate and another at the GRU Training School, appointed to the Foreign Section of the Scientific Research Committee, mainly as cover, it would seem, for his continuing work in the Directorate of Intelligence.

A full Colonel in the GRU at forty, Oleg Vladimirovich Penkovski had gone far. What is more, with considerable ability, good connections and a good record, he had every prospect of going further still. What, one may well ask, had got into him? Why did his British opposite numbers notice him sitting forlornly in the dreary cafés of the Turkish capital with a far-away look in his eyes? What, in the ultimate analysis, had induced him to turn his back on all this and, at appalling risk to himself and his family, secretly throw in his lot with the West? Was it simply dissatisfaction or was it something more than that?

In addition to the vast amount of secret material which he passed to the West during the months that followed, Oleg Vladimirovich also managed to record a series of personal reflections, a kind of *apologia pro vita sua*, giving, albeit in a rather disjointed way, his view of things in general, of the Soviet system and Soviet policy and of his own aims and aspirations. These throw a good deal of light on the way in which his mind was working.

'I began,' he says, 'as a good Komsomol ... I believed in the Soviet system and was ready to fight anyone who even spoke against it.' It was not until well on in the war that he began to take a different view. 'I became convinced,' he explains, 'that it was not the Communist Party which moved and inspired us all to fight all the way from Stalingrad to Berlin. There was something else behind us: Russia.'

This sudden awakening was followed, he tells us, by disillusion with the Party, with its leaders, with the ruling classes and finally with himself: 'Our Communism, which we have now been building for forty-five years, is a fraud. I myself am a part of this fraud; after all, I have been one of the privileged. Years ago I began to feel disgusted with myself ... I felt before and I feel now that I must find some justification for my existence which would give me inner satisfaction ... The Communist system is harmful to our people; I cannot serve a harmful system. There are many people who think and feel as I do, but they are afraid to unite for action. So we all work separately. Each man here is alone.'

Disillusion with a forty-year-old political system and with the type of politician and functionary it threw up might not, of itself, have been enough to tip the balance, to provoke so drastic a switch of loyalties. By the time they reach middle-age, most normal men have shed some of their earlier enthusiasms. What tipped the balance in Colonel Penkovski's case seems to have been something else: a genuine and deep-seated fear of nuclear war, the fear that, behind all his blustering and brinkmanship, Khrushchov might really mean business, and that the West might not take him seriously enough until it was too late. In this respect, of course, few people can have been better placed to form a judgement than Colonel Penkovski, aware, as he was, of Soviet strength and weakness, enjoying, as he did, access to his country's contingency plans for nuclear war, sharing, finally, the distrust felt by so many of his fellow-countrymen for the ebullient Nikita Sergeyevich Khrushchov, for whom he seems to have cherished an intense personal hatred.

The years 1960 to 1962, it will be recalled, marked a period of continuing crisis in East–West relations. After the shooting down of the American U2 plane in May 1960, Khrushchov abruptly broke off the Summit Conference in Paris and thereafter took a far tougher line with the United States. 1961 was the year of the Berlin Wall and of the crisis over East Germany, with Soviet and American tanks facing each other in Berlin, and, as Penkovski well knew, Soviet contingency plans ready for fighting a localized war in Germany. In September the Soviet Government, after constant references to new high-yield bombs, began nuclear testing in the atmosphere. 'Imagine the horror,' he wrote, 'of a fifty-megaton bomb with almost twice the normal explosive force.'

Finally in 1962 things were to reach a climax with the siting of Soviet offensive missiles in Cuba. For a time, the world seemed on the brink of war. Whether the conclusions Penkovski drew from his inside knowledge of these events were the correct ones is another matter. The fact remains that he drew them and that, together with his increasing disgust for the system of which he himself was part, they impelled him to take the action he did.

'From what I have learned and what I have heard,' he wrote, 'I know that the leaders of our Soviet State are consciously provoking atomic war. At one time or another they may lose their heads entirely and start an atomic war. See what Khrushchov has done over Berlin. 'In Moscow,' he continues, gradually working himself up, 'my life has been a nuclear nightmare. I know the extent of their preparations. I know the poison of the new military doctrine, as outlined in the top-secret Special Collection* – the

* The Special Collection referred to by Penkovski was a top-secret collection of studies by some of the younger Soviet generals, prepared at Khrushchov's request for the purpose of examining in depth the possibilities and practicality of a Soviet first-strike stance, verging on preventive nuclear war – a concept which does not seem to have appealed to the older marshals, most of whom were very sensibly inclined to place greater emphasis on conventional weapons.

plan to strike first, at any cost. I know their new missiles and their warheads . . . I must defeat these men. They are destroying the Russian people. I will defeat them with my allies, my new friends. God will help us in this great and important task.'

Perhaps, finally, in Penkovski's subconscious, another, subtler influence was at work. The KGB, it seemed, had, after twenty years of security checks, at long last discovered that in the Civil War his father had fought not for the Bolsheviks but against them. Inevitably, this discovery would count against him. (It seems to have lost him the post of Military Attaché in Delhi.) In other words, he would have to pay for another man's decision taken before he was born. But it was not only the injustice of this that rankled. The more he thought about it, the closer he came to the conclusion that his father's decision might after all have been the right one and that it was perhaps only proper that he should now be following in his footsteps.

Penkovski returned to Moscow well pleased with the results of his visit to London. 'During our sixteen-day period of work,' he noted on 16 May, 'a new alliance was created, an alliance of friendship and struggle for our common goal. I believe that this alliance will be eternal. God will help us in this great and important work.' Already his solitary musings had begun to take on an evangelical, an increasingly apocalyptic tone.

On returning home to his flat overlooking the Moscow River, he had carefully stowed away his Minox camera, film and accompanying instructions in a secret drawer, which he had contrived in his desk. During the weeks that followed he got down to work in a big way, methodically photographing large numbers of highly secret documents and technical manuals at the Ministry of Defence and GRU Headquarters, to both of which his rank and position gave him free access. What could be more natural, after all, than that a Soviet intelligence officer, who took his work seriously, should spend a certain amount of time consulting and working on secret papers?

On 27 May, Greville Wynne again flew out to Moscow to follow up the Soviet delegation's visit to London and discuss possible further exchanges. Having met him at Sheremetyevo Airport, Alex drove back with him to the Metropole Hotel and there handed him twenty rolls of exposed film – the result of a month's hard work. These Wynne passed the same day to the Moscow representative of the SIS for onward transmission to London. He also gave Alex a further supply of film and fresh instructions from the SIS. Alex's superiors, both in the State Committee and in the GRU were, it appeared, well pleased with the outcome of the delegation's visit to

London and perhaps even more so with the close relationship he had managed to establish with Greville Wynne, clearly a useful contact for a Soviet intelligence officer.

Before Wynne went back to London, he was told that Alex would be coming over again in July to attend the Soviet Trade Exhibition at Earl's Court. There was also to be a Soviet Trade Fair in Paris in September, which would give him (and his friends) another welcome opportunity of meeting Alex.

The Trade Exhibition only took up part of Alex's time when he visited London in July. Another important duty was to look after Madame Serov and her daughter Svetlana, who were on a private visit to London and whom General Serov had expressly entrusted to his care. At the airport, Alex tells us, he was much surprised to see with what genuine affection the General kissed his wife and his daughter goodbye. 'Somehow,' he writes, 'I found it hard to believe that this cold, hard-man with blood-stained hands could show such warmth to those near to him.'

With his previous experience of London, Alex was able to take his charges on a number of successful shopping expeditions, while in the evening he escorted them to restaurants and night-clubs, where he and Svetlana made a brave attempt at rock and roll. Both mother and daughter were delighted by all the trouble he took, called him by his Christian name and patronymic, Oleg Vladimirovich, and said that when they got back he must come and see them at their *dacha* near Moscow, where they had fresh strawberries all the year round and their own beehives.

Nevertheless Alex had plenty of time for other, more serious activities. Once again he found two British and two American intelligence officers waiting for him in a house not far from the Kensington Close Hotel, where he was staying; by now the Berlin situation had become critical and sometimes their sessions lasted as long as ten hours at a time. Nor, of course, did he neglect his normal reports to the GRU, passing them to Colonel Pavlov, the GRU's deputy Resident at the Soviet Embassy in London, for onward transmission to Moscow by diplomatic bag.

'In travelling from London to Sheffield (by the A1 route),' he wrote, 'I observed for the second time in the southern outskirts of the town of Stamford a military airfield, on which were based planes of the British Air Force and to the north of this same city a launch-site for the air defence. I had the opportunity to make a closer study of these targets, their location, their map references, etc. I made additional sketches of the targets, a description of which I am enclosing separately.'

[Sd] O. Penkovski, Colonel

Alex returned to Moscow on 10 August, having, it can safely be said, succeeded in pleasing everyone. From the Embassy, Pavlov wrote to Gvishiani, warmly commending Penkovski's work in London. He also now became a not infrequent visitor at the Serovs' *dacha* and at their apartment in Moscow, and sometimes even met Svetlana apart from her parents.

Meanwhile, to his Western contacts, his informed interpretations of Soviet policy and probable Soviet intentions were invaluable, as were the hard facts and detailed material which he was able to produce. In the fresh instructions they now gave him, special emphasis was placed on the collection of intelligence concerning the Soviet armed forces, missile troops, troops stationed in East Germany and also on Soviet preparations for a peace-treaty with East Germany. He was further given an assurance that, if he ever wanted or needed it, he would be granted asylum in the West. But once again, he returned to Moscow as planned. 'I must,' he wrote at about this time, 'continue for another year or two on the General Staff of the USSR, in order to reveal all the villainous plans and plottings of our common enemy. I consider that, as a soldier, with the task I have set myself, my place in these troubled times is in the front line.'

During 1961, Khrushchov, who four years earlier had abruptly dismissed Marshal Zhukov from the Ministry of Defence, continued to impose his personal defence policy on the military. Like certain Western politicians, he seems to have been attracted by the concept of a Bigger Bang for a Buck, which the more far-sighted professionals found disturbing for a variety of reasons. As a politician, he was no doubt also wary of possible Bonapartist tendencies on the part of the military.

The consequent discontent in army circles was, needless to say, only voiced in public once Khrushchov had been removed from office. Meanwhile, in his private jottings, Colonel Penkovski, writing as a regular soldier and a confidant of many of the marshals and generals involved and no doubt sharing their resentment, was becoming increasingly explosive on the subject of 'this scoundrel Khrushchov'. 'Having failed,' he wrote, 'to resolve the Berlin and other international crises to his own taste by shouts and threats, Khrushchov continues to struggle to gain time and uses the time thus gained to prolong the mad nuclear and missile armament race. As a General Staff Officer,' he went on, 'as a true fighter for peace and a soldier of a new army fighting for peace and democracy, I have reached my own conclusions as to the new Soviet military doctrine. Peoples of the world,' he concluded portentously, 'be vigilant!'

Not long after Penkovski's return to Moscow in August, Greville Wynne spent three or four days there, ostensibly to attend a French Industrial Fair. Penkovski had met him at the airport, seen him safely through the customs and then taken him to the Metropole Hotel. Once again the usual exchanges were effected, Alex handing over more rolls of exposed film and a broken Minox camera as well as some packets of information, and receiving in return a new camera and a fresh supply of film. Before leaving, Wynne also gave him a box of sweets.

A couple of weeks later, in early September, anyone who happened to be watching (and it is more than possible that someone was watching) would have seen three British children playing under the trees on Tsvetnoi Boulevard, one of the big new thoroughfares which run through the residential suburbs of Moscow, while their mother, the wife of the Second Secretary at the British Embassy, sat on a convenient bench. They had not been there for long when a passer-by – a sturdy, rather well-dressed man in his early forties with reddish hair, slightly flecked with grey – stopped to talk to the children and then, pulling a box of sweets out of his pocket, gave it to one of them. The child took the box to its mother and the Russian walked on.

In this manner Colonel Penkovski had managed to pass some exposed film to his Western contacts, without, he hoped, attracting undue attention. It was the Colonel's first Western contact with anyone other than Wynne and both he and the official's wife (whom he had met while in London) had been carefully briefed.

Though it had been decided that Penkovski should attend the Soviet Trade Fair in Paris in September, no firm date had as yet been fixed for his arrival. Wynne accordingly met one Aeroflot flight after another until, on 20 September, his patience was finally rewarded and Alex came bustling through the barrier with a broad grin on his face. With him he brought another big batch of exposed film. He was also the bearer of top-secret written instructions from the GRU and a long shopping list from Madame Serov, whose husband, after the usual official briefing, had invited him round to their apartment 'to receive', as he playfully put it, 'additional instructions from my wife' and had also graciously presented him with several jars of caviar for the journey.

In Paris, as in London, highly efficient arrangements had been made by the British and American intelligence authorities to ensure that Penkovski's presence there was put to the best possible use. A well-equipped, conveniently situated interrogation centre had been set up and every care taken to ensure that he reached it with the least possible risk of being seen. Once again, the Western intelligence officers he worked with during the weeks he spent in Paris were well satisfied with the answers he gave and the quality of the material he produced, which included, incidentally, full particulars of the GRU and KGB set-up in Paris together with a floor-plan of the Soviet Embassy, showing where their various offices were situated. In order to ensure that contact was maintained, the Second Secretary's wife was present at one of their meetings and future methods of communication in Moscow were worked out.

As usual, Alex did not allow any of this to interfere with the efficient performance of his duties at the Trade Fair, his social obligations to the Soviet Embassy, his duties as a Soviet intelligence officer (set out for him in a special directive from the GRU) or, for that matter, with his own personal enjoyment of the French capital, which offered, needless to say, abundant scope for a man with his abundant *joie de vivre.*

After spending nearly a month in Paris, Penkovski was due to fly back to Moscow on 16 October 1961. Once again his Western contacts had offered him the choice of not going back, guaranteeing him, if he wanted it, a secure future in Great Britain or America. The offer, for a man who appreciated the Western way of life as much as he did, was a tempting one, especially if you consider what he had already been able to do and the dangers he faced if he went back to his own country. On 16 October at Orly Airport his plane was delayed by fog and he had a moment of hesitation. But, when his flight was finally called and the actual moment came for him to go, his mind was made up and he pushed resolutely through the barrier towards whatever a doubtful future might hold for him. Had he not himself written, after all, that a soldier's place was 'in the front line'?

Within a week of his return to Moscow, Penkovski started to operate the new system of contacts with the West which had been agreed during his visit to Paris. At nine o'clock on the evening of 21 October he was walking along the Sadovnicheskaya Embankment near the Balchug Hotel, smoking a cigarette and holding in his hand a packet wrapped in white paper, when he was accosted by a man wearing his overcoat unbuttoned and also smoking a cigarette. 'Mr Alex,' said the man in English, using the code-name chosen for him, 'I am from your two friends, who send you a big, big, welcome.' And Alex handed him the packet.

This was the first of a number of packets passed in this way. For the next few weeks the material reaching London showed MI6 that Alex was working flat out for them. At the same time, he was leading his normal life: going to his office, keeping up with his friends in the Army, and also making the rounds of his favourite restaurants – the Baku, the Peking and the restaurant in the Park of Rest and Culture. In mid-November he took his wife, who was expecting a baby in February, for a holiday to Kislovodsk and Sochi, returning to Moscow on 18 December.

In late December and early January he met his Embassy contact again, and passed more film to her. As an experienced intelligence officer, he was naturally always on the look-out for possible surveillance. On 5 January, after he had handed over more film in the course of what was made to look like a casual meeting in a narrow side street near the Arbat, he noticed a small brown car with two men in it, hovering nearby, before swinging round and moving off into the Arbat. He noted its registration number: SHA 61.45. It might mean that they were being watched. Or it might not. At their next meeting a week later, there was no sign of anything suspicious. But a week after that there was the little brown car again, driven by a man in a black overcoat, as invariably worn by the civilian employees of the KGB and as recognizable to the initiated as the boots of a London policeman. There could no longer be any doubt that they were being watched. In a letter to a pre-arranged address in London Alex gave notice that for the time being there could be no more meetings with Mrs Chisholm.

But he did not let this obvious sign of danger stop him from transmitting material. Instead, he now used other methods. One was a system of *tainiks* or dead-drops, by which the material he wished to transmit was deposited in a pre-arranged spot from which his Western contact would in due course pick it up. But, despite its obvious advantages, it was necessarily an uncertain and not very satisfactory method, with the risk always that either the collector or the depositor might be observed or that something else might go wrong.

During February and March 1962 Alex used a whole series of such *tainiks*. One was in the doorway of numbers 5 and 6 Pushkin Street. Just inside the door on the right stood a dark green radiator with a three-inch gap between it and the wall. In the gap was a hook. The message for collection was to be hung on this hook in a matchbox, wrapped in light blue paper and taped with Sellotape. When he had something to send, Alex would first make a black mark on lamp post No. 35 on Kutuzovski Prospekt, then put the packet in the drop and then make two telephone calls to G3.26.87 and G3.26.94 each with a pre-arranged number of rings, hanging up when the number answered. Another drop was in the Vaganskoye Cemetery, near the grave of the poet Sergei Yesenin, who in the early exciting years after the Revolution had married the dancer Isadora Duncan and committed suicide at the age of thirty in 1925. There was one dead-drop in the entrance to an apartment block on Gogol Boulevard and another inside a doorway on Brusovski Pereulok. For the drops, places were chosen readily accessible to foreigners and each, as far as possible, was only used once.

Owing to his official position, Alex was invited to and authorized, in fact, encouraged to attend diplomatic receptions. Towards the end of March he twice met the Second Secretary's wife at British Embassy parties, handing over six rolls of film on 28 March and receiving fresh instructions from MI6 at the Queen's Birthday Party on 31 March. One ingenious dead-drop, which was never in fact used, was a special tin of Harpic with a false bottom, provided

by Greville Wynne and intended to be left in the lavatory of a British diplomat whose parties Penkovski sometimes attended. Yet another means of
communication with MI6 was by picture postcards of Moscow, which were
given to him already written, to be sent, in accordance with a pre-arranged
system, to a London address when he had a message to transmit. Thus, one
postcard, addressed to a Miss R. Cook, ran: 'I am having a very interesting
time and enjoying myself. There are so many interesting things here
that it is difficult to decide even where to begin. I'll see you soon. John.'
This, if sent, meant that he was likely to leave the Soviet Union within a
fortnight.

During the months that followed, Alex kept up his deliveries as best he
could. Another man might have broken off contact with the West and gone
to ground, at any rate for the time being. But the risks he was running do
not seem to have counted with him. By this time the Soviet Government
had already set in train the measures which were to lead later that year to
the Cuban crisis and, as Alex fully realized, the information he was sending
to the West was of vital importance.

Even so, the strain under which he was now working was considerable.
Ever since the beginning of the year it had been clear that the KGB (or
'Neighbours', as they were known to their not so friendly rivals of the
GRU) were taking an unhealthy interest in him. There had been the little
brown car at his meeting with the Embassy wife. And now there were signs
that they were continuing to probe into his background. 'Apparently,' he
wrote in January, 'the Neighbours have information that my father did not
die, but is abroad. This information cropped up at the end of 1961. An
immediate search of the place where my father was buried did not produce
anything. The grave was not found, nor any documents relating to my
father's death. The GRU are not especially concerned about this and
believe my father to be dead.'

Nor was this all. For some time Alex had been hoping to go to the
United States in April in connection with a Soviet trade exhibition. But
permission to make the journey was still not forthcoming. 'If all is well,' he
wrote, 'I will leave for the USA on 19 April. But at present things are
going badly. They are still searching for my father's burial place. They
cannot find it and therefore conjecture that my father is alive. Consequently
they will not in future send me on overseas assignments. The GRU consider these fears unfounded and defend me against all the Neighbours'
accusations. Everything will be decided soon.'

In London more serious thought than ever was by now being given to
the question of getting Alex out before it was too late. On one of his visits to
Western Europe there had been talk of picking him up by submarine in the
Baltic, which might make it possible to bring his family with him. He had

also been given a forged passport under an assumed name for use within the Soviet Union in case of an extreme emergency. Now a plan was evolved to bring him out hidden in a specially-built caravan. There was to be an International Trade Fair at Helsinki in September and the proposal was that two caravans, one specially fitted, should be sent there as part of a mobile exhibition. From Helsinki, if the Soviet authorities would agree, the caravans could be taken across the frontier to Leningrad for a brief visit and brought out again with Alex safely stowed away in one of them.

In June it was decided that Wynne, as Managing Director of Mobile Exhibitions Ltd, should fly out to Moscow to obtain permission from the Scientific Committee for the caravans to go to Leningrad. Alex, looking ill and worried, met him at Sheremetyevo Airport on 2 July and drove him to the vast modern Ukraina Hotel. 'I am under observation,' he said once they were in the car. In Wynne's room at the Ukraina, Wynne handed him a letter from London and they discussed possible means of escape. A day or two later Wynne saw Levin at the State Committee and obtained from him permission in principle to bring the caravans to Leningrad for a mobile exhibition.

That same afternoon Penkovski, who by now had delivered a second batch of material to Wynne, also had a talk with Levin, who, as he knew, was the KGB's representative on the State Committee. Levin told him that his people, meaning the KGB, were interested in the purpose of Wynne's visit. To this Penkovski replied that, in addition to talking to the Committee, Wynne would need to discuss his proposal for a mobile exhibition with the Trade Council or the Ministry of Foreign Trade. Levin said he knew this. He also knew that for some reason the KGB had become interested in Wynne. Later, Alex went off, undeterred, to an Independence Day party at the American Embassy, where he was apparently able to hand over to an American intelligence officer a detailed plan of recent Soviet missile construction.

Wynne was due to leave Moscow on 6 July. The KGB had been officially informed the evening before that as part of his official duties Penkovski was having dinner with Wynne at the Peking. After such official notification, it was considered the worst possible form for them to shadow officials or any foreigners they happened to be entertaining. But when, at about nine that evening, Penkovski arrived at the Peking, carrying a briefcase, he was surprised to see that Wynne, who had arrived before him, was under obvious KGB surveillance. He accordingly decided to go away without speaking to him. But it then occurred to him that Wynne might have something more to give him before leaving Moscow. He therefore made up his mind to go into the restaurant and have dinner with Wynne in full view of everybody. As he went into the lobby, he at once saw that Wynne was 'surrounded', in other words that the KGB men were either very bad at their job or were letting themselves be seen on purpose. He now went on into the restaurant, only to be told that there were no free tables. At this he decided to leave and walked out, telling Wynne to follow him. A hundred yards or so down the street, he turned into a large courtyard with a garden. Wynne followed him and so did two obvious KGB men. There was nothing more to be done. He told Wynne that he would see him off next morning, whispering to him to meet him at the airport first thing. And he made off. Later that evening Wynne met his principle Embassy contact at the American Club and told him that he had just seen Penkovski, who thought he was being followed.

Wynne was booked on an afternoon flight to London, but in view of what Alex had said to him he made it his business to be at Sheremetyevo at five-thirty next morning. He then simply sat and waited. Three-quarters of an hour later he saw a private car drive up with Alex in it. After parking it, Alex first walked straight past him to make sure they were not being watched and then came over and sat down next to him. He must leave immediately, he said. Pulling his rank and personal authority with the airport staff, as he still could, he then arranged for Wynne to be transferred to the very next outgoing flight to Western Europe, a Scandinavian Air Services flight to Copenhagen taking off in a couple of hours. For someone in his already precarious position it was a very brave thing to do. In order to get Wynne safely out of the country, he was compromising himself irretrievably. Nor, as Wynne's flight was called, did he forget to hand him the usual bulky package.

1962 was the year of the Cuban Crisis. Throughout July and August Alex not only carried on but redoubled his activities. The material he sent out concerning Soviet nuclear armaments and defences was of incalculable value to the West and, as things turned out, to the cause of world peace.

Taking the bull by the horns, he had on the very day Wynne left Moscow gone straight to his superiors to complain of the 'insolence' of the KGB the night before, explaining that they had prevented him from dining with an important foreigner, 'whom we respect'. And Levin, the KGB representative on the Committee, had duly expressed indignation at what had happened. Nor had his other colleagues on the Committee and at the GRU shown in any way that they had lost confidence in him.

'Things are going very well at the GRU and on the Committee,' he wrote towards the end of August. 'Serov, Smolikov, Gvishiani and other friends very much want to send me on another temporary duty tour abroad: either to Australia or Japan or the USA with the mobile book exhibition or to France with Rudnev and Gvishiani. They will try to talk the KGB and the Central Committee into granting the necessary temporary duty orders. If the KGB clears me of suspicion, they will sanction my travel.

'I have already grown used to the fact that I periodically notice some degree of surveillance and control over my movements. The Neighbours continue to study me. There is some reason for this KGB activity. I get confused by guesses and suppositions. I am very far from exaggerating the dangers. Still, I am an optimist and I try to weigh up the situation objectively.

'I am not disappointed in my life or my work. The most important thing is that I am full of strength and anxious to continue this work. To tell the truth about this system is the goal of my life. And if I succeed in contributing my little bricks to this great cause, there can be no greater satisfaction.'

On 5 September he had been asked to a party at the American Embassy and took some exposed film with him in the hope that he might find a suitable opportunity of handing it over. But none presented itself. On the following day he tried to make contact with the British but was again unsuccessful. Things were becoming increasingly difficult for him.

Back in London, anxiety for Alex was by now growing daily greater. Towards the end of September the two caravans were finally completed. But by this time it had been necessary to make a new plan and the decision was now taken that, in place of Helsinki, the caravans would go first to a trade fair which was being held that autumn in Bucharest and then, if the Hungarian Government agreed, to Budapest. If all went well, an invitation to take the exhibition to Moscow might follow.

Towards the end of October Wynne made his way via Bucharest to Budapest, where the Hungarian Government had given permission for the exhibition to be held in the grounds of the Trade Fair near the Danube. On the evening of 2 November he gave a party in a nearby pavilion to mark the opening of the exhibition. After the party was over, Wynne was standing outside the pavilion when he was approached by two men in trilby hats and dark raincoats. Two black saloon cars then drew up beside them, the door of one was opened and Wynne was bundled struggling and shouting into it. His driver, George Ley, tried to go to his help, but was held off at gunpoint. After a night in a Hungarian jail, Wynne was put on board a Soviet military aircraft and flown to Moscow, where he was at once taken to the notorious Lubyanka prison. There he was to spend the next six months. It was not until later that he realized that Penkovski had in fact been arrested some days before his own arrival in Budapest.

Wynne has himself vividly described the ordeal which he now endured: the scanty prison diet; the tension; the perpetual interrogation; the confrontations with Penkovski; the playing back of recordings of the conversations they had in his hotel room. But still he steadfastly refused to sign a confession.

After just over six months of intensive preparation, the trial of Penkovski and Wynne opened in the Supreme Court at ten o'clock on the morning of 7 May before the Military Collegium of the USSR. On a raised platform at one end of the courtroom, facing several hundred carefully chosen members of the public representing the Soviet People, sat the Presiding Judge, Lieutenant-General V. V. Borisolglebski, and two other generals in the role of People's Assessors, all three in uniform. In gold immediately above the head of the Presiding Judge hung the state emblem of the USSR: a hammer and sickle superimposed on a terrestrial globe and surrounded by circular sheaves of corn. To the left of the judges sat the prisoners in the dock, watched over by armed and uniformed guards. Immediately below them were the two counsels for the defence, Comrades Borovik and Apraxin. To their right were the film and television cameras. At the back of the court were the representatives of the foreign press.

After a few brief formalities, the proceedings began with the reading of the indictment by the Secretary of the Court, a major in the Administrative Service who sat with the judges. This stated that O. V. Penkovski had, 'as a result of moral decay, decided to become an agent of the imperialist intelligence services'. There followed a detailed and reasonably accurate record of his activities from his first meeting with Wynne until the time of his arrest (which had, it now appeared, occurred on 22 October, ten days before Wynne's own capture in Budapest). It also gave some account of the different letters and packets he had handed over and of their contents. On the strength of this, he was charged with high treason. As for Wynne, he was charged for his part with having transmitted to British Intelligence Penkovski's original offer to spy for them and with having subsequently provided him with a means of communication with the British and American intelligence services. Asked whether they pleaded guilty, both the accused said that they did – Wynne with certain reservations.

The remainder of the first day was taken up with Penkovski's examination by the Chief Prosecutor, Lieutenant-General A. G. Gorni, a bulky man, wearing spectacles. Under cross-examination Alex described in detail his first meeting with Wynne; his subsequent visit to London; how he had been recruited by British intelligence; the code-names of some of the British agents with whom he had worked; the packets he had handed over; and the methods he had used, including the dead-drops on Pushkin Street and elsewhere. What he did not even now describe was Wynne's true role in it all, declaring that he himself had made the first approach, that, before ever meeting Wynne, he had sought to make contact with the Western intelligence services and that, in the event, Wynne had had no knowledge of the contents of the envelopes he transmitted.

As Penkovski's interrogation continued, the attitude of the audience became increasingly hostile towards the prisoner. Towards the end of his cross-examination General Gorni asked Penkovski whether he realized the seriousness of his crimes and Penkovski replied that he did. Then Gorni asked him how he explained them, what it was that had led him to commit such crimes. 'The basest qualities,' he replied in a leaden voice, 'moral decay, brought on by constant heavy drinking, dissatisfaction with my official position in the State Committee (I did not like my work in the Foreign Section) and then certain inherited characteristics. These did not perhaps develop fully at first, but later weakened my morale and at difficult times drove me to drink. I lost my way, tottered on the brink and in the end went right over. Pride, vanity, discontent with my work, love of pleasure led me into the ways of crime. This is how it was and there is no excuse whatever for what I did. Moral baseness, utter depravity – I admit it all. Although I do not have a weak character, I could not take a grip on myself. Nor could I turn to my comrades for help. Instead I deliberately misled them by telling them that everything was all right, that I was fine. But in reality everything was wrong with me – spiritually, mentally and in everything I did.'

Next day it was Wynne's turn to be cross-examined. From every point of view it was important that he should maintain the illusion promoted by Penkovski that he had been no more than an intermediary between Penkovski and British intelligence.

'When you came to Moscow,' asked the Prosecutor, 'did you really not grasp that you were acting as a go-between for the British Secret Service and Penkovski?'

'I did not grasp it at the time, but afterwards I started to have serious doubts, which became even stronger after my return to England.'

'You mean that by then you had begun to have serious doubts?'

'Yes. Exactly. I had such doubts. With your permission l should like to say to the Supreme Court that at the time I knew absolutely nothing of these matters. What I am saying now may sound simple-minded to professionals, but I am a businessman and I had no idea how the Secret Service operated. Now I know.' (Laughter in court.)

'Defendant Wynne,' asked the Prosecutor a little later, 'after all this, did you grasp that what you were involved in was espionage?'

'Yes, in my own mind, I grasped that I had got caught up in something pretty nasty. In fact, I've already said as much.'

And in the afternoon Wynne, dapper in a black suit, white shirt and striped tie, went on to describe the threats used by British Intelligence to make him work for them and in general to present them as a powerful and sinister organization (thereby, no doubt, giving pleasure to everyone concerned: to the Prosecution, to the crowd and, back in London, to his friends at MI6, in this case only too glad to appear in the role of sinister bullies). At the end of the afternoon's session it was announced that the next morning's session of the court would be held *in camera* and would be taken up with evidence from technical experts.

The proceedings of the fourth and last day, 11 May, were again held in open court, most of the morning being given over to the evidence of two Jewish witnesses, Rudovski and Finkelstein, who were presented as booncompanions of Penkovski and called upon to testify to his dissolute way of life.

'Witness Rudovski,' said the Prosecutor, 'tell us about the evening when your girlfriends' shoes were used for drinking out of instead of glasses.'

'It did happen once,' said Rudovski, 'on the birthday of one of my friends, when we were with Penkovski and his girlfriend at the Poplavok restaurant in the Park of Culture. I did not have a girl with me and did not drink out of anyone's shoe. I don't know whether it was to show his love for the girl or whether it was a trick he had picked up in the West, but Penkovski really did pour wine out of the bottle into the shoe and actually drank it.'

Finkelstein said that he, too, had seen the prisoner drink out of a girl's shoe. Penkovski, he said, had few intellectual interests. He did not much care for art or the theatre, for politics or reading. On the other hand he was a great gourmet and keenly interested in women.

Had they so wished, the prosecution might well have rested their case on the mass of factual and material evidence already in their possession, including tape-recordings of conversations and the highly compromising contents of the secret hiding-place in Penkovski's desk: a forged passport, photographs of secret documents, three Minox cameras, the telephone numbers of foreign intelligence officers, a draft report to his foreign contacts, cipher pads, a note of radio frequencies for receiving messages from abroad and so on. In his summing-up, General Gorni made good use of these and of other more or less firmly established facts, enumerating the arrangements made for dead-drops and for the collection of their contents, and describing Penkovski's various transactions with members of the British or American embassy staffs or their wives, the instructions he received from them and the material he handed over to them.

As regards the dead-drops, a check had, it appeared, been carried out ten days after Penkovski's arrest. Half an hour after double rings to numbers G3.26.87 and G3.26.94, the American Assistant Air Attaché had been observed examining lamp post No. 35 on the Kutuzovski Prospect and later that same day one of his colleagues had been caught groping for a non-existent package behind the dark-green radiator in the entrance to numbers 5 and 6 Pushkin Street. General Gorni also mentioned the picture post-cards of Moscow with their seemingly innocent messages, which Penkovski was to use as a means of communicating with his contacts in England and of which several had been found lying unused in the drawer of his desk. If he changed his place of work, a view from the Kotelnicheskaya Embankment was to go to a Mrs Nixon, residing in Berkshire. 'I am having a pleasant time,' ran the message, 'and have even found that I like vodka. Moscow actually looks this way and you should see the size of the streets. I will give you all the details on my return. With love, Dick.' But, said Gorni, allowing himself a rare moment of grim humour, 'During this time he was not enjoying himself but looking uneasily around him and sweating with fear in the knowledge that the noose was closing in on him and that the end was near.'

Continuing his speech, General Gorni felt moved to say a few words about the CIA and the SIS. 'A leading role,' he said, 'belongs to the Central Intelligence Agency of the US. Like a giant octopus it extends its tentacles into all corners of the earth, supports a tremendous number of spies and secret informers, continually organizes plots and murders, provocations and diversions. Modern techniques are put to the service of espionage: from the miniature Minox cameras, which you see before you, to space satellites – "spies in the sky".

'The British Intelligence Service, which has been in existence for about three hundred years, is no less insidious and astute in its methods, but it attempts to remain more in the background. The activities of these major espionage centres against the USSR are connected and closely co-ordinated, as can be clearly seen in the present case. This does not, however, reduce the contradictions between them or their struggles against each other.'

The Prosecutor concluded his arraignment of Penkovski by stressing, as Penkovski himself had been obliged to do, his moral degeneration as the explanation of the crimes he had committed. 'In reviewing the present case,' he said, 'the question inevitably arises: how can it be that a man like Penkovski, who was born, was brought up, and received his education during the years of Soviet power, within our society, could so completely lose the moral qualities of a Soviet man, lose all sense of shame, conscience and elementary feelings of duty and end up by committing such serious crimes?

'A partial answer to that question was provided by Penkovski himself, when he pointed out, in his testimony in court, the base qualities which have finally put him in the dock: envy, vanity, a liking for a frivolous life, affairs with many women and moral decay, brought about in part by drink. All these blots on his moral character undermined him; he became first a degenerate, and then a traitor . . .

'Penkovski's utter selfishness and overwhelming ambition have long been apparent. He was forever striving to mingle with people of authority and influence, to please them and ingratiate himself with them. He positively gloried in his close relations with them.

'He indulged his tastes for high living at restaurants and drank wine from the slippers of his mistresses, habits he had learned in the night-clubs of London and Paris while Wynne was showing him the highlights of Western culture.

'He was naturally mercenary and, though well paid by the State and well provided for, with savings in the bank, his greed knew no bounds. He particularly enjoyed trips abroad. In fact, his dissatisfaction with his job and his bitterness came largely from the fact that he was not offered a job abroad.

'Of course, such degenerates, such renegades as Penkovski, who excite feelings of indignation and loathing in all Soviet people, are no more than a passing phenomenon in our society. But this example clearly shows the danger that lies in such survivals from the past, survivals brought to life by an ideology that is hostile to us. It shows, too, what they might grow into, if not taken in time and rooted out once and for all.'

Gorni next turned to Greville Wynne, again going through the evidence and again arriving at the inevitable conclusion.

There followed the speeches of the two Counsels for the Defence, Apraxin for Penkovski and Borovik for Wynne. Like General Gorni before him, Apraxin, having touched on Penkovski's war service and brilliant military career, attributed his downfall not to 'any difference of views' or 'private political theory', or 'lack of agreement with the policy of building a Communist society', or 'hatred for the people', but, quite simply, to his moral degeneration, to his love of 'souvenirs, trinkets, bracelets and French cognac' and finally to his Philistinism, which had led him to 'the logical end of all Philistines, namely crime'. 'I beg you,' he concluded though without much conviction, 'to let Penkovski live.'

On behalf of Wynne, Borovik took the line that his client had come to Moscow as a businessman and had unwittingly been trapped into serving as a go-between, who even then had never known what the envelopes he delivered really contained. He, too, asked for 'a just and humane sentence'. After this the two accused made their final pleas in closed session. The court then adjourned for the Judges to consider their verdict.

When the Judges reassembled three or four hours later, the courtroom was even more crowded than before with scores of extra workers who had been brought in to witness the grand finale. Beneath the glare of the flood-lights, with the television cameras whirring, the Presiding Judge then read out the sentences:

'Oleg Vladimirovich Penkovski, guilty of High Treason, to be shot and all his personal property confiscated. Greville Maynard Wynne, guilty of espionage, to be deprived of his liberty for eight years, the first three to be served in prison, the remainder in a harsh-regime correctional labour colony.'

When Penkovski's sentence was read out, the crowd applauded and hooted enthusiastically, while he, standing to attention, faced them. Wynne's sentence, which he received in the same way, was listened to with no more than a murmur of approval and a little gentle clapping. The court then adjourned and the prisoners were marched out.

A few days later, General Gorni gave an interview to *Izvestiya*. 'Penkovski,' he said, 'is dead. The sentence was carried out on 16 May, in the second half of the day . . . When it was announced to him that the Supreme Soviet of the USSR had rejected his plea for mercy and that he was to be executed, there was not a trace of the grand manner he had assumed in court. He met death like a despicable coward.'

From the courtroom Greville Wynne was taken back to the Lubyanka. Ten days later he was moved to the ancient town of Vladimir, 150 miles from Moscow, and there consigned to a special punishment prison, built by the Imperial Government not long before the Revolution to accommo-date political prisoners and used for the same purpose ever since. At Vladimir he was, by his own account, treated rather worse than at the Lubyanka and soon his health began to suffer from lack of adequate food. However, the weeks and months went by and still with amazing steadfastness he refused to admit that he was a spy.

Then, one day in the second half of April 1964, almost a year after his trial, he was again taken to Moscow and, after three days in a cell in the Lubyanka, driven to the airport and put aboard an aircraft. No explanation of the move was given to him. On landing, however, he realized that he was in Germany. Next morning at first light he was taken under guard in a yellow Mercedes to what looked like a frontier. On the further side of the barriers another car drew up – a black Mercedes. Out of it stepped a man in a light-coloured mackintosh, whom he at once realized he knew. With him was a dark, smiling, sturdily-built man with curly hair. Formal recog-nitions ensued and at 5.15 a.m. on 22 April 1964 Greville Wynne was duly exchanged for Gordon Lonsdale.

· · · · ·

The evaluation of intelligence material is, of course, a matter for the expert, but it is hard to resist the conclusion that Colonel Penkovski's contribution to Western knowledge of Soviet defence capability was a considerable one. It came, for one thing, at a critical time in history, when Nikita Khrushchov, volatile, dynamic and a gambler by nature, having settled to his apparent satisfaction the domestic affairs of the Soviet Union, was flexing his muscles in preparation for a comparable demonstration of forward policy in the field of foreign affairs.

In the space of a year or two there had been the showdown over the U2s, the Vienna Summit and the crisis over Berlin and East Germany. Penkovski's work for the West spanned the period from April 1961 to October 1962. The month of his arrest was also the month of the Soviet–American confrontation over Cuba. For a week or two world peace had hung in the balance. Thanks to the nature and extent of the information at his disposal. President Kennedy was, when it came to the point, able to call Khrushchov's bluff and by skilful diplomacy bring the crisis to a peaceful conclusion. Indeed it was on 28 October 1962, just six days after Penkovski's arrest, that Khrushchov finally told Kennedy that he was prepared to 'dismantle the arms which you describe as offensive' and bring them back from Cuba to the Soviet Union. There can be little doubt that much of the information at President Kennedy's disposal came from Oleg Penkovski, as had much of the information which enabled the Western Allies to handle the earlier crisis over East Germany as successfully as they did.

There can be little question of the quantity or indeed of the quality of the information produced by Penkovski. By virtue of his rank and position in the GRU he could and, as we know, did have access to a wide range of secret material, including full particulars of Soviet orders of battle and troop dispositions, missiles and all other nuclear and conventional armaments. Furthermore, he was informed or could inform himself as to the workings of the whole of the Soviet intelligence and counter-intelligence networks. Thanks to his useful military and political connections, to his position at the heart of the Soviet ruling class, he was also as well-placed as anyone to form an estimate of the probable intentions of the Soviet Government and High Command and of current trends of opinion and to follow the ever-changing interplay of personalities. And all this information he was willing to place unreservedly at the disposal of the Western Allies, thus enabling them to assess Soviet intentions and capabilities far more accurately than they could otherwise have done. Little wonder that at the first hint that a man of his calibre might be prepared to talk, the Western intelligence services and the British Secret Service in particular at once set the necessary machinery in motion to contact him and give him every opportunity to do so.

What, in the ultimate analysis, were Penkovski's reasons for behaving as he did? From Greville Wynne and from his own writings, we know enough about him to say with reasonable certainty that he was not actuated by mercenary or indeed selfish motives. Such material rewards as came his way were in any case minimal – a thousand roubles or so for expenses. He had, too, by Soviet standards enough money, a good job, a happy family life, and an excellent position in society. On occasion, it is true, he seems to have hankered after the bright lights and free and easy intercourse of the West, but these he could (and did) enjoy at fairly frequent intervals as an organizer of trade fairs and trusted officer of the GRU. It was certainly not necessary for him to do what he did in order to get taken to a couple of night-clubs in London or Paris. Indeed, if the delights of life in the West had been all that he was concerned with, he could have seized an early opportunity to defect and spend the rest of his life in the West as a pensioner of MI6 and the CIA. Instead of which, with his eyes wide open to the probable consequences, he chose to stay in the Soviet Union and continue to work there for the West, when the dangers of doing so were obvious to anyone.

In the light of what we know we thus return to the conclusion that his motives were those which emerge from every line of his writings. He had come to detest the system of which he himself was part. He had even less liking for the KGB, of which he had seen so much at such close quarters. He was disillusioned by Soviet society, especially in its higher echelons, of which, again, he was part. Finally, both as a regular soldier and as a critic of the regime, he had conceived an almost obsessive loathing for Khrushchov and was rightly or wrongly convinced that he was preparing to plunge the world into nuclear war. For all these reasons, he had come to believe with an almost manic fervour that it was his duty to the Russian people and to humanity to do everything in his power to strengthen and help the West in the hope of avoiding war and bringing about the eventual overthrow of the Khrushchov regime. To achieve this end, he was in the ultimate analysis prepared to sacrifice his life, his family, his reputation and everything that in the past he had held most sacred and calmly face the misery, agony and degradation of a treason trial. Clearly the man we see here was not just a disgruntled or disappointed middle-piece officer, who was prepared to do his superiors a bad turn out of spite or greed. That he should have been so ready to take the risks he did points to a deep, almost religious conviction of the rightness and justice of his cause, to a belief, of which we occasionally catch a glimpse, that God was on his side.

A good many Soviet citizens at all levels of society are no doubt to some extent disillusioned with the system under which they live. Of late, the dissident, the internal emigrant, has become a regular feature of Soviet life.

The difference in 1962, however, was that Penkovski had the courage of his convictions and translated them into effective action, while most other dissidents preferred to stay safely submerged – at any rate until such time as it was the done thing to attack Khrushchov, who, once he had been overthrown, immediately became fair game for all the politicians, senior generals and others who up to then had nursed more or less secret grievances against him.

Looking back fifteen years later, it is possible to see that for the Soviet authorities the Penkovski affair, at every stage in its development, presented a whole series of appalling problems. Even when the KGB had at long last become aware that something fishy was going on, it was by no means easy for them to know what to do.

A quarter of a century, it should be remembered, had gone by since the great purges and treason trials of the 1930s when, under Stalin, the NKVD itself had been shown to be as vulnerable as anyone else. Genrikh Yagoda, their former Chief had, early in 1938, stood in the dock on a charge of high treason side by side with the men whom barely two years before he himself had arrested, and the long arm of retribution had reached right down into the depths of his department until 'Purge the Purgers' had become the most popular cry of all.

Under Nikita Khrushchov, the power of the KGB had to some extent been curbed and, when it came to witch-hunting, it was no longer quite the same merry free-for-all it had been under Stalin. The caste system, too, had by now increasingly crystallized with all that this implied and it had become almost inconceivable that a high-ranking officer like Penkovski with a key position in the GRU and an almost equally strong one in the Party should be even remotely suspected of a serious misdemeanour. It was thus that, when in July 1962 after more than a year of intensive espionage, Penkovski found that he and Wynne were being followed and watched by the Neighbours, his immediate reaction was to complain of this to his superiors who, in their turn, showed and quite possibly felt a corresponding degree of outrage at this altogether unwarranted encroachment on their privacy and privileges.

It was, no doubt, this social and professional inhibition, as much as anything, coupled of course with Penkovski's own acute awareness and expertise as a trained intelligence officer, that accounted for the astonishing fact that he was able to spy for the West for almost a year and a half before retribution finally overtook him. And spy on an unprecedented scale, working painstakingly through the secret files of the Ministry of Defence, photographing literally thousands of vital documents on all the most sensitive subjects and, in addition to the welcome surprise-packets he delivered to them, thrice placing himself day after day, for hours on end, at the disposal of trained Western interrogators so that they could cross-question him on any aspect of Soviet policy they chose.

Little wonder that, when those concerned eventually put two and two together and the day of reckoning finally came, it should have been on such a spectacular scale and that, in addition to a Marshal of the Soviet Union (Penkovski's old friend Varentsov), General Ivan Alexandrovich Serov, the Head of the GRU, should himself have bitten the dust, not to mention several hundred smaller fry in his department. (In view of what we know, it is perhaps also scarcely surprising that several British and American diplomats should have had to leave Moscow rather suddenly at about the same time.)

But worse still in a way was the problem that arose once the spy had been caught. Soviet treason trials have always been elaborately staged set pieces, carefully designed to convey a significant and edifying message. But in this case the message, though significant, was scarcely edifying.

Stalin, it is true, had never been unduly worried about such things. In the space of a few years, the pick of the Party and Government and the flower of the Red Army, had all been shot as traitors. And the message that came across, though admittedly implying a disquieting state of affairs, had in the event been blindingly clear: they had all been wrong and Stalin had, as usual, been right.

But things were no longer quite as simple as that. Had not Khrushchov himself only six years before denounced Stalin as a mass-murderer, a homicidal maniac? Had there not even been some suggestion that in future Soviet justice should bear a closer relationship to ordinary justice, should try to stick more closely to the facts?

And the facts, in this instance, were just about as unpalatable as they could be.

No wonder that in court every effort was made to play down Penkovski's importance and the importance of the material he had handed over, to present him as being a colonel on the Reserve rather than on the active list and keep quiet about his membership of the Communist Party, and to try also to present the secrets he had betrayed as having been, in the main, not military, but commercial or economic.

But in a sense hardest of all for the prosecution to explain were his motives, the motives that had led someone in his position to do what he had done. It was to explain this that they sought so painstakingly to represent him as degenerate and dissolute, bringing his two Jewish cronies to bear witness in this sense. But here again the evidence produced, that he had once been known to drink wine out of a girl's shoe, that he often went to the cinema and to football matches and rarely read good books, was scarcely calculated to carry conviction, especially in a world where so many of his social equals and superiors publicly indulged in foibles that were so very much more spectacular. Nor, if he really had been so degenerate and so dissolute, would it have been easy to explain how he came to be entrusted with such important work. And, even after its true nature had been carefully masked, it would surely have been difficult to deny that his work had been anything but important.

It has, of course, been suggested that the sentence of death passed on Oleg Penkovski was not in fact carried out, and that instead he was sent to some remote part of the Soviet Union for further interrogation and there managed in the end to take his own life. This may be so. The KGB must have had plenty more questions to ask him and far stranger things than that have happened in Russia.

It has also, inevitably, been suggested that the whole thing was an elaborate plant on the part of Soviet Intelligence, an act of deliberate provocation, designed to mislead and confuse the West and perhaps also to place in Soviet hands a prisoner worthy to be exchanged for their own star performer Konon Molodi, alias Gordon Lonsdale. This I find harder to swallow. From what we know of him and from his own writings, Alex comes alive in the round, not as a fictional character, but as a real man with weaknesses, it is true, for companionship, bright lights, good food and pretty girls, but also with deep convictions.

Whether he was right in believing that the help he gave the West could serve to overthrow Khrushchov, or whether, from the West's point of view, it was even desirable to overthrow him, is another matter. What he sought to do was in any case achieved a couple of years later, quietly and at a higher level, by Khrushchov's own colleagues without producing any very startling differences in Soviet foreign or domestic policy.

Today it seems on the whole more likely that change in the Soviet Union, if and when it comes, will be brought about slowly as the result, not of a sudden upheaval, but of a gradual process of evolution. Nor does it seem very probable that Khrushchov ever really intended to push his policy of brinkmanship to the point of nuclear war. What does seem certain is that, thanks to the secret information available to him during those eighteen critical months, it was possible for President Kennedy accurately to evaluate Soviet intentions and capability and so call Khrushchov's bluff. With the result that both countries were in the end pulled back from what by then seemed the verge of nuclear war. That, it appears, was largely Penkovski's doing and that, in all conscience, is more than most people can hope to achieve in a lifetime.

When, eighteen months or a year after his execution, Penkovski's collected writings were published in the United States and Great Britain, they were received with extreme indignation by the Soviet Government, who at once declared them a complete forgery and addressed vigorous protests to all concerned. Doubts as to their authenticity were also freely expressed by a number of well-qualified Western commentators, while others were equally convinced they were genuine. Possibly the aptest comment came from a leader-writer in the London *Times*: 'The difficulty about anything connected with espionage,' he wrote, 'is that both forgeries and denials are part of its stock in trade.' As for the Soviet press, they too rose nobly to the occasion, getting their own back by revealing in all seriousness that the Great Train Robbery had in fact been engineered by an impoverished British Secret Service as a means of overcoming its perennial shortage of funds.

Epilogue

THE SPY WHO NEVER WAS

Before laying down my pen I must confess to one serious disappointment. I have long been fascinated by the well-known story of the Watchmaker of Orkney, concerning Wahring or Oertel, the German spy said to have been responsible for the sinking of the *Royal Oak* at Scapa Flow in October 1939.

Captain Alfred Wahring, the story ran, was a German naval officer who, having seen the German Grand Fleet scuttled at Scapa in 1918, was left with a feeling of overpowering resentment and swore that sooner or later he would have his revenge. As a first step, he went to Switzerland, took out a Swiss passport under the name of Albert Oertel and learned the trade of a watchmaker.

In 1927 Albert Oertel, by now a skilled watchmaker, moved to Great Britain, was in due course naturalized British and set up shop as a jeweller and watchmaker at Kirkwall in the Orkneys, not far from Scapa Flow. Meanwhile he kept in touch with German Naval Intelligence. It was thus that on the outbreak of war in 1939 he was able to send by radio, pigeon or possibly the unsuspecting GPO, a message to German Naval Headquarters to say that no boom and no adequate submarine-nets were blocking the eastern approach to Scapa Flow. As a result of which, just twenty-one years after the scuttling of the Grand Fleet, a German submarine, following up this useful morsel of intelligence, succeeded in entering the anchorage and torpedoing the *Royal Oak*, guided according to one version by Wahring or Oertel in person who on the night in question drove at high speed along the shore of Scapa Flow, signalling the while with his headlights to Captain Guenther Prien, the commander of the German submarine. It was even whispered that the episode had eventually led to the enforced resignation of Sir Vernon Kell, for some thirty years Head of MI5 and spy-catcher in chief.

Though a sad business for the Royal Navy (not to mention MI5), it seemed to me that artistically this was as neat a spy story as one could wish for and I accordingly decided to look into it in some detail and see whether it would not make another chapter for this book. I even had visions of an octogenarian Wahring or Oertel emerging from his well-deserved retirement to give me a first-hand account of his carefully prepared and most successful exploit.

It was at this point that I began to run into difficulties. It was true that the story, much as I have told it, had appeared in the spring of 1942 in an article by Curt Riess in the Philadelphia *Saturday Evening Post*.

It was equally true that after the war no less a person than Walter Schellenberg, the head of German intelligence, had recounted it in his memoirs, while Allen Dulles had told the same story to a graduating class of CIA agents, promoting Wahring to admiral for the occasion. But there the trail, so promising at first, seemed suddenly to peter out. There were references here and there to Oertel or Wahring, some by highly respectable historians, but they could all be traced back to either Schellenberg or Riess. There was no trace of any Wahring, Wehring or Oertel in the records of either the German Kriegsmarine or of the Abwehr. Nor was there any trace of a Swiss or German watchmaker in Orkney, the only known watchmaker on the island coming from a family of Orcadians who had been watchmakers for seven generations. On the other hand, the story had certainly reached Orkney, though it was indignantly refuted by the inhabitants. Moreover, it seems to have been believed, by the Admiralty's Naval Intelligence Division – for a time, at any rate.

What conclusion is it possible to draw from this somewhat tangled skein? The conclusion ultimately arrived at by the Admiralty seems to have been that soon after America entered the war, the story of Wahring or Oertel was deliberately planted in the United States by the Germans for the purpose of making the British look foolish, an emigrant from Central Europe being used for this purpose. Simultaneously the story started to circulate in Orkney.

What had made British Naval Intelligence inclined to believe it in the first place? Probably the fact that the Germans clearly knew there were no submarine nets at that particular point and that intelligence of this kind could not simply have been derived from aerial reconnaissance. It could only have come from someone on the spot. Which leads one to the conclusion that the successful sinking of the *Royal Oak* was in all probability not the work of a single spy, but rather the result of a lot of careful work immediately before the war by German Naval Intelligence and in particular by Section SKL3 of the Naval High Command.

It is certainly clear from his war memoirs that Admiral Doenitz knew that no proper boom or anti-submarine nets had been laid at the northeastern approaches to Scapa Flow and that on the basis of this information he had from the start planned a raid on the Royal Navy's anchorage there. Admiral Canaris, the chief of the Abwehr, seems equally to have ordered Commander Menzel of his naval section to carry out a reconnaissance of Scapa Flow. Likewise an Abwehr agent who visited Kirkwall with the German merchant navy in August 1939 reported that there were inadequate anti-aircraft defences in Orkney; that it was being said in Kirkwall that the defences of the anchorage were very poor; that the boom and anti-torpedo defences needed repairing; and that to the north east they were practically non-existent.

There remains, however, one curious and unexplained incident: that of the driver of a car flashing his headlights in the blackout by the shores of Scapa Flow on the night of 13–14 October 1939. Of the existence of Oertel or Wahring there is no trace. But of the fact that a motorist with his headlights full on was stationed in the vicinity of Kirk Sound at 1.20 am on 14 October as Captain Prien's U-boat was approaching and then drove off at top-speed in the direction of Scapa Flow, we have very definite proof. First, because it was independently reported to British Naval Intelligence and secondly because it was specifically recorded by Captain Prien in the log of his submarine. 'I must assume,' he wrote in his entry for that time and date, 'that I was observed by the driver of a car which stopped opposite us and drove off towards Scapa Flow at top speed.'

Who, one wonders, can the mysterious motorist have been? There is of course the possibility that he was simply a careless Orcadian, on business or pleasure bent, who could not be bothered with the blackout or for that matter with enemy submarines. On the other hand, Mr Richard Deacon, the well-known authority on spies and spying, has suggested that he could have been a German agent sent without Captain Prien's knowledge by the Abwehr or German Naval Intelligence to check on Prien's conduct of the operation or even for devious reasons of his own, to frustrate it. Had the Germans acted immediately on the intelligence at their disposal, they could probably have sunk not one, but three major ships at Scapa. But possibly, as so often happens, they were dubious as to the quality of the information they had received, finding the story of British unpreparedness hard to credit. Or else Captain Prien, believing that he had been sighted, felt that he had better not spend too much time there.

This leaves us not very much the wiser as far as the mysterious motorist is concerned, while as for Wahring or Oertel, we are reluctantly forced to the conclusion that he simply did not exist, being in all probability no more than a figment of the collective imagination of the dirty tricks department of the Abwehr. Once again one is left with the uneasy feeling that fiction is superior to fact.

335

Much as I should like to do so, I find it hard to draw any very valid or even instructive general conclusions from the cases we have considered in the course of this prolonged excursion into the field of espionage. Spies are human beings and human nature is moved by the most diverse motives.

In a sense Wahring or Oertel, the spy who never was, is perhaps the most revealing case of all. Had he existed, his story would certainly have had a place of honour in any manual of espionage or anthology of spies. He could have been held up to students of the subject (as indeed he was, and by no less a person than Mr Allen Dulles of the CIA) as an example of careful long-term planning and patience rewarded, as a perfect model for keen young spies. But in fact he did not exist. German Naval Intelligence achieved their object by other means. The necessary work was done by other less dramatic but no less effective methods, notably by the careful accumulation of various scraps of information, painstakingly put together to provide a complete picture.

Whether we like it or not, we live in a technological age and may soon have to face the fact that the space-satellite or spy-in-the-sky, the cunningly placed microphone and the purloined cipher-machine are gradually taking the place of the seductive, sable-coated countess travelling first class on the Orient Express.

We live, too, in an age of shifting loyalties, which in a way has complicated counter-espionage. Things are no longer what they used to be. Even members of the ruling class do not always run true to form. Though working for a foreign power, neither Philby nor Penkovski regarded himself as a traitor. The one, we may assume, looked forward to a blissful Soviet Britain; the other was sustained by the no less improbable vision of a democratic Russia, duly provided with a House of Commons, real night-clubs, department stores to rival Harrods and an army run by generals rather than politicians. And this at a time when only an utter cynic would say that we were in fact moving uneasily towards a hideous synthesis of the two.

But despite the difficulties that beset them, one would be wrong to suppose that the secret services of the world are as yet likely to put up their shutters or even pool their secrets. For those who enjoy that sort of thing, it is all still too much fun. Human nature does not change. Greed, sex, self-dramatization, the love of excitement are still powerful motives. So is patriotism. And so are the new ideological loyalties which have to some extent superseded it. Nor can nature resist the urge to ape art. However lamely, real life, when it gets the chance, invariably follows fiction.

And then one has to admit that every now and then this spy or that still comes up with the jackpot – Sorge, for example, or Penkovski – though often only to have his unparalleled scoop labelled, like Sorge's, 'Doubtful and Misleading Information'.

Just over a hundred years have passed since Mata Hari, the archetype of the beautiful spy, was born to her bourgeois Dutch parents. Great traditions die hard. Surely we can safely assume that somewhere, on this side or that of the Iron Curtain, some no less glamorous figure is waiting to step into those elegant, well-made shoes in which she took such pride and show for all to see that the romantic tradition which she, poor thing, so gallantly upheld, is not entirely dead.

ACKNOWLEDGEMENTS

The author and publishers would like to express their gratitude to the individuals and organizations below for their generous help and advice and for permission, in certain cases, to use copyright material from their published works:

Albin Michel for material from *Souvenirs* by Pierre Bouchardon; Robert Hale Ltd, Christie & Moore and the author for material from *Inquest on Mata Hari* by Bernard Newman; Hodder & Stoughton for material from *Queer People* by Basil Thomson; Sam Waagenaar, whose book *The Murder of Mata Hari* proved one of the most useful starting points to the author's researches; the Editor of *Vogue* (USA) for material from the edition of 15 December 1913; the Editor of the *Tatler*; Anne Hogg for her research; Robert B. Asprey for his help and material from *The Panther's Feast*; Hutchinson Publishing for material from *Azef, The Russian Judas* by Boris Nicolaievsky; William Deakin and Richard Storry, and Chatto & Windus, on whose excellent book, *The Case of Richard Sorge* the author has relied extensively in chapter four; Ewen Montagu and Evans Brothers, London, for much essential material from *The Man Who Never Was* by Ewen Montagu, whose latest book, *Beyond Top Secret U* (Peter Davies), casts further fascinating light on the highly successful deceptions practised by his committee in World War II; André Deutsch Ltd for material from *I Was Cicero* by Elyeza Bazna (1962), *Memoirs* by Franz von Papen (1952) and *Operation Cicero* by L. C. Moyzisch (1950); Curtis Brown Ltd for kind permission to reproduce material from *My Silent War* by H. A. R. Philby; André Deutsch Ltd and the authors for material from *Philby* by Page, Leitch and Knightley (1969); Hamish Hamilton Ltd and Patrick Seale Books Ltd for material from *Kim Philby, The Spy I Loved* by Eleanor Philby (1968); Macdonald & Jane's Ltd for material from *The Missing Diplomats* by Cyril Connolly; Doubleday & Co. Inc. and William Collins & Sons for allowing the author to make copious use of material from *The Penkovsky Papers* by Oleg Penkovsky with Frank Gibney; Greville Wynne for sparing the time to discuss his experiences with the author; for their help, the *Sunday Telegraph*, who own the copyright to Greville Wynne's articles, material from which has been used in *The Penkovsky Papers* (Collins); Donald McCormick (Richard Deacon), to whom the author is much indebted for his version of the Scapa Flow story related in the Epilogue; the staff of the Bibliothèque Nationale, Paris; the staff of Beaverbrook Newspapers Library; the staff of the London Library; and the staff of the British Library. The author's warmest thanks are also due to Sheila Macpherson and Alex MacCormick for their patient help with the preparation of the text.

The illustrations have been used by kind permission of the following: Popperfoto 1, 5, 7 and 8; Topix 4; Radio Times Hulton Picture Library 2 and 3; and Keystone 6.

While every effort has been made to make due acknowledgement, any appropriate omission will be gladly rectified in subsequent editions.

SELECT
BIBLIOGRAPHY

Allard, Paul, LES ENIGMES DE LA GUERRE, Paris, 1933
Asprey, Robert B., THE PANTHER'S FEAST, London, 1959
Bazna, Elyeza, I WAS CICERO, London, 1962
Bizard, Leon, SOUVENIRS D'UN MÉDECIN, Paris, 1923
Borkenau, F., THE COMMUNIST INTERNATIONAL, London, 1938
Bouchardon, Pierre, SOUVENIRS, Paris, 1953
Bulloch, John, and Miller, Henry, SPY RING, London, 1961
Burtsev, V. L., MEMOIRS, Berlin, 1923
Carr, E. H., A HISTORY OF SOVIET RUSSIA, London, 1958–64
Colette, MY APPRENTICESHIPS, London, 1957
Connolly, Cyril, THE MISSING DIPLOMATS, London, 1952
Cookridge, E. H., SPY TRADE, London, 1971
Cookridge, E. H., THE THIRD MAN, London, 1974
Cooper, Duff, OPERATION HEARTBREAK, London, 1950
Coulson, Thomas, MATA HARI, COURTESAN AND SPY, London, 1930
Deakin, F. W., and Storey, G. R., THE CASE OF RICHARD SORGE, London, 1966
Dillon, E. J., THE ECLIPSE OF RUSSIA, London, 1918
Driberg, Tom, GUY BURGESS: A PORTRAIT WITH BACKGROUND, London, 1956
Fisher, John, BURGESS AND MACLEAN, London, 1977
Gerasimov, A. V., TSARISM OR TERRORISM, Paris, 1934
Hoare, Geoffrey, THE MISSING MACLEANS, London, 1955
Houghton, Harry, OPERATION PORTLAND: THE AUTOBIOGRAPHY OF A SPY, London, 1972
Johnson, Chalmers, AN INSTANCE OF TREASON: THE STORY OF THE TOKYO SPY RING, London, 1965
Kisch, Egon Erwin, DER FALL DES GENERALSTABSCHEFS REDL, Berlin, 1924
Ladoux, Georges, LES CHASSEURS D'ESPIONS, Paris, 1920

Ladoux, Georges, MES SOUVENIRS, Paris, 1937
Longuet, J., and Zilber, G., LES DESSOUS DE LA POLICE RUSSE, Paris, 1909
Lonsdale, Gordon, SPY: TWENTY YEARS OF SECRET SERVICE, London, 1965
Lopukhin, A. A., MEMOIRS, Moscow, 1923
Lucas, Norman, THE GREAT SPY RING, London, 1966
Lucas, Norman, SPYCATCHER, London, 1973
Massard, Emile, LES ESPIONNES A PARIS, Paris, 1922
Meissner, Hans Otto, THE MAN WITH THREE FACES, London, 1955
Monroe, Elizabeth, PHILBY OF ARABIA, London, 1973
Montagu, Ewen, THE MAN WHO NEVER WAS, London, 1953
Moyzisch, L. C., OPERATION CICERO, London, 1950
Newman, Bernard, INQUEST ON MATA HARI, London, 1956
Nicolai, W., THE GERMAN SECRET SERVICE, London, 1924
Nicolaievesky, Boris, AZEF, THE RUSSIAN JUDAS, London, 1934
Page, Leitch and Knightley, PHILBY: THE SPY WHO BETRAYED A GENERATION, London, 1969
Papen, Franz von, MEMOIRS, London, 1952
Penkovsky, Oleg, THE PENKOVSKY PAPERS, London, 1965
Petrov, V., EMPIRE OF FEAR, London, 1956
Philby, Eleanor, KIM PHILBY: THE SPY I LOVED, London, 1968
Philby, Kim, MY SILENT WAR, London, 1968
Presles, Alain, and Brineau, Francois, Articles from LE NOUVEAU CANDIDE, Paris, 1962
Purdy, C. A., BURGESS AND MACLEAN, London, 1963
Rees, Goronwy, A CHAPTER OF ACCIDENTS, London, 1972
Richer, Marthe, I SPIED FOR FRANCE, London, 1935
Rivière, P. L., UN CENTRE DE GUERRE SECRÈTE: MADRID, Paris, 1936
Ronge, M., KRIEGS UND INDUSTRIALSPIONAGE, Vienna, 1930
Schellenburg, Walter, MEMOIRS, London, 1956
Seale, Patrick, and McConville, Maureen, PHILBY: THE LONG ROAD TO MOSCOW, London, 1973
SUDEBNI PROZESS PENKOVSKOVO I VINNA (Official report on Penkovsky trial), Moscow, 1963
Thomson, Basil, QUEER PEOPLE, London, 1922
Trevor-Roper, H. R., THE PHILBY AFFAIR, London, 1968
Trevor-Roper, H. R., *New York Review of Books*, 19 February 1976
Vassiliev, A. T., THE OCHRANA, London, 1950
Waagenaar, Sam, THE MURDER OF MATA HARI, London, 1964
Willoughby, Charles, H., SHANGHAI CONSPIRACY: THE SORGE SPY RING, New York, 1952
Witte, S., MEMOIRS, London, 1921
Wynne, Greville, THE MAN FROM MOSCOW, London, 1967

SIR FITZROY MACLEAN, British Member of Parliament from 1951 to 1974 and former Under-Secretary of State for War, entered the British Diplomatic Service in 1933, serving in the Foreign Office and the British embassies in Paris and Moscow. While in the Soviet Union he undertook several notable journeys to the Caucasus and Turkestan, then a forbidden zone for foreigners.

During World War II Sir Fitzroy served with the Special Air Service Regiment in the Western Desert, taking part in a number of that unit's now famous raids behind the enemy lines. In 1943 he was parachuted into German-occupied Yugoslavia as Brigadier commanding the British military mission to the Partisans and Winston Churchill's personal representative to Marshall Tito.

Among his best known books are *Eastern Approaches*, in which he has recorded some of his experiences, *Back to Bokhara*, and *To the Back of Beyond*. His home is in Argyll, Scotland.